IMPROVING THINK TANK MANAGEMENT

IMPROVING THINK TANK MANAGEMENT

PRACTICAL GUIDANCE FOR THINK TANKS, RESEARCH ADVOCACY NGOS, AND THEIR FUNDERS

RAYMOND STRUYK

RESULTS FOR DEVELOPMENT INSTITUTE

ISBN-13: 978-0-9864213-2-7
LCCN: 2015905529

Cover Design by James Arneson
Typeset by MK Ross

Printed in the United States of America

PREFACE

Want to change the world? Start—not with armies or money or power—but with an idea whose time has come. But ideas don't come unbidden. Throughout history, small groups of people, starting with the germ of a concept and developing it into a roadmap for practical action, have had incredible impact.

Think tanks, although that term dates from the 1950s, have been around forever. Ancient Greece was rife with them. Today, 4,500 of them have been counted around the world—and that is probably a huge underestimate. Other sources of new knowledge, such as academia, are good at coming up with fresh ideas. But think tanks are particularly good at getting ideas from the research world into the minds, words, and actions of impactful people making decisions affecting millions of lives.

This wonderful book by Raymond Struyk is a must-read on how to create and manage effective think tanks. The evidence, insights, lessons from experience, and practitioner's tips and tricks of the trade that are carefully laid out here are relevant for almost any think tank anywhere—and nowhere more so than in developing countries, where the need for more and better think tanks is greatest.

I do not say that lightly. As the founder and current leader of a young think tank that has experienced rapid and sustained growth over the past six years—and as an alumnus of one of the original think tanks of the post-WWII years, the Rand Corporation—I wish I had had this advice-packed volume close to hand every step of the way. It could have saved me much time and many missteps—in everything that comes up in the daunting work of crafting a thriving and productive institution—from the lofty terrain of strategy-setting, to the arcane details of constructing an indirect cost rate, to the delicate fine-tuning of incentives for staff motivation, to worrying about quality control for written products.

Part of the rationale for preparing this major reworking of the second edition of Ray's earlier book—and for investing more in getting the word out about it—is to help think tank managers, funders, board members, and other stakeholders to benefit from the many nuggets of down-to-earth wisdom it contains. And none more so than the brave souls, so important for their countries' future, who spearhead think tanks where they can make massive difference, whether in Asia, Africa, Latin America, or even in the already well-endowed high-income countries.

This edition is better than its predecessor in several respects

- o Struyk makes improving management more compelling by highlighting examples of southern think tanks that have strong practices and including case studies of how specific think tanks moved from weak to strong practices—what motivated them to make the change, the problems encountered, and the benefits realized. These are supplemented with numerous vignettes that illustrate other important points.

o The book focuses squarely on think tanks but it offers lessons for research-advocacy organizations and organizations funding think tanks. The hope is to create a common understanding across these three populations of what constitutes strong management practices.

o Also, Struyk includes strong examples of policy and procedure statements from well-managed organizations for a number of key management tasks. The idea is make it easier for think tanks to implement these by providing well-crafted and tested statements that a think tank manager can work from to develop a statement that suits its particular circumstances.

For readers who are not familiar with Raymond Struyk's experience in working with think tanks, it is worth noting that he is one of the few true experts on think tank management. He learned on the job as he directed research centers at U.S. think tanks and large technical assistance projects in multiple transition and developing countries. There he relied upon local think tanks as key subcontractors, under a philosophy that it is important for international aid projects to build capacity that remains when a project concludes. In Russia and Hungary he worked with local teams to create a think tank and was their mentor during the early years. He has carried out numerous assessments of think tank operations and conducted in-depth interviews with dozens of think tank managers.

So, read and learn. And don't make a move in the think tank world without this new classic on the subject.

David de Ferranti, President
Results for Development Institute

For
Bill Ausman
mentor and friend

ADVISORY BOARD[1]

K.Y. Amoako
Founding President of the African Center for Economic Transformation

Goran Buldioski
Director, Think Tank Fund, Open Society Foundation

Mwangi Kimenyi
Director, Africa Growth Initiative in the Global Economy and Development at the Brookings Institution; formerly, Founding Executive Director of the Kenya Institute for Public Policy Research and Analysis

Ruth Levine
Program Director of the Global Development and Population Program at The William and Flora Hewlett Foundation; formerly Vice President at the Center for Global Development

Nadeem Ul Haque
International Monetary Fund; formerly President of the Pakistan Institute of Development Economics

---

[1]   Listed are a member's present position and, where appropriate, a former position that best illustrates the member's connection with think tanks.

ACKNOWLEDGMENTS

In preparing this book I have had an enormous amount of help from many generous people.

The Results for Development Institute (R4D) was a partner throughout the book's development, beginning with the proposal. Courtney Tolmie was a fine colleague in providing useful and thoughtful comments. She worked particularly hard to acquire the case studies critical to the book and conducted a series of interviews with African think tanks about their practices. She handled a host of organizational necessities. Courtney is also to carry out an assessment of the effects the book's publication may have on think tank exposure to strong management practices. Mame Annan-Brown, R4D's Director of Communications, did a terrific job identifying and working with our publisher and structuring the book's marketing plan. Mame was ably assisted by Henna Mahmood, who provided general support and drafted some text boxes. Gina Lagomarsino gave me ideas from her vantage point as Chief Operating Officer.

David de Ferranti, R4D's president, was thoughtful from the start and was exceptionally engaged in constituting the Advisory Board and participating in its meetings. David additionally gave me access to an array of the Institute's administrative policy and procedures documents and permitted their use in the book.

Our Advisory Board, whose members are listed on the previous page, was engaged and thoughtful, providing excellent comments at the introductory meeting and on book drafts thereafter. Goran Buldioski, beyond serving energetically on the Advisory Board, was instrumental in identifying think tanks that could contribute quality case studies of strong management practices, made a think tank survey by the Think Tank Fund available for my use, and generally provided insightful advice.

Ruth Levine, at The William and Flora Hewlett Foundation and a member of the Advisory Board, gave really excellent feedback from the proposal stage to the end of the project. Her deep experience at think tanks combined with her current experience at the Foundation gave her a particularly advantageous perspective. I and my colleagues at R4D are very grateful to the Foundation for its support.

Kwame Owino, executive director at the Institute for Economic Analysis in Kenya reviewed an advanced draft of the book and provided fine comments and highly useful observations based on his management experience.

A special thanks goes to Hans Gutbrod, who 1) had the idea for the book as a follow-on to, but very different from, *Managing Think Tanks* and 2) provided resources to explore and develop the concept. Hans also remained an active source of ideas during the writing.

Over the years dozens of think tank executive directors, senior managers, and others in many countries were remarkably cooperative and open in interviews I conducted with them—in particular, the additional interviews on specific topics conducted for this volume. Several senior managers at the Urban Institute (Washington, D.C.) participated in interviews on areas under their responsibility and were extremely generous in dealing with follow-up requests. These include: Margery Austin Turner, Senior Vice President for Program Planning and Management; Deborah Hoover, Director for Human Resources; John Rogers, Executive Vice President, Treasurer, and Chief Financial Officer; and, Bridget Lowell, Vice President for Strategic Communication and Outreach.

Nadezhda Kosareva and Alexander Puzanov at the Institute for Urban Economics in Moscow were generous in responding to questions and in describing challenges they confronted in recent years and the corresponding management actions taken.

At the International Development Research Centre (IDRC), Peter Taylor provided access to a wide range of data, case studies, and other materials generated by the Think Tank Initiative project that very substantially enriches the presentation. Katy Stockton was unfailingly efficient and cheerful in dealing with a seemingly endless stream of requests. Samar Varma and Sheeba Varghese at the IDRC New Delhi office were welcoming and provided wonderful help in setting up interview appointments for me with a dozen South Asia think tank executive directors at a conference in spring 2014.

The Global Development Network allowed the use of data collected by NORC at the University of Chicago on 15 think tanks that participated in a mentoring program it administered.

I am grateful to NORC at the University of Chicago for allowing me to excerpt and edit materials from several of its personnel policy statements. Jeffrey Telgarsky cooperated in many ways and Samuel Haddaway generated a series of tables from various survey data sets with his usual efficiency, competence, and good humor.

Several mature think tanks allowed me to include some of their policy and procedures statements in annexes and draw on them for the text. In some instances contributors asked that a contributed statement not be attributed to them. I cite these as from an unnamed think tank. Regardless, I very much appreciate these organizations sharing these internal materials with me and you.

Enrique Mendizabal, editor of *On Think Tanks*, was extremely cooperative in helping get the word out to the think tank world of work on the book generally and, in particular, announcing the call for case studies.

The book was very substantially improved by the case studies contributed by eight authors. While each is named with the case study s/he authored, I thank them all for their cooperation in accepting the request to generate the studies and being so cooperative in carrying them out and responding to questions.

Many others provided an idea, permission to use material, a key piece of information, or participation in an interview—all of which together made a huge difference to the book. They include: Vladyslav Galushko at the Open Society Think Tank Fund; Christopher Miller; Ann van Dusen; Chris Hamilton; Dongseok Kim at the Korean Development Institute; Sonny Mumbunan and Chitra Septyandrica at Article 33 in Indonesia; Hoseana Lunogelo (Economic and Social Research Foundation); Nidhi Sabharwal (Indian Institute of Dalit Studies); Ajaya Dixit (Institute for Social and Environmental Transition); Clement Ahiadeke (Institute of Statistical, Social and Economic Research); Bitrina Diyamett and Constantine Deus Shirati (Science, Technology and Innovation Policy Research Organization); Shaymaa Kadry (IDSC-Cairo); Ognian Shentov (Center for Democracy Studies); and Sarah Ssewanyana and Birabwa Aliro Elizabeth Koli (Economic Policy Research Centre-Uganda); Jai Asundi (Center for Study of Science, Technology and Policy-India); Subrat Das (Center for Budget and Governance Accountability-India); Nidhi Sabbarwal (Indian Institute of Dalit Studies); Ajaya Dixit (Institute for Social and Environmental Transition-Nepal); Manoj Panda (Institute of Economic Growth-India); Sultan Hafeez Rahman (Institute of Governance Studies-Bangladesh); Dushni Weerakoon (Institute of Policy Studies of Sri Lanka); Hari Nagarajan (Institute of Rural Management Anand-India); Shekhar Shah (National Council of Applied Economic Research-India); Raghava Suresh (Public Affairs Centre-India); Abid Suleri (Sustainable Development Policy Institute-Pakistan); and Udan Fernando (Centre for Poverty Analysis-Sri Lanka); Andrew Onokerhoraye and Job Eronmhonsele (Centre for Population and Environmental Development-Nigeria); Ebere Uneze and Drusilla David (Centre for the Study of the Economies of Africa-Nigeria); Felix Murithi (Kenya Institute for Public Policy Research and Analysis–Kenya); Kwame Owino and Oscar Ochieng (Institute for Economic Affairs-Kenya); Abdoulaye Diagne (Consortium pour la Recherche Economique et Sociale-Senegal); and Ebere Uneze (Center for the Study of the Economies of Africa-Nigeria).

Felicity Skidmore did her typically great job editing the volume. She both improved the book and was a fun colleague to work with.

CONTENTS

Building a Productive Staff

Core Operations

---

1   The policy and procedure statements contained in the annexes marked with an "*" here and in the text are available in a Word format on the website: http://r4d.org/improving-think-tank-management

List of Tables

List of Case Studies[2]

---

2   Case Studies and Boxes appear at the end of each chapter in which they are included.

List of Figures

List of Boxes[3]

---

3   Boxes and Case Studies appear at the end of each chapter in which they are included.

Contents

Abbreviations and Terms

Annex x.x*	Annexes marked with an "*" are examples of strong policy and procedure statements. These are published separated in Word format at http://r4d.org/improving-think-tank-management
CASE	Center for Social and Economic Research – Poland
CBPS	Centre for Budget and Policy Studies – India
CD	Center Director
CDFE	Center for Democracy and Free Enterprise -- Prague
CDG	Center for Global Development – U.S.
CEE	Central and Eastern Europe
CEE-6	Refers to 6 think tanks in the region whose executive directors were interviewed in-depth on management topics, the results from which are drawn upon in the text discussion
CSD	Center for Study of Democracy – Sofia
CIPPEC	Center for the Implementation of Public Policies Promoting Equity and Growth – Argentina
CIS	Commonwealth of Independent States (a union of countries in the Caucasus and Central Asia that were in the former Soviet Union)
CPS	Cost policy statement
CSG	Center for the Study of Democracy - Bulgaria
CSO	Civil Society Organization
DfID	Department for International Development – U.K.
ED	Executive Directors
EPRC	Economic Policy Research Center – Uganda
EOs	Example organizations
EU	European Union
FTE	Full time equivalent
GDN	Global Development Network
GDN-15	Refers to 15 think tanks that participated in a GDN mentoring program that included monitoring surveys whose data are drawn upon in the text discussion
Expert	Expert Institute of the Russian Union of Industrialists and Entrepreneurs - Moscow
HR	Human resources
IDSC	Information and Decision Support Center of the Cabinet of the Government of Egypt
IET	Institute for Economy in Transition – Russia
IFI	International Finance Institution
IT	Information technology
IUE	Institute for Urban Economics – Russia
KDI	Korean Development Institute -- Seoul
MPs	Members of Parliament
MRI	Metropolitan Research Institute – Budapest
PD	Project Director
PETS	Public Expenditures Tracking System
PEC	Policy engagement and communications
PO	Participating organization
PROs	Policy research organizations

QC	Quality control
RA	Research assistant
RAOs	Research advocacy organizations
R4D	Results for Development Institute – U.S.
SME	Small and medium enterprises
Stage 1,2, and 3 think tanks	Chapter 1 introduces three stages of think tank development based on number of full time researchers and the presence of communications specialists. Stage 1 think tanks have 10 or fewer full-time researchers and may lack a dedicated communications specialist. Stage 2 and Stage 3 are larger but are not distinguished by numerical staff count or composition but rather on the degree of overall development.
SMERU	The SMERU Research Institute – Indonesia
TAP	Transparency and Accountability Project
TARKI	Social Research Institute - Budapest
Team leader	The person managing a group of researchers working together. In a large group there may be sub-leaders. Team leaders are often called Center Directors or Department Heads.
TTF	Think Tank Fund of the Open Society Institute
TTI	Think Tank Initiative at the International Development Research Center
TTI-48	Refers to 48 think tanks that participated in the TTI program that included monitoring surveys that data from which are drawn upon in the discussion.
TTI-EX-2012	The summer 2012 meeting in South Africa of 50 leaders and staff from think tanks and other members of the think tank community to discuss strengthening management and communications practices
TOR	Terms of reference
UI	The Urban Institute – U.S.
USAID	U.S. Agency for International Development

CHAPTER 1
Management Matters

> Think tanks are independent, usually private, policy research institutes containing people involved in studying a particular policy area or a broad range of policy issues, actively seeking to educate or advise policy makers and the public through a number of channels. As such these organizations compete in two separate markets: that for funding and that for the opportunity to provide policy advice.[1]

This classic definition of think tanks appropriately stresses their primary objectives. And there is ample evidence that think tanks are making a significant contribution to the policy process.[2] They are expanding the number of policy options considered to address a nation's problems, providing hard facts and analysis to empower smaller players in the political process and informing the public on key issues of the day.

While emphasizing these outcomes is often appropriate, typically overlooked is the reality that, to be successful, think tanks must execute three tasks effectively: conduct rigorous policy research, engage closely with the policy community to activate the research findings, and manage the organization effectively. My focus in this book is on the third task, which is often the most neglected. If management is not very effective, success with the other tasks becomes even more daunting.

Consider the likely negative effects for a think tank of the following conditions resulting from weak management: low staff morale and impaired productivity, weak quality control, a significant share of resources being poorly deployed in the absence of a basic system for tracking expenditures, or a dysfunctional governance system wherein members of the Board of Directors intervene in day-to-day staffing and procurement decisions the chief executive should be handling. In our competitive world, the

---

1   Definition is a slightly edited version of that by Stone (2000) as augmented by Buldioski (2010b). Many definitions of think tanks exist and most state that they are non-profit organizations. See Pautz (2011), for example, on why emphasis on legal status is misplaced; also Mendizabal (2013d). One can still argue, however, that nonprofit status is often a convenient signaling device for indicating institutional motives. An interview on this topic with Andrew Selee is referenced here: Selee (2013b).

2   See, for example, Court and Young (2007), Struyk and Haddaway (2012), Johnson (2000), Langsford and Brownsey (1992), McGann (1999), Rich (2001), Smith (1991), Stone, Denham, and Garnett (1998), Struyk (1999), McGann and Johnson (2005),and Telgarsky and Ueno (1996).

stronger the management the more effective the think tank will be in achieving its primary objectives.

The list just enumerated may sound familiar; indeed you may be thinking that failings like these are experienced by for-profit consulting firms as well as think tanks. Actually, think tanks' goals differ from other organization types and have fundamental effects on the execution of an array of management tasks. For example, when assessing success a consulting firm's board relies very heavily on financial performance, i.e., profit and associated indicators. Think tanks' boards focus primarily on the institution's effectiveness in the policy arena and inputs to this performance, especially staff quality and the targeted communication of policy-relevant results. Think tanks' orientation to the public good has fundamental effects on the type of worker they attract compared with those at consulting firms and they have a strong influence on the type of incentives that stimulate senior researchers, e.g., success in improving the lives of a significant number of poor through better social service administration or being a public figure, compared with greater remuneration favored by their consultant counterparts. Important operational divergences also exist between think tanks and advocacy NGOs, which are described below. In short, think tank management differs importantly from various for-profit and nonprofit counterparts. Think tank management is my focus.

In the past few years, think tanks themselves and their funders have begun to recognize more fully the cost of poor management and have taken steps to address identified weaknesses. In part this reflects the maturing of large cohorts of think tanks founded in the past 25 years (described below) and the growth of many—a trend that has permitted greater professionalism in management as full-time management positions are created.

- In Baku, the European Union in 2013 funded a group led by the Economic Research Center to provide training and mentoring to local think tanks and research advocacy organizations to strengthen a range of management functions—including human resources (HR) and accounting, as well as communications.[3]

- The Policy Association for an Open Society (PASOS)—an association of think tanks in Eastern Europe, the Caucasus, and Central Asia—gave strong attention a few years ago to improving management through a series of studies and, perhaps more importantly, joint member discussions as to what constitutes strong practices in a number of areas and how to implement them.

- The Think Tank Initiative (TTI) organized their three-day TTI Exchange 2012 largely devoted to addressing a wide variety of management issues—with think tank leaders swapping experiences and lessons on such topics as enhancing organization governance and the role of Boards of Directors in think tanks, how to attract and nurture quality think tank researchers, and balancing commissioned work and long-term research. About 70

---

3   This kind of local technical assistance for management improvements is sorely needed and the Baku program could serve as a model for others. A description of the activity is in Annex 1.1.

participants, including senior leaders from about 50 think tanks, gathered in South Africa for a series of lively presentations and debates.

- "On Think Tanks," the industry's go-to blog, regularly features posts on management questions that consistently elicit thoughtful comments.
- In a capacity building program administered by the Global Development Network, 10 of the 15 participating think tanks reported receiving major institutional development funding during 2009-2010 (described further below).

The following conclusion by Jacek Kucharczyk and Piotr Kazmierkiewicz (2007), based on their on-site, in-depth survey of 12 Western European think tanks' management practices, provides an excellent summary of the fundamental issue:

> A striking fact is that all the interviewed representatives of think tanks were aware of the distinctive task of running an institution of this kind and thought in terms of best ways to apply general management techniques to fit the specific characteristics of think tanks.... The awareness of the need to reflect on the management practices of one's own think tank is the first step towards running it better. (p.6)

Beyond the think tank community's heightened interest in improved management, recent exogenous developments add urgency to increasing operational efficiency and effectiveness.[4] The political scene is evolving in many countries and the role of think tanks along with it: 1) factual knowledge is less valued, driven in part by a rise in partisanship; and, 2) with greater political polarization, more think tanks are becoming politicized and evolving at least partially into "guns for hire," with results and recommendations no longer based squarely on strong, disinterested research.[5]

The past few years have also witnessed a surge in the aggressive dissemination of seemingly analytic information in the form of blog postings and twitter tweets, along with other postings of "facts" that have no valid research basis. Think tanks are often not keeping up in getting timely, short messages out that are linked to valid research, thereby losing standing in policy debates. These patterns call for a more active think tank role. But external funding for this kind of activism is in short supply.

The reality is that resources may be available only for think tanks that improve their management

---

4   Medvetz (2012) provides a more general analysis of the position of U.S. think thanks in the evolving community of institutions influencing and making policy. To paraphrase, his focus is on the formation of the space of think tanks, a hybrid and highly dynamic institutional arena situated at the nexus of the political, academic, economic, and media fields. (p.213)

5   The "guns for hire" issue has become sufficiently acute that a new blog was established in early 2014 to report on and promote think tanks' transparency in their revenue sources. See www.transparify. org. An early post on the site addresses directly whether think tanks are turning into lobbyists; Bruckner (2014).

of basic tasks—to free the essential (overhead) resources while keeping overall operating costs constant or nearly so.

MY OBJECTIVE IN WRITING THIS BOOK

My goal here is to respond to and deepen managers' interest in strengthening their operations by providing concrete, comprehensive advice and examples of good practices and how they can be achieved. Managers in transition and developing countries are my greatest concern, because they have fewer local advanced-management organizations to emulate. I present and analyze numerous real world examples of current practices and exemplar practices and discuss how to implement improvements. Thus, my focus is on not only the objectives of management improvements but also ways to achieve them.

My sense from working with several dozen think tanks over the years is that think tank leaders often have exaggerated views of the costs of change—in terms of disruption to the usual work flow, staff resistance to change, and actual expenditures. At the same time, managers have tended to underestimate the benefits of implementing stronger management practices. Consider the following examples of investments that think tanks have recently made to improve their operations. These come from among the nine case studies commissioned for this book (which are presented later):

- The Institute for Urban Economics in Moscow determined its overhead or indirect cost rate through a rigorous process. The rate's validity was confirmed by the U.S. Agency for International Development (USAID), which formally awarded the Institute a rate certification that is recognized by all U.S. agencies. The Institute has used the rate in successfully negotiating its contracts with sponsors beyond the U.S. government. Additionally, knowledge of the composition of its overhead spending permitted management to intelligently rein in overhead spending when the Institute faced a sharp revenue decline.

- When senior managers at the Bandung Institute for Governance Studies in Indonesia observed that presentations made by some of its staff lacked focus and did not take sufficient account of the range of views likely held by their audiences, the managers designed and implemented a process for vetting presentations in advance. The process entails more rigorous preparation for presentations either being made to government officials or addressing particularly sensitive budgetary issues. One of the benefits is giving presenters greater confidence in delivering their remarks and responding to questions during ensuing discussions.

- The Center for the Implementation of Public Policies Promoting Equity and Growth (CIPPEC) in Buenos Aries, a fairly large think tank, has systematically developed policy and procedure statements for a wide range of its internal operations including HR, finance, communications, strategic development, and the monitoring and evaluation of its work. Its "White Book" has increased consistency in the way many operations are executed—including, among others, quality control, charging time to types of work, authorship, and a range of staff activities such as the annual performance appraisal and allocation of "performance incentives." Longer term effects include efficiency gains and improved staff morale.

- Praxis, a think tank in Tallinn, through careful analysis of possible strategic opportunities, decided to launch the Praxis Academy, a training center that provides training to government officials and NGO staff in Estonia and elsewhere in the region. By explicitly linking the training offered to the findings of its research, it is able to offer high quality tuition while indirectly influencing policy. In the past two years, the Academy has contributed significantly to Praxis's bottom line and increased work satisfaction among staff who decided to become part-time teachers in the program.

In short, designing and implementing strong management practices can be undertaken with reasonable effort and the rewards can be significant. Funders should encourage think tanks with which they work to strengthen specific practices, at least in part out of the self-interest that their awardees will be more productive.

WHO SHOULD READ THIS BOOK?

This guide targets three audiences: think tanks; research advocacy organizations; and those institutions that fund them, particularly the donor community. Although the institutional contexts differ among these organization types, the management principles are widely applicable to all three.

Think Tanks

Over the past 25 years, beginning roughly with the collapse of the Soviet Union hegemony in Eastern Europe and then of the Union itself, the number of think tanks and research-advocacy organizations has expanded sharply worldwide, particularly in the 1991-2000 decade.[6] While many have remained quite small, focused on specific policy questions, a significant number around the world have reached, or will soon reach, what might be termed the "second stage of development." Based on my work with think tanks, in this book and elsewhere I use the criterion 10 or fewer than full-time researchers with at least one communications specialist consistently employed as an indicator that a think tank has reached Stage 2 of its development.[7]

---

6   McGann (2013) estimated that in 2012 there were about 6,600 think tanks in the world. Based on a sample of 4,348 who responded to his questionnaire, he found 61 new think tanks were created annually on average during 1971-1980, 142 during 1991-2000, and 69 during 2001- 2007. Given the elasticity of the research-advocacy organization concept (discussed below), no estimates are available for this group. My sense is that conditions influencing the creation of think tanks and research-advocacy organizations are similar and therefore the growth patterns of the two groups were similar over the past 25 years.

7   A comprehensive 1997 survey of think tanks in Eastern Europe found that about 30 percent of think tanks included met this criterion. The survey is reported in Freedom House (1999). Among CIS countries, only Belarus and Ukraine are covered by the directory.   Similar data on this point for think tanks around the world have not been found. Information on current staffing at 59 think tanks from transition and developing countries is presented in the next chapter.

Stage 2 institutions are at the point where they move from a low, often highly variable level of operations and a small number of sponsors to a higher level of activity (i.e., larger staff, more projects, greater specialization and professionalization in management and support leadership positions, and more opportunities in the policy process and for educating the public on current policy issues). Think tanks in the third (and final) stage of development are established, significant players, typically with strong management systems. In the United States, the Brookings Institution and the Urban Institute are good examples of Stage 3 think tanks. Developing and transition countries have examples of think tanks approaching or perhaps even at Stage 3 status—including, for example, SMERU and the Center for International and Strategic Studies in Indonesia. Because of the difficulty of distinguishing between Stage 2 and Stage 3 think tanks, I use the convention below of referring to the whole group as being in Stage 2-3.

A substantial share of Stage 1 think tanks that remain small organizations focus on a few policy areas. Over time they are able to professionalize some key management functions, often with experienced individuals handling multiple areas (such as HR and general office management, including oversight of the IT expert). Even at Stage 1, organizations can adopt some strong practices at low cost. They can, for example, adopt the annual staff assessment form discussed in Chapter 2 and included in Annex 2.1*, or they can rigorously implement the flexible advice on quality control in Chapter 6.

As think tanks reach Stage 2 of development, they must alter their management and financial systems to gain efficiency and effectiveness. But managing the transition to a higher activity level is difficult at best. Even an excellent policy analyst or advocate who is a think tank executive director cannot make up for a primitive financial management system that does not permit the institution to control its costs or ensure that available revenues are used for priority tasks.

I direct much of my advice to typical Stage 2 think tanks, although I have found that sophisticated advanced Stage 2 or even Stage 3 think tanks in the developed world often fall short in some management practices and can benefit from management guidance as well. One reason is that senior administrative staff and officers, including the president and senior vice president, sometimes take on their roles without having a think tank or research institute background. While there *are* similarities with conventional consulting firms, there are also very important differences. The key point is that, although an executive director need not have expertise or substantial knowledge about all management areas, the management team collectively must possess comprehensive management knowledge, with responsibilities distributed to match.

Institutional characteristics can make an important difference in particular management tasks. Size, for example, really matters. This is especially true for the Board of Directors' role, where at small organizations they can be part of the management team because of the lack of other management resources. Where size has critical effects, I provide special advice for the smaller organizations. Another major difference is between groups that are essentially fully funded by the government ("government think tanks") and those affiliated with a university ("university think tanks"). The main management effects of these arrangements are in governance and some personnel policies. Governance is affected by the composition (and therefore the views and priorities) of the Board of Directors, which may significantly affect an institute's agenda. The effects on personnel policies arise most deeply if think tank staff is subject to 1) government or university salary and benefits schedules and regulations governing performance incentives and 2) annual review procedures. There may also be limitations on fund raising activities—for example, payments from for-profit organizations may be prohibited to government think tanks because of possible conflicts of interest. Since very little systematic information is available on government and university think tanks in general, and even less on their management practices,[8] individual think tanks of each type should be prepared to tailor my strongly worded practice descriptions to their specific situations. (See additional comments in Chapter 7.)

In sum, think tanks of all sizes and levels of sophistication can find information in this guide that will foster improved management although, as noted, the smaller and younger institutions are my primary focus.

Within think tanks, my primary audiences are the executive directors, senior administrators (such as the directors of human resources, finance, and communications), and directors of research groups, whom I refer to as team leaders or center directors.

Research Advocacy Organizations

Research advocacy organizations (RAOs) are nonprofit public interest advocacy groups and trade and professional membership NGOs. They differ from the more traditional advocacy organization in that they emphasize an objective evidence-based approach to their work. They often have the same goals as the more traditional advocacy organizations but generally—though by no means always—use more sophisticated analytic techniques and devote a smaller resource share to advocacy as opposed to research. In the United States, Stage 3 RAOs include the American Association of Retired Persons advocating for the elderly and the American Hospital Association working to advance its members' views. The international World Wildlife Fund is a traditional advocacy organization. In Indonesia, advanced Stage 2 RAOs include PATTIRO (Center for Regional Information and Studies).

It is important to recognize that NGO membership organizations, such as a bankers' association, differ from think tanks along several dimensions, including:

- *Staff*: Some have numerous volunteers; some have large associated service delivery operations with specialized staff.
- *Fund raising*: Beyond seeking funds for policy research, many rely on membership dues as a principal funding source, and some conduct mass funding drives not related to membership

---

8   There appears to be no information even on the simple question of how large a share of think tanks falls into these categories. McGann's (2013) global ranking report, for example, does not provide data. The survey obtains information about these types of think tanks and names the best government affiliated and the best university affiliated think tanks. But counts of such organizations are not published.

or policy research.

- *Management*: In membership organizations the elected presidents, and perhaps some VPs are mostly only marginally involved in day-to-day operations with a strong management team running operations; the professional managers can face challenging situations when honorary leaders want major changes.

Even so, I make a point of including RAOs in the audience for this guide because they do engage in the policy research function and the standard NGO management guides devote little, if any, consideration to this important task. Table 1.1 lists the chapters, and where appropriate the specific sections, that I think will be most useful to RAO managers. Depending on a particular RAO's interests and organization, other sections may merit attention as well.[9]

Table 1.1 Sections of Particular Relevance for Research Advocacy Organizations

Chapter		Comment
Number	Topic	
2-5	Staff policy --performance incentives, annual assessments --staff training --position descriptions, performance standards --hiring and organizing the research team --developing team leaders	These chapters focus primarily on research staff, although administrative and communications staffs receive significant attention. Certain types of incentives (authorship) and performance review criteria (success in policy promotion) are special to the policy research function. Multi-mission organizations can consider creating a wholly owned policy research NGO to avoid multiple and possible conflicting practices for different parts of the organization
6	Quality control of written products and various presentation types.	Applies exclusively to policy research operations. Entire chapter of interest.
9	Developing a forward looking policy research and engagement agenda and organizing moves into new areas	In multi-mission organizations may need to coordinate this agenda process with activities of other missions.
10	Whether to accept grants and contracts from government agencies	The interactions between the policy engagement mission and others (e.g., service delivery to disadvantaged groups) may have a major impact here. Possible conflicts of interest strengthen the argument for a policy research subsidiary.
11	Financial accountability and sustainability—case for and mechanics of time management system and development of a technically defensible overhead rate.	Both actions would likely require adjustments throughout the organization (hard to implement a time management system only for the policy research team).
12	Monitoring performance, section on indicators of performance from the public policy perspective	Such indicators could be added to existing ones that track aspects of operations to inform management of policy related outputs and outcomes. Should not conflict with monitoring of other performance areas, presuming that various operations are treated (at least implicitly) as cost centers.

---

9   A major consideration, not explicitly addressed here because of RAOs' diversity, is how treatment of the policy research department interacts with departments concerned with an RAO's non- policy research and advocacy missions.

Funders

Institutions that give grants and contracts to think tanks have two broad motivations for doing so. One is simply to have them conduct a policy research, survey research, or demonstration project or evaluation. This is essentially a fee for service arrangement. The second is broader and includes an interest in sustaining the organization *per se* and supporting its development. Governments, multilateral organizations (such as the World Bank), some bilateral aid agencies (such as USAID and the prime contractors working for them), and some foundations that hire local think tanks typically have the first motivation. In instances where technical assistance is provided to a think tank without any project-specific funding, the second motivation is obviously dominant.

Some donors believe they are supporting a think tank's development simply by contracting with it. But how think tank executive directors actually view their relations with different funder groups has not been systematically explored. To help fill this gap, I had the chance at a Spring 2014 conference in New Delhi to conduct structured interviews with executive directors or senior managers from 12 South Asia think tanks based in five countries on exactly this question. I asked these executive directors about each of five funder types: multilateral organizations (e.g., World Bank, UN agencies), international foundations and foundation consortia,[10] domestic foundations or persons/firms who individually make large contributions, bilateral aid agencies, and national and subnational governments. My focus was on the executive directors' experiences in the past two to three years with specific funders in each group with whom the organization had worked, e.g., the World Bank and/or the Asian Development Bank among multinationals. Typically eight or nine funders were named per think tank across the five groups. My data include 28 assessments of relations between the think tanks and international foundations and nine assessments of relations between the think tanks and domestic foundations or individual patrons. While the sample is small and certainly not representative, these reports nonetheless provide a useful initial picture.

Two points emerge from the interviews that bear specifically on relations with different types of funder:

- *To what degree is a particular a funder "actually concerned with the development of your think tank"?* Responses classified about 50 percent of the international foundations as "very concerned" but classified another 30 percent as seeing the relationship in purely transactional terms (i.e., the foundation is simply purchasing services). Almost all (94 percent) of multi-national organizations and all bi-lateral interactions were classified as seeing the relationship as purely transactional. Based on 23 cases, work for domestic government agencies was always seen as purely transactional.[11]

---

10   The Think Tank Initiative, described below, is in this group. The Initiative is administered by the International Development Research Centre, a Canadian aid agency that also contributes funds to the program. The bulk of the funds come from several foundations.
11   Only five observations pertained to domestic foundations.

- *How thoroughly do different types of clients review analytic reports (as opposed to progress or administrative reports)?* About 75 percent of the projects funded by multi-nationals credited their sponsors with providing thoughtful, detailed comments vs. about 60 percent for international foundations, 45 percent for domestic government agencies, and 40 percent for bilateral agencies.

Several executive directors were clear that they are very cautious when engaging with multilateral agencies and international foundations. They have little expectation that projects from these types of organization benefit them in ways beyond use of the project's outputs for their own ends and those of their clients—a consideration that naturally influences their decision calculus when considering the tradeoff between bidding on a competitively released project from a multilateral vs. negotiating for a foundation award that is not, at least explicitly, a competitive procurement.

In fairly rare cases, foundations and bilateral aid programs are motivated only to further the development and competence of their grantees as institutions, with the accent typically on training and mentoring rather than research support. Notable examples are the Think Tank Initiative (TTI), funded by private foundations and developed-world aid agencies, and the Open Society Foundation's Think Tank Fund. A significant number of think tank–strengthening technical assistance projects have also been donor funded, with contractors—both for-profit and not profit—engaged as implementing agents.[12] Overall, however, it is fair to say that administrative practices in many think tanks are weak partly as a consequence of limited donor interest in management performance.

Goran Buldioski, director of the Think Tank Fund, summarizes the typical differences in perspective between project funders and funders providing core or institutional grants (2013).

- Donors who award core and institutional grants, unlike their peers who underwrite projects, have a fuller picture of the organizations they support. Given that most core support commitments last longer than two years, the relationship between the donor and grantee, provided it is properly developed, can develop to be trustworthy. This is not to suggest that project donors cannot develop deep relationships with their grantees. It is simply the somewhat discrete nature of project support that is usually short that allows for shorter attention span and focus on a peculiar policy problem and not so much on the overall organization picture. As a donor who gives both types of grants, I could experience and empathies [sic] with both types.
- This allows the donor to look at the capacity building needs of the organization as a whole and not just focus on separate individual needs as most specialized capacity builders do.

---

12   For a discussion of implementing NGO agents' relations with civil society organizations, including think tanks, see the essays in Hulme and Edwards (2013).

However, the many donor-grantee relationships I have been able to experience warn me not to draw too rosy a picture.

- There is clearly a negative side to this relationship. For example, some donors rush to bundle their funds with the advice they give or render; and grantees, too often, accept the advice in fear not to lose the funds. Donors must be careful not to fall into the trap of confirmation bias and not confuse acceptance of their ideas with actual agreement.

I offer additional commentary on think tanks' views of think tank-funder relations in Chapters 10 and 11, based on my 2014 executive director interviews noted above.

The information in this guide can be used by think tank and RAO supporters in two ways. The first way is to help funders and their agents to be confident that the organizations they support can carry out the project work to be done. As the size and duration of a project increases, the stronger is the required due diligence. Relevant areas of concern include staff policy (Do policies cover the essential elements to protect employees and the organization?); quality control (Is there risk to the funder from a weak vetting process?); governance (Is the management set up sound?) and financial management (When the need arises, will you be able to know how your money has been spent?).

The second way this guide's information can be used is when funders are approached by a potential grantee to support institutional development and want to understand if the areas for the proposed improvement are clearly needed and will have a significant payoff from a development investment. For example, further development of the HR function—in part addressing staff retention—may be critical for attracting and retaining highly capable researchers. Many of the essential HR policies and procedures may exist on paper with the real issue being one of administration. In this case, institutional investment may still be warranted but should be sharply targeted and limited to that purpose. Alternatively the grantee may be requesting funds to add social media to its communications package, without any analysis of whether this is the most important change that could be made to its communications operations; does it consistently prepare project-level communications plans? Careful, informed consideration and discussion of various options are clearly in order.

The foregoing makes clear that this guide is designed to help funders recognize strong management practices and, where practices need improvement, know options available for addressing issues identified. This guide provides ideas on specific steps that funders could take. The guide does not, however, discuss how a funder's program for working with an array of think tanks might be structured.

To highlight the most important points I have for funders, the final section of all succeeding chapters contains a "For Funders" set of summary statements designed to help with carrying out essential due diligence and fostering development. An important word of advice at the outset is about how to use the "For Funders" sections. The ever more commonly accepted rule for donors is that money spent on capacity building is wasted unless there is clear think tank leadership buy-in.[13] A program officer or equivalent can often get a sense of an executive director's view about the way some management practice is currently executed by assessing whether the director is already aware that better practices are available and that s/he is lagging behind. Another way of making this assessment is to see whether, in a subsequent discussion about plans for the future, the director spontaneously brings up making improvements in the specific practice at issue or is simply saying what s/he thinks the officer wants to hear.

Also important to keep in mind, and often overlooked, is that certain essential management improvements, such as strengthening the quality control program and improving staff incentive structures, are inexpensive to implement and could be encouraged in the context of a research grant—although explicit buy-in remains essential.

The "For Funders" statements are complemented in each chapter with similar statements for think tank and RAO managers under the heading "Strong Practices," which immediately precede the "For Funders" sections.

CONCRETE DATA AND EXAMPLES ARE BEST

The principles of good management can seem clear and direct when written on a page, but they come to life best when a manager sees them applied to a situation to which s/he can directly relate. I furnish the text liberally with examples, not only from my personal experiences and those of my colleagues at the Results for Development Institute (R4D), but also from three primary information sources: 1) survey data compiled from 59 developing and transition think tanks in developing and transition countries (sometimes referred to as 'southern') on their current practices; 2) case studies commissioned for this guide; and 3) additional examples provided to me through the variety of sources listed later in this chapter.

My Sources on Current Practices

Reviewing actual practices of think tanks in developing and transition countries has two objectives. First, the data give readers a reasonable idea about the current state of management: one can see the range of practices in use. Second, the data demonstrate that some of these think tanks have strong practices in essentially every aspect of management considered—confirming that a high performance level on every task can already exist within this peer group and is within the grasp of many others.

When I wrote an earlier book on think tank management (Struyk 2006), there was essentially no systematic information on think tank management practices. Indeed, information was even lacking on such basic facts as the size and composition of think tanks' staffs. Since then the situation has changed sharply.

---

13   For example, Buldioski (2012)

I draw on survey data from three primary sources to elucidate current practices and to provide basic facts such as think tanks' staff size distribution and funding sources. Such facts are important to give executive directors and their governing/advisory boards an idea of where their organizations stand in relation to their peers—something not previously possible. These facts provide basic information on significant management issues: How does their ratio of communications to research staff compare with those of others? How about staff turnover? What about the extent of their dependence on international donors for support? Funders will also find this type of basic information highly valuable for placing in context the think tanks with which they work.

Two of these data sources were generated in only the past few years: 1) the GDN-15 series of surveys of 15 think tanks in multiple regions that participated in a think tank mentoring program during 2008-2013,[14] and 2) the TTI-48 surveys of 48 think tanks that have participated in a broad capacity building program launched in 2008 and scheduled to extend to 2017. The third data source, CEE-6, consists of information from structured in-depth interviews of six think tanks in 2000 in Central and Eastern Europe on a limited range of management practices that, though dated, provides important details not elsewhere available.[15] None of these samples are representative of the international or regional think tank populations. (More information on these data sets is presented in Annex 1.2.)

Case Studies

The case studies were chosen and commissioned in the following way. First, I defined 16 topics on strong practices or improvements in think tank management for which I thought concise summaries of actual cases would be particularly compelling and informative for think tank managers. Then my colleague at the R4D, Courtney Tolmie, and I solicited and commissioned the case studies. Throughout the process, would-be contributors could suggest additional topics, two of which were commissioned. Case study authors were to generate a 700-1,000 word statement, roughly following an outline we provided. Authors of accepted case studies received $500 and the commitment that their names and institutional affiliations would appear with the case studies in the book.

In soliciting case studies we first made an open call by posting solicitations on several think tank-oriented blogs, including "On Think Tanks" and "Politics & Ideas." The Think Tank Fund and the TTI sent out notices as well. We then solicited cases from think tanks that we understood from working with them to have a strong specific management practice or to have made a particular management improvement. In the end we commissioned nine cases studies, eight of which appear as Case Studies in the book, with the ninth included as an annex to this chapter as an example of a local think tank mentoring program. The Case Studies expand significantly on the detail of management practices and are an important part of the overall narrative.

---

14   Participating think tanks are listed in Annex 1.2. They are drawn from five diverse regions: Central and Latin America, sub-Saharan Africa, South Asia, Southeast Asia, and the Caucuses.
15   I also make limited use of information from a 2012 survey of 41 Think Tank Fund grantees from Eastern Europe, the Caucuses and Central Asia (Think Tank Fund 2012).

Policy and Procedures Statements

Readers may be convinced about making changes to improve some management tasks, but then be daunted by the effort required to write the essential concrete policy or procedure statement. To lower the cost of change, I include example statements as annexes. As one might imagine, not all think tanks are ready to make their policies and procedures available for public consumption after having invested substantial resources in their development. But a few have been very generous in this regard. Most of the statements included here come from well-managed U.S. think tanks; the rest come from African and Eastern European organizations. (Annexes containing policy and procedures statements are marked with an asterisk, e.g., Annex 2.1*, and are published on-line in Word format to facilitate their use.)

Other Sources

In 2012-2013 the TTI, as previously mentioned, was the subject of an external evaluation. The evaluators solicited "stories of change" from the participating think tanks, which could select their own topic. The evaluators gave some ideas and prompts for items the various topic groups were to cover. The following statement from the evaluators provides an example:

> For stories of changes in the way the organization works, or the people in it behave, or the behavior of external actors has changed: what are the reasons for the change involved? This could include: internal structures, incentives or drivers of change, external factors, significant events, etc. What is the evidence to support your analysis of the reason for change?

TTI provided us with 24 "extended stories," five of which reported on management improvements germane to the topics I cover in this book.

The discussions at the TTI Exchange 2012, a gathering of about 70 leaders from around 50 think tanks who gathered in South Africa to discuss management issues among others, were very useful. I reviewed them as on-line videos.

I also monitored postings on management topics and related comments on prominent think tank blogs for the past couple of years. The postings often offered an alternative way for management to address a challenge, raised a new management issue, or provided additional information on a range of topics of interest. Following the blogs certainly stimulated my thinking.

Finally, senior staff—executive directors, chief operating officers, research directors, HR directors and communications directors—at U.S. and other think tanks were good enough to meet with me and offer remarkably open and useful responses to a range of questions on specific operations that helped fill in gaps that arose while I was drafting the text. Statements of actual policies and procedures were supplied upon my request by a half dozen think tanks.

WHAT'S COVERED?

"Management" can mean different things to different people. I have adopted a deliberately narrow definition that encompasses core think tank management tasks. Perhaps clarification is best approached in this instance by saying what is not covered. Executing research *per se* is not. Nor is the specific design and implementation of communications strategies in support of policy engagement. With the advent of multiple new digital communications channels, including social media, a detailed exposition of organizing and delivering content and fostering effective engagement would constitute a disproportionate share of this book; full treatment awaits another book by another author. Chapter 5, in discussing team leaders' responsibilities for policy engagement, conveys key principles for designing project-level (in contrast to institution-level) communications plans. Basic points on an institution-level strategy appear in Chapter 9 in the context of developing a think tank's strategic plan. The numerous points where communications is addressed are listed in this book's index.

Many other key administrative tasks essential to both research and communications are given full attention—with more space devoted to staff policy, acquisition, motivation, and training than to other themes. Given the centrality of capable and productive staff to think tank success, this is to be expected. Moreover, the fact that staff costs consistently account for 60-70 percent of think tank expenditures makes achieving strong staff performance critical. Quality control is also thoroughly covered. Strong practices are obviously essential, if only for defensive purposes (i.e., to shield a think tank's reputation from degradation). But my accent is on the opportunity for products that are improved more than is typically possible from reviewers' comments. I also introduce an innovative paradigm for realizing these opportunities.

I cover think tank governance, particularly the Board of Directors role, because of the invaluable support it can provide the executive director, including advice on fundamental challenges confronting the institute. To achieve this, the Board must be kept focused on the think tank's strategic plan and comprehensive financial and policy effectiveness oversight rather than everyday management tasks. In another chapter, I address the challenges of internal management—i.e., making sure decisions (ranging from which projects to pursue to how to structure staff incentive systems) are thoughtfully considered and made on a timely basis—and ways for information to flow both from management to staff and from staff to decision makers.

I devote Chapters 9 and 10 to developing a forward looking policy research agenda and for the institution to set the conditions for being innovative in its choice of topics. I take a particularly careful look at the tradeoffs involved in whether or not a think tank should take contract funding from government agencies.

The final chapter pair covers financial management and monitoring performance, respectively. The focus in the chapter on finances is on making certain that the resources available to a think tank are spent as intended.[16] I make a strong case for the presence of a system for tracking how staff allocates its time and capturing non-staff spending on a project-level basis; remarkably, such tracking is very seldom done. I also detail how to construct and implement an overhead or indirect cost rate and argue strongly that the current funders' practice of selecting an arbitrary overhead rate of 10-20 percent that it will pay is shortsighted and stimulates poor accounting practices. The last chapter, on measuring and tracking the multiple dimensions of think tank performance, includes a wide array of indicators of the outputs and intermediate outcomes of the communications operations.

HOW TO USE THIS BOOK

This is not a cook book full of ready-to-bake recipes. Rather, it is an idea book for addressing a wide range of management questions. For key tasks confronting think tank managers at various levels the text lays out principles and examples for addressing them. It is not a compilation of various ways each task might be done in different environments such as a think tank being a political think tank, one supported by a government agency, or being embedded in a university. I expect many readers in these circumstances will want to, and should, adjust the implementation of the principles in a way that best fits their institution's specific needs.

I imagine two likely types of readers. The first type is someone who is comparatively new to the world of think tank management and will read it through to get a general grounding on the issues involved and approaches to addressing them. One example is a new foundation program officer with responsibilities for programs working with think tanks in developing and transition countries. Another example is a businessman who has accepted the appointment to a think tank's Board of Directors; s/he is more likely to delve into the chapters on management topics with which s/he is less familiar, such as developing a policy work program or quality control for research products. A senior researcher recently appointed to be a center director or team leader (a level above principal investigator) is another likely example.

The second reader type is a manager who is confronting a specific problem and seeks ideas on how to address it. I believe helping in such cases will be the book's dominant role, and hope this guide will be kept close at hand for think tank managers to use as a continuing reference. The chapters are substantially self-contained, facilitating their use in this way. I have included a detailed table of contents and index to facilitate finding specific topics of interest expeditiously. Many operational details are provided in the annexes.

The "Take Aways" for think tanks concluding each chapter highlight the most important points on the features of a well-managed think tank. Organizations where these attributes are missing have work to do to gain efficiency and probably effectiveness. These lists are concise to emphasize the

---

16   Basic financial management issues, e.g., controls to prevent theft, etc., are not covered as there are many books available on these topics.

few points made. The chapters' text contain additional, second tier points. Lastly, and as noted earlier, this book is addressed to multiple audiences within a think tank and should be readily available to senior managers, including the communications chief, HR director, and senior financial officer, as well as team leaders.

The observations for funders in the Take Aways focus on what to look for and ask about in order to understand how management tasks are actually being executed. They also give some ideas on engaging with think tank leaders on a management topic, should this be thought to be desirable.

BUILDING A
PRODUCTIVE STAFF

CHAPTER 2
Motivating Staff for Higher Productivity and Increased Retention

Staff quality is a key determinant of success for all service organizations, but for think tanks it is fundamental. Senior researchers and policy analysts provide ideas about which of the problems facing their countries an institution can profitably address, direct analysis on those problems, and proffer policy responses to them. Senior researchers are also an institution's representatives for engaging policy elites in debates about the effectiveness of the action the institution proposes. Probably the most visible and intense competition in the labor market is for those with the qualifications to be senior researchers. But, in fact, competition is typically sharp as well for the best IT and communications specialists, in addition to strong administrators in finance and HR.

Think tanks must be better at staff motivation and management than the competition, because they generally are not able to match salaries with a share of the competition. In some countries the private sector—banks, consultancies, and other businesses—are the main competitors who can pay more; in others it is international organizations, ranging from the World Bank to contractors working for aid agencies.

The importance of a think tank's mission and brand, as noted in the last chapter, is hard to overestimate. But the energy, zeal, creativity, and dedication think tank staff brings to their work, and the satisfaction they derive from it, are far from preordained. Personnel management policies and actions make an enormous difference. Beyond the personal relations established among the institute's head, other members of senior management, and individual staff members, other important factors include compensation, working conditions, nonmonetary rewards for good work, and the staff assessment system in place—with prominence going to the quality of feedback on performance. Strengths in one area can be offset by weaknesses elsewhere. In analyzing such factors as staff turnover, morale, and productivity, it is essential to go beyond the compensation or performance assessment system to look at the whole array of an organization's interactions with staff.

Despite their importance, however, little information has been compiled—much less customized guidance—on such fundamental topics as staff turnover rates of think tanks in developing and transition countries and the personnel policies of even Stage 3 think tanks. But think tanks and the donors that support them should have a keen interest in staff motivation, given the role high-caliber, well-motivated staff members play in ensuring strong institute performance.

This chapter's perspective on staff motivation begins to fill the gap. While my focus here is primarily on research staff, communications staff also gets special attention because of the very large recent increases in the types of communications tools and the soaring number of individual products released by institutes. This trend is especially marked when social media releases are added to the traditional reports and policy briefs. Note that I defer specific discussion of team leaders (sometimes called center directors) to Chapter 3, where they are the focus my discussion on ways to attract and on-board staff.

The chapter begins by providing basic information on think tank staffing patterns, so readers can place their organizations' staffing patterns in a wider context. I then examine core principles derived from a combination of the human resources management literature—particularly the literature for private organizations (including NGOs)—and think tank leaders' commentary on their practices. This preliminary discussion provides an essential road map for think tanks in designing their own systems. I then contrast these practices with those that six Eastern European think tanks (in the former Soviet bloc) that have been operating for a decade or so have used to motivate their staffs.

One key difference between NGO staff (including think tanks) and staff in most government agencies or for-profit firms is how the two alternative types approach motivation and productivity. The spirit of this difference is captured in Letts, Ryan, and Grossman (1999):

> [Nonprofit-sector staff] are deeply committed to the social causes their organizations address and are inspired by the possibility of "making a difference." Thanks to this asset, the human resources challenge is different from that of most for-profits. Their biggest challenge is not to attract motivated people—such people will seek out nonprofit opportunities—but to channel their energy so it advances the organization's mission and goals. (p.107–8)

STAFFING PATTERNS IN SAMPLE THINK TANKS

I begin by describing full-time staffing patterns for think tanks from both the GDN and TTI samples. I then provide more detailed information on staffing patterns for both full- and part-time staff at the GDN think tanks, followed by a discussion of turnover.

General Picture: Major Differences between Stage 1 Think Tanks and Others

Table 2.1 shows full-time staff for the GDN-15 and TTI-48 think tanks combined. The data break out Stage 1 think tanks (those with 10 or fewer than full time researchers) from larger (and often more mature) Stage 2–3 organizations. (As noted, since I am uncertain if any of the larger think tanks meet my strict definition of Stage 3 organizations, I group them together into a single category.) The size difference between the two groups is substantial, with Stage 1 organizations averaging 17 full-time staff—less than half the 58 full-time head count of their larger counterparts. The differences are particularly great for research staff, where the full-time staff ratio was over 4:1.

Table 2.1 Mean Number of Full Time Staff by Position Type at GDN-15 and TTI-48 Think Tanks[a]

Full-Time Staff Category (2009/2011)	GDN and TTI Combined		
	<=10 FT Researchers	>10 FT Researchers	All
Research staff	**5.7**	**27.9**	**19.3**
Senior	2.2	8.2	5.9
Mid-level	2.6	9.3	6.7
Junior	1.0	10.4	6.7
Communications/PR Staff	**1.6**	**3.4**	**2.7**
Senior	0.5	0.9	0.7
Mid-level and junior	1.1	2.4	1.9
Administrative technical staff	**3.9**	**8.6**	**6.8**
Senior	1.4	2.5	2.1
Mid-level and junior	2.5	6.1	4.7
Survey operations staff	**1.7**	**4.1**	**3.1**
Interviewers	1.1	1.4	1.3
Supervisors	0.3	1.3	0.9
Data entry/cleaning staff	0.3	1.4	0.9
Support staff	**4.0**	**14.4**	**10.4**
Secretaries	1.5	7.1	4.9
All other support (drivers, coffee, boys, etc.	2.4	7.3	5.4
All Staff	**16.9**	**58.3**	**42.1**
#Orgs in Category	**23**	**36**	**59**

   a.   Staff counts are for 2009 for GDN and 2011 for TTI think tank.

The differences in number of full-time staff in non-research positions between the two size groups are much narrower. For communications staff, for example, Stage 1 think tanks averaged 1.6 staff versus 3.4 for the larger size group. The difference for administrative staff in absolute terms is about the same for the two groups; but the smaller organizations still had over six full-time administrative staff, suggesting that there are several critical support positions that need to be staffed by trained professionals regardless of size beyond some very small minimum. Accounting and IT positions come readily to mind.

Table 2.2 provides a more nuanced view of think tank staffing, drawing on GDN-15 data for both full- and part-time staff, where part-timers' level of effort is converted to full-time equivalents (FTEs). Separate information is shown for the Stage 1 group (8 think tanks) and the larger group (7 think tanks). The "larger" organizations are, as before, very much larger, averaging 52 full-time staff vs. somewhat under 9 for Stage 1 think tanks, and a total of almost 60 FTEs vs. just under 24 for the Stage 1 group.

Table 2.2 Organization Size and Staff Composition of the GDN-15 Think Tanks, 2009

Staff Category	≤10 FT Researchers[b]		>10 FT Researchers		All	
	Mean FT[a] Employees	Mean PT[a] Employees (FTE equivalents)	Mean FT Employees	Mean PT Employees (FTE equivalents)	Mean FT Employees	Mean PT Employees (FTE equivalents)
Research staff	**3.8**	**8.9**	27.9	**0.6**	**15.0**	**5.0**
Senior	2.3	3.5	8.1	0.6	5.0	2.1
Mid-level	1.0	2.8	7.7	0.0	4.1	1.5
Junior	0.5	2.6	12.0	0.0	5.9	1.4
Communications/PR Staff	**0.4**	**0.3**	**4.6**	**0.0**	**2.3**	0.2
Senior	0.3	0.1	1.6	0.0	0.9	0.1
Mid-level and junior	0.1	0.2	3.0	0.0	1.5	0.1
Administrative technical staff	**2.1**	**0.1**	**6.3**	**0.0**	**4.1**	0.0
Senior	1.0	0.0	2.3	0.0	1.6	0.0
Mid-level and junior	1.1	0.1	4.0	0.0	2.5	0.0
Survey operations staff	**0.8**	**5.8**	**1.4**	**7.6**	**1.1**	6.6
Interviewers	0.4	4.5	1.0	5.7	0.6	5.1
Supervisors	0.1	0.6	0.4	1.1	0.2	0.9
Data entry/cleaning staff	0.3	0.6	0.6	0.7	0.4	0.7
Support staff	**1.6**	**0.1**	**10.7**	**0.0**	**5.9**	0.1
Secretaries	0.5	0.0	3.4	0.0	1.9	0.0
All other support (drivers, coffee boys, etc.)	1.1	0.1	7.3	0.0	4.0	0.1
All Staff	**8.6**	**15.3**	**52.0**	**7.9**	**28.4**	**11.8**
# Orgs in Category	8		7		15	
Mean % total staff that is part time	65.0		13.3		38.6	
Mean % research staff that is part time	70.0		2.1		36.0	

a. FT = full time; PT = part-time expressed in full-time equivalents (FTEs).
b. The number of full-time researchers is based on the average number of researchers during the 2009-2011 period.

Particularly conspicuous is the far greater relative importance of part-time vs. full-time staff for Stage 1 think tanks, accounting for nearly 64 percent of total FTEs staff vs. only about 13 percent for the larger organizations. The difference is equally striking for research staff, where the Stage 1 group averages 70 percent of FTEs that are part-time vs. only 2 percent for the larger think tanks. The challenges to Stage 1 think tanks of having such a large share of part-time staff are obvious, with maintaining high quality products perhaps the most daunting.[17] A clear indicator of the ability of the larger organizations to afford greater specialization is in the number of communications and

17   Chapter 6 outlines practices for written report reviews that apply equally to the out-sourced work as to that done by in-house staff.

public relations staff. Stage 1 think tanks averaged slightly less than one FTE in these positions vs. the larger think tank average of 4.6, all of them full-time. Obviously Stage 1 organizations are struggling to get their messages out. The larger organizations are more visible in the policy community—and presumably more effective, as well.

Greater professionalism is also evident in the administrative staff head counts, as suggested earlier. While the larger think tanks averaged 6.3 full-time senior administrative and technical staff, the Stage 1 organizations averaged 2.1. Stage 1 think tanks also have a high incidence of full-time workers in the administrative and technical positions—2.1 full time positions compared with 0.1 part-time FTEs. In other words, there is an administrative core staff working at Stage 1 organizations with a composite full- and part-time research staff.

Turnover Is Significant

Staff turnover rates are of genuine concern to management because of the financial cost and lost productivity associated with hiring replacement staff and on-boarding new staff members. The TTI-48 data set contains information on turnover, both across all positions combined and for individual positions. See Table 2.3 for all staff combined and research staff separately, disaggregated by firm size as measured by staff. Given the small numbers involved, the turnover rates are inherently very volatile.

Table 2.3 Full-time Staff Turnover for All Staff and Selected Positions at TTI-48 Think Tanks, During 2010- 2011

Panel A. All Staff[a]

	<=10 FT Researchers	>10 FT Researchers	All Think Tanks
# Staff Who Left as a Percent of Full-Time Staff	20	15	17
# Staff Hired as a Percent of Full-Time Staff	23	18	20
Number of Full-Time Staff	21	59	45
Net Change in Number of Full Time Staff	+0.4	+1.3	-0.6

   a.   Three observations were dropped where the turnover rates appeared unrealistically high.

Panel B. Research Staff[a]

	<=10 FT Researchers	>10 FT Researchers	All
# Staff Who Left as a Percent of Full-Time Staff	13	20	18
# Staff Hired as a Percent of Full-Time Staff	32	22	25
Number of Full-Time Staff	7	28	20
Net Change in Number of Full Time Staff	+1.1	+0.3	+0.6

   a.   Three observations were dropped where the turnover rates appeared unrealistically high.

The overall turnover rate for the one-year period was about 18 percent—i.e., 17 percent of staff departed and 20 percent equivalent of the base year staff were hired. Nevertheless all this turnover, with farewell parties and new staff receptions, generated little net change in the total staff count. Among researchers, the percentage newly hired (at 25 percent) was higher. For comparison with western think tanks, Simon Maxwell, long-time head of the Overseas Development Institute, estimates the typical turnover rate among British think tanks at 25 percent (Mendizabal 2011). This suggests that average turnover rates may be roughly similar among think tanks in western and other think tanks.

The distribution of staff hired and departed over the previous year as a percentage of total staff (see Table 2.4) indicates that turnover volatility was by no means typical of all think tanks. Full-time staff arrival and departure rates were under 10 percent for about 40 percent of these think tanks and the rate over 40 percent for only about 10 percent of think tanks. Think tanks with departure rates of over 40 percent very likely need to re-analyze the incentives they have (or don't have) that support staff retention.

Table 2.4 Percentage Distributions of Staff Hired and Staff Departed at TTI-48 Think Tanks in All Positions as Percent of Full Time Staff[a]

Distribution of # Staff Hired as a Percent of Full-Time Staff	TTI – All
0% to 5%	13
6% to 10%	24
11% to 20%	22
21% to 40%	27
41% to 75%	13
Distribution of # Staff Departed as a Percent of Full-Time Staff	
0% to 5%	22
6% to 10%	22
11% to 20%	31
21% to 40%	13
41% to 75%	11

Note: In the both panels of this table, 3 observations were dropped because they reported 75% or higher turnover with more than 4 total full-time staff. Sample size is 45 think tanks.

PRINCIPLES OF STAFF MOTIVATION

Successful practices for motivating staff use two kinds of motivational tools. The first consists of specific rewards, such as higher salaries and exposure to leading figures in the policy community (as when a senior staff member makes a presentation to the think tank's Board of Trustees). The second encompasses the counseling and mentoring inherent in a good annual performance appraisal. These are detailed in the next two sections. The types of motivational tools I describe are distilled from a combination of actual think tank experience and the extensive literature on staff motivation. Such tools work best when the think tank has an overall plan for their use and team leaders develop a specific plan for each staffer within the organization's overall incentive plan.

Staff members in all positions are more likely to perform well when they fully understand what is expected from them. Supervisors should set these expectations and ensure they have been well understood by the staff member when s/he first joins the organization and, again, at each annual performance review. The importance of this step is reinforced when one recalls that many researchers have been trained, and perhaps employed, in academic settings where success is not contingent upon the timely delivery of research products, participating in communications campaigns, and completing assignments within budget.

To effectively communicate performance expectations, the supervisor must first define them clearly for him/herself. The time to do so is when the position and the qualifications for it are being first defined. (This definitional task is thoroughly covered in the Chapter 3 when discussing the hiring process.) For a new hire, the job description and the on-boarding orientation are the two critical inputs. It is also good practice for the manager to commit his/her expectations to paper—a few bullet points can often be sufficient—with a copy given to the staffer during a discussion to establish a common understanding of their meaning. For staff already on board, the assessment and annual goals set in the performance appraisal process define the performance expectations.

REWARDS AS MOTIVATORS

Theories on staff motivation can be divided into two groups of motivational structures: those that rely heavily on external rewards and reinforcements (extrinsic or monetary), and those that rely on factors internal to the staff position (intrinsic or non-monetary), as shown in Table 2.5. Intrinsic incentives either reward by recognizing, or facilitate the doing of, good work and enhance the analyst's self-satisfaction and sense of self-worth. Monetary rewards are certainly also related to performance, but in a way that is external to the work itself.

Table 2.5 Major Staff Incentives Used by Think Tanks

Monetary (extrinsic)	Non-monetary (intrinsic)
Salary	Working conditions; support
Bonuses	Authorship
Fringe benefits	Conference attendance
--health insurance	Participation within the organization-e.g., team meetings
--pension contribution	Promotions (requires a career ladder)
--sabbatical	Awards
	Presentations to the Board
	Participation in policy meetings
	Chances for professional growth
	--enriched job content through mentoring and training
	--subsidized job-related courses
	--time to work on publications

To extend this point, experts in human resource management of both for-profit and nonprofit organizations generally feel that adequate base pay is essential to retaining staff and for basic motivation. But other kinds of rewards are more important in motivating staff to higher levels of achievement. For example, Letts and colleagues (1999) state that good pay "is more a protection against dissatisfaction than a source of motivation for the long term. Pay cannot substitute for the satisfaction of producing results" (p.123). A case study of a program to reduce staff turnover implemented by Fleet Boston Financial documented the very high impact of nonfinancial rewards complemented by reasonable pay increases (Nalbantian and Szostak 2004).

Monetary Rewards

Compensation is usually defined as base pay plus fringe benefits and rewards, particularly bonuses, which can be paid either annually or episodically to mark special achievements during the course of the year.

The standard among Stage 3 think tanks for "base pay" is the monthly salary.[18] Organizations operating under tight budgets and uncertainty often turn to other schemes designed to shift the risk of "meeting payroll" each month from the organization to staff. One such arrangement is to pay researchers only when they have work to do. At the start of a new project, management in effect defines a scope of work and enters into a fixed price contract with each researcher involved. A variation on this theme is to pay a small monthly salary plus a project-specific contracted amount.

Sometimes annual bonuses, paid out in good financial years, are part of annual compensation to avoid building the higher payment into the base salary.

---

18   Annex 2.2* contains the statement on Salary Administration for the Urban Institute, a Stage 3 think tank that follows this policy.

Most staff members prefer the certainty of a defined monthly salary, and the structure of remuneration is an important factor in selecting an employer, other things equal. The Economic and Social Research Foundation (ESRF 2012) in Tanzania stated one consequence of its support from TTI as follows: "We are now happy that by paying [adequate] salaries to key researchers IDRC [TTI] has helped us to strengthen human resources in the research department."

Kucharczyk and Kamierkiew (2007, 16) make a useful observation based on on-site interviews about management practices at European think tanks: "the further away an institution moves from the academic to the 'consultancy' model, the more important direct financial incentives become." Without question, salary is a key consideration for all staff, as the level of payment substantially determines analysts' quality of life away from work and represents the value of their work to the organization. Salaries paid to staff at all levels depend on their individual productivity and market rates for persons with their skills. Meeting market conditions frequently causes apparent inequities between staff with seemingly similar qualifications as defined by years of experience or the highest university degree earned, but valued differently by the market (e.g., the IT specialist with a Master's degree typically commands a higher salary than the HR specialist with an MA degree).

It is important for think tank management to recognize *and* reward productivity increases. A small survey of a half-dozen Eastern European think tanks in about 2000 (characteristics described in Chapter 1) found that four of the six executive directors said staff productivity was "good" but could improve. Productivity increases are likely to be very great among research assistants in their first couple of years on the job—as they learn software packages and research protocols and become knowledgeable about the specifics of working at a particular institution. But too often junior staffers shift firms simply in order to get a significant pay increase—a negative outcome because replacing them may be more expensive than a salary increase in terms of the all-in cost of attracting and training new staff. Such extreme productivity gains are likely in other entry or near-entry positions as well, such as in the communications team, IT personnel, and perhaps accountants. Again, high turnover due in part to the failure to financially recognize productivity gains pushes these staffers to achieve higher pay levels by switching organizations. The staff turnover rates reviewed earlier in this chapter are high enough in some cases to encourage senior managers of those think tanks to seriously consider what might be done to get another one or two years of service from their younger staff members.

At the other end of the spectrum, productivity increases are usually quite modest among long-established senior researchers and directors of support departments. And very often they receive correspondingly modest percentage salary increments, albeit on a large base.

Explicit pay-for-performance schemes, such as bonuses, do not get good marks generally in public sector organizations and have seldom been adopted in nonprofits (Liner et al. 2001, 15–16). They often are of questionable value even at for-profit firms (Kerr 2003). A severe limitation is the difficulty in defining goals and achievements precisely. For example, if a senior policy analyst's recommendations for a new program are not accepted by the parliament, how does the evaluator sort out the roles of the myriad actors involved? Researchers working under an incentive system to maximize their income will be motivated to produce many reports of just-acceptable quality for the client, loose standards that could impair the think tank's reputation and cause it to lose clients over time. Other often-noted problems include employees perceiving a weak link between performance and pay increments, a lack of integrity in the ratings, and inequities in the resulting pay patterns. In short, these systems seem to have frequently sent more negative than positive signals to staff (Perry 1991), although many companies have in fact improved staff performance by implementing such systems (McAdams and Hawk 1994).

Bonus payments appear particularly controversial within the think tank community. At a discussion session after presentations on staff retention at TTI EX 2012, there seemed to be general agreement with a statement by a participant from South Asia who described his institution's unsatisfactory experience with bonus payments to research staff. To paraphrase:

> At first giving bonuses for special achievements went well. But soon staff began to petition for a bonus for doing what was really just part of their jobs, nothing extraordinary. It became a real headache and we discontinued them. (Mensa, 2012)

Better received by TTI EX 2012 participants was the creative use of fringe benefits to both attract and retain staff. Many countries have national health programs that provide officially free-of-charge medical care, with firms making premium payments (whole or in part) to the health care system. In some cases the quality of care is unsatisfactory, particularly the long wait times to see a doctor. In such environments, contracting with a private health provider can be extremely attractive to staff. Often the think tank gets a lower premium per person or family insured than an individual or family applying alone for coverage, which strengthens the value of employer-provided vs. individually purchased coverage.

Financial incentives in the form of pension contributions and sabbaticals for researchers can be structured to increase retention rates. Again at TTI EX 2012, starting a modest pension contribution (in addition to state-mandated contributions to the public pension system) after three years' service was cited as being very well accepted. Not discussed in that forum but well-regarded by some private businesses and many universities is the sabbatical after seven or more years' service—although leaves of two months on full pay or four months on half-pay may be much more realistic for think tanks than the whole semester or year off that many universities offer (Dunn and Norton, 2013, 70).

Together the pension contribution (after three years' service) and the sabbatical (after seven) could provide a quite strong retention package. To conserve on overhead spending, these awards could also be limited to particular groups of analysts and perhaps senior managers.

Nonmonetary Awards

In contrast to monetary rewards, most think tanks have never really thought about such awards in a systematic, i.e., strategic, way. This is unfortunate because the very nature of policy research suggests the primacy of factors intrinsic to the job, particularly for the researchers.

Note that successful policy researchers/analysts need to execute three tasks well: be strong researchers; be good managers of research if they are to rise above the research assistant level; and be good promoters of the policy recommendations that emanate from their research, in written presentations and, at least as important, in person. Most think tank analysts receive their greatest rewards from doing high quality, policy relevant research that is recognized as such, and from successfully engaging with policy makers so that their work improves public policy and the lives of the people affected by it. So an important question for the think tank manager becomes: How can the institution best facilitate high quality work and reinforce recognition for it, so that analysts are well-satisfied with their positions and, thus, likely to continue to be productive and stay at the institute?

My general answer is to use intrinsic rewards. Although my focus is primarily on research staff, I also pay special attention to communications staff to illustrate some important differences in how to think of incentivizing groups other than researchers. My discussion of non-monetary rewards first considers the content of and rationale for some of these awards and then turns to strategic considerations.

Working conditions. Typically, when one hears "working conditions," one thinks of physical conditions—office space quality, the extent of crowding, and the degree of privacy (and quiet); availability of conference rooms for meetings of various sizes; the quality of the floor plan (does it contribute to staff seeing each other casually to encourage interchange?); and the appearance of the building where the think tank is housed.[19]

Space and layout are important, of course, but at least as important is the quality of the assistance that supports the research and communications functions. This includes such things as the array of state-of-the-art software for statistical analysis, mapping, and other functions; the efficiency of internet access; access to modern computers, generally; the quality of printers available; ready access to the literature relevant to projects under way, particularly access to international journals and books; and, for senior researchers, the quantity and quality of the research assistance. I turn again here to ESRF's response to its TTI support: "Good working conditions contribute very much in retaining and motivating workers to perform their duties effectively."

It is easy for an organization as a whole, particularly for smaller think tanks, to get used to poor working conditions. But the reality is that staff in such conditions will be less efficient than their

---

19   Mendizabal (2013e) offers some ideas on office space for think tank use. Allen and Henn (2007) provide an analysis of how coworker location affects the frequency of communication.

better-equipped counterparts and the organization less attractive as a place to work. Think tanks with poor working conditions are, thus, more vulnerable to losing good staff to other think tanks than if their working conditions were better. I fully recognize how difficult it can be to find the resources for upgrading such systems. But, as discussed in Chapter 11, defining a realistic overhead rate and getting funders to pay it can be a major part of the solution.

Authorship. Few topics can be as contentious as determining who will be listed as report or article authors and the order in which they are listed. This is understandable: the stakes are high. Without question, authorship of published documents, especially publications in international peer reviewed journals, is extremely important for researchers' reputations and their value in the market. The "rules" regarding authorship are stated in a number of places. I think the following statement, taken from the Urban Institute's policy, covers the topic well:

> In general, the authors of a book, report, paper or article should be those researchers who have made *significant* intellectual contributions to the research, including, but not limited to, formulating the research design or concept, analyzing and interpreting the data, and writing or rewriting substantial parts of the manuscript. Another condition of authorship is that contributors must be able to explain and answer questions about the research. As a rule of thumb, it's the quality and importance of the intellectual contribution that determines authorship, not the amount of time spent on the project…. Keeping in mind each project member's interests and abilities and their match with the research task at hand, Principal Investigators are encouraged to provide opportunities for staff to make significant intellectual contributions.

Think tanks have a strong incentive that they should recognize for research team leaders to be generous in determining authorship, as the Urban Institute policy clearly encourages Principal Investigators to be. Including someone as an author rewards hard work and creates a valuable credential for the individual involved. But it also strengthens the person's profile for inclusion in future proposals and adds to the institute's stature. Obviously, younger researchers included as authors generally value this very highly.

Promotion. Being promoted from one professional level to another is a genuine achievement and is highly valued by those staff members who succeed. It makes sense, therefore, for even small think tanks to define multiple levels within each job category—researchers, communications experts, IT experts, financial staff, and so on. Not all defined positions in the "job ladder" need to have someone in them; but the very existence of a job ladder with several positions creates the opportunity for staff to be explicitly judged and recognized as succeeding against an objective standard.

Annexes 2.3* and 2.4* present illustrative job descriptions for research and communications positions at the Urban Institute. Also highly relevant is the description of the Institute's overall salary administration system in Annex 2.2* that places annual salary increments in context.

The researcher ladder has five well-defined rungs. The career path is clear. The descriptions are clear and explicit about the research tasks at each level. They are, however, essentially silent on the responsibilities for policy engagement and the communication of research findings to the wider policy community,[20] which I regard as a conspicuous omission. (This criterion receives greater emphasis in the requirements for promotion to the senior staff levels.) Active engagement with the policy community is more important today than ever before; job descriptions need to be explicit on researcher responsibilities in this area. A recent analysis of policy engagement and communications (PEC) practices in a dozen African think tanks agrees with me on the need for emphasis on policy engagement, concluding that "researchers already have tightly packed agendas and are unwilling to take on communications work" (TTI, 2013). Those working actively with these think tanks opined that reviewing job descriptions to include communications activities might be order.

The Urban Institute's pattern for communications positions differs sharply from that for research staff. Nine different communications positions are defined, excluding the overall leader (who is a vice president). The positions are mostly specialty positions, for example, web specialist, infographics specialist, and content and social media strategist. There is a short ladder for editors, with the editorial/production editor supervising the production editor. The blog editor (Metro Policy Editor), in contrast, reports to the Director of Digital Marketing. Such shorter or single-step ladders in communications complicate recognition of clear advancements in skill acquisition.

Figure 2.1 is an organization chart for a large communications team, designed for this book by a think tank communications vice president, using the same number of positions as in the Urban Institute team but with some adjustments in their arrangement. (There is a side-by-side listing of the two sets of positions in Annex 2.4*.) The major division in the chart is between digital media and other communications forms (which are grouped under the Director for External Affairs). The job ladders remain single step or short.

---

20   Annex 5.1 contains the job description for a team leader or center director, in which these communication responsibilities are well-developed.

Figure 2.1 Illustrative Communications Staff Org Chart

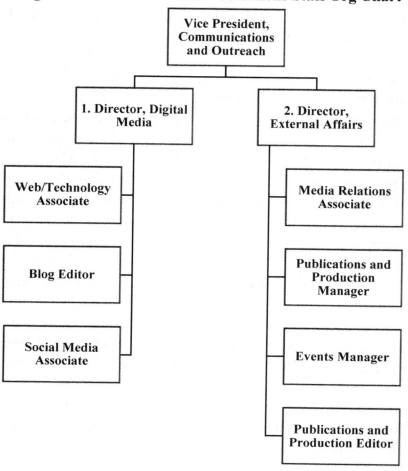

Several administrative areas also have short job ladders at larger organizations. Annex 2.5 shows ladders and corresponding responsibilities for three areas at a Washington think tank with about 70 staff:

- Accounting: Staff Accountant, Senior Staff Accountant, and Budget, Grants and Contracts Manager

- General administration: Administrative Coordinator, Program Coordinator and Executive Assistant.

- Operations: Operations Program Associate, Operations Manager, and Chief Administrative Officer

Note that this organization does not have a ladder for human resources, with there being a single HR officer.

Where a job ladder is absent, management must clearly define increases in responsibility and level of work without necessarily changing the job title—for example, by naming an analyst as the Principal Investigator on a project, providing a research assistant for lower-level tasks, or permitting the analyst more freedom in meeting with clients and policymakers. Or in the case of the blog editor, give him/her more responsibility to interact directly with researchers on questions about a candidate posting being too politically charged.

In communications where job ladders are routinely short, what attributes do managers seek in candidates? A WonkComms (2013) panel in December 2013 addressed exactly this question. Communications directors from three think tanks, two London-based and one in New York, participated. In spite having teams that ranged in size from 15 to 3 full time communications staff, the views were remarkably similar. Both look for someone with a core area of expertise who is clearly willing to adapt to new tasks and cheerfully cooperate with colleagues. A "core skill" includes: editing and writing well and quickly; sound technical knowledge (e.g., HTML); and good telephone manner (talking to editors, etc.) where PR is a big activity in the group. Other traits emphasized by one or more of the participants were to understand the policy process (i.e., the dance among policymakers, their staffs, and those providing policy advice) and being engaged in a policy topic without it becoming a passion, which leads to overselling to editors and overinvesting communications resources in one project's dissemination.

Equally important is how positions in think tank communications groups are sold to applicants. All implicitly or explicitly noted the great responsibility (and freedom) given to everyone on small teams. Another universal selling point for think tanks can be the idealism of working on issues important to the lives of their fellow countrymen. Many staff members find working for an important cause deeply satisfying. Finally, for those with a greater understanding of contemporary communications practices, the challenge of "cracking the short content problem"—how to make blog entries, for example, simultaneously informative, accurate, and catchy—can be attractive.

Conference attendance, awards, making presentations to the Board of Trustees and more
All of these activities contain a significant element of awarding good work; in some cases, e.g., conference attendance, there is an element of investing in the staffer as well.

Awards. The use of awards, where a staff member or team is publicly recognized for special accomplishment and given a gift (often nominal), seems to depend on the Executive Director's personality as well as the organization's. Modest one-off cash bonuses for consistently extraordinary work also go here.

Awards to individuals can be a very useful tool, especially in larger organizations where it is harder for individuals to stand out. It is important, however, that the choices of awardees be clearly justified and the awards presented with some ceremony. Awards to support staff, because they seldom get into the policy world's limelight, are especially effective.

Awards to teams as well as to individuals send the right signal for researchers to assume a cooperative attitude. An annual team award for the project with the greatest policy impact is one example. A major western think tank has two annual "President's Awards," for example: one for the best policy research of the year and the other for the best public communications. Both can go to teams as well as individuals and awardees are listed on a plaque in the organization's entryway.

The first rule in organizing awards is to be: 1) inclusive in selecting the team that considers to whom awards should be given and 2) very careful and thoughtful about choices. Ponder the pros and cons of awards to various individuals and jealousies that could be created. Such complications are the reason many organizations shy away from making awards, except for one or two of the "greatest annual achievement" type.

Presentations to the Board of Trustees. Board meetings often include a senior staff member making a presentation on a particularly interesting or policy-important project. Being selected to make such a presentation is typically viewed as a distinct honor. Most think tanks include presenters as guests at the dinner, lunch, or other social events held in conjunction with the Board meeting itself. Seating arrangements are such that staff members of the organization are mixed with Trustees. This gives staff the chance to chat with these luminaries and make a policy point or two, especially if asked the right question.

Conference attendance. Conferences can be a significant opportunity to gain knowledge on the topic of the conference and to network with peers. For researchers, peers are other analysts and policy makers with a clear interest in the conference's topic. For support staff, the peers are from the same professional group. When a staff member is invited to give a presentation at a conference, there is little question about the organization supporting the invitee's participation, so long as s/he can be counted upon to make a strong presentation. If there is any question about the invitee's ability, then a manager will have to be given responsibility for working with the staff member, including listening to and commenting upon a dry run presentation. Overall, this represents a significant investment in the invitee and one likely to be highly valued by him/her.

Decisions on attendance as a non-presenter are more complex. The more directly relevant the conference topic is to that on which staff work consistently, or are working at the time, the stronger is the case for being there. Supervisors vary sharply in their views about the utility of their staff attending many conferences because of the opportunity cost of their other work. Consequently, non-presenting attendance is often viewed as a reward for good work. For senior support staff, permitting conference attendance is particularly appreciated as a clear recognition of their professional status. Most conferences also provide highly valuable information on trends in the specialty area of the staff involved, which often yields significant benefits to the think tank more generally.

Participation within the organization (e.g., team meetings). The literature on the effects of a range of personnel practices on staff performance in administrative settings devotes significant attention to the effects of staff participation in an organization's decision making (Perry, Mesch, and Paalberg 2006). Findings indicate that the effects of such participation on staff retention are substantial, but have little effect on staff productivity. Events such as staff meetings, where all staff members feel free to contribute, are common and can be very effective in communicating information to staff and generating a sense of community, both of which can influence retention and productivity. For larger organizations, staff meetings by work group, research division, or finance department, are more successful than all-staff meetings. Research team meetings on particular projects are also effective for building team spirit and for efficient project execution. (I include more on team meetings in Chapters 3, 5, and 8.)

Professional development. The last four entries in the nonmonetary column in Table 2.5 focus squarely on increasing skills and competency. "Enriched job content through mentoring and training" will typically be enormously attractive to junior staff in both research and administrative positions. As discussed in greater detail in the Chapter 3, staff training consists of both formal training events and on-the-job training (OJT). The importance of well-structured OJT is hard to overestimate, although at most firms and think tanks it is organized haphazardly and therefore fails to realize its potential (Bowsher 1998; Rothwell and Kazanas 1994).

But mentoring efforts are not always effective. Remarkably, most established researchers think of themselves as natural and effective mentors without ever giving much thought to what effective monitoring requires. Some senior researchers, in fact, are natural and generous mentors. Others are less so, but even some of those can be encouraged to spend time explaining concepts, methods, and results related to their projects to lower level staff working directly on the project. Sometimes this takes fairly strong encouragement from team leaders to be successful. But sometimes is just does not work, in which case the team leader can at least rotate research assistants (RAs) among the senior researchers, so every RA experiences some productive mentoring.

Participation of mid-level research staff in policy meetings has both longer-term investment and immediate professional stature effects. A senior analyst taking a less seasoned colleague to policy meetings is a particularly superior form of mentoring. The more junior colleague learns how to prepare for such meetings, how these discussions flow, and the type of follow-up that is appropriate—a most effective way of "learning the trade." Policy meetings in some countries can include testifying before official parliamentary committees or government commissions. Again, extremely valuable lessons can be drawn from such an experience. And beyond the learning value comes recognition from those with whom the meetings are held, as the senior person is in effect vouching for his/her more junior colleague. My own experience leads me to emphasize how important it can be for the senior person to explain to the junior colleague his/her expected role in the meeting. (I have had at least one junior colleague become so talkative from nerves that a meeting's productivity was much lower than it should have been.)

Needless to say, many senior analysts closely guard their policymaking contacts, as is to be expected. But at some time the less senior colleague will be ready for a more public role than simply being a strong analyst and writer. The institution can either help him/her move into the policy community or risk his/her departure to another think tank where s/he will have this role. In sum, senior management needs to keep aware of reputational developments and adjust workloads and public exposure accordingly.[21]

Incentive System Administration

Some of the incentives listed in Table 2.5 clearly involve significant potential financial commitments by the think tank, which must be carefully assessed before adoption. Many can have substantial impacts on the overhead rate and, thus, the organization's competitiveness. Senior management, and possibly the Board of Trustees, must establish a framework for deciding whether to include an incentive in the organization's incentive package and the amount of money to authorize for each incentive type chosen, which fall into several relatively homogeneous groups for budgeting purposes:

1. *Significant recurring monetary awards.* These include fringe benefit items beyond mandatory social payments—such as bonuses, private health insurance, supplementary pension contributions, sabbaticals, and time awarded to work on non-funded projects. The last item could be particularly substantial when, for example, an analyst is awarded several months' funded time to write a book.

2. *Costs of realizing or sustaining desirable conditions.* Included here are the physical plant; furniture; computer system, software, and other IT investments; and training budgets.

3. *An overall budget for a group of incentives with comparatively modest costs.* Included here would be conference attendance (local and international), staff awards, and small amounts of time to prepare publications.

4. *Incentives with few cost implications.* Authorship credit, participation within the organization, presentations to the Board, and enriched job content through mentoring fall into this category.

While incentives in items 1 and 2 involve significant budget as well as policy decisions for management, those in items 3 and 4 require comparatively less funding but institution-wide policies are to be set. Two types of decision must be taken for the less costly incentives. One is whether to offer the incentive at all where there is a choice (authorship is not such a choice, nor is at least some level of participation within the organization; these are simply facts of life). The second type of decision is that senior management must decide on: 1) the total resources to be made available for all incentives in this class and how to allocate them among competing opportunities, and 2) policy

---

21   It is worth noting, however, that the importance of such introductions may be declining because of the rapidly increasing ability of mid-level analysts to become known through social media and blog postings.

on awards without a monetary element (authorship, participation in the life of the institution, presentations to the Board, and awards/recognition fall into this category.)

My experience is that few think tanks approach incentive decisions on such an organized basis. A common outcome is to find the incentives they adopt rather more costly as a package than envisioned when the decision was made. To avoid this trap, the first step is to decide what your objectives are and what you have in total to spend, given overhead costs and the extent of price competition in the organization's market. Only then should an organization begin allocating funds. It may well be that, beyond seeking a generally productive staff, the primary goal is retention of highly productive senior analysts. Alternatively, the primary perceived problem may be low productivity and high turnover among lower level research staff. Clearly, very different incentive mixes are appropriate to address each. Focusing the available resources where they have real impact is critical; if this is not done, a few staff will feel somewhat better about working at the institute but the problems will remain.

Once the incentive structure and budget have been set, the major question becomes who decides on making awards that are not awarded universally—either to all staff or to all staff in certain positions groups (e.g., all senior analysts, all accountants). My vote is to decentralize as much of this decision making as possible to team leaders. They know their team members better than senior management and they can see when an intervention may be particularly effective. A simple and equitable way to make the allocation to team leaders is based on the share of their group's annual staff salaries to total staff salaries in the groups participating in the allocation scheme. (Salaries are better than head count because most awards are valued primarily in staff time; the all-in costs of even international conference attendance, for example, are often dominated by staff compensation.) It may be that management decides to include administrative offices among the groups participating in the decision process. Separate money pots for research groups and administrative offices give management a desirable degree of flexibility in setting average award amounts.

The final incentive issue is how managers allocate the incentive funds given them to use. Allocations need to be both: 1) equitable (similarly performing staff receive similar benefits but not necessarily the same awards) and 2) given in recognition of good work and to promote greater productivity. A senior manager at a Stage 3 think tank made the useful observation that larger think tanks likely share these resources more equitably among staff than their small counterparts, because the larger ones are almost certain to have more written guidelines governing the reward distribution.

None of these decisions is easy to make. Managers I know have found it useful to prepare a matrix with staff listed across the top and incentives, including promotions, down the left-hand side. The matrix has three columns for each staff member—the prior two years and this year—so the manager can easily keep track of what s/he has done for each staffer over time. It is useful to enter both that an award was made and its cost to the institute. The matrix also comes in handy when senior management wants to discuss how the manager has used his/her allocations in the past year or two.

There is, of course, always the danger of favoritism or discrimination. The positive effects of an award system can quickly dissipate if staff believes the allocation process is unfair. So I strongly encourage executive directors to require that logs of the type just described be kept up-to-date and that s/he examine them a couple times a year to check for clear cases of favoritism toward or discrimination against individual staffers. Just knowing that their logs will be checked will strongly encourage award givers to think carefully about the way they distribute them among staff.

Creating and administering an incentive system is a major task demanding, at least in the development stage, a good deal of time from the HR Director, senior management, and team leaders. They will all have views on which incentives will be most effective with which staff groups and which most need the stimulation. Taking the time for a full discussion is well worth it in terms of creating a team that pulls together, rather than competitively, to increase staff productivity and retention.

ANNUAL PERFORMANCE EVALUATION

A strong appraisal system is one used primarily as the basis for discussion between supervisor and employee on the employee's record of achievement, the suitability of the employee's goals for the future, and a plan for how the supervisor and organization can help the employee achieve agreed-upon new goals. Glen (1990, 2) had this to say about the performance appraisal process:

> It is hoped that data are gathered by systematic observations, not only to accurately measure current performance, but also to reinforce strengths, identify deficiencies, and feedback necessary information of changes in future performance. The purpose is to measure progress, differentiate between levels of performance, pinpoint training needs, validate rewards, and identify promotable employees.

Many think tank directors are unenthusiastic about annual evaluations. "I know my staff and I really don't need this" is a frequent reaction. My reaction is quite different. I am highly dubious that any manager can keep in mind accurately the diverse accomplishments of even a couple of subordinates over the period of a year. I have also found reading the self-assessment part of the forms of my own direct staff enlightening. And not remembering is not the only danger; supervisors can also be totally unaware of some activities their subordinates have carried out. Not remembering and not knowing combine to produce a systematic tendency to underestimate what a particular staff member has done. In addition, institutions owe it to their employees to be very thoughtful in using the only time in the year when there is a focused conversation about actions necessary for a particular staff member's future development. The annual performance evaluation should be used to have a conversation that leads to a sensible plan for the coming year and sets concrete goals.

The better assessment systems get substantial employee input on setting goals and describing accomplishments (Lee 1996; Wilson 1994). But it is important to note that these assessments, though used to inform the salary review process, do not drive it. Stated differently, salary adjustments and other rewards should not be in conflict with assessments, but rewards should not be based exclusively on those assessments.[22] Mechanistic "score sheets" used to determine salaries generally cause more staff problems than they address.

A comparatively new wrinkle in assessments is rating the performance of teams rather than individuals (Heneman 2001, chapter 8). For think tanks with teams whose workers are almost exclusively executing a large project over multi-year periods, such team ratings may be somewhat useful. Individual assessments, however, will very likely remain the rule because there are so few multi-year, full-time team projects.

An array of rating systems and procedures for employee assessments is available to think tanks that can be seen in the next section and learned about elsewhere.[23] The essential point to make here is a more fundamental one: An effective assessment process is critical for generating information on which to base rewards and to develop a program to assist staff with professional development. Increased professional development, in turn, raises achievement and job satisfaction—and motivation. Goal setting, which should be a key part of any assessment, has been linked to higher productivity (Perry, Mesch, and Paalberg 2006, 509).

Example of a Strong Annual Assessment Process
The Urban Institute has a strong assessment process that is well worth taking time to look at with some care. Annex 2.1* presents three relevant documents from the Urban Institute's HR department: 1) a memo to all staff explaining the procedures involved in the year's performance assessment; 2) the assessment form used for nearly all staff that is completed by the person being reviewed and by the reviewer; and 3) the memo to Senior Fellows, the Institute's most senior researchers, giving guidance about the essay they are to write about their accomplishments in preparation for their review meetings with the Institute's president.

These are complemented particularly by the first document in Annex 2.2* the Institute's salary administration policy, which places the performance review process in perspective. It reviews such

---

22   This is the system used by several Western think tanks I am familiar with. A number of well-managed corporations use the same procedure, including the General Electric Corporation (Glen 1990, 3). Lee (1996) and Ledford (1995), among others, also strongly support separating assessments from the formal salary adjustment process.

23   Alternatives are discussed in Rabin and others (1985, 184–94) and in Chapter 7 of Heneman (2001). A specific type of evaluation worth mentioning is the so-called 360 degree performance evaluation. This system is designed to give managers feedback from a variety of sources with the goal of improving the manager's performance. So, for example, a middle manager, would be rated by the people s/he supervises and other managers with whom s/he has frequent contact in addition to his/her supervisor. This system was introduced and has achieved substantial acceptance in business. In more recent years, however-er, careful analysis of these systems has called their efficacy into question. See, for example, Toegel and Conger (2003) and Bracken and Rose (2011).

items as position classifications, salary ranges for a position, salaries for newly hired staff, pay increments, promotions, and the reclassification of positions.

The all-staff memo is particularly useful for think tank managers because it lays out the whole assessment process. It notes the various steps and tasks of both those being reviewed and the reviewers. Performance ratings are also described and the purpose of the appraisal discussion between staffer and supervisor is outlined. The importance of both parties signing the document is emphasized (if the staffer disagrees with the assessment, s/he can appeal; signing simply confirms that s/he has read the review). Finally, the relation between the assessment, on the one hand, and promotions and reclassifications, on the other, is explained. The Institute holds meetings where new staff can learn more about the process; new supervisors also receive instruction.

The initial step in the actual review process is the employee preparing his/her self-assessment. This covers the first two pages in the nine page assessment booklet (which is now used on-line at the Urban Institute). The first item prompts the staffer to list his/her outputs during the year. For researchers this includes publications (that today would include blog postings), presentations, fund raising, and involvement in the policy process (included under "special external activities"). There are also helpful prompts for administrative and technical staff. (I think the form could be improved with a specific prompt for those in the communications group.)

The assessment booklet is quite thorough in other areas as well, prompting the staffer to outline if the goals set last year were realized, and to list new responsibilities and skills acquired, major accomplishments over the year, goals that the staffer would set for the next year, and more. Then comes a series of questions designed to set up the discussion with the supervisor (questions 7-10) and a request to attach an up-to-date resume.

The second step is the supervisor's turn. Part 1 of this begins with the supervisor commenting on the staffer's self-assessment and goals proposed for the next year. The supervisor then takes stock of the staffer's strengths and weaknesses and is asked to make "a suggestion [that], if followed, would enhance the employee's performance, strengthen skills, or improve the employee's opportunity for advancement or career growth." This is a series of demanding questions and requires real thought by supervisors to prepare useful productivity-improving replies.

Part 2 of the supervisor's part requires him/her to check boxes with five point scales (plus "cannot assess" and "not applicable") on performance strength in various areas (e.g., quality of work, productivity, technical skills, writing skills, interpersonal skill, and other areas). There are 11 areas assessed for all staff, an additional four areas for research staff, and four more for supervisors and managers (such as the quality of their supervisory skills and financial management of projects and other activities). The supervisor is then requested to give an "overall assessment" or summary of the staffer's performance.

Worth noting is that some think tanks state explicit performance standards for various positions, although the more common practice is for the rater to infer reasonable standards for the duties listed in the relevant job description. Annex 2.5* displays the standards used for a series of administrative positions at the Results for Development (R4D) Institute in Washington. (These should be of additional interest to the reader because they imply the content of the corresponding job descriptions, which I did not find readily available for these positions.)

The final assessment element is the meeting between supervisor and staffer, which happens only after the staffer has had a minimum of 24 hours to read and digest the supervisor's comments and ratings. Given the extensiveness of preparation for the discussion, this provides a genuine opportunity for real mentoring and for lesson learning on both sides. The result is in effect an "individual development plan," which sets development goals for the next year and covers changes in the type of work the staffer will be doing, if any, as well as training to be undertaken.

Note that the Institute's assessment process does not result in an overall numeric performance score, although Part 2 of the rater's section would lend it to quantification. The Institute's view is that assessments are too complex to reduce to one or two numeric scores.[24] Likewise, the system avoids "stack ranking" (i.e., when staff in each group, such as research assistants, are explicitly ranked from highest to lowest performance). Stack ranking systems tend to be used to identify weak performers who are often then candidates for replacement. But it is possible that such a ranking could, even within a rating group where everyone is performing at a "fully satisfactory" level, still be used to force the weakest out. For this reason, such systems have come under substantial criticism in recent years and, in my view, should be avoided.[25]

Assessment Systems in the Context of Compensation Decisions

How do performance assessments affect compensation decisions? The first point concerns the context in which individual staff compensation decisions are made. Market conditions are very important. If support for think tanks from foundations is down or expected to fall next year because of generally poor performance of endowment earnings, for example, price competition among think tanks for the smaller pool of grants can be expected to be more intense, including on prices for proposed work. Finally, the inflation rate is always relevant in determining percentage pay increases. All these factors must be considered when the institution sets an overall average percentage staff increase. Typically, the target announced—say 3.5 percent—is actually less than the actual target because there are always special or unexpected cases that push the average above the target by 0.5 percent or so. The decision on the target rate is typically made by the executive

---

24   Fox (1991), Rabin and others (1985, 183–84), and Wilson (1994, ch. 9) also list problems with mechanistic assessment processes. Lee (1996) reports that 60 percent of 218 corporations surveyed reported using a narrative evaluation with an overall numeric score; the second most frequently used system was numeric scoring.

25   For a layman's discussion of such systems, see "Ranked and Yanked," *The Economist,* November 16th, 2013, pp.69-70, North American print edition.

director in consultation with senior managers or the executive committee if there is one.

Within relatively homogeneous groups of workers—defined by task, level in the organization, degree of experience, and the market demand for their group's services—the performance assessment typically plays an important role in informing the "salary administration committee" about each person's performance in the past year and expectations for the future. There is, however, no simple lock-step relationship between the appraisal and an individual's salary increase. Some committee members give more weight to some factors than others, even within the same institution. A complicating factor is that the performance appraisal and the contents of any recommendations for promotion are both critical in making the case for a promotion, with promotions nearly automatically carrying larger salary increases than good performance alone. The overall general rule in making a salary decision is to weigh each staffer's performance relative to: 1) that of his/her peers (as defined in the first sentence of this paragraph) and 2) his/her expected future contributions.

Lastly, the salary review committee needs to be attentive to any possible patterns of discrimination. It is easy for women or ethnic minorities to be paid less, perhaps implicitly on the misconception that their opportunity cost is lower. The HR director should be tasked with looking over the patterns of salary increments and actual proposed compensation levels and to report any unusual patterns to the committee prior to the next year's salaries being finalized.

THINK TANK PRACTICES

This section covers the same two interlocking topics as the previous section—monetary and nonmonetary incentives and staff assessment—examining practices at the CEE-6 Stage 2 think tanks. I rely on this information because more up-to-date survey information on personnel practices with equivalent detail is lacking. In a few places I can supplement the CEE information with limited data from the GDN and TTI surveys and information from other sources.

Incentives and Annual Assessments at the CEE-6
To add to the brief introduction on the CEE-6 think tanks in the previous chapter and Annex 1.2, each institute's name, year of establishment, and number of full-time researchers in 2000 are shown in Table 2.6. The number of full-time researchers ranged from 10 to 53. Obviously, the practices of such a small number of organizations provide only a rough idea of actual practices in the region, but they are useful for demonstrating the range of practices at relatively young think tanks.

Table 2.6 Six Eastern European Think Tanks: their Location, Year Founded, and Staff Size in 2000

Institute	Location	Year founded	Number of full-time research staff
Metropolitan Research Institute (MRI)	Budapest	1990	11
Social Research Institute (TARKI)	Budapest	1985[a]	31
Center for Study of Democracy (CSD)	Sofia	1990	20
Institute for Urban Economics (IUE)	Moscow	1995	38
Institute for the Economy in Transition (IET)	Moscow	1990	53
Expert Institute of the Russian Union of Industrialists and Entrepreneurs (Expert)	Moscow	1991	10[b]

[a] TARKI shifted its main operations to a for-profit basis in 1997, although it also retains its nonprofit component.
[b] Includes the president, executive director, and eight team leaders. All other research staff are contracted for individual projects

Incentives. I start with *monetary incentives.* Box 2.1 gives a thumbnail sketch of the systems used to determine basic pay and bonuses (where applicable). Reading through the systems highlights the striking complexity of many. Only two have traditional simple salary schemes, CSD and IUE (the middle two in the list). The others embody some sort of incentive payment, consistent with the view of salary's key role in staff retention and motivation. Some incentive payment plans are designed in part to promote marketing and work acquisition; but such plans may create incentives that are negative from the organization's perspective. Staffers at IET and TARKI working on fixed-price contracts, for example, have a strong incentive to do the minimum required to fulfill the contract. Team leaders at TARKI and Expert have clear incentives to press clients for a maximum price and to minimize the effort in producing the deliverables contracted for—all to maximize profits and their own net pay. Obviously, senior management should make every effort limit such behavior, given that clients are less likely to be interested in future contracts if they face a high price for only a modest product.

Box 2.1 Compensation System for Researchers at Sample Eastern European Think Tanks, around 2000

Institution	System
MRI	*All staff.* Beginning in 2001, employees receive 75 percent of base pay on a monthly basis. Twice yearly, management assesses the share of time charged to billable projects. If the share is greater than 75 percent over the whole period, then the person receives the other 25 percent of base pay. Staff can bill any number of hours (beyond 40) and receive extra pay for the additional hours worked. But at least 75 percent of time charged must be billable. Researchers are divided into two project teams, each directed by a managing director. Individual compensation depends significantly on the performance of the whole team.
TARKI	*Project directors or team leaders.* Total compensation consists of base salary and bonuses. The bonuses can be substantial—as large as or even larger than the base salary. The bonus is determined by the net profit on projects carried out by the project director. Project directors generally negotiate contracts and are responsible for fulfillment. The net profit is split between the organization and the project director based on a formula known to all parties. *Senior and junior researchers.* These employees also have the opportunity for payment beyond the base salary. Project directors negotiate with junior staff for blocks of time within which specified tasks are to be done (e.g., two months to conduct a particular analysis). In effect, staff members are given fixed-price contracts. Staff members are able to take commitments for more-than-nominal full-time work and thereby raise their total compensation.
CSD	*All staff.*[a] Monthly base salary plus the 13th month's payment. Payment rates are changed during the year as needed, in light of both inflation and the need for merit increases (i.e., there is a constant salary review process).
IUE	*All staff.* Salaries are set through an annual salary-setting process associated with a comprehensive staff assessment process.
IET	*All staff.*[b] Compensation is based on three components: a small base salary; principal income, from participation in specific projects, is determined as a fixed-price contract between the project leader and the employee; and bonuses on contracts where funds are available at the end of the contract and the quality of work warrant, as determined by the project leader.
Expert	*Team leaders.* Payment has two parts: a small monthly salary and payment for directing projects. The team leaders control staffing and execution of the project, including determining the pay for all staff. Team leaders' compensation for a project is agreed upon with the executive director.

[a] Excludes the board of directors—president, executive director, and director of research—and the staff in the survey research unit. The latter can receive bonuses largely based on the volume of overtime committed to projects.
[b] Excludes senior management.

These systems also engender other significant risks. One is wide swings in month-to-month salaries, creating tensions and difficulties in managing household finances for the workers involved. Another is fomenting resentment between those staff members who do less well in the competition for bonuses compared to colleagues who are "big winners." Such resentment can easily result in staff departing in frustration.

In early 2013, I did an assessment of the effectiveness of a three-year institutional grant from the Think Tank Fund to European Initiative-Liberal Academy Tbilisi (EI-LAT). This is a Stage 1 think tank with a small research team, and they contract out to consultants for report input or whole reports for which EI-LAT has a contract but not the in-house capacity. One research-advocacy organization I talked with praised EI-LAT's oversight of the consultant firms they engage, saying that they were much better than others at enforcing quality control standards. I took this to be evidence of the challenges of quality control when think tanks issue fixed-price contracts for research, whether to in-house staff or to external consultants.

Four factors related to *nonmonetary incentives* at the six think tanks are shown in Table 2.7— quality of the research facilities, authorship policy, presence of career ladders, and encouragement of staff to publish. Broadly, the included think tanks demonstrate a significant range of practices:

- In terms of office quality and space and computer support, there are think tanks at both ends of the range: for four of the six, office space is generally viewed as a strong positive while computing was not much beyond "OK." But the other two think tanks are weaker for offices and stronger for computers than the first four.

- Authors of reports are listed on title pages in five of the six.

- Staff is encouraged to publish at all six.

- Staff classification practices are weak. Only three of the six organizations have formal classification systems for researchers, meaning that positions are not explicitly defined at the other three. Since promotions can be used to reward staff, the lack of career ladders denies management one important reward option.

Table 2.7 Motivational Factors at Six Eastern European Think Tanks around 2000

Motivational Factor	Conditions at Sample Think Tanks[b]
Rating of research facilities[a]	
--Office space per person	4 rated theirs as superior, 1 competitive, and 1 average
--computer and internet support	1 superior, 1 above average, 4 comparable
Authorship policy	
--Names of authors shown on title page of publications?	5 yes, 1 no
Formal classification system for research positions (e.g., junior, mid-level, senior or project leader)?	3 have no ladder/classifications
--number of levels, where levels are present	3 had a ladder: one each with 3, 4, and 5 steps
Staff encouraged to publish?	6 yes

a. Compared to similar organizations.
b. These are self-ratings by think tank management on conditions at their institution compared with competitors.

Other nonmonetary incentives did not play a very large role at these think tanks. At some level, all helped staff prepare publications, attend conferences, and participate in training. But with a few exceptions these activities were not viewed explicitly as rewards; rather, allocation tended to go to the most suitable person for other reasons. Sometimes, for example, support for writing a paper was given to someone who was without project coverage for the moment and needed the work. Travel to an international conference was clearly viewed generally as a reward, but who was chosen to go was sensitive to language skills.

There is very limited information in the GDN and TTI data sets on incentives. The baseline (2009) TTI survey included questions about the quality of facilities and IT infrastructure. (Conditions may well have improved since the survey, in part due to TTI support.) The responses are shown in Table 2.8.

Table 2.8 Percent Distributions of Ratings of Facilities and IT Infrastructure by the TTI-48 Think Tanks

	TTI		
	≤10 FT Researchers	>10 FT Researchers	All
Quality of Facilities (2009)			
Highly suitable	0	13	8
Suitable	50	57	54
Somewhat suitable	33	23	27
Unsuitable	17	7	10
Quality of IT Infrastructure (2009)			
State of the art	6	13	10
Functional	50	70	63
Somewhat operative	22	13	17
Outdated	22	3	10

Regarding facilities, 13 percent of Stage 2-3 organizations rated these as "highly suitable;" no Stage 1 organizations gave such a high rating. About half of the organizations gave a "suitable" rating and about 27 percent gave the lower "somewhat suitable" scoring. Ten percent stated that the facilities were simply unsuitable. There was weak praise for IT infrastructure, with the majority (63 percent) of all respondents rating the quality as "functional;" only 8 percent of all organizations (and none of the Stage 1 group) gave a "state of the art" rating. Overall, the ratings suggest that most of the think tanks could usefully make upgrades in these areas to enhance staff morale and productivity. The question, of course, is if this would be the most effective use of the organizational resources available, given other needs.

All six CEE think tanks recognized staff achievements in some way. Most often they did so through an announcement at an institute seminar, working session, party for a new publication, successful conference, winning of a big contract, or a successful policy outcome. IET made some of these announcements in the bulletin it publishes. At IUE, management and department directors annually selected the best analyst in a staff classification (e.g., expert, senior expert) and announced the award at an end-of-year staff gathering.[26]

- *Staff Assessments.* Despite the centrality of formal assessments in providing staff with feedback on their performance and offering a forum in which to discuss employees' future development, only three of the six CEE institutions had any sort of formal assessment in 2000 (Table 2.9).[27] Respondents at institutes without a formal assessment process stated that their organizations are small and that feedback to staff is more or less continuous, making a formal process unnecessary. They maintained these positions even when questions were asked about possible problems with supervisors who wanted to avoid the potential conflict of giving negative reviews. Two of the organizations making this statement each had over 20 researchers at the time, suggesting that managers may not really have had detailed knowledge of each staff member's activities and performance (an issue I stressed earlier).

Table 2.9 Annual Staff Assessment Practices at the CEE-6 Think Tanks, around 2000

Practice	Conditions at Sample Think Tanks
Is there an annual staff assessment process?	3 yes, 3 no
For those with an annual process:	
--Does it include a self-assessment by the staff member?	1 yes, 2 no
--Does the supervisor complete a form or prepare a written statement?	1 yes, 2 no
--Are results of the assessment discussed with the staff member?	3 yes
--How closely are salary decisions tied to assessment results?	3 related
--How tightly are various rewards tied to the assessment results?	2 substantially, 1 very little

By way of comparison, in 2009 half of the reporting TTI think tanks and one-third of the GDN thought tanks had "an annual or other systematic performance appraisal system." Most of those with a system reported that supervisors consulted the reviews of a researcher's products in making the ratings.

At two of the three CEE institutes with formal assessments—MRI and TARKI—the assessment consisted of a discussion between one or two members of senior management and the researcher. There was no formal staff input into the discussion (e.g., a written statement of accomplishments during the year); nor did the supervisor prepare a written statement of management's views. And no written record of any sort was produced for future reference on goals set or other plans.

Only the IUE had a full staff assessment system in place. Its process was initiated by the staff member, who completed a written statement about his/her accomplishments during the year,

---

26   Among the limited sample of 28 TTI think tanks for which we have information on "incentive and award systems," about half reported some type of system being in place, with nearly all stage 2-3 organizations having them. It is unclear if these systems included monetary as well as non-monetary awards.
27   About half of the 28 TTI think tanks responding in the 2009 survey also said they had a formal system in place.

changes in responsibilities and capabilities, goals for the coming year, and suggestions for how the supervisor can help the employee achieve them. The evaluator—the team leader—completed a complementary assessment form. The two documents then formed the basis for the interview discussion between the employee and the team leader. The interview covered, among other things, the supervisor's views about what training the analyst needs in order to be more productive or to advance in the organization. IUE's process paralleled those of Stage 3 think tanks.

All three institutions with some type of formal assessment systems used the assessments to inform decisions about pay increases during the annual consideration of staff compensation. Only IUE, however, used the assessment results as a primary input for determining who should receive noncash rewards.

How do the practices just described compare with those generally in effect at well-managed Stage 3 think tanks? The record is patchy. Specifically:

- Staff assessments were a weak point. Only three of the six organizations had an annual review process in place. In only one of these was there written input by both staff member and evaluator; importantly, however, the results of this process did feed into training and salary adjustment decisions.

- Compensation structures were diverse, with a surprisingly high incidence of incentive schemes. Only two compensation schemes were consistent with typical practice at Stage 3 think tanks. Three of the schemes were directed at increasing potential staff payments; one focused on generating projects to pay for staff time. These types of incentive plans are little used in the West. Their use by the CEE organizations is likely attributable to relatively unseasoned leaders testing incentive structures they viewed as creative and rational, even though there was little evidence of their effectiveness at hand.

- Even though rewards were used to some extent by five of the six CEE organizations, rewards were underused compared to what could potentially be done and what the personnel management literature documents as good practice. These findings show little evidence of an overall reward strategy present.

Does the fact that the staff practices of the six think tanks differed in many respects from those generally accepted in Stage 3 organizations mean that these organizations should have revised their personnel management? Several factors on the positive side should be noted here. First, the leaders of the six generally believed that their practices were well suited to their specific organization—its structure, size, and particular operating style—at the time. They also placed a premium on informality and an atmosphere of democratic collegiality. This attitude, the perceived unequal competition with businesses for their better staff, and the generally low priority assigned to addressing administrative issues may have been the principal factors producing the personnel practices observed. Also important is that the think tanks studied were all producing high-quality work and succeeding in having it used in the policy process (Struyk 1999).

On the more negative side, the success of the less-developed personnel systems at five of these organizations appears to have been heavily dependent on the particular personalities and styles of key managers. Most think tanks, especially young ones, are very much creatures of their founders. If staff motivation continues to depend on this type of personalized operating style as the organization matures, there arises the real danger of a turbulent transition when new leadership eventually comes. To avoid this possibility, maturing think tanks should work to adopt the more systematic practices common to Stage 3 organizations without disturbing their essential operating styles.

TAKE AWAYS

Strong Practices

Characteristics of a well-managed think tank in this context follow.

- Basic pay is based on a standard salary system with paid sick and holiday leave.

Simpler schemes are almost always better. Salary plans that introduce uncertainty are disliked by staff for obvious reasons, may lead to weak performance (when the incentive leads staff to rush to complete assignments to maximize actual remuneration per hour), and higher turnover than standard plans.

- Bonus systems are avoided.

There is no evidence that bonuses work well for think tanks. In addition, opinion in the think tank community is generally opposed to their use, even if some organizations may have had a positive experience with them.

- Monetary incentives beyond base pay, such as health insurance and retirement contributions, are adopted only when: 1) the objective for each benefit is clearly defined, 2) a determination is made that the institution can afford them in terms of higher overhead rates, and 3) the incentives selected are structured to maximize their effectiveness in reaching the organization's particular goals.
- Senior management, consulting with team leaders, decides on which nonmonetary incentives to use. They also establish and promulgate organization-wide policies (such as authorship) as necessary. Team leaders make award allocation decisions for their groups, with periodic oversight from senior management.
- An annual performance assessment system is in place and includes written self-assessment input from the staffer, written assessment from the supervisor, and discussion between the two in which career development and increased productivity are the focus.\

For Funders
Look carefully for:

- *The structure of pay to research staff.* Are bonuses awarded? Are fixed price contracts on a per project basis in use? (Administrative staff typically enjoys a regular salary program.) Consider what perverse incentives a nonstandard structure may entail for the quality of work you will get from the funding you are providing.

- *Annual staff assessments.* These days a solid three-part process is accepted standard practice. The absence of such a system is a red flag indicator of a bad overall institutional attitude toward personnel management. Ask specifically about the absence of a standard system; the answer may be revealing about the executive director's attitude toward staff (i.e., "the director knows best" or similarly deleterious attitudes).

Perhaps to do:

Where your involvement will be significant and multiyear, and no comprehensive staff assessment program is in place, make the case for implementing one. Offer the executive director partial support for implementation of a stronger system and judge the enthusiasm (effective demand) of his/her response.

Some funders give special attention to the equal staff treatment regardless of gender, religious affiliation or ethnicity. If this is of particular interest, as a start the distribution of staff at various positions by gender and among prominent ethnic groups could be requested from the organization and compared with the distribution of the same classes in the general population or, better, among university graduates if the necessary local data are available. In countries where preparing such information is not standard practice, just requesting the information may be viewed as highly intrusive and may be resisted or at least resented.

CHAPTER 3
Hiring and Organizing the Research Team

This chapter addresses matters important to realizing the goal of an effective research staff. I begin with the significant question of how to structure research staff—in particular whether, given a series of conditions, it is better to think of research teams vs. senior fellows working with a research assistant or two. Second, I discuss how to approach the decision to hire a particular senior research candidate. Executive directors consistently report challenges in finding and hiring senior researchers experienced in rigorous analysis and policy engagement. What attributes are most important and what inducements may attract them?

The chapter ends by addressing certain provisions that are prudent to include in staff employment contracts and a related ethics policy statement new employees should sign. A strong contract and clear mutual agreement on conflicts of interest, inappropriate political activities, and similar matters dramatically lessen the chances of misunderstandings and conflict down the line. Admittedly, these are not the most glamorous management issues. Paying consistent attention to them, however, may avoid protracted staff disputes that can undermine both staff morale and productivity.

OPTIONS FOR STRUCTURING RESEARCH STAFF

Even if a think tank is producing high-quality work under its research staff structure, work may still be done more efficiently and with greater staff satisfaction if management adopts an alternative structure for some or all of its research and policy analysis. It is often the case that particular structures adopted some years ago and possibly for particular reasons are no longer optimal for the current maturity of the organization. The discussion here is also relevant for recently established organizations. As they begin to grow obvious questions arise, such as: 1) whether to have a research director who oversees all projects, possibly delegating some authority, or a couple of distinct groups each with its own head, where one group works on the institute's most important topic consistently and the other covers other areas; and 2) what is the appropriate mix between full-time and part-time researchers.

Alternative Models
Perhaps not surprisingly, several distinct arrangements for structuring analytical and policy work have emerged among think tanks over time. I have distilled the following from interviews and on-site observations at about 40 think tanks in around 10 countries. These models result from a complex interaction between two distinct aspects of how think tanks conduct their research: research organization and staff structure.

Research Organization can come in two different models:

- *The "solo star" model.* Under this model, notable and influential researchers work largely independently, with the aid of one or two research assistants. Stars focus on a particular topic (e.g., international economics, agriculture); and the research they produce is more often "soft," in the sense that it involves little if any primary data collection, limited manipulation of large secondary data sets, and little complex statistical analysis. The results are usually published under the star's name. In the United States, for example, institutions that conduct *solo star* work have senior researchers with strong connections to government, Congress, and academia.

- *The team model.* This model typically consists of a core team that gets highly specialized help from other centers or consultants, for example, sampling expertise. Think tanks that select this approach tend to conduct large-scale research projects, program evaluations, and demonstration and pilot projects. The work more often includes original data collection and other field work; statistical analysis is frequently complex and rigorous. Simulation model development is routine.

The team model exists in two different forms. The first occurs in larger organizations where research activity is carried out in centers or departments, each of which has a topical or geographic focus. Within the centers teams are formed to execute projects. The Center is a permanent larger team of specialized experts. The second model is more common in smaller organizations, in which analysis teams are formed around specific projects. In both cases individual researchers typically work on more than one project at a time, because projects seldom require full-time work over their complete lifespan. For example, teams frequently have "down time" during the data collection phase of a project involving a large household survey.

Staff structure can also take two forms: reliance almost exclusively on full-time staff or a smaller full-time core staff plus various forms of supplemental staff *(visiting fellows,* who are usually some type of part-time or full-time distinguished visitor employed for a specific project; and *consultants,* who are journeymen experts engaged to work on specific projects, often with the think tank's resident staff). Visiting fellows are a standard fixture in western Stage 2 and Stage 3 think tanks. Most are faculty members who take leave to lead two-to-three year projects important for their research or to spend a year or two providing extra expertise to an ongoing research program. The advantage of this system is that visiting fellows are often very senior analysts who would be almost impossible for a think tank to recruit as regular staff. A disadvantage is that such senior academic-oriented scholars require extensive attention by resident senior staff to ensure their full integration into the organization's work.[28]

---

28   Selee (2013, 74-5) discusses these arrangements.

Two variations in these arrangements can be distinguished:

- *Very dominant resident staff*; some supplemental researchers may be present but are not integral to the institute's operations

- *Blends of resident staff, visiting fellows, and consultants*; in some instances only a minority of the analysis is performed by resident staff.

To inform the discussion of factors for management to consider in deciding on a research staff structure, the next section presents information on think tank staffing patterns.

Staffing Patterns of Think Tanks in Developing and Transitioning Countries

A common model for Stage 1 think tanks is a small core team of researchers who of necessity work flexibly across a range of topics. Where necessary, either because of capacity or expertise constraints, consultants or associates are also engaged to work on individual projects. In contrast, Stage 3 organizations generally are organized into centers or teams for management reasons—with those with relatively broad policy topic coverage organized into issue-based centers, while those occupied with international affairs or security organized into groups based on geographic area.[29] Such centers also include stars or integrated teams depending on the type of research conducted.

The data presented in Chapter 2, Table 2.2 for the GDN-15 think tanks confirms these patterns. Among Stage 1 think tanks, part-time researchers expressed in FTEs outnumbered full-time staff by a ratio of 4:1. Even the senior researcher category averaged 2.3 full-time and 3.5 FTEs engaged part-time. In sharp contrast, hardly any part-time researchers are engaged by the larger think tanks, indicating a clear preference for the full-time staff model. It is also clear that these same think tanks prefer the teams organization model to the stars model, as indicated by the 2.5:1 average ratio of mid- and junior-level to senior researchers.

A late 1990s study of staffing arrangements in 21 think tanks with at least seven full-time researchers in Armenia, Bulgaria, Hungary, and Russia provides another data point (Struyk, 2006, 117-8). These think tanks clearly favored the full-time staff model over the one with a small core staff and a large number of part-time researchers. Only two reported having more part-time than full-time researchers. In short, in the Eastern Europe-CIS regions think tanks also favored a model in which resident staff is dominant.

A few think tanks, including the Indian Institute for Dalit Studies (IIDS 2012) and the Center for European Policy Studies,[30] have satisfactorily used a community of researchers model where a cadre of geographically dispersed analysts and a relatively smaller number of resident analysts

---

29   Kucharczyk and Kazmierkiewicz 2007, 16; Struyk 2006, 117.
30   www.ceps.eu and Struyk, Ueno, and Suzuki (1993).

work on projects together. In the case of IIDS, the focal point of the recent collaboration was a set of studies on discrimination in the housing market. The Science, Technology and Innovation Policy Research Center (2012) reports a poor experience with a similar arrangement, however, suggesting caution in its use.

Which Model Is Best for Your Institution?

Senior management should consider five factors when determining the best arrangement for a particular think tank.

Project Type and Size. The larger the share of a think tank's workload that consists of projects requiring a range of staff skills and significant data collections (e.g., program evaluations, demonstration and pilot projects, and technical assistance projects), the stronger the argument for a team model, which normally requires a core of resident staff to manage the projects and provide the necessary coherence and organization. For example, consider a pilot project that works with local governments to improve the targeting of locally administered social assistance programs. The project requires that a team design and implement the pilot projects and then carry out rigorous implementation or process evaluations to determine whether pilots are successful. A team of six or more professionals could be engaged on such a project part-time for more than two years.[31]

The situation is very different in cases where a think tank emphasizes policy analysis that exploits secondary data or a limited amount of qualitative information; in such cases the solo star model is more appropriate. For example, consider a project addressing questions involving a country's foreign policy. In a typical case tasks would include substantial literature review, perhaps examination of internal foreign ministry documents, and possibly interviews with members of the policy elite. A single star researcher would be appropriate for such a project, with the help of an able research assistant or two.

While associates and consultants can be solo stars as well as resident staff, the credibility of the think tank itself depends on the quality of core cadre of resident senior staff. This is why it is unusual to find a solo star model that is not based mostly on resident staff.

Workload Variability. Two kinds of variability are relevant here: variation in the total volume of work and variation in the topical mix and analytical requirements of the work to be done, even when the overall volume is about the same. The greater the variability in both cases, the greater is the challenge to the institution's management to maintain a long-serving core staff. To tackle this important issue, managers must make every effort to: 1) keep full-time staff at work on appropriate projects during funding troughs, and 2) recruit and train needed additional staff promptly during peak periods.

---

31   Note that the team members could conduct elite interviews but would generally not carry out household or other large-scale surveys. Sampling and survey experts, along with interviewers, would have this responsibility. The team would, however, be responsible for managing the survey process to ensure that it met project needs.

Keeping full-time staff when there is considerably less than full-time coverage is a terrible drain on an institution's financial reserves, however. If senior core researchers are flexible about the topics they will work on and are quick learners, variability can be weathered with a minimum of staff dismissals and hiring of consultants to work on new topics. Generally, though, the greater the workload variability, the stronger is the case for having a comparatively limited full-time resident staff and relying more heavily on intermittent staff, associates, and consultants. Even then, regular staff may have to be hired on "at will" contracts. Many Stage 1 organizations are faced with high funding variability and limited financial reserves, making this type of arrangement necessary to protect their financial situation.

Staff Flexibility. An institution's agenda may change substantially from year to year, even though total work volume is relatively stable, because of shifts in the relevant policy priorities and interests of those funding the institute's work. Retaining a number of senior resident staff over time remains desirable even under these difficult conditions, because the institutional knowledge and loyalty of resident analysts and the continuity they provide are crucial assets.

But how does management deal with the possibility that entrenched senior staff members may be unwilling to work effectively on new topics? Senior staff may also have the wrong skill set for a new project, but this is less frequent than unwillingness to shift the focus of his/her work away from a favored topic or line of analysis. To convince a senior analyst to make the change and remain with the organization takes sensitive guidance by senior management. That said, however, the very substantial investment a researcher must make to become thoroughly conversant with the issues and literature in a new area should not be underestimated.

Obviously, the more flexible the senior staff is in working on different topics, the better the case for having a relatively large ratio of resident to short-term staff. Still, senior management may well have to supplement their resident staff with short-term experts to maintain high-quality analysis on topics that are new to the resident staff but important to the institution.

Tax and Social Fund Implications. In a number of countries there are important differences in the cost to a think tank between hiring the same person as a staff member and hiring him/her as a consultant. This arises because of differences between staff and consultant hires in the employer's responsibilities for paying contributions to various social funds (e.g., health insurance, pension). Consultants are typically cheaper to the think tank because no social payments on behalf of consultants are required. But in a market where most think tanks and consultancies are using consultants for a significant share of all work, a think tank may have little choice but to compete for consultants and push up compensation levels.[32]

---

32   Although economic theory suggests that consulting rates should rise to be the equivalent of all-in staff compensation or more because of the intermittent nature of consulting work and the need for the consultants to take care of their own social fund contributions. In many countries this appears not to be the case, however, for reasons that are not clear.

Institutional Reputation. A think tank's choice among the resident staff, consultant, and distinguished visitor models will depend substantially on the institution's reputation. The more prestigious the think tank, the easier it will be to attract a senior policy analyst or researcher to be a resident visiting fellow. If the institution has yet to establish itself among the first echelon of think tanks in its country, however, hiring such senior people as consultants may be the right strategy to add staff strength and strengthen the institution's reputation. The following caveat is important, however: resident staff members have strong incentives to do excellent work and otherwise act to build the institute's reputation. Consultants, in contrast, typically act to maximize their hourly wage rate from assignments, making them less likely, other things equal, to delivery exemplary work. To avoid this outcome, core staff needs to be particularly vigilant in controlling the quality of consultants' work throughout the project in question.

Other Pieces of Advice
Most think tanks would do well to review their staffing and research structure arrangement every few years. Preparing careful characterizations of the institution's situation for each of the five factors listed above is a useful starting point for these deliberations. Here are four further bits of advice.

First, take care not to have too large a share of visitors. The public does not closely associate visitors with the host organization; typically they retain their public connection with their home institutions. Their strong work reflects well on the think tanks visited, but many audiences will not necessarily think of the organization as having particular capability in the subject areas where visitors had the lead. In short, too many visitors can weaken your brand.

Second, think not only about the institution's current requirements but also about the goals the organization is striving to attain in the next few years. Is it trying to shift from being heavily concentrated on technical assistance projects to doing more policy research? Is it striving to make evaluations of government programs a substantial part of its agenda? The institution's goals need to be reflected in how the structure of the research operation evolves.

Third, be flexible. There is no need to adopt any single model as the sole structure for conducting research. As noted, major think tanks in the United States and Europe use more than one model depending on the task to be done. Different models should be adopted to fit particular circumstances, even within the same institution. That said, it is nonetheless useful for a think tank to define the general approach it will take to structuring its research—that is, a model that is believed to be effective in current operating circumstances unless there are good reasons for change.

Fourth, be creative. For example, some think tanks find that while the resident staff/team model generally works well, each team cannot be fully self-sufficient. One common problem is that an institution's research teams need help with econometric aspects of a particular evaluation or analysis, but no in-house team needs a full-time econometrician (or expert on regulation or governance) for its own projects. In this case, think tanks are wise to employ an econometrician (or other specialist) who acts as an in-house consultant to all the research teams when needed, as well as carrying out his/her own projects. Sampling and survey experts can be used across teams and project in the same way.

ATTRACTING SENIOR RESEARCHERS

My context for the focus on senior researchers here is the challenge that many think tanks face, particularly in developing and transition countries, in recruiting and retaining such staff. In watching the video of the discussion session, "How to Attract and Nurture Quality Researchers," at the TTI EX 2012 Conference,[33] I was struck by the consistency of the senior-researchers-are-hard-to-attract theme. I heard no challenge to it and have seen the same point made elsewhere.[34] Interviews with think tank leaders in 2013-2014 reinforce this theme. Competition from the for-profit sector for highly trained individuals is intense.

The views expressed at that conference and elsewhere are borne out by the limited data we have. Table 3.1 shows the percentage distribution by region (Africa, Asia, and Latin America) of responses by the TTI-48 sample to a four-response question on the difficulty in finding qualified senior researchers (practically impossible, have to work hard but good people are available, average difficulty, or not difficult). Think tanks in all three regions gave responses indicating considerable difficulty. Latin American institutions averaged the lowest—with 83 percent of responses in the two highest categories, compared with Asian institutions at 94 percent and African ones at 85 percent.

Table 3.1 How difficult has it been to find qualified senior researchers?
TTI-48 think tank (percentage distributions)

Responses	Region			All
	Africa	Asia	Latin America	
It is practically impossible to find qualified people	5	6	0	4
We have to work very hard to find them, but good people are available	80	88	83	83
I would say about "average" in difficulty	15	6	17	13
Not difficult	0	0	0	0
Other	0	0	0	0

In circumstances where a think tank must often make substantial commitments to sign a senior researcher, managers should structure the hiring process to enhance the chances of make a very good decision. This starts with being clear about the attributes your institution most wants to fill the open senior researcher position with. This, in turn, depends in good part on how research operations are organized: "teams" or "stars"? In the team model, the person with the greatest experience with

---

33   See Mensa (2012) for the session discussion. For other relevant sessions see Ofori Mensah (2012) and Kulasabanathan (2012).
34   Ibeanu (2008, p.3), for example, makes this point for Nigerian think tanks. The same point was made by Echt (2012) in a different context.

complex projects is likely to be preferred over someone who has concentrated on solo research.

Annex 3.1* includes a "Request for Position/Job Specifications Form" that should be used routinely to enumerate the specific tasks to be done and necessary qualifications. The qualifications are separated into four groups: education, experience, skills, and "other qualities desired." The person completing the form is asked to rank the importance for recruitment of these various qualities.[35] Completing the form carefully—and getting agreement on it from senior management for a position as key as senior researcher—can clarify thinking and focus the search for candidates. The process often leads to a discussion of the kinds of trade-offs the institution would be willing to make if no perfect candidate is found. Those who interview candidates should be asked to give their assessments in a uniform format that facilitates comparisons not only across interviewers but also across candidates.

Participants at the 2012 TTI EX session noted earlier offered important attributes for high quality senior researchers, including:

- Necessary education credentials, a good publications record
- Strong communications skills
- Being passionate about their own areas of expertise and about making positive change in the country
- Ability to think in a multidisciplinary context
- Strong research ethics
- Ability to deal with alternative views
- Being a good mentor
- Being able to multitask.

In another TTI EX session, Nancy Birdsall, head of the Center for Global Development, cited a further attribute: government experience, which gives analysts greater realism about program administration and the difficulties generally of achieving policy change (Birdsall 2012).[36] Several of these attributes fall into the "other qualities desired" category in the job specification form. There is no question that this is a demanding list and trade-offs among attributes will be necessary. Management should also be aware that the true depth of some of these qualifications (e.g., ability to deal with alternative views, being a good mentor), can only be determined through open

---

35   The Annex also contains a useful example of a policy statement on establishing a new position.

36   No one mentioned candidates' political orientation, i.e., liberal or conservative. Murray Weidenbaum, who worked for U.S. think tanks of both orientations, believed that think tanks hire staff already sympathetic to the organization's broad views. Similarly, donors give to think tanks whose views are consistent with theirs, rather than try to fund an organization to reorient its policy perspective. Weidenbaum (2009, 55)

conversations with the candidate's former colleagues.

Participants at the 2012 TTI EX session on attracting and nurturing quality research also offered ideas on the kinds of inducements likely to attract these researchers—including long-term contracts, high salaries, guaranteed time to work on research topics of particular interest, offering a collegial work environment, and permitting those who wish to have a voice in institutional management to do so. They also discussed how and where to search for candidates—including: 1) attracting them from the diaspora, and 2) developing senior researchers over time by recruiting new PhDs and mentoring and otherwise fostering their development. Candidates from academia can potentially be attracted, at least temporarily, by the presence and true availability of capable support teams—not only research assistants and statisticians for their research, but also a communications team to assist in policy engagement activity (Echt 2012).

Finally, two institutes participating in the TTI made the point in their Stories of Change statements that favorable institutional visibility and reputation are key ingredients in attracting capable researchers. One spoke of the need for strong participation in international and domestic conferences for this purpose.[37] The importance of an institute's "brand" in attracting senior people is also made by Selee (2013, 78). This is an important point: brand and the visibility it engenders matters. This is amply evident in the boasting among think tanks in getting a high rating in the University of Pennsylvania's *Global Go To Think Tank Report* (e.g., McGann 2012), despite various critiques of the methods employed in making the ratings. Obviously, high rankings boost their images and facilitate attracting good people. Equally obviously, there is certainly an important role here for the communications team in boosting a think tank's ranking.

The span of these ideas and comments certainly suggests that practices in this very special labor market may differ importantly among countries. They also suggest that think tanks particularly hard-pressed to recruit experienced analysts may be taking on sizable medium-term financial commitments in doing so, which they could have difficulty fulfilling if they face a significant downturn in turnover. One member of the advisory board for this book spoke at one meeting, for example, about the recruitment of senior researchers as having a potential negative impact on financial sustainability.

In considering options for finding high quality senior researchers, I think it valuable to pass along lessons enunciated by Simon Maxwell, the long-serving leader of the Overseas Development Institute in the U.K. on developing strong analysts:[38]

> We eventually settled on a strategy of 'growing our own' young researchers, recruiting youngish people and helping them adjust to our work pattern... some went on to be among our best senior researchers. Average age [of research leaders] fell...

---

37   See Ahiadeke (2012) and Dixit (2012).
38   The interview was in 2011 with Enrique Mendizabal (2011).

A word of caution, though. A strategy based on developing younger staff does place a premium on having enough more experienced people to manage and mentor. Sometimes this was a challenge for us, especially as we grew into new areas. At one point, we invested substantially in leadership (not management) training, for me and some other senior staff, with follow-up coaching, to help us all do better and shaping the Institute and supporting its staff.

Some think tanks in developing and transition countries have pursued the "grow your own" strategy by sponsoring tertiary education for young analysts. Usually the contract between the analyst and the think tank requires that, when the analyst completes training, s/he works an equivalent number of years for the institution that subsidized the training. The Korean Development Institute (KDI) had such a program for many years beginning in 1973, for example, when the country was still poor.[39] KDI management rates that program (see Box 3.1) as a strong success.

Some executive directors believe that promising fresh PhDs true mentoring can be a compelling sales point—particularly now, when there is growing appreciation that mentoring needs to go beyond producing technically proficient research to include pointers on how to network: 1) in the policy arena and 2) among one's professional peers both in-country and within the region. In 2013, an executive director of a Stage 2 African think tank told me his institute had engaged a highly capable woman with an international education and related experience to help just such staff establish professional networks in the region to promote their visibility and policy effectiveness. The promise of learning how to write for policy audiences is another area where mentoring can be highly attractive to savvy young research staff. In addition, many will need guidance on making the transition from academia to the "consulting world," where deadlines and budget constraints are binding and time allocation must be carefully managed.[40]

Lastly, an often overlooked source of senior staff is the ranks of retiring senior civil servants who are analytically capable. Some may be induced to retire early. They can provide an experienced perspective on many questions. Perhaps most important, they will understand the workings of the government policy process and actual administration of government programs. Some may also be good candidates for short-term assignments on program design and administration questions.

---

39   In 1970 per capita GDP in Korea was under USD 9; in Japan it was USD 206. By 2007 Korea's GDP was over USD 25,000.

40   In a blog posting, Leandro Echt (2014) lists the three principal challenges that Arab world researchers face. These problems appear to me to be faced by young researchers in the majority of transition and developing countries. They are: (1) restrictions on access to essential data; (2) a lack of funds for young researchers to attend international conferences [important for both knowledge acquisition and networking]; and (3) the tendency to produce a large number of analyses at the expense of doing so at a relatively low quality standard. An experienced, energetic mentor could work with a younger colleague to address all the points to some degree.

CONTRACTUAL RELATIONS BETWEEN THINK TANK MANAGEMENT AND ITS STAFF

In turning to contractual relations between think tank management and the organization's staff, I am taking a broad view that includes both the employment contract and supplemental institutional policies addressing ethical matters (which are frequently not part of the formal employment contract). Because senior staff members, particularly senior researchers, are often public figures and may have access to more institutional resources than other staff, this section applies particularly to them and their senior managers, although there are lessons here that apply to all staff.

Employment Contracts

The content of employment contracts typically receives little attention in think tank management discussions. This is understandable given the major differences among different countries' labor laws that must be respected. At the same time, many forms of risk arise from behavior not covered by labor codes but are important for think tanks to guard against. For example, a senior researcher using his/her institution's name in support of a candidate for political office, though legal in labor law, is typically strictly forbidden by think tank policies. Think tank management has an obligation to protect itself against reputational risks such as this, whether the harmful actions are committed intentionally or not.

What does a labor contract signed upon entry typically contain? The contents can be quite brief. The following list is fairly typical, whether the items are included in the document signed or attachments to it or referenced by it:

- Minimum provisions stipulated by national law covering a listing of the value and structure of the financial package, including benefits and time-off for vacation and holidays, and possibly other matters

- The title of the position (consistent with the job description the candidate has reviewed), the group in which the person will be working and the name of his/her supervisor

- Special provisions, which could include: 1) such items as payment of educational expenses (even for international study) or a percentage of time to work on research topics of the employee's own choosing and 2) expectations for mentoring younger staff or participating actively in communications campaigns.

Contracts do not have to specify the length of the appointment in all countries. Neither of the two think tanks for which I worked, for example, stated the length of appointment in the appointment letter. Rather, the appointment was open-ended. The actual statement used in such agreements is something like the following:[41]

---

41   The statement is a composite of those from two cooperating think tanks as moderately edited by me.

It has been our experience that an employment relationship is successful as long as both parties are mutually comfortable and satisfied. Accordingly, both you and DEEP ANALYTICS [a fictitious U.S.-based think tank I also use in further examples below] will have the right to terminate your employment and all related compensation and benefits at any time, with or without cause or notice. This is called employment "at will," and only the Director of Personnel has the authority to alter the arrangement.

Length-of-contract is an extremely important contract provision that protects the institution. Open-ended "at will" contracts give the think tank the flexibility, subject to national labor laws, to dismiss staff when financial conditions demand it. The Urban Institute, at which I was working at the time, suffered the shock of several major government contracts being canceled in the early 1980s, supposedly "at the convenience of the government" but actually for political reasons. The only way it survived was by taking advantage of the ability to dismiss staff as needed using the two-week notice period stated in its letter of appointment. Staff count was cut from around 350 to 140 in 11 months—a wrenching experience for all. But the organization survived and prospered again within a few years. Several other U.S.-based Stage 3 think tanks suffered the same fate and also survived.

On the other hand, lack of a stated period of employment lowers staff sense of an obligation to remain, although fear of creating hard feelings on the part of the think tank from which the analyst is planning to move—which could become fodder for the rumor mill—may lead to second thoughts.

Three things are worth noting here: 1) Specified performance periods, even when stated in the employment contract, are typically difficult to enforce in a court of law. 2) In countries where "at will" arrangements are not legal, managers need to be sure that appointment letters are explicit about permissible reasons for terminating an appointment prior to the contract's end date. 3) Contracts should contain "escape clauses" that make it possible to curtail education and other specially promised benefits when required by the institution's financial condition. Think tanks will work hard not to renege on such promises, however, because doing so entails very substantial reputational risk.

These points notwithstanding, it is important to recognize that in some countries "at will" contract provisions will be a strongly negative factor for candidates assessing a job offer. As Echt (2012) says, "In a market characterized by high levels of informality, finding a civil society organization in which to enjoy some stability is attractive to researchers...."

Other Employment Provisions

Beyond the employment contract, which can be as simple as a single-page letter of appointment, there are other important conditions for working at a think tank that management should codify in a policy statement. Every new staffer should be made aware of such a statement. And anyone being offered a position should read it carefully before signing the employment contract. Directly after signing the contract, the new hire will likely be asked to agree in writing that s/he has read the employment conditions and agrees to them.

Box 3.2 lists major items included in a Statement of Ethics and Business Practice Standards for the fictitious DEEP ANALYTICS Think Tank mentioned above.[42] Several provisions are worth further discussion here.

The last three paragraphs under *Conflicts of Interest*, for example, cover three very important points:

- Requiring the employee to notify DEEP ANALYTICS about any non-compete, non-disclosure, or similar agreements with a prior firm
- Prohibiting the employee from working for or advising another firm when the service would conflict with DEEP ANALYTICS business interests or adversely effect the staffer's job performance
- Prohibiting consulting assignments or employment with other survey research or social science research organizations.

Smaller think tanks, or even larger ones, that adopt a staffing model where researchers are only paid when there is work for them will need to adjust the second two provisions. Even if prohibitions are not in order, it is good practice for such organizations to require knowledge of projects their staff members are working on for other firms.

Three additional provisions of the Box 3.2 Statement are also of note:

- *Research Misconduct* explicitly prohibits plagiarism. This is an increasing problem as it becomes ever easier to cut-and-paste text from documents on-line.
- *Use of Copyrighted Material and Intellectual Property* defines 'work made for hire,' making it crystal clear that work done for the institution is the institution's property (i.e., a staff member is not at liberty to publish his/her work elsewhere without explicit permission from that institution). Such permission is generally given, but authors are being encouraged by management to follow the relevant formalities, in part so management can confer, if appropriate, with the analyst about the most policy-effective place to showcase certain results. (As a general matter, I think the DEEP ANALYTICS policy is unfair to authors. There are a variety of rights-sharing arrangements available that are more reasonable.[43])
- *Political Contributions* prohibits working for candidates for public office or the use of

---

42   This statement is based on provisions from policies of two stage 3 think tanks.

43   The Creative Commons web site (http://creativecommons.org/) outlines a series of licensing arrangements and provides guidance on which is appropriate under varying circumstances.

DEEP ANALYTICS resources in supporting any campaign, including devoting work time to a campaign. The staffer can make contributions of his/her own funds to a candidate. Most think tanks pride themselves on producing policy results that are nonpartisan. Obviously, staff being actively associated with one candidate or party will damage the institution's credibility as a politically disinterested policy adviser and could have significant deleterious effects on its funding from foundations and international organizations that wish to stay out of local politics.

Think tanks with such ethics policies in place generally take them very seriously. A typical concluding statement in such a policy states:

> Violations of this policy may result in disciplinary action up to and including termination of employment, and/or referral for criminal prosecution. Individuals who violate standards may also be required to reimburse DEEP ANALYTICS for losses or damages resulting from the violation. In addition, an employee shall be subject to disciplinary action, including termination of employment, if the employee fails to cooperate in an investigation or deliberately provides false information during an investigation.

The items in Box 3.2 are worth studying in detail. Even though they constitute a formidable list of prohibitions, think tanks really do need to impose them on their staff to maintain their independence and to operate within the law. It is good management practice to: 1) make sure incoming staff are aware of these policies and 2) remind them of these provisions annually with a simple email statement to minimize policy violations, the vast majority of which will be unintentional.

TAKE AWAYS

Strong Practices
Characteristics of a well-managed think tank in this context follow.

Attracting highly capable senior analysts is essential for a think tank to succeed in its mission. Capable, articulate senior analysts are a key element in maintaining a strong image in the policy arena as a thought leader and effective communicator.

- A very carefully developed recruitment strategy is in place, starting with defining and prioritizing the attributes candidates should possess in light of the institution's evolving research program. The set of inducements that can be offered to attract good staff are determined through a combination of effectiveness in attracting strong candidates and the financial liabilities the institution can reasonably take on.

- A comprehensive ethics policy is in place to help protect the organization from malfeasance and reputational risk, even if inadvertent. As a standard part of the on-boarding process, all incoming staff signs a statement that they have read, and understand, the ethics policy.

Every few years, Stage 2 and Stage 3 think tanks should review how researchers are organized for conducting policy research projects efficiently, taking into account anticipated future work as well as current projects. The solo star model, for example, can result in underemployed research assistants and is an ill-suited staffing structure for bidding on larger, more complex projects.

For Funders
Look carefully for:

- *The challenges facing the institution in attracting highly capable senior researchers and its recent record in doing so.* Such staff is essential to the institution's ability to produce high quality, creative analysis. Follow-up with a query on the inducements being offered and get a sense if large, potentially risky financial liabilities have accrued or are likely to evolve as a result of recruiting efforts.

- *The institute's ethics policy statement.* This should be checked for completeness. Also inquire about how it is promulgated to all staff. A nonexistent or weak policy statement is a very real but largely unnecessary liability for the think tank and, though to a much lesser extent, for those funding it.

- *Are senior researchers trying to cover too many topics or leading too many projects?* A result of recruiting challenges can be key staff being stretched too thinly with research quality and policy engagement suffering or an exhausted colleague departing. From the funder's selfish perspective it means that the quality of the research you support may be weak, but there are broader negative institutional effects as well.

Perhaps to do:

- If the organization does not have a strong ethics policy in place, requiring them to implement one could be part of a grant package, though the implementation burden should be low. Resistance to implementation may signal the presence of ongoing questionable practices.

Box 3.1 Sending Young Researchers Abroad for Tertiary Education

The Korean Development Institute (KDI) was created in 1971 as an independent, government-supported think tank dedicated to helping that government develop effective economic policies. Indeed, KDI was the "brain trust" for the Economic Development Bureau, which directly supported the president's office in defining and refining the country's development policy (Studwell 92-127). At that stage in Korea's development there was an acute shortage of trained economists and other social scientists in the country.

Every year starting in 1973, five to six university graduate KDI researchers, selected based an evaluation of their ability and work performance, were sent to study at U.S. universities. After completing master's degrees, they returned and continued to work for KDI. Of these researchers, KDI again selected those who excelled and provided them with additional supports to complete doctoral degrees abroad. Later, they returned with a doctoral degree to become principal research fellows at KDI.

Expenses in the early years (1972–1976) were paid from a USAID fund, which was then under control of KDI management. Later, KDI raised its own funds to continue the program. It was a great benefit for KDI researchers, who were very satisfied with it.

The agreement was that researchers completing the academic assistance program would return to KDI and work there for the same period they spent on the program. Many stayed at KDI beyond the required period and most of the others moved to prestigious universities. Additional regulations for a domestic study assistance program for employees were introduced in 1977 for MA-level work, in recognition of the improvement of Korean universities tuition. The program was concluded in 2001.

KDI rates the program as a clear success: "…the program provided great opportunity not only to strengthen the capability of individuals but also to build better, productive research environments for KDI as a whole. The participants who returned with doctoral degrees actively engaged in many important research projects, and their advanced knowledge and expertise delivered quality outcomes on those projects. Externally, the program served to enrich the Korean society by letting KDI's competent experts contribute outside the institute, such as schools, research institutes and government offices. With these benefits, the program has been evaluated to be very successful and worth it."

Source: Personal correspondence with Dongseok Kim, Senior Vice President, KDI, summer 2013.

Box 3.2. Representative Statement of Ethics and Business Practices Standards at the U.S.-based DEEP ANALYTICS [fictitious name] Think Tank

Conflicts of Interest

A conflict of interest exists when an employee:

- Has an outside interest that materially encroaches on time or attention that should be devoted to the affairs of DEEP ANALYTICS;

- Has a direct or indirect interest in a relationship with an outsider that:
  - is, or may be, implied or construed to be inherently unethical;
  - makes possible personal gain due to the employee's ability to influence dealings;
  - renders the employee partial toward the outsider for personal reasons or otherwise inhibit the impartiality of the employee's business judgment in DEEP ANALYTICS dealings;
  - places the employee or DEEP ANALYTICS in an equivocal, embarrassing, or ethically questionable position; or
  - reflects on the integrity of DEEP ANALYTICS;

- Uses DEEP ANALYTICS property in a manner that is inconsistent with its intended business purpose;

- Discloses proprietary information to unauthorized persons; or,

- Takes personal advantage of an opportunity that properly belongs to DEEP ANALYTICS.

Employees are required to notify DEEP ANALYTICS about any non-compete, non-disclosure, or any similar agreements that are binding on them from previous employers. Employees are also required to notify DEEP ANALYTICS about any resulting litigation or claim against any sponsor of DEEP ANALYTICS or the reasonable anticipation thereof.

Employees are not permitted to engage in any outside or secondary employment, including serving in an advisory capacity or as a Board member for another organization, when that service conflicts with DEEP ANALYTICS business interests or adversely affects job performance.

DEEP ANALYTICS employees may not accept consulting engagements or employment, paid or otherwise, with other survey research, social science research organizations, or private firms unless explicitly approved in writing by the Executive Director.

Gifts and Gratuities

DEEP ANALYTICS employees may extend invitations to meals and events to sponsors or vendors in recognition of the business relationship, as long as these invitations do not constitute reciprocal agreements or restrain competition. The expenses associated with hosting external events must be charged to an unallowable expense category and may only be approved by a Department Head. *Employees may not give gifts of any kind to a sponsor.*

Research Misconduct

Research misconduct is any intentional act that has the effect of reducing the accuracy or quality of data or findings. Examples of research misconduct include data falsification, inappropriate data destruction, and inappropriate interviewing practices. Plagiarism is strictly against DEEP ANALYTICS policies and is forbidden.

Ethics, Confidentiality, and Business Practices

Records retention

It is a violation of this policy for anyone to intentionally destroy, alter, mutilate, conceal, cover up or falsify any records, documents or tangible objects that are involved in or could be involved in a U.S. government investigation or prosecution of any matter, or in a bankruptcy filing. In the event of such an investigation, prosecution or filing, DEEP ANALYTICS must retain all related e-mail, e-mail attachments, and documents retained on computers, as well as hard copies of all related records.

Use of Copyrighted Material and Intellectual Property

DEEP ANALYTICS's policy is to adhere to laws concerning copyrights, including those governing use of computer software. Violation of copyright laws can result in damage to DEEP ANALYTICS's image and in severe financial penalties. Therefore, DEEP ANALYTICS staff must not copy or use computer software, articles, publications, or other audiovisual materials in violation of copyright or license agreements. Adherence to the following guidelines will ensure that DEEP ANALYTICS is in compliance with copyright laws and license agreements with regard to computer software, articles, publications, and other audiovisual materials. Employees should be aware of, and abide by, limitations on use of copyrighted material.

Work produced by DEEP ANALYTICS employees and representatives shall be a work made for hire within the meaning of the Copyright Act of 1976. DEEP ANALYTICS shall hold all rights to the manuscript without limitation and may register the copyright in its name. Employees and DEEP ANALYTICS representatives hereby transfer all rights, title and interest worldwide to any such written product, data, or any other information or materials to DEEP ANALYTICS.

Political Contributions

DEEP ANALYTICS shall not participate in any political activity on behalf of any candidate for public office. As an organization, DEEP ANALYTICS neither favors nor endorses any political party or candidate at any time. DEEP ANALYTICS employees will refrain from any political activity on behalf of DEEP ANALYTICS in support of any candidate for political office. DEEP ANALYTICS will not reimburse employees for any contributions they make to a political candidate or for a political purpose. DEEP ANALYTICS funds and assets (including employee work time) will not be contributed, loaned, or made available to political parties or the campaigns of candidates for Federal, state, or local office or to foreign political parties, candidates, or communities.

Anti-Trust Laws

This country's anti-trust laws prohibit agreements or actions "in restraint of trade" or restrictive practices which may reduce competition without providing a beneficial effect to consumers. Violations include agreements or understandings among competitors to: fix or control prices; boycott specific suppliers or sponsors; allocate products, territories or markets; and limit the production or sale of products or product lines.

Employees and DEEP ANALYTICS representatives should not discuss these matters with representatives of other companies and should report attempted discussions initiated by others.

Confidential information

DEEP ANALYTICS places a high priority on the preservation and protection of its confidential and/or proprietary information. Reports, data, documents or other products prepared by or with the assistance of staff members or consultants are the property of DEEP ANALYTICS. This also includes all records and files maintained by or housed on DEEP ANALYTICS's property during and after employment at DEEP ANALYTICS.

Confidential information includes, but is not limited to, financial information, payroll and personnel records, computer passwords and security codes, research, business strategies, computer software, technology, databases, vendor supplier information and any other information in connection with DEEP ANALYTICS that is not publicly disclosed. Unless expressly authorized by DEEP ANALYTICS, or as required as part of the employee's duties on behalf of DEEP ANALYTICS, an employee is strictly prohibited from using, disclosing, sending, transmitting, or otherwise disseminating any DEEP ANALYTICS proprietary of confidential information.

CHAPTER 4
Organizing Staff Development: University Courses to Affinity Groups

Training needs arise from on-boarding new staff and from the need to improve staff quality. Most think tanks experience significant staff turnover, particularly at the junior researcher level and among lower level support staff—as people leave, and are replaced, and in some cases, as the institution expands. Consequently, a great deal of time is often devoted to providing on-the-job training to new staff (i.e., training where one worker explains to another the institution's policies on such items as formatting documents, archiving statistical analyses, working with clients, and the IT system). Some of this training can be done more effectively by designating experienced staff for several relative newcomers at the same time, rather than each new staffer "shadowing" a more experienced colleague.

Ongoing skills improvement is essential as well to enhance productivity and staff satisfaction. Here tools such as active mentoring, self-teaching affinity groups, in-house seminars on projects under way, and IT department sessions on software updates all have a role to play. Sending staff to external short courses as well as university courses is another key resource.

Opportunities for skill enhancement are legion. Many new researchers do not have strong grounding in policy analysis or in program monitoring and evaluation—skills that are very likely to be needed at most think tanks. Most have also had only limited experience with the main statistical analysis packages such as SAS and SPSS. It is certainly possible for support staff and researchers to gain competence gradually through mentoring from their peers, but using colleagues alone can be inefficient. Colleagues do not always have time to explain carefully, not all colleagues can answer the questions posed, and the explanations almost certainly will be less thorough than would be optimal. To avoid wasting resources and potentially frustrating staff, think tank management must give careful thought to defining the best mix of in-house and external training options.

This chapter presents ideas on a program of training for support staff and policy researchers. The next section discusses the development of an annual training program. Following this is a discussion of how to organize such a training program, with considerable attention given to in-house and comparatively informal approaches. I then present information I have been able to assemble on current think tank practices and a case study of an exemplar orientation program. The chapter concludes with "Take Aways" for think tank leaders and For Funders suggestions.

FORMING THE ANNUAL PROGRAM

Staff training consists of both formal training events and various forms of on-the-job training (OJT). The importance of OJT is hard to overestimate, although at most firms and think tanks it is organized rather haphazardly and therefore fails to realize its potential (Bowsher 1998; Rothwell and Kazanas 1994). That said, think tanks can and should take a variety of steps to encourage effective OJT as well as relying on more structured formal options.

Basic Considerations

In principle, there are two types of training needs: 1) organizational needs and 2) needs to improve individual staff performance.

Training for organizational needs is usually driven by two forces: the organization's future business strategy (explicit or implicit) and the requirements of its current programs (Bowsher 1998; Ban, Faerman, and Riccucci 1992). Many think tanks are beginning to value the role of rigorous program evaluation. This will lead them to start investing in building capacity by sending a senior researcher, for example, to one of the short courses offered by the International Initiative for Impact Evaluation.

Training for individual performance improvement is driven primarily through the annual performance assessments. A standard HR task is to go through the completed assessments to compile a list of the training needs agreed by the employee being assessed and by the assessor. This training increases the employee's skills, but the new skills may be only generally applicable to current or future institutional assignments. At a think tank that does modest work on banking policy, for example, an employee might take a think tank–financed course on sophisticated bank-risk management. This would be helpful as broad background for the current and expected assignments, but is likely to be even more prized by the employee as deepening his/her human capital.

Most think tanks understandably emphasize training focused on concrete skills gaps. More general training is often used as a reward for particularly valued employees.

Where HR does not systematically collate training needs identified in the performance assessments, an alternative is a set of discussions with team leaders and directors of administrative departments about their views on areas of a particular staff member's weakness.

Development of a training program can be relatively formal or informal, but the literature indicates that it should be clearly and specifically defined, however it is developed or delivered (e.g., Rothwell and Kazanas 1994).

Program Content

The most obvious division in training content is between analysts and support staff, although even here exceptions to the rule are easy to find. A translator on staff may improve his/her performance by attending a research-oriented workshop on program evaluation to learn the concepts and the vocabulary, for example, and then use these new skills in his/her non-research job of translating project reports. Nevertheless, distinct groups with comparatively homogeneous training needs can be identified and the training events for them defined. Table 4.1 lists separately generic types of training for analysts and support staff. For both there are three types: general orientation, human capital building, and tools more specific to the position.

Table 4.1 Types of Think Tank Staff Training

For Researchers	
General orientation	<ul><li>Mission and primary activities of the institute, organization of work</li><li>Goals and philosophy, work style, and ethical standards</li><li>Importance of high quality work and how the quality control system works</li><li>Guidance on how to work at a think tank—for example, working on multiple projects simultaneously, working within budget constraints</li><li>The time sheet system</li><li>Annual performance appraisal: purpose, goals, timing</li><li>Review of benefits—health and life insurance, vacation and sick leave, tuition support for job-relevant courses</li><li>Staff documentation, labor book and other government forms, other HR topics listed under orientation for support staff (Table 4.2)</li><li>Introduction to the organization's IT system and associated training</li><li>Introduction to the communications team and its activities and products, and who is responsible for what activities</li><li>"How to be a consultant"</li></ul>
Tools	<ul><li>Basic software—the in-house computer system, e-mail, archiving, report formats</li><li>Statistical packages (e.g., SPSS, SAS), Excel, Microsoft Project, and so on</li><li>Making presentations, including preparing PowerPoints; related quality control</li><li>Communicating in brief—writing policy briefs and blogs, giving effective media interviews</li></ul>
Human capital building – areas emphasized	<ul><li>Public policy analysis, including effective writing for policy recommendations</li><li>Program evaluation</li><li>Financial analysis of investment projects—for example, communal services, roads, mass transit, housing</li></ul>
For Support Staff	
General orientation	<ul><li>Goals and philosophy, work style, work rules, and so on</li><li>Rules for document handling, company formats, archiving documents, processing travel expenses, and so on</li><li>Review of benefits—health and life insurance, vacation and sick leave; tuition support for job-relevant courses</li><li>The time sheet system</li><li>Annual performance appraisal: purpose, goals, timing</li></ul>
Tools	<ul><li>The institution's text editor program</li><li>Basic software—the in-house computer system, e-mail, archiving, report formats</li></ul>
Human capital building	<ul><li>Policy on attending short courses to enhance skills</li></ul>

General orientation.

For research staff. Three areas should be covered in the orientation for analysts: 1) the organization's mission and primary tasks; 2) the basics on working at the institution, including HR matters, IT systems, and the like; and 3) how to be a successful "consultant" for lack of a better phrase (i.e., how to be responsive to one's clients, be they internal or external to the organization, and other "good performance practices").

Orientation for researchers should be designed to acquaint new research staff with the organization's goals and operating style and to introduce favored work patterns. Think tanks have a wide range of activities, so their orientations should be as diverse as necessary to suit.

At a think tank that strongly emphasizes econometric research, the "work at the institution" part of orientation of new researchers will likely focus on the following in addition to HR matters and the like:

- The importance of high-quality analysis
- How to judge data quality
- The way the institution's projects are organized and the need for teamwork in executing them
- Where to find help with computing, statistical, econometric, and similar issues.

At a think tank that predominantly conducts and evaluates technical assistance projects to improve the performance of local governments, in contrast, the orientation will concentrate on good practices working with local officials and nongovernmental organizations in a technical assistance pilot project. Broad topics could include:

- understanding municipalities' incentives for participating in pilot projects
- approaching an administration
- working with local officials
- building trust in a relationship
- understanding "demand-driven" technical assistance.

The second area within General Orientation includes a host of administrative issues listed in the first panel of Table 4.1, beginning with point five.

The third area of orientation, "how to be a consultant," is quite generic and targeted at educating new hires to certain systems and expectations (last item in the orientation list). Many analysts in their first job with a think tank have never worked on projects with a hard budget constraint (i.e., the analyst has only so many days to complete a task and should not charge additional hours to it). This discussion must include information on what to do if it appears that the time allocated will not be sufficient to accomplish the task and, just as important, what to do if it is possible to finish the task within fewer hours. Also extremely useful is an open discussion of ways to organize one's work and measure progress. Equally important is advice on meeting the demands of working on multiple projects (possibly for multiple supervisors) at the same time—and what to do if there are conflicts in the demands placed on the analyst. Another topic deserving discussion is the importance of completing time sheets daily, to ensure project costs are properly tracked.[44]

For support staff. A more detailed orientation agenda for support staff is shown in Table 4.2. Topics include information on the goals and philosophy of the institution, guidance on how to complete a host of practical tasks, and resources available to the staff. Note the additional topics in Table 4.2 for a new communications staff hire.

Table 4.2 Orientation for Institute Support Staff

Introduction
• Definition of a think tank
• Mission, main directions of activities
Staff Documentation
• Labor book and/or other government documents
• Contents of the labor agreement, consistency with national laws
Office Documents
• Formats for different types of documents—letters, reports, activity reports for sponsors
• Maintenance and format of address and contact lists
• Archiving documents
Participation in Staff Education Program
• Responsibilities for reminding designated staff to attend, including monitoring travel schedules
Introduction to the Library and Accessing Institute Reports
• Ordering institute publications for distribution
• Arranging for a large number of publication copies for big events
• Using the library and the automated card catalogue
• Getting to know the library collection, including periodicals
Introduction to the Communications Program
• Major communications group activities
• Who does what in the communications group
• Responsibilities of researchers and support staff in submitting documents for posting
Documentation for Domestic Business Trips
• Travel advances
• Expense reports
• Importance of billing trips to the correct projects
Documentation for International Travel
• Visa arrangements—letters of invitation, rules of different embassies
• Travel advances
• Expense reports
Computer Network and Office Equipment
• Introduction to the computer network, including protocols for backing up
• Copy machine operations (operations, paper to use, etc.)
• Scanner operations
• CD-ROM recording
• Telephone system
Additions to support staff training for Communications Staff
• Communications program goals and the overall communications strategy
• Project level communications plans and execution
• Working with researchers
• Communications activities

---

44   See Chapter 11 for a discussion of time management systems.

Surprisingly, few think tanks have the kind of orientation programs just outlined. The result is that new staff members waste a large amount of time "learning by doing," when they could be contributing to projects and support tasks. Another unfortunate result is that researchers are likely to be less effective in the policy engagement process than if, from the start of their employment, they understood and used the resources available to them from the communications team.

The HR team may have only a modest role in making presentations to all new staff. But it has an extremely important role in organizing all orientation sessions, as described in the section later in this chapter on Organizing Training. If HR staff does not oversee that all groups carry out the sessions assigned to them, there is a good chance that some of the sessions will never take place. In addition, HR has the role of grouping new hires for general sessions where appropriate, for example with IT and communications, and making certain the new hires actually attend them.

Human capital building.

For research staff. Most junior and mid-level researchers arrive at think tanks with basic or stronger quantitative analysis skills and significant knowledge of one sector of the economy. So, for example, a typical new researcher could have a higher education degree in economics and three years of experience in the transportation sector. During those three years the researcher will have mastered information on the sector's legal and policy environment and analyzed secondary data on trends in, for example, ridership, costs, and revenues for different transportation modes. But the same researcher could lack competence in policy analysis and program evaluation techniques, as well as lacking knowledge of other sectors.

Limited competence with policy analysis and evaluation is typical in most transitional and developing economies because of the structure and content of their higher education systems. But to be strong performers at think tanks, most analysts need to be competent in these areas. Moreover, depending on the composition of the institution's work program, new researchers may need additional training. For example, if a think tank works consistently on analyzing the economic efficiency of alternative investments—for example, in water and sewerage facilities, district heat plants, or transportation improvements—the research staff will need to be able to perform financial analysis of investment projects. In short, the specific mix of training appropriate for a think tank depends on its work mix.

Tools for the research and support staffs.

"Tools" training generally increases staff productivity rather than providing competence in whole new areas (such as program evaluation or sophisticated desktop publishing). Table 4.1 above lists examples of such training for both researchers and support staff.

For research staff, importantly, the list for researchers includes presentation skills, with the use of PowerPoint featured. This training module should also contain good practices on structuring presentation development and delivery techniques. Note also that training in the statistical package used by the specific think tank is listed here. Limited formal training in this software affords new staff an impressive head start in their early work with the package.

For support staff, the "tools" training examples in Table 4.1 are aimed at helping staff gain proficiency with the computer system and with often-used software, particularly the text editor used by the institution. Where a staff member shows promise, "tools" training can and should be supplemented with human capacity building mentoring or short courses.

The items listed in the Table 4.1 should be taken as plausible ideas. Each think tank will know best what kinds of training should be offered, depending on its work program and the formal training of its staff. Note that the in-house training done by the IT department, communications group, other administrative staff leaders, or senior researchers is often at the introductory level. If staff needs full competence in using Power Point or Word, then a short-course acquired on the market is usually appropriate.

Follow the Plan

A challenge to think tanks in most transitional and developing economies is integrating training opportunities offered by donors (sometimes held at international venues) into the think tanks' own training programs. This can be difficult, because the donor opportunities are typically offered on only a few weeks' notice and are sometimes not on the highest-priority topics from a particular think tank's perspective. Nonetheless, their low cost and coverage of topics not addressed by local education programs often make them attractive to staff and managers, particularly as rewards for good performance.

That said, attendance usually comes with a high opportunity cost in work not getting done. Key staff members attending several multi-day, off-site training events can seriously impair a team's ability to meet contractual obligations and to be sufficiently active in policy engagement at critical moments.

Managers' first act should be to determine if the subject of the training has been independently identified by the think tank as high priority and is included in its training plan. If so, the decision is obvious. If it is not included, participation makes sense only under extraordinary circumstances. Note that in declining an invitation, the fact that the conference's topic is not included in the training plan can be cited.

When staff returns from such trainings, they should at an absolute minimum share the materials received with relevant colleagues. Much better would be that, within a couple of weeks of returning, they give an informal presentation to interested colleagues designed to share the key knowledge gained. Knowing they will make such a presentation upon returning home usually has the effect of making training event attendees more attentive during the training. (Actual experience with such knowledge sharing is reviewed below.)

Keep It Simple

I can readily imagine many readers literally cowering at the prospect of having to develop the annual plan. Such fears are likely misplaced, particularly after the first year. Plan development can be really quite simple once the content has been decided. "Content" in this case has three dimensions: 1) what is to be among training activities, i.e., within each of the three areas just discussed; 2) how each will be taught (external provider, e.g., university, or offered in-house, in which case who will teach each needs identification); and 3) how often each presentation, workshop, or course will be offered. The results can be easily summarized on a spreadsheet. To facilitate plan development, the next section addresses various options for structuring the training.

ORGANIZING THE TRAINING

Presenting a training program of the type just described requires attention to several organizational issues. Four of the more important ones are discussed in this section, ranging from determining which staff members should receive each type of training to funding for the training involved.

Getting Started

Identifying training needs. Training needs of think tanks will vary substantially depending on their size, level of staff turnover, and main directions of their work. No standard training program suits all think tanks. The comments below build on the earlier section on training needs identification.

The actual training program adopted will depend on the organization's own training resources, needs identified, and number of people to be trained in a given period. The last factor clearly influences the cost of a training event per staff person trained (if training is done by staff), how often certain training events should be offered, and perhaps whether the training should be done in-house. Small think tanks could explore pooling their resources with similar organizations to conduct some of the more commonly needed human capital–building workshops not offered by universities or other vendors.

Holding a special meeting of senior management and team leaders every year or two is often an effective way to define evolving broad training needs. A key input is management views on any new policy research area initiatives being planned. The meeting will be more productive if participants are given an illustrative list of possible training topics in advance, to stimulate thinking. The training agenda can be kept within feasible bounds by using as inputs to the deliberations the expected value of the annual training budget and the cost of typical events. During such discussions, some participants tend to confuse the training needs of individual staff members with the needs of the staff overall; a clear separation needs to be maintained when inputs are on the table. This discussion has to be about needs *at the institutional level.*

The actual plan should be based primarily on the results of the training requirements identified in the annual performance reviews plus: 1) needs likely to arise from strengthening the capabilities of new hires and 2) the results of the senior management deliberations just described. At some level this is a wish list that will in the end have to be checked against the funding available for training.

Deciding who should do the training. This is a broader topic than may first appear. The identity of the trainer is generally conflated with how the training is organized. It is more useful to distinguish among three training options: informal training, in-house "tool" training (such as a one-to-three hour session on efficient use of a Microsoft Office product), and formal training. This is discussed further below.

Orientation Training

Many readers can probably remember an orientation session that consisted of someone from HR greeting you, then going over certain HR topics such as benefits and what you had to do to sign up, and finishing with wishing you well in your new job. Sadly, this is still the industry norm.

An effective orientation program consists of many more parts (i.e., separate sessions, each led by the appropriate, knowledgeable person). Once the topics have been set, which should be done by senior management, the various departments should decide which topics each will cover and which are best assigned to the new hire's supervisor. The following ideas on allocations are only suggestions. (Decision making on this type of issue is discussed in Chapter 8.)

For researchers, the HR person should cover the topics that are general or clearly in the HR domain, which include many of those listed under orientation in the "For Researchers" part of Table 4.1. Other think tank departments should take on other areas listed in the table in separate sessions. IT should handle the subjects in its domain, for example. The same holds for communications, both because this is the group with the expertise and also because it is critical that researchers look to this group for support and advice from the outset.

Some of the topics to be covered should be discussed individually with each new staff member. In particular, the first four topics listed in Table 4.1 should be covered in detail by the new hire's Team Leader/Department Head. This would also be a good time for the leader to spell out his/ her expectations for performance in the new hire's specific position. Other topics, such as the institution's mission and philosophy, could be addressed by the Executive Director or other appropriate senior manager with several new hires at the same time.

In the orientation session led by the Director of Communications, the role of the communications group is explained and its tasks and tools outlined. Here researchers are told such things as when to begin consulting with the communications team on engaging policy community stakeholders in a particular project and developing a corresponding communications plan for disseminating results. An important element should be the communications group's role in the institution's social media contributions and any blogs the institute hosts. Additionally, because the communications group often maintains the library (and may control the purchase of books and journal articles), the library's structure, holdings, and services should be on the agenda.

For support staff, the topics listed in table 4.2 would sensibly divided among HR, finance, and communications as appropriate.

The IT group can and should provide a basic introduction to the IT system, the services the group provides to various departments, the trainings regularly on offer, and who handles which tasks. An overview of the software available is essential, as is a brief introduction to the short courses or seminars the IT group gives on commonly used programs, such as Microsoft Power Point and other Office products, and the schedule on which they will be given over the next couple of months.

Case Study 4.1 describes the orientation program developed for its interns by the Center for the Study of Democracy (CSD) in Sofia. Its structure and content are broadly applicable to on-boarding new research staff. CSD has given a great deal of thought to on-boarding these individuals, orienting them thoroughly, and mentoring them during their six-month visits. The program is a major recruiting vehicle for the Center.

Ongoing Training

On Site Options. The vast majority of all training is informal (i.e., OJT). It essential to take explicit account of this resource in developing the training plan; it is also appropriate to ask if training needs can be met efficiently and thoroughly in this way before turning to formal options. Again, this is a topic for the annual or bi-annual managers' meeting devoted to staff training. At least three forms of informal training should be considered beyond the two traditional forms of OJT (the "buddy system" or a new worker shadowing a more experienced partner).

- *Mentoring*: the conscious, systematic teaching by a more knowledgeable staff member (a principal investigator, head of the Communications group, etc.) of a less experienced colleague to increase his/her skills. This differs from the simple training that occurs on a peer-to-peer basis where the knowledge shared is typically of a relatively simple mechanical task, such as how to structure the specific command in using a statistical package. Being a good mentor is becoming an increasingly important job requirement for senior researchers, as I have noted in previous chapters; and, the requirement for mentoring is increasingly being added to senior researcher job descriptions. For researchers, mentors have to think about how to expand a lower level researcher's skills step-by-step over time. For example, a research assistant who has been doing good basic statistical analysis for 18 months may now be ready to be given the assignment of interpreting results and writing up his/her interpretation (perhaps in bullet form to start).

- *Internal seminars:* an often overlooked resource for less senior researchers and for members of the communications staff who will be responsible for helping design and implement policy engagement programs for the research results. For research assistants the exposure to new topics and methods can be very important and welcomed. It is likely that research staff slightly higher on the ladder will not attend many of these unless they are required to—a case of short-term pressures overriding long-term benefits. Seminars should be held over the noon hour where possible, to minimize disruptions in standard schedules, and staff encouraged to participate.

Internal seminars offer an important opportunity for relationship building between members of the communications team and the researcher-presenters. In many think tanks there is some estrangement between these two groups, which can make engaging the researchers in planning and executing communications plans difficult. (Examples of friction include researchers perceived by the communications team as haughty and communications staff perceived by researchers as "dumbing down" or over simplifying the research at issue.) Attendance by someone from the communications team is valuable—to show respect for the work and to learn enough about its substance to make them more efficient in thinking about targeting the campaign—as is attendance by advocacy NGOs that may be possible partners in promoting the policy recommendations.

- *Affinity groups:* a group of individuals with a shared research interest who self-organize to meet periodically, usually monthly, to discuss a topic of common interest. Such groups could include those interested in spatial mapping software, for example, or studies about teachers' and health professionals' absenteeism. Generally, someone volunteers to lead the discussion for the next session and does background work to provide the introductory comments. Sessions are usually held over the lunch hour.

The potential role of each of these training options is substantial and, when senior management is confronting the list of training needs, consideration should be given to these tools as well as to more formal options. *A word of caution:* There is typically significant demand for such courses, but it is worthwhile at the outset to send a menu of possible events to staff asking them which they are "very likely" to attend. Experience shows that positive response rates are usually much higher than actual turn outs, and a step-by-step approach is warranted in developing such a training series.

"Tool training" events are internal events organized and typically taught by institute staff. I gave the example of an event on computer software above. Using specific social media tools is another good target. And there are many opportunities in the software realm. Similar tools training could be organized for analysts (e.g., on logit model estimation).

A badly underserved need is in the communications area for senior and mid-level researchers to be trained in giving interviews to television or radio reporters, and on making the two-to-three minute video presentations on current topics of high policy interest that are then posted on the institute's website, Facebook, or other forums. These can be one-to-two hour trainings, assisted by videos of strong and weak performances made before the session. Many researchers operate under the illusion that they are by nature smooth respondents and presenters. It may require reviewing the video of a recent short presentation or interview involving a researcher with poor delivery for him/her to see the very different truth. Untrained, many give answers that are simply too long, do not respond to the question asked, and/or wander into topics extraneous to the question.

Management can expect significant resistance by senior researchers to participating in short communications workshops. One way to encourage them is to inform all who should attend that the institution's Executive Director will participate and s/he expects others to be there as well. Alternatively, the Executive Director may need to have a quiet word with those most needing the help, encouraging them to participate.

All the training options discussed thus far are those internal to a think tank. But this does not mean they are costless. Far from it. The staff time needed to prepare a good presentation on a software package, or on how to be a good media respondent, is significant. Unless such events are held during participants' private time (e.g., lunch hour or outside usual working hours), staff costs are incurred here as well, unless the training can be viewed as relevant to a current research project and staff time billed accordingly.

What about training courses (i.e., those requiring more contact time between students and teachers or a higher degree of expertise available on staff)? The argument for offering a course in-house with senior staff being the lecturers is greater the larger the number of students who will attend and the closer the match between the course topic and the experience of a senior staff member. So, if 10 staff should take the course and someone on staff has taught it in the past, offering the course in-house makes sense. The further one moves from this ideal situation in terms of fewer students and lower existing experience of potential in-house instructors, however, the stronger the argument for reimbursing staff for taking a course offered by a university or other outside vendor. Reimbursement usually depends, as it should, on passing the course.

Off Site Options. The two broad options available are attending either: 1) classes at local universities or staff training organizations (to acquire computer skills or greater proficiency in accounting, HR, social media in communications, and other skills); or 2) on-line courses covering the same topics. On-line courses are defined here as similar in content to their traditional classroom-based counterparts. In particular, I am excluding donor-supported one-off on-line training sessions in communications, research skills, or other areas that are part of capacity building programs.

Generally, three conditions govern whether a think tank will reimburse the student for taking a course of this kind:

- Its content is directly related to the staff member's responsibilities
- HR approves the staffer taking the course prior to course registration
- The staffer passes the course.

In approving course attendance (and potential tuition reimbursement), the HR officer will generally check with the applicant's supervisor on relevance.

The advent of on-line courses has the potential to expand sharply the range of readily available courses. But little information exists on think tanks' use of these. Hints are available from interviews that a team from the Results for Development Institute conducted in spring 2014 with six executive directors of think tanks located in Anglophone Sub Saharan Africa.[45] Half reported a few staff taking such courses. Notable points from the interviews include:

- Staff members were self-motivated to take the courses; that is, they identified and enrolled in the courses. Taking the on-line courses was not part of the think tank's training plan, if it had one.

- Although most courses were free, fees were charged for some. The fees were reimbursed by two think tanks—in one case where the course subject was "of interest to it" and in the other where the subject was in the training plan.

- Students completing courses were often awarded a certificate. (The interview did not inquire as to whether tests were administered.)

For many on-line courses, think tank managers will face the challenge of judging whether staff taking the on-line course has mastered the material covered. Major course purveyors such as Coursera (www.coursera.com) have taken significant steps to ensure that the registered student is uniquely doing the course work for courses for which the student wants certification of successful completion.[46] Still, some question whether they are really foolproof.

Selecting participants. It is useful to distinguish among three levels of a staff member's need to participate in a particular training event:

1. Staffer cannot properly do his/her current job, or a job for which s/he has been identified as the best candidate, without the knowledge to be imparted in the training—i.e., a critical skills gap.

---

45   The interviews were done in conjunction with an April, 2014 workshop for a TTI-supported project on Policy Engagement and Communications.

46   Worth noting is the following quotation from the Coursera web site: "You acknowledge that the Letter of Completion, and Coursera's Online Courses, will not stand in the place of a course taken at an accredited institution, and do not convey academic credit. You acknowledge that neither the instructors of any Online Course nor the associated Participating Institutions will be involved in any attempts to get the course recognized by any educational or accredited institution." https://authentication.coursera.org/auth/auth/normal/tos.php. It is commonplace that on-line students are permitted to use notes, the textbook, and other resources in taking tests, resources normally denied those taking classroom courses. This complicates comparison of the extent of course content mastery in the two regimes. See, for example, Colvin et al. (2014).

2. Learning the material covered in the training will enhance the ability of the staffer to do his/her job and it may prepare him/her for future promotion or assignment.
3. Training is not directly relevant to the staffer's responsibilities and it is unclear if it will be needed for future assignments.

Most think tanks I am familiar with readily support training in the first two categories but generally not the third, although requests are examined on a case-by-case basis. Staff in the first category must take and pass a course or move to another position where mastery of the topic is not necessary or leave the institution. Staff in the second category usually are encouraged by their supervisor to take the course. If the annual staff performance assessments are being done well, staff members in the first two categories will be clearly identified in the goal statements.

Funding the training. To create and maintain a training program, the organization must make adequate provision for training expenses in its annual budget. For think tanks, the presence of an annual training budget will usually signal that there is explicit provision for training as an overhead expense item. Most organizations include an allowance for staff training when determining the size and composition of the overhead rate. This, then, is a reliable source of funding—one whose value for the year is usually known at the beginning of the year. (Of course, the funds actually available will depend on the think tank's success in meeting its planned fund-raising goals for the year. But most institutions can forecast the likely range of funds raised with some confidence.) Typically, overhead funding forms the core of training resources. [47] (Overhead rate calculation is discussed in Chapter 11.)

A second source of financial support is training events included in project budgets. Project resources can be used in at least two ways. First, many think tanks work collaboratively on projects with outside advisers, often from North America, Western Europe, or Australia, who contribute special expertise to a project. Knowledgeable advisors can be asked to give a seminar on the project's research subject. In addition to the one-time benefit to staff from such seminars, the materials distributed can serve as the basis for future similar presentations by institution staff. Second, project funds can be used to support staff attendance at training events directly related to project execution. Those attending such training can then become a resource person on this topic at their own think tanks. Analysis of the extent of sharing of information gained at skills acquisition workshops of the GDN project presented in Annex 4.1 indicates a high degree of sharing and suggests that such "multiplier effect" may be more important than generally appreciated.

Finally, staff can contribute some of their own time in attending the training events, rather than charging the time to project or overhead accounts. The lunch hour, as noted, is an excellent time to hold short training events, where staff can eat lunch and participate in the training at the same time. Some institutions also schedule training near the end of the day, so that most of the training

---

47   In the corporate world, the rule of thumb is for training expenditures to equal about 5 percent of payroll (Bowsher 1998, 76).

takes place after normal working hours. This "cost sharing" is generally a good idea; but care must be taken not to undermine staff morale by imposing this condition too often, or at times when the opportunity cost is especially high, such as holiday seasons.

In thinking about funding for training, it is very important to be realistic about the cost side. Many think tanks try to run a training program on the cheap by adding formal teaching responsibilities and frequent class participation requirements without any corresponding compensation. This leads not only to resentment and poor morale, but probably also to lower quality course content and poorer student receptivity and retention than if staff could charge realistic time to these activities.

THINK TANK PERSPECTIVES ON TRAINING

As with so many areas of think tank management, systematic data on actual practices is very limited. This section draws on interviews of a few think tank leaders and two studies that provide quite different perspectives on broadly defined training at think tanks (see Chapter 2 for the general characteristics of the two groups of think tanks involved). The first is from 2000 data on HR practices at six Central and Eastern European (CEE) think tanks. The second is from 2010-2011 data on such practices at 15 think tanks in the GDN sample.

While I found no survey data on the think tank experience in developing annual plans, in a 2014 interview we learned that the Consortium pour la Recherche Economique et Sociale in Senegal has recently created such plans with the support of its TTI funding. Staff preferences are taken into account and the plan includes both internal training on computer skills and writing, for example, as well as external courses eligible for funding.

The CEE-6 Think Tanks

Two central findings stand out from the experience of the CEE-6 think tanks: 1) the importance they assigned to training varied widely, but 2) those who did value it were quite active (see Table 4.3). Free international trainings were a major part of all programs, as were in-house seminars (for most of them).

Table 4.3 Staff Training in CEE-6 Think Thanks, Data for the Year 2000

Training issue	MRI	TARKI	CSD	IUE	IET	Expert
Importance generally assigned by management to additional training for research staff	High	Low	Marginal	High	High	Marginal
Is there a specific line for staff training explicitly included in overhead charges?	Yes, but not a separate item	No	Yes	Yes	No	No[a]
Is an annual training plan developed?	No	Yes, focused on in-house events	No	No, but needed training is defined[b]	Yes, every six months, for allocation of international opportunities	No
Who participates?	NA	Senior management and team leaders	NA	NA	Senior management	NA
Is the plan developed at the beginning of the fiscal year?	NA	Yes	NA	NA	No	NA
How is the decision on allocation of resources made?	In response to donor offers and staff requests	Little activity; in response to staff requests	In response to staff requests	Needs are defined as part of staff assessment process	In response to opportunities from donors[c]	In response to donor offers
How important are training events sponsored by other organizations?[d]	Very important	Marginal	Marginal	Very important	Very important	Very important
Percent of research staff attending at least one training event or course per year	~50%	5 to 10%	5 to 10%	~50%	~50%	10 to 15%
Are there formal in-house training events?	No, but there are monthly staff seminars on ongoing projects	Yes; internal seminars on methodological topics	Few	Yes; in-house seminars on substantive topics and methods	Yes; internal seminars on substantive topics and methods	Yes; internal project review seminars and brainstorming sessions on methods

a. But there is a line for staff travel; travel typically constitutes most of the cost of attending training events and conferences held outside the home city.
b. The definition occurs as part of the staff assessment process.
c. The department head makes decisions about attendance at domestic conferences and seminars with training content.
d. Includes events sponsored by donors.

CSD, Expert, and TARKI management teams did not assign formal training a high priority, and a correspondingly small share of staff participated in training outside the organization in a given year. Management of these think tanks had the view that they hired capable people who would not need much training. Senior researchers at TARKI and CSD taught at some of each country's most prestigious universities, so there was a general feeling they were keeping abreast of developments in their disciplines.

Even so, Expert and TARKI had in-house training programs (see below). Training expenses were estimated as less than 1 percent of total institute costs, excluding the cost of staff time for participation. These institutions relied primarily on hiring well-trained staff who already had the requisite skills.

The other three institutes assigned greater importance to staff training, with about half the research staff participating in conferences or formal training events during a year. IUE, for example, spent the equivalent of 3 to 4 percent of its turnover on training, including external and internal funding. Nevertheless, divergent practices among these three organizations are evident. IUE and IET came the closest to having a fully defined training plan. In IUE's case, a comprehensive picture of training needs was a product of the staff assessment process and formed the basis for training activities, although a formal plan was not prepared. International opportunities sometimes met these needs and supplemented the other training. (As noted, international travel was often allocated as a reward for staff who would use the training in their work).

Abundant international training activities were available everywhere. (Remember that international funders were heavily engaged in the region around 2000, when the data were collected.) IET made a plan for use of these resources about twice a year. At both IUE and IET, much of the structured training was accomplished through staff participation in international conferences or explicit training activities. These were funded either as an element in contracts or grants awarded to the organizations or by discrete offers from international sponsors for particular events. IUE also sent staff to local (Russian) training events, and on occasion contracted with an expert organization for specific training (e.g., training in the financial aspects of project analysis) when an extant course could not be found.

With respect to in-house training events, four of the six—TARKI, IUE, Expert, and IET—conducted a program of seminars on substantive and methodological topics. In all four, staff—especially junior and mid-level staff—were strongly encouraged to attend. MRI had monthly staff seminars at which results of ongoing projects were reviewed; these seminars also conveyed information on technical topics and informed staff about the range of work going on at the institute.

The GDN-15 Think Tanks
The questions on training in the survey of GDN think tanks include a very important one about the number of staff who received training in a range of areas over the period April 2010 to November

2011 (i.e., the time between two monitoring surveys for the evaluation of mentoring programs).[48] The specific question wording was:

> **Between April 2010 and November 2011,** did staff participate in training workshops or courses in the following areas where you think the result was a significant increase in their competence? *If not, enter "0". The point about increasing their competence is critical; we all know that there are many trainings that review what is already known or make a small incremental contribution to the knowledge base. We are looking for training experiences that made you think that the staff member could do tasks they previously could not do.*

Hence, the emphasis was on skill enhancement, no matter how many staff participated in courses or workshops. In reviewing the responses it is relevant to remember that the GDN program was providing several types of analytical training during the survey response period.

The results (see Table 4.4) show that two-thirds of these think tanks reported increased skill in at least one analytic area and as high a share reported improvement in at least one communications area (next to last column). In analytic skills, about six different staff benefited; for communications the figure is somewhat over three (last column). Over such a short period, these are substantial figures.

---

48   Training experience was not covered in the TTI surveys used in this analysis.

Table 4.4 Improved Skills at GDN-15 Think Tanks during April 2010 – November 2011

Improved staff skills[a]	=<10 FT researchers (Stage 1)		>10 FT researchers		All think tanks	
	% of Think Tanks Responding	Mean # of Staff (Non-Zero Responses)	% of Think Tanks Responding	Mean # of Staff (Non-Zero Responses)	% of Think Tanks Responding	Mean # of Staff (Non-Zero Responses)
Analytic skills	**88%**	**2.7**	**43%**	**14.3**	**67%**	**6.2**
How to analyze questions in a specific area, e.g., budget analysis in the health sector	75	2.2	57	10.3	67	5.4
Statistical analysis	50	3.8	29	3.5	40	3.7
Econometrics or similar skills in sociology, psychology, etc.	38	1.3	43	4	40	2.7
Program evaluation	38	1.3	57	11.5	47	7.1
Using SPSS, SAS, or similar statistical package	63	3.6	57	5.8	60	4.6
Communications skills	**88**	**2.9**	**43**	**4.7**	**67**	**3.4**
Public relations topics: working with the media, organizing events, targeting audiences	50	1.5	57	4	53	2.8
Communications-improving writing for web site or other documents, learning about alternative formats and products, matching products to audiences, etc.	75	3.5	43	4.7	60	3.9
Other	13	1	0	0	7%	1

a. Staff was to have significantly increased their competence in an area to be included.

Staff at Stage 1 think tanks participated at a higher rate than those at larger organizations. Of Stage 1 institutions, 88 percent had staff who improved analytic skills and the same share improved communications skills. This compares with only 43 percent in both categories at larger organizations.

Within the analytic area, analysis of issues in particular areas (e.g., health, and learning statistical packages such as SPSS) had the highest share of think tank staffs gaining skills, with 67 and 60 percent, respectively, for all think tanks combined. Forty-seven percent of think tanks also reported staff gaining skill in program evaluation. Particularly among the larger think tanks, numerous participants took advantage of this type of training. These facts are consistent with such institutions working to strengthen the rigor of their quantitative analysis, which was generally weak at the time these countries joined the GDN program.

The participation rates in the communications area are similarly high. Sixty percent of these think tanks had staff who improved their skills in general communications skills and 53 percent in the communications area. Among these think tanks, about 3 staff members benefitted from each type of training on average—a tribute to the evolving importance to think tanks of communications activities.

In sum, very substantial staff capacity building was ongoing among several of these think tanks more than a decade ago.

TAKE AWAYS

Staff training is an often neglected source of improved productivity at think tanks. Far from a luxury, investment in training is a rational economic decision for boosting staff efficiency. But it is more than this. Staff who acquire new knowledge and skills are more satisfied with their jobs, which improves morale and staff retention. Organizations with good reputations for staff training opportunities have an edge in recruiting staff as well.

Strong Practices

Characteristics of a well-managed think tank in this context follow.

- An annual training plan covering new "tools" mastery and human capital development is developed based on: 1) the agreement reached between supervisor and supervisee on capacity development in the annual performance assessment, 2) senior management's plans for new initiatives, and 3) input from research and administration managers.

- A line item for training is included in overhead calculations and an affordable plan developed within this budget envelope. The plan need not be elaborate, but even creating one in outline will provide a structure and focus.

- Internal resources in a variety of formats are used where possible to deliver training, with mentoring (and mentoring quality) a priority issue for managers. Other informal training through in-house seminars and affinity groups are supported by management.

- Workshops, short courses, university classes, and on-line courses are used where specifically needed, and financial support is restricted to topics directly relevant to each worker's tasks.

For Funders
Look carefully for:

- *Whether the overhead rate includes a line item for training.* Both its presence and its absence send important messages. In either case, ask whether the institution prepares any kind of annual training plan, even a notional one.

- *What kind of orientation is in place for new hires?* This includes topics covered, who participates, and how orientation activities are organized. Prompt the respondent about topics not readily mentioned, because s/he may think of orientation narrowly (i.e., as the initial greeting meeting for new staff), rather than a series of sessions held over time covering a range of specific topics.

Perhaps to do:

- Resist the temptation to invite and even pressure individual staff, such as communications directors, to attend training events without informing or, *much better*, consulting the executive director about his/her staff participating. (On the other hand, notifying management and relevant staff of the forthcoming courses that are open for a think tank's staff is very valuable.)

- If you are designing a think tank mentoring program, try to schedule training events as far in the future as possible to permit think tanks to include them in their training programs. Providing detailed descriptions of course content will facilitate think tank assessment of the extent to which the planned course will meet its needs. It would be even better to share a draft of the contents with a request for comments on how the course could be adjusted to better meet probable invitees' needs.

- Because most training and the most relevant training for staff is defined through each member's "personal development plan" and carried out on site, consider funding think tanks' own training operations, i.e., essentially provide matching budget support to make these plans a reality. This would certainly stimulate preparation of strong performance assessments and development of annual training plans. Grants could include one-time funding to set up a strong annual assessment program that would generate personal development plans agreed by the staffer and supervisor as needed.

- Getting involved in a think tank's training program only makes sense if you are planning a multi-year and a fairly intensive relationship is probable. It can be too easy to get drawn into micro-management discussions. If you do get into such discussions, make every effort to place them in the context of overall staff policy, especially career paths and retention.

Case Study 4.1 Orientation Program, Center for the Study of Democracy

The Center for the Study of Democracy (CSD), based in Bulgaria, has a robust, well-defined, and standardized policy for welcoming and mentoring newly hired interns, which frequently results in extending offers of: 1) permanent positions as general researchers and/or experts in particular fields at CSD or other institutions, 2) admission to elite graduate schools, or 3) funding schemes for additional employment and/or education. About 20 interns come to CSD annually. Internships are generally for a three-month period. CSD interns are usually reimbursed via scholarship schemes from their host universities or via EU funding—though on occasion CSD provides a modest wage to exceptional performers.

In order to incorporate the accumulated employee management best practices in the management of interns, CSD applies a number of standardized practices in the intern orientation process. This is also done in the interest of equal treatment of all interns regardless of gender or ethnic origin. CSD is committed to adhering to the values of diversity management, which the institution believes are best reflected in a standardized common approach to employee orientation which seeks, at the same time to identify the specific needs of incoming interns.

On-boarding
Prior to the intern's arrival, the following information is provided to him/her:

- List of necessary documents (statements of availability and commitment, confidentiality agreements, etc.) if any;
- Information regarding life in the city (stores, tips regarding apartment rentals, traffic and transportation, safety and cultural tips, etc.) dress code information (i.e., a description of the "business casual" style);
- Contact point information (i.e., internship manager and mentor)

Usually orientation is conducted for individual interns. During the first week after the intern's arrival, the following procedures are followed:

- "First Day Welcome" and Orientation, including:
  - Meeting the whole team and the organization's program board (i.e., the Directors of each of the four CSD Programs – Security, Economic, Sociological and Law)
  - overview of the organizational structure, systems, and processes

- Introduction to/overview of the organization's work
- Introduction to on-site canteen and identification of foods the intern is unable to consume due to dietary/health or religious concerns
- Interview with the mentor to establish common work interests and potential synergies, including:
  - Setting an initial agenda (and refining it, as necessary, to fit intern's needs);
  - Explaining tasks/projects and their relation to the work of the organization (i.e., their context)
  - Clearly identifying roles and responsibilities (with special attention to the intern's role in each project)
  - Describing mentor's commitments and identification of preferred mentorship style; (average time spent on mentoring each intern is approximately three hours per week);
  - identifying performance expectations
  - Introducing the calendar of planned events and key dates
  - Discussing logistics and any other matters
- End of the week get together and welcoming party with all staff invited.

In all cases when interns are hired, CSD uses standardized templates and procedures for developing intern action plans as well as mentorship plans to guide the intern's supervisor(s)—while clearly identifying the expected timeline(s) and performance indicators that would determine successful completion of the internship. The action and mentorship plans provide an initial assessment of the strengths and opportunities provided by the internship for both the intern and the organization. Such an assessment includes identifying:

- What the intern expects to gain from the mentoring relationship
- What are the intern's career or academic goals
- What type of duties the intern is expected to perform
- Expected level of independence and self-learning/development (alternatively, the intern's preference for formally structured work); an assessment of what sort of mentorship style would work best for the intern (i.e., one that either includes detailed day-to-day instructions and feedback or provides instructions and feedback on demand)
- Most suitable learning style for the intern (e.g., by reading, listening, seeing, or doing)

- Time the mentor and the intern are able to commit to the mentorship
- Professional and practical opportunities provided to the intern
- Provisional timeline for completing each project (subject to amendments related to ongoing progress)
- Commonalities between the organization's areas of expertise and current projects, and the intern's professional interests.

The Internship Experience

Interns take part in all planned events (workshops, conferences, round tables, etc.) of the department they are assigned to. On average, the program average is three events each month. If interns express interest, they can also attend or participate in events organized by other CSD programs/departments. They have full access to the calendar of planned events via the CSD intranet.

CSD attempts to match interns' professional aspirations to their assignments. Having developed, over the past two decades, into a major think tank including several programs with expertise in fields as diverse as economic policy, energy policy and sustainable development, immigration policy and human rights, IT and innovation, anti-corruption, and international relations and security policy, CSD attracts diverse talent indeed. As a minimum, CSD always guarantees interns the ability to produce policy briefs (with supervision and feedback where needed) or policy notes on a topic relevant to the intern's educational background and/or future professional goals.

In recent years, CSD has developed its capacity to manage large-scale international projects, which can take place in up to all 28 EU member states and requiring the publication of reports for each of the countries involved. It is, thus, often possible to match the talents of incoming interns to tasks that form part of such large current projects. Given the diverse fields in which CSD has developed its expertise, and the multiple countries where such large projects are implemented, interns based in countries other than Bulgaria are frequently given the option to conduct research in their country of origin and/or current residence.

CSD staff provides international interns with Dropbox access to key project documents and mentors, and manages them via Skype when they cannot be present in Sofia the whole time. Their initial "virtual" training and orientation often includes familiarizing them with the standardized methodology for producing country reports so that (on the assumption they are top performers) they can, under the guidance of senior experts, contribute and eventually even co-author the report for the country in which they reside. This allows them to gain extremely useful experience and provides them with mentorship by international experts in addition to CSD project managers.

Measuring Success

CSD does not have a strict or formal system of performance measurement for interns. The basic indicators measuring the success of the internship experience are:

- Number of publications to which the intern has contributed or which s/he has authored
- Number of events to which s/he contributed;
- Number of project development contributions (i.e., grant/proposal writing)

In addition to the above, CSD also takes into consideration the results of the exit interviews, during which the interns' levels of satisfaction is gauged and feedback solicited so as to improve the internship programs in future. CSD also considers the number of applicants who apply, although it does not place great significance on the number as long as there is no alarming negative trend (i.e., the focus is on maintaining stable inflows of interns to make sure we can devote sufficient time to each individual).

Nikolai Tagarov
Center for the Study of Democracy
Sofia, Bulgaria

CHAPTER 5
Creating Team Leaders

Team leaders—think tanks' middle managers for research—are second in importance only to the think tanks' presidents. Team leaders, who are called many things in different think tanks—center directors, department heads, program managers—direct groups of researchers ranging from two or three analysts to more than 20 people. They usually are the principal investigators for projects where they are actively involved. As soon as an organization has an analytic staff of at least 10 people, teams are usually formed and team leaders are designated—sometimes formally, sometimes informally.[49]

In large departments, other project directors report to team leaders.[50] Thus, there can be two levels of "team leaders" within a department: the overall team leader and project directors. The former have a much wider range of management responsibilities than the latter. In the following, I distinguish between the two levels only where important differences are involved.

Duties of team leaders at Stage 2 and Stage 3 institutions include carrying out projects, keeping staff productively employed, maintaining a positive work environment, ensuring the high quality of reports, being active in the policy process, and acquiring new business. The role of team leader can be described as having five general elements: to set objectives, manage, and coordinate the team so it does its best work; to interact effectively and creatively with clients; to provide resources to the team; to link the team to the rest of the organization; and to be a contributing team member.[51]

Ideally, team leaders at think tanks will possess a formidable array of attributes. They should:

- Have solid research and policy skills in order to direct staff and be a leader in the policy development process

- Be a thought leader

- Have the strong interpersonal and leadership skills essential in getting the most out of the team

---

49   One type of think tank does not follow this model. This is an organization composed of senior scholars who work substantially alone on research projects, sometimes aided by a research assistant. These scholars may be grouped into divisions or centers, but merely as an administrative convenience. This is discussed further in Chapter 3.
50   To be clear, the team leader positions discussed here are permanent management positions. In contrast, many organizations today form teams to address a specific task and disband them when the task is accomplished.
51   Based on Rees (2001, 86).

- Be good project managers—that is, know the volume of resources needed to carry out a project and how to schedule and organize these resources effectively

- Have strong organizational skills to keep the team fully and productively employed, meet deadlines, and maintain product quality

- Be effective in marketing the team's skills to existing clients

- Be innovative in assessing the needs of existing and new clients and identifying new policy issues and activities for the group to pursue.

This list is, naturally, very similar to that for the sought after qualities for senior researchers outlined in Chapter 3. The critical difference is that one hopes to attract a true thought leader, as discussed further below.

Box 5.1 provides a more concrete version of a team leader's duties and responsibilities. (More detail is provided in Annex 5.1.) This excellent statement was framed very recently by a Stage 3 think tank that asked not be identified, to address what it saw as an insufficient description of its center directors' tasks. In Box 5.1 I call this organization the Data Policy Institute (DPI).

Four of the responsibility areas in Box 5.1 stand out, calling out tasks often overlooked or under emphasized when a team leader position is discussed with candidates. First is *institutional leadership*, i.e., responsibility for working with one's fellow team leaders and senior management to realize the think tank's shared vision. Second is *external engagement,* the responsibility to work actively in engaging the full range of stakeholders and working with the communications team to advance the institute's policy positions. Third is *fundraising*. Time and again new team leaders get too tied up in guiding research, mentoring, and policy engagement, at the cost of raising funds. Strong fundraising requires a vision, forward planning, good intelligence, active marketing, and excellent proposal writing. Last is *staff mentoring and recruitment.* It is hard to overemphasize the need for team leaders and other senior researchers to work steadily to expand the skills and qualifications of junior and mid-level staff.

Few team leaders excel in all these areas, which is hardly surprising. What is surprising is that almost no think tanks appear to have even informal programs for training or mentoring team leaders to help ensure they will be effective. In a typical situation, a good researcher who seems reasonably well organized, sufficiently affable, has been effective in the policy arena, and has some taste for marketing is promoted into the team leader position when it comes open. From that point on, the team leader is learning by doing, with some support from the president or research director if the new team leader is observed to be struggling. Most team leaders are eventually able to perform their jobs to a reasonable standard, but a significant share perform marginally—too well to be reassigned but too poorly to satisfy the needs of their staff and the think tank.

Think tanks can improve the effectiveness of these essential managers by explicitly working with would-be or new team leaders on a series of tasks for which they will be responsible. This chapter presents steps senior management can take to develop the highly effective team leaders they need, based on practices in private industry and observations of successful think tank team leaders.

That said, senior management must be ready to reject marginal candidates, internal and external. Focus passed-over internal candidates on research and involve them in the rewarding work and visibility of policy engagement. It is typically worth the wait to find a strong external candidate when all internal ones are only questionably qualified.

I organize my discussion into two sections. The first, *addressed to senior managers*, briefly discusses the qualities senior management should look for in a team leader and how management can help team leaders do their jobs better. This is the one area where differentiation between the roles and corresponding qualifications of team leaders and project directors must be taken into account in filling a particular position. The second part, *addressed to team leaders*, describes a series of tasks team leaders have to carry out, carefully giving pointers on performing these jobs effectively and efficiently.

SENIOR MANAGEMENT'S ROLE

A think tank's leadership is responsible for recruiting team leaders. In some cases this is easy, when an obvious candidate is already on staff, usually in the group s/he will direct. But often it is necessary to recruit from outside the organization. We know from think tank directors' comments at the TTI EX 2012 highlighted in Chapter 3 that identifying and attracting senior researchers is challenging; finding those with a taste and capability for management is doubly so. Despite the difficulties, the candidates should be rigorously judged against a set of explicit criteria. Once the selection is made, senior management can take several actions to increase the odds of the new team leader succeeding.

Selecting a Team Leader

The requirements for succeeding as a team leader are demanding. Useful criteria for assessing candidates are listed in Table 5.1. This set of qualifications is generally accepted and covers all the key attributes noted above. The table also shows the relative weights I assign to the various attributes, which are more subjective than the criteria themselves and will be explained below. The essential point is that senior management should assign weights to this or a similar set of qualifications to facilitate reaching agreement among themselves in assessing candidates. (The form in Annex 3.1 can be modified slightly to array these factors and weights.)

Table 5.1 Weights Assigned to Desirable Attributes of Team Leaders

Weight assigned[a]	Attribute
25	*Substantive knowledge, analytic skills, and policy acumen*—is extremely familiar with topic area, has years of experience; is conversant with main statistical techniques, and has strong understanding of policy issues and policy engagement
20	*Interpersonal skills*—is a natural leader and proven mentor; will be a productive participant in management meetings
16	*Initiative and vision*—seeks out opportunities both for funding and in the policy arena; thinks of ways to strengthen staff; is good at anticipating changes in policy priorities and client needs
16	*Effective with external audiences*—enjoys dealing with policymakers of all persuasions and is effective with them; strong communicator
13	*Fundraising skills*—has demonstrated competence leading proposal teams and no aversion to responsibilities in this area
10	*Growth potential*—is intellectually creative and flexible; appears to have strong management skills
100	Total points

a.   In a scoring exercise the weights can be used as the maximum number of points assigned to each attribute.

I assign the highest weight to *substantive knowledge, analytic skills, and policy acumen* (25 points). This is because, above all, the team leader must be a true expert in the topic for which s/he is leading the team *and* understand the broad policy environment and how to operate effectively within it. Without these qualities, the team is likely to do work that is not cutting edge and the team leader will be forced to do too much learning on the job. Thorough knowledge is essential for providing intellectual leadership to the rest of the team. (Only in rare cases are departments led by team leaders sufficiently large that management tasks alone constitute a sufficient work load to be fundable through management hours charged to individual projects plus modest resources for management from overhead accounts.)

But substantive knowledge is not enough. The candidate must also have proven skills in the relevant policy arena. Anyone who has worked with researchers knows only too well that many have great difficulty making strong connections between their analysis and specific policy questions. A few researchers develop into strong policy analysts. But many are simply not interested.[52] Ideally, a team leader is a "thought leader" in his/her policy field. Such a leader deeply understands the policy status and needed developments in the sector in which s/he works. S/he understands the policy changes needed for significant improvement in the government's policy approach and where program delivery effectiveness can be improved. S/he clearly sees the key next two or three policy development steps essential for improvement. (This is discussed further within factor three, below.)

The second highest weight I assign to *interpersonal skills* (20 points). This may seem strange in a

---

52   See the commentary in TTI (2013).

profession where an individual researcher's qualities, such as technical facility and the ability to make effective presentations, are so highly valued. Nevertheless, the justification is clear: a team leader with poor interpersonal skills can reduce the team's productivity and may even destroy a team by causing good people to leave. I know both Stage 2 and Stage 3 think tanks where this has happened within a team before the president decided there was simply no alternative to reassigning or dismissing a technically competent, policy-effective team leader who made life miserable for subordinates. As Bunkder, Kram, and Ting (2002) point out, a true leader must be approachable, build team spirit, and motivate the team.[53] This requires a degree of emotional maturity that is often lacking in young analysts, although this type of maturity is not highly correlated with age.

How can management gather information on the interpersonal skills of candidates for a team leader position? If the candidate is already on the think tank's staff, there should be ample opportunity to make the assessment. Signs of potential problems include the staffer being a loner (i.e., preferring not to work on team projects or not volunteering to help others); being constantly critical, especially if the criticism is done without a clearly constructive purpose; or trying to avoid responsibility for the quality of products or for making presentations. Naturally, significant interview time should be spent ascertaining the candidate's interest in dealing with day-to-day management tasks.

Outside candidates are harder to judge. There are ways, however, to gather information besides the candidate's interviews with the top people at your think tank. Possibilities include the following:

- Ask staff or other experts in the particular field—who are known by staff at your think tank and have been at conferences and policy working sessions with the candidate—about the candidate's style. Was it cooperative and constructive, competitive, or even destructive?

- Check with people who have worked with the candidate about the candidate's working style and relations with coworkers. It is often difficult to make inquiries of workers where the candidate is currently employed, but experience in earlier positions is also relevant. The best opportunity is if someone within the hiring organization can ask a personal friend at another institution where the candidate has worked.

- Have the candidate interview with two or three people who will be on his/her team. Sometimes candidates will be quite aggressive in these meetings, and other times they send a clear signal of their own superiority. Either is a worrisome sign. Get candid feedback from your staff.

- Invite the candidate to give a seminar on a topic in his/her area of expertise; make sure questions are asked and observe the responses carefully.

Initiative and vision, the third key attribute on the list, is closely related to the thought leadership discussed above (16 points). I would have ranked this second but wanted to emphasize the importance of interpersonal skills to thought leaders actually realizing their promise. Sought here

---

53   On the distinction between leaders and managers, see Kellerman (2004).

is the person who can imagine with some accuracy the "over the horizon" central policy issues emerging in his/her topic area. This is not a matter merely of careful thought or perspicacity; rather such knowledge comes from probing conversations with policy community members across the board—including, usually most importantly, the very senior government officials and MPs (or trusted staff working directly with them). Initiative is critical to exploiting the insights, i.e., to generating the resources with which the team can carry out the first round of policy research—often entailing clearly defining: 1) the issue, including bringing the relevant data to define its magnitude, 2) a range of policy actions that could address the issue, and 3) the set of criteria by which alternative solutions should be judged. Evidently, these are very demanding tasks, but the payoff to being the "first mover" on an important issue is often great.

The fourth attribute on the list is being *effective with external audiences* (also 16 points). Accomplished team leaders must enjoy the interaction with government officials, NGOs, and legislators. They must be very good presenters at conferences and in small groups. If possible, the candidate should be already recognized in his/her policy community as an expert. And even if the candidate is not yet at such a level, his/her views on policy issues should be cogent, well founded, and compelling. Interviews, a seminar at the hiring think tank, and public presentations offer a good idea of what to expect.

Although I give the two final attributes listed in the table somewhat lower weights, they are still important. Take *fundraising skills* (13 points). It is fair to say that many senior staffers truly dislike writing proposals and meeting funders. Some senior professionals recognize that the real conceptual work—defining and fleshing out the main idea and associated hypotheses—is the heart of proposal writing and enjoy this aspect of the task. But if a team leader candidate is not a strong proposal writer, or views writing them with distaste, this attitude is likely to be tacitly communicated to the team, creating a poor environment for such work.

Interacting with funders varies, of course, with the personality and professionalism of the funders as well as what team leaders bring to the relationship. Typically, team leaders have much stronger technical competence than the program officer. Some team leaders are natural mentors and enjoy explaining element of the analysis of interest to the officer and do it well. Others find it a bit boring and their (possibly condescending) attitude can show through. Team leaders with a poor attitude toward program officers obviously make sustaining long-term relations with funders difficult. As with many of the necessary attributes, this one is hard to judge without direct observation (current staff) or a very open and knowledgeable reference for those not on staff. A possible informant could be a donor program officer who works with both your and the candidate's institutions, who might be willing to offer an opinion in light of the probable benefits and costs to both organizations of the candidate relocating. One question to candidates that sometimes yields useful information is about the nature of the relationship they seek to establish with major funders and how they go about doing it.

The first five points on Table 5.1 concentrate, as the discussion above makes clear, on the candidate's demonstrated qualities. The sixth and final attribute—*growth potential* (10 points)—is in the future but is important, especially for younger candidates. What can one look for as signs of growth potential or lack of it, which is subjective and tricky to judge in practice? Table 5.2 reproduces a list standards for judging potential compiled for for-profit firms (Charan, Drotter, and Noel 2001). The left-hand column lists attributes for persons with substantial potential; the right-hand column lists those for a person who is likely to develop further to only a limited degree.

Table 5.2 Standards for Judging Potential

Substantial leadership potential	*Limited leadership potential*
• Exhibits broad and deep range of operating, technical, and professional skills	• On balance, exhibits operating, technical, and professional skills that are acceptable for current level
• Exhibits sound managerial skills	• Demonstrates little effort to build new skills but keeps current skills sharp
• Demonstrates leadership skills consistent with the team leader position	
• Regularly works at developing new skills and abilities	• Aspires to stay with the institute, but does not demonstrate much interest in assuming larger challenges
• Aspires to higher-level challenges and opportunities	• Is motivated to do what is needed in the current job
• Demonstrates high interest and energy in the institute's work	• Understands the current job
• Is oriented to the success of the whole institute, not just this team	• Is focused primarily on technical success

Source: Based on Charan, Drotter, and Noel (2001, exhibit 10.1).

These standards should give managers a good idea of a candidate's potential. Clearly, it will be easier to apply them to internal than to external candidates. For internal candidates, the results of past performance assessments and discussions with their raters are important inputs, as noted. But even candidates outside the organization can be asked about their interest in management, as well as about their skills and experience. Candidates might be asked, for example, how they would handle certain tasks, such as planning the work of the team, thinking about new directions for the team's work, or delegating responsibility for certain jobs.

In comparing alternative candidates for team leader it is useful for two or three leaders at the hiring institution to explicitly and independently rate each candidate, using the same set of factors. The group should then discuss their respective ratings and explore the reasons for any differences. While nothing completely eliminates the risk of making a poor choice, such group reviews of multiple candidates at the same time have proven effective.[54]

Supporting the New Team Leader

Making the transition from being a productive policy analyst to being a team leader entails a sharp

---

54   For a detailed and lively review of what is known on practices leading to effective decisions, see Heath and Heath (2013).

change in thinking.[55] Most people want to continue doing the things they know they are good at and enjoy. But the new team leader must learn to reallocate his/her time—shifting it away from research and toward management tasks. This is often very difficult for first-time managers—who are not only being asked to devote less energy to the very work that has made them successful to date but must also learn to delegate responsibility. Table 5.3 outlines the range of changes in skills, time allocation, and work values inherent in moving from being an individual contributor to being a team leader.

Table 5.3 Work Program Changes Inherent in Moving from Team Member to Team Leader

Team member	*Team leader*
Skills	
• Technical or professional proficiency • Team play • Relationship-building for personal benefits, personal results[a] • Using company tools, processes, and procedures	• Planning—projects, budget, team • Job design • Selection of team members • Delegation • Performance monitoring • Coaching and feedback • Rewards and motivation • Communication and climate setting • Relationship building up and down and with clients for team's benefit • Business acquisition
Time allocation	
• Daily discipline • Major project responsibilities and meeting due dates for projects[a]	• Annual and monthly planning—budgets, projects • Making time available for subordinates—both at team leader's own request and theirs • Setting priorities for team • Making communication time with other parts of organization and clients
Work values	
• Getting results through personal proficiency • Producing high-quality professional work[a] • Accept the institution's values	• Getting results through others • Success of team members • Managerial work and disciplines • Success of unit • Self as manager • Visible integrity

Source: Charan, Drotter, and Noel (2001), table 2.1.
[a] Items to be sharply reduced when person becomes a team leader.

---

55   This section draws generally on Dotlich and Cairo (1999), Charan and colleagues (2001), and Conger and Benjamin (1999).

Given the major changes involved in becoming the new team leader, support from the think tank's leadership is crucial. Timely help with taking up the new duties can save an enormous amount of frustration on all sides. The following section briefly outlines how senior managers can facilitate a transition from senior analyst to the team leader position.

Define the Job Carefully. A typical real-life scenario is for a staff member to be a policy analyst one day and a team leader the next. The think tank's president or research director may meet with the team to make the announcement and outline the team's work program and prospects for the coming months. But the new team leader will have little in the way of a detailed understanding of the new responsibilities—the specific tasks s/he must carry out. Many think tanks do not have a written job description for this position; where such descriptions exist, they tend to be quite general. The new team leader is expected to know what to do from having watched other team leaders in the past. In fact, the new team leader's appreciation of his/her responsibilities is heavily dependent on the management style of the former team leader—in much the same way as new university professors tend to mimic their own professors' style. The more open the former leader has been in discussing the group's overall work, plans, and tasks, the better prepared the new occupant of the position will be for the job.

Thus, the think tank president or second-in-command can help the new team leader enormously by providing a written job description and a supplementary list of concrete tasks that are the team leader's responsibility. The task list should also give an idea of how often each needs to be done. Such tasks might include preparation of quarterly projections of staff coverage under existing and expected grants and contracts, monthly activity reports due to certain clients, quality control for reports produced and presentations to be given, and monthly travel schedules for members of the team.

Beyond this, senior management should be clear about the expectations for the team. Marketing and revenue generation by the team is certainly one topic. A useful context for the revenue target is the monthly billings required to maintain the team at its present size. Another topic could be the president's ideas about the future direction of the team's work—which will directly affect the team leader's marketing and hiring activities.

Being clear about the tasks for which the team leader is responsible has at least two advantages. First, it keeps the new team leader from constantly being surprised by new requirements. Such unexpected additional duties can be particularly disruptive if the team leader carefully allocates his/her time. Second, such clarity gives both president and team leader a common understanding about a core set of activities for which the team leader is to be responsible, establishing one basis for monitoring the team leader's performance.

How to Help. Senior management needs to monitor the team leader's performance carefully but as unobtrusively as possible during the first six to twelve months and provide regular feedback and coaching to help the team leader make the transition.

Monitoring Performance. Management can use an array of documents to monitor the team's activity: time sheets to check the allocation of time charged by the team and team leader, staff coverage projections, project-associated travel records, peer reviews of the team's products, and the team leader's monthly activity report for the team. In addition, discussions with the team leader can be used to determine how the team leader is using team staff (changes in specialization, travel patterns) and whether s/he is marketing the team's and the organization's services effectively. Equally important is feedback from team members on working relations, the atmosphere within the team, the team's productivity, and their reactions to the team leader's style.

Obtaining client feedback is also key. Where the new team leader has taken over projects already under way, clients will be happy to be asked by senior management how the transition is going. Direct client input is extremely valuable in forming an overall idea on performance.

What kinds of problems may be encountered? They fall into two groups: those indicated by the outputs of the team and those more directly associated with the team leader's style. Examples of both are listed in Box 5.2. These two types of problems differ sharply in the ease with which they are identified and can be addressed.

Problems with the team's results are clear red flags—the think tank's very integrity is at stake. Such problems require immediate attention. In principle, management should be able to identify most of the problems easily. The possible exception is quality control: if all the peer reviewers are drawn from within the team and are reluctant critics, and the team leader does not take an active interest in this process, research product quality problems could go unnoticed for some time—until a client complains or an outside analyst criticizes a report.

Output problems, with the exception of marketing, can also be handled in fairly straightforward ways, mainly by improving the organization of the work. Senior management can give pointers on how to do this and perhaps suggest the team leader enlist a team member to help track schedules for accomplishing various tasks.

Unproductive behaviors are more difficult to identify and address. They may be harder for management to discover because they may be confined within the team. Team leaders can also have strained relations with support departments, possibly because of perceived poor performance on the departments' part—such as finance (tardiness in pursuing receivables, excessive time to review financial proposals), contracts (too slow in reviewing draft agreements or inflexible on contract conditions), and HR (insufficient effort in recruiting for an open position).

Once identified, such problems may resist easy correction, because they often have to do with the team leader's basic attitudes and personality attributes, rather than insufficient vigilance or energy in carrying out the basic research management functions. Charan, Drotter, and Noel (2001) suggest several ways for senior management to gain insights into the success of a new team leader's transition from being a "contributor" to being a manager and leader. Three techniques seem particularly look promising:

- *Understand how the team leader is allocating his/her time.* The allocation of time offers a good window on understanding the value the team leader places on different activities. There should be significant time devoted to planning, discussions with individual staff members and the team as a whole, and marketing. Compared with team members, team leaders should spend less time on direct research and report writing.

- *Listen carefully to how managers evaluate subordinates.* Excessive negative comments about staff members or fixation on a single performance dimension are both reasons for concern.

- *Review plans team leaders develop (in written or oral form) from a values standpoint.* Plans often tell where the manager is placing the greatest emphasis. It may be that too much of the team's time is being devoted to research and analysis—the topics of greatest interest to the team leader—and too little to marketing and team member coaching. The quality of the team leader's plan is also important. A muddled plan signals either poor thinking or a low value on planning in general, both are causes for concern.

Extensive, open discussion with the team leader every month or two can provide a good deal of the needed information—on the assumption there is a good working relation between him/her and the senior manager with whom the discussions are held. Discussion is also an opportunity for the team manager to ask questions about how to handle certain problems. The team manager should be strongly encouraged to take personnel issues to the HR director as soon as they arise. Early advice on how to proceed often saves much more management time later on the same issue.

Addressing Significant Problems

Once a significant problem is identified, how can senior management help?

Start with Management Itself. Senior management is the boss. When a problem is detected, senior management should first examine its own actions toward the team leader to be certain these are not contributing to the problem. For example, have senior managers been guilty of:

- Micromanaging the leader, sending the signal that they are doing the handling, scheduling, and planning and giving the leader little space to try innovations in running the team?

- Doing a poor job of communicating expectations for the team or making shifts in the direction of the think tank without due notification?

- Providing inadequate resources to the team and hence undermining the team leader's ability to get projects completed on time?

- Bypassing the team leader to give assignments to individual team members, thereby undermining the leader's authority and reducing the resources available to him/her to carry out the team's research and analysis?

Self-awareness on the part of senior managers will prevent them from unintentionally undercutting and discouraging the team leader and may prevent conflict.

Coaching. Almost inevitably, the new team leader will make mistakes. Proper monitoring permits identifying missteps before they lead to serious problems. There is no substitute for one-on-one coaching from the new team leader's boss. "Coaching is personal help given to develop skills and improve a person's way of working. It is a highly practical activity concerned with today's task, not a future job" (Leigh and Maynard 1995, 141). The literature on coaching outlines a general process for a "coach" (e.g., one of the think tank's top people) to work with a "client" (the team leader) once a problem is evident.

The old saying that leaders are made, not born, sums up the discussion presented here. Most think tank directors have learned this lesson over time. Developing an efficient, reliable team leader usually requires a significant up-front investment in the kind of activities outlined above. Although expensive, such investment typically carries a high rate of return.

Examples of Mentoring for Managers

Little is known about actual think tank practices in this area. The few surveys of think tank management practices have not included questions regarding team leadership, in part because responses would be difficult to pre-code or for respondents to express succinctly. I have found two examples through discussions with think tankers that are highly instructive.

At *The Urban Institute*, a large Washington, D.C. Stage 3 institution where I worked for many years, considerable attention is given to on-boarding new team leaders, who the Institute titles Center Directors (CDs). A new CD meets monthly with the Executive Vice President (no. 2 in the organization) and the Senior Vice-President for Research (no.3) each month during the first year, for a scheduled one-hour session. These meetings can extend into the second year if either side wants to continue.

The focus is on management topics. The new manager has the floor at the beginning of the meeting to ask as many questions as s/he may have. When this is finished, the VPs discuss aspects of four critical parts of the CD position: research quality, staff morale and productivity, finance (both controlling costs and raising funds), and communication of results.[56]

I interviewed these two Institute VPs for the book, and both rated these meetings as highly productive.

Abt Associates is a huge Stage 3 for-profit consulting firm headquartered in Cambridge, Massachusetts that conducts policy research, mostly for U.S. government agencies. The firm is

---

56   CDs now meet alone with only the two VPs above (not the president) to discuss common issues and problems. Discussions have tended to be more open without the president's participation.

interesting in the mentoring connection because of the resources it devotes to training new project directors (PDs). These are staff members who lead projects—a step below team leaders although some of them may have broader management responsibility. Abt has worked on developing a course for new PDs for many years and has fielded several iterations of it. The firm is so large it can afford to develop the course and offer it for each group of new PDs.

The latest version runs for six full days spread over a three-week period. Topics covered include: client relations, managing contracts and subcontracts, managing the project schedule, managing the project budget, leading the project team, and delivering a top quality project. The large amount of staff time and resources the firm devotes to development and offering the course speaks to the value the firm assigns to PDs having this training.

TEAM LEADER TASKS

This section provides pointers to team managers on executing their tasks, which have been divided into four groups: planning and controlling staff utilization, client relations, project execution, and staff productivity.

Planning and Controlling Staff Utilization

For a typical research or technical assistance project executed by think tanks, the great majority of costs are for staff inputs. Staff costs are typically around 70 percent of total costs. It follows that controlling staff inputs is key to keeping projects within budget. Similarly, making certain work is available for team members in the months ahead is the most important element in ensuring the team can continue to work at its current level. This section reviews ways for team leaders to track staff utilization during project execution and to assess future team coverage.

The first step to controlling time charges to a project is for the team leader to prepare a careful plan for executing the project that budgets specific time allocations for each person who is to work on the project. Equally important, the task the person is to do and the amount of charge time available to do it must be clearly communicated to each staff member. Thereafter, control is a matter of monitoring staff time charges, comparing them with progress on the task, and making allocation adjustments as needed.

As simple as this sounds, projects at many think tanks, including Stage 3 institutions, regularly get into trouble because of poor staff time monitoring. The result can be large cost overruns that are damaging, sometimes severely, to the think tank's financial health. A time sheet or time management system is the heart of the cost control process (as presented and discussed in Chapter 11). The key point here is that timely reports to managers, generated from weekly or bi-weekly time sheets submitted by the staff, give project managers accurate information to control staff effort going into a project and to take quick action where needed to control hours charged.

Planning future staff use is just as important as controlling staff utilization on current projects.

Neglecting this kind of planning can result in several kinds of problems:

- *Funding short falls.* Where there are looming shortfalls in staff coverage, the team should be especially active in generating new projects. If the team leader is not aware of the impending fall-off in work, a serious coverage problem is likely to ensue, possibly requiring some staff to be put on part-time work or even let go. Team leaders and senior management knowledge of coverage problems ahead will strongly affect whether they bid on projects that might otherwise not be of strong interest (as discussed in Chapter 10).

- *Overbooking.* At the opposite extreme, the team leader may bid on too many assignments, because managers assume a lower probability of success than justified by experience in order to control the risk of a funding shortfall. While this is a happier situation than coverage problems, it generates its own strains. Because no think tank wins every proposal submitted, most research staff is overcommitted in the future in terms labor requirements embodied in undecided proposals. When the team wins a higher share of proposals than it anticipates, at least one or two key team members will indeed be overcommitted. The most obvious impact is pressure on staff to work exceptionally hard to meet all contract or grant requirements—stressful work conditions that create significant possibilities of a drop in quality. An organization can address this issue by bringing on consultants to help although, as discussed below, this entails substantial management costs in preparing terms of reference and exercising quality and schedule control over the products consultants are to deliver.

Senior managers are understandably most unhappy to learn that a team leader has encountered any of these situations through negligent forward planning. Some think tanks use an explicit projection process to help team leaders do their forward planning. Table 5.4 shows a composite form based on forms used by several think tanks. The form is to be completed by team leaders for each staff member for the next three months, because projections should be done at least every calendar quarter. In a particularly dynamic environment, where new proposals are being regularly submitted and the results of others are being announced, more frequent updating is necessary for the team leader to have a realistic view of the situation.

The top part of the form shows coverage on current projects. The lower portion is for prospective projects, usually those for which proposals are outstanding. Based on past experience with the client or on discussions with the client about this particular proposal, the team leader should be able to assign a probability to various grants or contracts being won and adjust the projected coverage accordingly.[57] Summing the staff person's coverage over the current and expected projects provides the team leader with a realistic assessment of the coverage situation for each staff member for the

---

57   For example, a proposal may include 30 days of a researcher's time. The team leader estimates the probability of success in competing for the work at 0.6. So the expected number of days of coverage could be assessed as 18 (30 x 0.6).

next three months (i.e., until the next update of the form and new coverage estimates).

Table 5.4 shows that a fictional staff member, Richard Jones, has very good coverage for the three months beginning in April 2013. Indeed, for the first two months Mr. Jones is overcommitted (see the bottom two rows). His workload is particularly acute in May, when he will have 11 more days committed than work days, should the team in fact win the contract to provide technical assistance to NGO service deliverers. The team leader should use this information to consider who else on the team could work on one of Mr. Jones's projects, should all commitments come into force. The team leader might also consider trying to get the client's permission to delay some deliverables for one of those projects.

Table 5.4 Example of Forward Planning Staff Chart

Staff person name:	Richard Jones				
Department:	Local government				
For the period from:	April 1, 2013 to July 1, 2013				
Completed by:	Andrei Suchkov				
			Month		
Project Name	*Project Number*	*1*	*2*	*3*	*Total Days*
Ongoing Projects					
Legislation on nonprofits	00127-00	10	8	2	20
Loc Gov housing TA	00136-00	9	9	9	27
Subtotal		19	17	11	47
Projected projects					
TA to NGO service deliver		–	8	8	16
Proposal preparation		3	5	–	8
Asst to MinFinance	OV	2	–	–	2
Subtotal		5	13	8	26
Totals					
Actual/projected work		24	30	19	73
Work days in month		21	19	20	60

Who should complete this form? Experience shows that individual staff members often lack realistic information on proposed projects. Frequently they are not involved in preparing the proposal or in discussions about the likelihood of winning, leaving them in a bad position to complete the lower part of the form. This type of situation usually leads to inflated estimates of coverage. It is, thus, generally more reliable for the team leader to complete the forms for all team members.

Before turning to a new topic, it is worthwhile to address the team leader scheduling of his/her own time. Often one of the most disruptive changes for a new manager is the amount of time s/he now spends in meetings—both scheduled meetings, usually with other managers or staff meetings, and "drop bys" when staff members seek guidance. This drumbeat of meetings makes it very hard to assemble time blocks to work on analysis or writing or just thinking ahead. This can be deeply frustrating. One way to preserve some time blocks is to establish office hours, defined as when the team leader is either available for unscheduled meetings or when his/her door is firmly closed. It is simple to post these times on a publicly accessible Outlook calendar a day or two in advance so team members readily have the information. Graham (2009) outlines other options for creating real "work time."

Client Relations

Clients, and their staffs, are the entities who give grants or contracts to the think tank to carry out policy research projects. (See below for the important difference between this type of client and the so-called "policy client.")

There are two distinct elements to client relations: interactions while the think tank is executing a client-supported project and more general relations that have a marketing objective, directly or indirectly.

The client-relation tasks during *project execution* are the same for all clients. Beyond delivering strong work on time, these are the common sense steps the team leader should be taking:

- Be very responsive to requests for information about the project and related matters.

- Keep the client informed and up-to-date. This goes beyond submitting a mandated quarterly report. If there are important project developments, or the plans call for an event or policy engagement campaign coming up, offer to meet with the project officer at his/her office or for a coffee somewhere. Project officers want to be involved, to have their opinions asked and not just be a mail drop. They will have views, often very useful, about whom to invite to certain types of events, say a public roundtable discussion, and where to hold them.

- The Golden Rule of good client relations is "no surprises." Make certain the project officer knows well in advance of any publicity—even blog postings—about the project so s/he is not caught off guard. There is no person in the world who enjoys being congratulated on a grantee's strong blog posting when s/he has not seen it because s/he did not know it was to be posted today. It is bad enough for simple information or reporting positive results; for bad news it is simply unforgivable. Generally be open with the project officer about impending "issues" in the project (e.g., that a senior researcher is thinking of leaving the project and how you are thinking of addressing this problem if it comes to pass).

A major challenge to team leaders conducting policy research projects is that they really have two audiences: the sponsor and the policy client (not a client in the strict sense but an audience the think tank and funder are both desperately trying to reach).[58] The policy client is, of course, a range of actors—government officials, elected representatives and their staffs, advocacy NGOs, and front line program managers—with the mix varying with the specific policy topic. The interests of sponsor and policy client do not always coincide. One source of divergence can be the desired content of project reports. When the sponsor's representative is relatively new to the country, whether resident or not, s/he will not have had time to learn fully the ins-and-outs of the government's structure, including the distribution of specific tasks among agencies, or how social programs, for example, are structured and operate. This can create tension in the way reports are written: the sponsor's representative appreciates more detailed background information in the text, while policy clients want succinct, to-the-point reports that assume basic program knowledge.

There is no question that balancing these interests is tricky. One way around it is, in effect, to produce two reports—the full report and an extended policy brief for the policy makers (who can refer to the longer document if they want to). Note: it is important to deliver both at the same time to avoid the policy clients thumbing through the main report and deciding it is just too detailed in its program descriptions to merit investing their time.

Similar tensions can arise in organizing events. The PEC plan could call for a small meeting with senior government officials to advance the case for a certain reform. The sponsor's representative may want to expand it with his/her own participation, or even further.

Beyond specific projects, client relations are essentially *marketing focused*. The first point, of course, is that marketing involves more than responding to RFPs issued by a client. Many researchers hate the idea of "client relations" and consequently really do just wait for RFPs to arrive. You can do that, but expect to: 1) receive a smaller volume of RFPs for solicitations where competition is limited than others who work harder on marketing (agency project managers typically select three organizations to compete for the work); and 2) have to write stronger proposals to win than think tanks whose staff are more familiar to those judging the proposals. Awarding grants and contracts is a perilous business for the client, with many projects producing very average results. Naturally, clients tend to favor those who have delivered well for them in the past and with whom they already have a good relationship.

---

58   Government agencies that fund a think tank for a project whose findings and recommendations they will directly use in their operating role are appropriately termed clients in the strict sense.

Andrew Selee makes a very strong point: "Fundraising is, at its core, about building a network of people who share the organization's mission and want to participate, either actively or vicariously, through its work" (2013, 76). It is essential, therefore, to keep a line of contact open with actual and potential clients to establish and maintain a working relationship and hopefully gradually draw them into a commitment to the type of organization you represent. What actions make sense (i.e., indicate an interest in the client or his/her organization without appearing obsequious)?

- Put them on the mailing list for your digital newsletter, and for any blogs your think tank moderates that are on topics of *specific* interest to the client.

- Make it a point to attend events occasionally that the client representative is very likely also to attend, and be sure to greet him/her and have a substantive exchange, assuming you have something relevant to report.

- Be sure to attend events the client is sponsoring. Organizers are sensitive to turnout for their events and remember who attended. You should also be clear that you or others at your think tank would be willing to participate actively in future events.

- Discuss with your team new projects of possible strong interest to the client given the areas in which it has been funding work. If you think it has merit, prepare a one- or two-page overview, share it with the client, and suggest a meeting to discuss it. Most of the time these "good ideas" do not go far. But taking the time to prepare a thoughtful note certainly documents interest and possibly creativity.

My spring 2014 interviews with South Asian think tank executive directors, introduced in chapter 1, provide another interesting idea. When discussing the comments they received from their clients at government agencies, they divided the staff at agencies into two groups: those who were technically proficient and provided useful comments on technical reports and those who were not technically strong and did not. In the latter case, some said they found it useful to offer a briefing on the report where intuitive descriptions of the analysis could be given without "talking down" to officials. The respondents viewed this as an important element in building relations with these officials that, along with other actions, often led to contracts being issued to them on a noncompetitive basis.

Obviously, there are limits to the amount of time a team leader can devote to marketing, particularly event attendance. So make choices carefully and where possible send other team members—but be sure to brief them on what they should do on the marketing side. Even so, some well-placed marketing by the team leader of the kind outlined above is still essential.

Project Execution

The six tasks essential to project execution are listed in Table 5.5. Several of these are discussed below, particularly elements where a new team leader is likely to have limited experience.

Table 5.5 Six Steps of Project Execution

1. Define the policy objectives.
Prepare a clear statement of the policy question(s) being addressed and the corresponding research questions or hypotheses to be addressed. It is often wise to bring in stakeholders at this stage for discussion and confirmation of questions being addressed.

2. Define the analytic approach.
For a research project, this includes further developing the hypotheses to the extent needed, determining the data sources for testing the hypotheses, and defining the analysis to be done. For a technical assistance project, tasks include working with the client to define the reforms needed to accomplish the objective; identifying needed legal changes, if any; choosing the approach to execution-training and/or pilot projects; and assessing results.

3. Schedule the project.
Outline the time line for the project and corresponding milestones. Determine who will be working on the project at what points. Schedule travel, training events, seminars, and all reports.

4. Develop the communications strategy.[a]
Based on the policy questions being addressed, work with the communications team and consult the institution's Executive Director to identify the persons or organizations with the greatest interest in the issue (and who are therefore those most willing to be the "champion for change") and define a communications strategy for reaching them. Compare this to the explicit requirements of the contract or grant, and reconcile differences as needed.

5. Control the quality of the work.
Schedule start-up, mid-term, or end-of-project seminars as needed. Identify the depth of review needed and a peer reviewer; allow time in the schedule for the review. Think about sharing drafts with other stakeholders to 1) get their input on findings and 2) build interest in the work and pave the way for possible future cooperation in communicating results. Give explicit attention to controlling work quality of subcontractors.

6. Communicate the results.
Transmit results both to the client and to the primary policy audience (if these are different and if the contract permits disclosure of results to someone other than the client).

a.   This task appears in the listing to be quite delayed. In fact, it should be addressed during the time the prior three tasks are being executed.

Defining objectives. The cycle begins with defining the policy objective—which may or may not be well-articulated in the terms of reference for the research or technical assistance grant or contract—and the corresponding hypotheses to be tested, if any. This is the point to elaborate the implications of particular possible results. Say, for example, the contract is to evaluate the effectiveness of a conditional cash transfer program. Beyond stating the primary and secondary policy objectives, it is good to consider the implications of a particular finding. If the program is not working well, the first question will be how to improve it. To respond in an even limited way to this question, the project will need to gather at least basic information on program administration at both the field office and head office levels, as part of the survey work.

Scheduling the project. This is the time-sequencing of resource inputs into the project. Scheduling staff input is critical: the team leader must seek both to not waste resources by having researchers underemployed during some periods and to insure against delays that arise because too few staff are available to work on the project at critical points. Such major events as surveys, seminars, and report submission dates must also be scheduled.

Elaborate project management regimes, now computerized and widely available, are used in the construction industry, for example, to schedule subcontractors, labor, and the arrival of materials on the job site. These systems are far more elaborate than needed for nearly all research, evaluation, and technical assistance projects. But preparing simple charts and corresponding milestones is very useful for guiding projects.

Figures 5.1 and 5.2 exemplify simple scheduling charts prepared by the Urban Institute for a training project in Poland. The project called for the contractor to: (1) prepare case studies to be used in the training; (2) organize all aspects of the training, including hiring and briefing qualified local trainers; and (3) deliver the training in multiple sites in two principal phases, with follow-up training to the main training in each phase. The project was on a compressed seven-month time frame, requiring a comparatively large contingent of trainers.

Figure 5.1 Activity Schedule

Activity (work)	Months from Project Inception						
	1st	*2nd*	*3rd*	*4th*	*5th*	*6th*	*7th*
A. Field Investigation and Study Items							
Task 1. Project Start-Up							
Task 2. Needs Assessment/ Final Work Program							
Task 3. Selection of Training Participants							
Task 4. Venue Selection							
Task 5. Training Material Preparation							
Task 6. Team Training							
Task 7. Case Study Preparation							
Task 8. Phase 1 Training							
Task 9. Phase 2 Training							
Task 10. Training Follow-Up							
Task 11. Study Tour							
Task 12. Training Evaluation							
B. Report Completion and Submission							
1. Needs Assessment/Final Work Program (Task 2)		X					
2. Workshop Evaluation Form (Tasks 8 and 9)		X					
3. Phase 1 and Draft Phase 2 Training Materials (Tasks 8 and 9)		X					
4. Phase 2 Training Materials (Final) (Task 9)				X			
5. Case Studies (Task 7)	X	X	X	X			
6. List of Study Tour Participants (Task 11)					X		
7. Evaluation Report (Task 12)							X

■ Full-time activity

▨ Part-time activity

Figure 5.2 Time Schedule for Professional Personnel

Name	Position	Reports due/ activities	Months							Number of Days
			1	2	3	4	5	6	7	
K. Alison	Trainer	Training		█			█			37
M. Borkowska	Trainer; Environmental /Economics	Training	▓	▓	▓	▓	▓		▓	85
T. Driscoll	Trainer; Water	Training		█						35
D. Edwards	Trainer	Training		█						35
A. Eymontt	Trainer; Environmental	Training		▓	▓	▓	▓		▓	85
B. Ferrone	Trainer; Roads/Schools	Training		█						35
G. Frelick	Trainer	Training		█	█					45
A. Grzybek	Trainer; Economics/ Energy	Training		▓	▓	▓	▓		▓	85
A. Law	Trainer; Procurement	Training		█			█			35
M. Lebkowski	Trainer; Finance	Training		▓	▓	▓	▓		▓	85
R. Marcola	Trainer; Finance	Training		▓	▓	▓	▓	▓	▓	85
B. Markiel	Trainer; Environmental	Training		▓	▓	▓	▓	▓	▓	85
R. Milaszewski	Trainer; Water /Economics	Training		▓	▓	▓	▓	▓	▓	85
G. Mikeska	Trainer; Project Manager	Training, Mgmt.	█	█		█	█			79
A. Muzalewski	Trainer; Economics/ Waste	Training		▓	▓	▓	▓		▓	85
A. Pecikiewicz	Trainer; Project Manager	Training, Mgmt.	▓	▓	▓	▓	▓		▓	140
J. Pigey	Trainer	Training		█		█				35
F. Rosensweig	Trainer	Training, Mgmt.	█	█					█	27
B. Ruszkowska	Trainer; Environmental	Training		▓	▓	▓	▓		▓	85
D. Wallgren	Trainer; Solid Waste	Training		█		█				35
T. Wojcicki	Trainer; Finance/Roads	Training		▓	▓	▓	▓		▓	85

█ International trainers

▓ Local Trainers

Full-time: Pecikiewicz and Ruszkowska (all others are part-time)
Reports due: end of project, Activities duration: 7 months

Figure 5.1 shows the timing of execution of each of the 12 tasks (top panel) and the schedule of report completion and submission (lower panel). Figure 5.2 shows the corresponding staff inputs. In this project, the trainers and managers are engaged full time when they are working on the project, so the scheduling is simple relative to the situation where staff is working part-time over an extended period. When staff is scheduled to work on a part-time basis over multiple weeks, team leaders should conduct more detailed planning with each staff member as to when their time is needed.

Charts of this type, which are easy to construct and update, are an invaluable tool for team leaders in organizing their team's work, especially when multiple projects are being executed simultaneously. I have found that even this fairly simple level of complexity and detail has been sufficient to guide quite large ($30+ million) multiyear technical assistance projects successfully.

Developing PEC strategy. Armed with the information developed in the first three steps, this is the time to address policy engagement. As Chapter 1 makes clear, this book is not the place to fully cover the development and execution of a PEC program.[59] But it is relevant in any discussion of a team leader's role to cover the four fundamental points team leaders need to know and adhere to if they are to enjoy success in developing PEC strategies: develop the PEC plan early; remember that PEC development is a team sport; the strategy depends heavily on the specific issue; and you must target, target, target to the audience(s) you wish to influence.

1. *Develop the PEC plan early in the project.* There are multiple advantages to doing this. One is that analysts can prepare products knowing how these are going to be used in the communications campaign. For example, if a policy brief is needed, the executive summary to the main report can be written with this repurposing in mind. Another advantage is that members of the policy community identified as critical to achieving reform can be approached to develop rapport or deepen a relationship during the project period. The team leader can work with advocacy NGOs seen as allies for policy reform. Toward the end of the project, the decisions made in developing the strategy are revisited to confirm that the basis for decisions made then are still valid.[60]

2. *PEC development is a team sport.* Developing the PEC plan requires a team effort: the research team leader, the communications team, and the executive director or someone s/he thinks knows the policy turf better in this particular case. Perspectives and knowledge from all vantage points are essential to identifying critical actors—and how they might best be influenced. Communications teams should implement targeting and communications channels decisions, but team leaders should work closely with them in designing the programs.

---

59   On various aspects of communications programs see D.N. Scott (2011), N. Scott (2012), and Georgalakis (2012). Struyk (2006), Chapter 5, describes a seven-step process for developing a program- or project-level communications plan.

60   In a blog post Andrea Ordonez (2014) encourages this kind of early start, emphasizing the impact it can have on drawing out the research's policy implications. A specific "to do" list is included.

3. *The PEC strategy depends heavily on the specific issue.* Bardach (1984); Stone, Maxwell, and Keating (2001); Greenberg, Linksz, and Mandell (2003, 48–58); Court and Young (2006) and many others have argued that the context in which research is produced fundamentally affects the utility of the results to policymakers—if the issue under study is a "hot" topic, the work may be influential, even if it is not packaged terribly well. Great research, in contrast, even if ably presented, may receive no attention if: 1) the policy question it addresses is not prominently on the agenda of the government or legislature and 2) the think tank does not work quietly behind the scenes with lower level staff and policymakers to make an effective case for change.

Political scientists speak of "windows of opportunity" for policy changes (Hall 1990; Kingdon 1984). The early days of a new government are often cited as such a moment. There are similar windows for the effective use of research findings in the policy process—that is, when an issue is prominently on the nation's agenda and under active consideration (Garrett and Islam 1998). In reality, there are multiple types and degrees of opportunity, as illustrated in Table 5.6 for national-level policy issues. The opportunities in the table are differentiated by how prominent the issue is, whether the issue requires action by the government or legislature or by a lower-level government agency, and timeliness or urgency (i.e., if the issue is under active consideration).

Table 5.6 Types of Policy Issues from a Communications Perspective

Opportunity	Target audience
Prominent policy questions under current discussion	Key members of the government and the legislature and their staffs; influential intermediaries[a]
Policy question likely to be prominent and taken up in the mid-term	Administration and legislative branch staff and intermediaries
Second-tier policy matters (e.g., those addressing improved administration of a program) under active discussion	Key program administrators, interest groups, intermediaries
Second-tier policy matters likely to receive attention in the mid-term	Key program administrators, interest groups, intermediaries
Identification of a new, potentially prominent policy issue	Senior members of government and legislators with responsibility for the area, relevant advocacy NGOs, intermediaries, the public

[a] Intermediaries include relevant advocacy nongovernmental organizations (NGOs), think tanks and consulting firms working in the area, donor organizations, and individual experts and lobbyists.

The most prominent public policy issues are the purview of senior government officials and the legislature. Within the legislature, its leaders constitute the key players. Members of the government and legislative leaders are assisted by their staffs and by such intermediaries as advocacy NGOs, think tanks, and individual experts and knowledgeable lobbyists.[61] When issues of national importance are under active consideration at this level, it is critical to deliver advice just then.

61   Saywell and Cotton (1999) and Lomas (1993) comment on the importance of such intermediaries in the policy development process. Stone (2000) specifically addresses the role of think tanks in this process.

Box 5.3 describes a situation where the Institute for Urban Economics in Moscow enjoyed the unusual position of being asked to contribute analysis very quickly to help address a top priority policy question: changing the way in which retiring Russian officers received their retirement housing from an apartment built by army construction battalions (construction of which entailed a great deal of corruption and was years behind schedule) to a system where the officer received a voucher s/he could use to purchase a dwelling of his choice on the open market.

The research-to-policy bridge was absolutely direct. It was the most inside of insider games. Still, the Institute went on to provide a strong information campaign so as to educate government officials and NGOs to the potential of vouchers as a policy tool.

Nicolas Benequista (2014), summarizing discussions among mentors of a recent communications capacity building project in Anglophone Africa, rightly points out that a quiet, discrete approach is often also the most effective one in cases where the issue being addressed is likely to be controversial to the government. Informing and consulting with the key government players should begin early in the project's formulation and continue throughout the project. As Benequista says, "More often than not, this approach will eventually win over one or two sympathetic allies to the value of doing independent, methodologically sound research on the topic."

Second-level issues are another matter, and will be dealt with by lower-level government officials—although the ultimate disposition of a question may require cabinet approval. Implementation of the results of many program evaluations comes at this level. Regulatory changes are also often in this category.

One example of effective research and communications on a second-tier problem comes from the Center for Democratic Development (CDD) in Ghana in its work on teacher absenteeism. In this case, CDD decided that mobilizing public opinion and speaking directly with government officials and other key stakeholders was the best approach.

CDD's analysis of teacher absenteeism provided compelling evidence of several diverse factors contributing to the absenteeism, including several that invited relatively simple remedies. CDD released its report in July 2008 using a strategy carefully calculated to draw public and media attention. It organized a series of media encounters with participants from Parliament, the Ministry of Education, and Ghana Education Service (which employs and supervises teachers), the Ministry of Finance and Economic Planning, the United Nations Children's Fund, the Ghana Association of Teachers, the Ghana National Association of Graduate Teachers, and other civil society organizations working in education. CDD researchers also participated in live radio discussion programs with directors of basic education as well as officials from Ghana National Education Campaign Coalition. (Radio is a key medium because of low TV ownership rates in rural areas.)

The strategy worked. The media reaction was enthusiastic, and six newspapers published major stories. CDD created a media guide for journalists to engage politicians and policymakers on the issues in the run-up to the December 2008 presidential and parliamentary elections. (Kosack, Tolmie, and Griffin 2010, p.88)

On making use of policy results on second-tier issues, Platt (1987) points out the importance of networks (or researcher advocacy organizations), such as professional associations, in informing administrators and generating a consensus for change. Worth stressing is that the involved policy communities are typically very well defined and often comparatively small groups of persons with direct program administrative responsibilities.[62] In short, partnering multiplies the resources brought to the communication task and creates additional opportunities for direct interaction with decision makers.[63]

Critically, analysts need to take the long view when working on issues of this type. It is possible that one single incident of poor administration will get into the press a year or two after a project is completed and create an opportunity for research findings to play a key documentary role in pushing for reform. In such cases a quick blog posting, including a link to the research report, can often be effective in reminding players of the prior work and stimulating action.

Finally, there is a third class of policy topic—the newly identified issue. Box 5.4 gives an example from India of an expenditure monitoring project that uncovered two un- or underappreciated issues on the targeting of health and education transfers from the national government within the state of Karnataka. In this case, the communications task is to inform the people as well as policymakers to generate pressure for the new issue to be addressed, which was in fact done in the Karnataka case.

Besides the prominence of the issue, a key dimension defining the relevant communication audience is the issue's place on the policy agenda—is it currently under consideration? On the agenda but unlikely to be considered before next year? Not on the agenda? In other words, is this the moment of opportunity? If it is a hot topic, the think tank should design concise products and work hard to communicate results to the most senior policymakers and their advisers. If the political environment is very restrictive, as in Azerbaijan and Uzbekistan, working directly with these officials could be challenging, since the government is so closed to outside input; but it may be the preferred option. A highly visible publication or the think tank's executive director commenting publicly on the issue and the policy recommendations could well ensure the recommendations' rejection.

---

62   Likewise, Huberman (1994) stresses the importance of researchers finding the right vehicle to reach frontline administrators (or in his case, teachers) to act upon research findings.

63   One useful summary statement on this point by true experts is: "Organizations seeking to scale their impact should look to a network of allies, not just to the departments within their organization's four walls, as the engine of change." Crutchfiled and McLeod (2008, 126).

If the policy question is not on the current agenda, it is still important to communicate analytic findings to relevant audiences for at least two reasons. First, strong early analysis of an issue can set the terms of the future debate. Experts in a field, in and out of government, may come to think of the issue as it is depicted in early analyses. An analysis by Andrew Rich (2001) on the influence of U.S. think tanks is insightful. While think tanks with a conservative perspective are much more active day to day in the national policy process than their more liberal counterparts, Rich does not see conservative organizations as necessarily more influential. The reason is that the liberal think tanks do more of the basic analysis and number crunching, while the conservative think tanks offer greater argumentation but less new information. In effect, the liberal think tanks are more successful at framing the way the issue will be considered—an extremely powerful advantage in a policy debate.

The second reason is the extreme importance of transmitting analytic results to the key intermediaries for a particular topic—whether the advocacy NGOs, administration and legislative staff members, donor organizations, think tanks, or experts who will be consulted when the issue gains prominence. Bardach (1984) refers to these organizations and individuals as "information banks" or "storage cabinets."[64] These are the resources key decision makers will consult once the issue matures. It is the job of these intermediaries to be informed, so they will informally catalogue and store quality entries on a topic to have on hand when the issue does move up the agenda.[65]

Many think tanks fail to differentiate sufficiently among policy issues along the lines suggested in Table 5.6; in other words, their communications strategy is too undifferentiated. For example, half of the GDN-15 think tanks reported that they do not devise a PEC strategy for each project; they tend to use the same vehicles to disseminate their findings, regardless of an issue's prominence or timeliness. Yet the lesson implicit in the research literature is that the first step in developing a strategy for a project is to understand the policy prominence and timeliness of the issue in question.

4. *Target, target, target.* This is the final fundamental point team leaders need to adhere to in developing their PEC strategies. The overriding conclusion of the foregoing discussion is the necessity of determining deliberately and carefully those persons and organizations that will be the primary targets of the PEC campaign and then design a program directed to them. In other words, conduct a rigorous stakeholder analysis.[66] As noted, it is possible that, in some countries for some issues, the most effective PEC will be to meet privately with key government officials and provide quiet support to them as they advance the policy position you favor through the system. The report may be placed on the website in due

---

64   Greenberg and colleagues (2003, 47) refer to this information gathering as "inventory creation."

65   This formulation is consistent with the "knowledge utilization school" that views knowledge as cumulative. Accumulated research findings over an extended period change decision makers' views of both the causes of problems and the utility of alternative policy interventions. See, for example, Sundquist (1978).

66   A concise explanation of this analysis and an example are given in Morse and Struyk (2006), Chapter 3.

course, but only if it is unlikely to upset the "insider approach" deemed the best chance for success.

In other cases, a very different approach can be effective in reaching the same audience, for example:

> In its last two years in office (2010-2012), the Saakashvilli administration in Georgia became relatively closed to leaders of civil society NGOs and think tanks. One think tank, the European Initiative-Liberal Academy Tbilisi (EI-LAT), developed a communications package that succeeded in getting messages through to the administration. EI-LAT's executive director realized that senior officials were not only following social media very closely but were sensitive to stories reported there, as well as in the conventional press, which was quite free of government restrictions although it did engage in some self-censorship.
>
> EI-LAT's communications strategy for major projects was to partner with relevant civil society NGOs and hold effective, high profile events that were well covered by the social and other media. The "buzz" created by this approach got policymakers' attention and opened doors.[67]

Quality control. Because of the wide range of products now developed by many projects, a uniform quality control system centered on the peer review process has become both inefficient and costly. Nearly equivalent results can be achieved on average faster and at lower cost with a different approach—one that tailors the type of review to: 1) the product's importance to the think tank's reputation and 2) the extent of review underlying documents have already received. Team leaders should also play a central role in ensuring quality control by being the ones who decide on the level of review required for each product and taking personal responsibility for the adequacy of that review. (See Chapter 6 for a detailed discussion of these and related issues.)

The relevant point here is the important role the team leader plays under such a review system. To discharge these responsibilities effectively requires that s/he knows well in advance when each product will be ready for review, so a decision can be made on the nature of the review necessary and the resources for the review organized in a timely way.

A good practice is for the team leader to assign a research assistant, secretary, or other lower level administration person working with the group the task of reviewing the list of deliverables

---

67   My interviews in Tbilisi in February 2012 as part of an assessment of a grant to EI-LAT from the Open Society Think Tank Fund. Information on media freedom came from published Freedom House ratings and Jones (2013).

required under each new grant and contract, make a schedule of due dates and, based on these, dates by which the product must be ready for review. These dates can be the basis for organizing each document's or presentation's review. The same person should check periodically with project directors on possible changes to the delivery schedule.

Importantly, exercising quality control often creates a rich opportunity for mentoring. When a product review contains significant criticism, for example, the team leader can volunteer to examine the comments in detail and discuss them with the author. Usually, the team leader's greater experience gives him/her a broader basis for interpreting such comments and suggesting how to address them. The report's author is very likely to truly value help given in this way.

Managing consultants and subcontracts. All think tanks turn to consultants or subcontractors to supplement their resident staff. Often a think tank bids on a project for which it has some of the required experts but not all, and adds a consultant with the missing expertise to the project team. Less frequently consultants are added to augment the number of experts working on a project, even though the think tank has capacity in all the necessary fields. When projects involve a survey and think tanks do not have the necessary in-house capacity, survey firms are engaged as subcontractors to conduct them and often also supply the expertise to draw statistically valid samples.

Whether to engage a consultant vs. a subcontractor depends on where the expertise is found, the configuration of expertise sought, and its cost. For basic analysis and report writing in a particular area, consultants are generally preferred, because the task is a limited one for someone with specific expertise, only a single person or two are needed, and the price is lower than for subcontractors, mostly because of lower overhead costs. When whole areas of a project are being contracted out, however, hiring a subcontractor has the advantages of outsourcing task management and acquiring some degree of guarantee that the firm will produce an acceptable product, even if one of the firm's experts fails to perform well for any reason.

Regardless of whether a consultant or subcontractor is sought, the think tank must execute three tasks well to obtain a good product: prepare a strong Terms of Reference (TOR), carefully select the consultant or subcontractor, and exercise rigorous quality control over the draft products it receives.

Writing the TOR. The main point to make here is the necessity of writing a very clear and unambiguous statement. Such a statement has several components:

- Sufficient information about the overall project that the consultant/subcontractor can understand how their responsibilities relate to the rest of the project

- Information on who is working on related tasks, their contact information, and encouragement or the requirement to coordinate with them if there is need to do so

- A statement on the work to be done, beginning with the specific objective of the work, and continuing with the type of analysis to be performed, identification of certain data sets to be used, and possibly encouragement or a requirement to seek out other reliable information, including the conduct of interviews or other original data collection

- Description of the report to be produced: anticipated length, type of evidence to be presented, format to be followed (no point spending staff time reformatting a consultant's report; provide a style sheet)

- The schedule on which the work is to be done, including due dates for any intermediary products or progress reports, the draft report, and the final report

- A statement on the review to which the report will be subject and the duty of the consultant to respond fully to reviewer's comments as a condition for the report's acceptance

- A listing of any other responsibilities, such as attending project staff meetings or participating in an end-of-project conference

- A statement on the amount and timing of payments to be made and any possible penalties for poor performance, including late delivery of the product or inadequate work quality.

Subcontractor selection. In selecting a consultant or subcontractor management should look for the same technical attributes as when hiring a senior analyst (see Chapter 3). But an additional, and all important, factor is the consultant's reputation for finishing work on schedule. Most of the individuals and firms being considered will provide references and these should be checked. Of particular interest are: work quality and timeliness, the ability to work well with other team members, openness to criticism, and willingness to revise a draft product as needed.

Quality control. Strong consultants take genuine professional pride in their work and consistently deliver products that need little further work to be accepted formally by the client. Unfortunately, there are consultants who work to maximize their hourly wage rate by doing as little work as possible to satisfy the client. A favorite tactic of this group is to reuse materials from other projects, even some quite inappropriate to the task ordered. A think tank needs to be vigilant, and even demanding when necessary, to ultimately receive a strong product.

Because of the not uncommon tendency to submit weak work, rigorous quality control is essential. The next chapter on quality control (Chapter 6) relates how the strong reputation of a Georgian think tank for quality control influenced a subcontractor to submit first-class work. The chapter also presents a scoring sheet that can be used as a check list of quality control aspects to assess.

Maximizing Team Productivity

New team leaders face a number of concerns. Promotion to the new position is certainly welcome, but it comes with challenges, especially for someone promoted internally. Often the biggest worry is how to handle the people who were previously the team leader's peers or friends. How they will respond to the new leader as an authority figure is an open question and depends critically on the team leader's conduct.[68] The challenge is to exert authority while being careful to enhance the self-esteem of each member of the team.

Teamwork has two dimensions: task and social. The task element concerns work the team is to do: to gather and analyze data, prepare reports, prepare and deliver seminars, or in the case of technical assistance work with local officials or NGOs to implement pioneering projects. The social dimension concerns how team members feel toward one another and their membership in the team (Rees 2001). The team leader must be equally concerned with both dimensions. If the social dimension is neglected, the team's productivity will be impaired, perhaps severely.

This section first discusses the changing context in which a team leader must function—the evolving relationship among bosses and workers occurring around the world. I then address how team leaders can handle four specific issues that are the keys to their overall performance.

Changing workplace, changing leadership styles. Many organizations have evolved from places where staff members were generally told what to do to places where employees are involved in figuring out and deciding how best to accomplish key tasks. The change is especially noticeable in the knowledge industries, where well-educated workers are demanding an alternative to an authoritarian leadership style. This style was common in the West until 20 or 25 years ago; in Eastern Europe, the Commonwealth of Independent States, and parts of Africa and Asia, however, relatively authoritarian leadership styles are still found.

Table 5.7 highlights the differences between the traditional leadership style and the more facilitating role being adopted by progressive organizations. The contrast is striking between the controlling style—in which strong direction and problem solving by the leader are central; and the more open, consultative, and thoughtful process—in which responsibility is more widely shared.

Table 5.7 Characteristics of Alternative Leadership Styles

Controlling style	Facilitating style
• Tells	• Listens
• Sells	• Asks questions
• Directs	• Directs group process
• Decides	• Coaches
• Solves problems	• Teaches
• Sets goals	• Builds consensus
• Uses authority to get things done	• Shares in goal-setting
	• Shares in decision making
	• Empowers others to get things done

Source: Rees (1999, 55).

---

68   To paraphrase Leigh and Maynard (1995, 156), leadership style is "how the leader relates to people and influences her team."

The reason organizations have pushed managers to change their style is straightforward: more inclusive and consultative styles result in greater staff productivity, longer staff retention, and stronger research and policy results. Workers in such organizations contribute more by making suggestions on how to do things, are happier in their work, and are more willing to accept additional responsibility and work longer and harder (Leigh and Maynard 1995; Rees 1999; Conger and Benjamin 1999).

But basic manager tasks have not changed (they remain the five listed in Box 5.1 earlier in this chapter). And a facilitating manager still does not give up the ultimate responsibility for making decisions. In other words, compared with a traditional leader, a facilitating team leader consults more with team members, allowing them to provide information and interpretations; but the team leader must still reserve the right to make the final decision.

Developing a team that is substantially "self-managing" in this sense can be challenging. In countries and organizations where a facilitating style is novel, team leaders may find it particularly hard to solicit the kind of input and cooperation they are seeking and is needed for this management style to be truly effective. The best advice is: take it a step at a time. Leaders can encourage participation by asking for opinions and ideas and by being good listeners; more responsibility can be assigned downward. Over time, what seems a new style will become routine and staff are likely to respond by participating more fully.

Experience suggests several signs the team leader can look for to confirm that the leadership style outlined above (and discussed further below) is working and that a positive team spirit is emerging (Leigh and Maynard 1995, 105ff). Three have particular application to the research and analysis teams and teams implementing technical assistance projects at think tanks:

- *Supportive relationships.* Staff members help each other in various ways. These include sharing information and other resources, as well as directly assisting in completion of a task, such as volunteering to read a draft report.

- *Personal investment.* Team members "take ownership" of the team's work. They feel directly responsible for the quality of the work and are willing to go beyond the routine work effort to achieve the team's goals.

- *Permissive encouragement.* Team members generally react positively to new ideas advanced by their peers on how to do the work or proposals for new areas of work. It is a "yes" rather than a "no" culture; jealousy over who has the ideas tends to be minimized.

A team exhibiting these characteristics will be effective in its work and rewarding to the team members as a place to work.

Making jobs in the group interesting. A team leader can design the positions he/she controls, particularly those of more senior staff, in ways that make them more or less interesting. "Interesting" means having a relatively wide range of latitude along three dimensions:[69]

- *Span of accountability.* This is the range of trade-offs used in evaluating the person's performance. For example, as pointed out in Chapter 2, for senior staff raising funds, the quality and quantity of research, the degree of success in the policy arena, and performance in managing projects (on time and within budget) are paramount. The greater the flexibility in assessing performance across these dimensions, the more able the staff is to pursue one area this year and another next year, thereby maximizing both their job satisfaction and their value to the organization.

- *Span of influence.* This concerns the role of the staff member in the group and in the overall organization. Obviously, the greater opportunity s/he has to provide input into analytic questions, policy issues, and management decisions, the more self-satisfying the job will be. The team leader can explicitly seek input in preparing performance assessments; peer review of reports and practice presentations is another obvious area for staff participation.

- *Span of support.* This refers to the amount of help an individual can expect from the rest of the organization. A senior analyst needing a research assistant is an obvious example. But there are other potentially important inputs—secretarial services, advice from an expert econometrician, editorial services, and advice from the communications team come readily to mind. A senior analyst having such resources on call, perhaps after a planning session with the team leader, can remove some of the drudgery and uncertainty from a project. Other support questions: When preparing a proposal, does the finance department produce the budget on time and cooperatively? Is the proposal reviewed by top management quickly so time crises are avoided? Does the accounting department handle invoicing professionally to avoid alienating the analyst's client? Clearly, how these tasks are done has a substantial impact on job satisfaction as well as on productivity.

Goal Setting. Experts on team management stress the importance of teams having articulated goals that transcend completion of project-specific tasks (Rees 1999; Leigh and Maynard 1995). Goals provide a unifying theme for the project-based work, help orient day-to-day work of the team, and can be very important in generating the kind of team cohesiveness described above. Cleverly set goals can provide a richer meaning to successfully executing individual projects, as staff sees completion of each project as building something more important. In short, goals make more concrete the general vision that guides a team's work and can even inspire a team's efforts. A vision is the grand picture, what the team aspires to. Goals are steps to achieving such a vision.

Team-level goals flow naturally from a think tank's and the research group's strategic plans. Chapter 8 continues this discussion by describing a strategy development process in which each

---

69   These dimensions are listed in Simons (2005) but the context and examples here are original.

team provides a key building block for the overall strategy. Each specifies the research agenda and accomplishment targets the team can use to mark progress over the plan period.

Guiding team meetings. Gatherings of a team can be opportunities for improving productivity, sharing information, increasing knowledge, and strengthening coordination and teamwork. In short, team meetings constitute an important management tool. In reality, most team leaders meet too infrequently with their teams; and when meetings are held, they are often unproductive. Lack of productivity, indeed, probably explains the infrequency of staff meetings.

Rees (1999, 126–27) describes four prototypical types of meetings:

- *"Tell 'em, sell 'em" style.* The team leader comes prepared to inform team members of decisions already made. There are explanations and discussion to be sure, but the purposes are to inform and to solicit support.

- *Information-dissemination style.* The team leader uses the meeting to inform everyone of what is happening in the department and in the larger organization. There may be reports, prepared in advance or spontaneous, from team members. Issues of all sorts can be raised at such sessions, but they are seldom discussed in much depth or resolved.

- *Participative, "free-for-all" style.* These loosely run events give participants plenty of time to contribute and discuss topics tabled. However, little progress is made on resolving issues or making decisions, because the team leader does not have the skill to guide the discussion to closure or does not want to. Frustration is common among team members seeking clear direction. A prime cause for lack of closure in such cases is the absence of a clear agenda for the meeting. This kind of meeting provides active interaction, but to no particular end.

- *Focused, participative style.* These meetings are focused, since their objectives are clear at the start. The main information reports are delivered by persons notified of their role in advance. Other bulletins can be contributed. The team leader keeps the discussion focused on resolving the issues on the agenda, whether reaching a decision or having a healthy discussion. The meeting may wander on to other topics from time to time, but the team leader is able to bring it back to the agenda and concentrate on reaching the objectives. At the same time, the team leader draws people out and gets their opinions in order to generate support for the conclusions reached. Sufficient time is allowed for thorough discussion without running over the meeting's allotted time.

Clearly, the final model is the one team leaders should strive to deliver. Possibly the single most important factor driving the success of a team meeting is having a thoughtfully developed agenda beforehand. The discipline of preparing an agenda will make the team leader check that the meeting is really needed and to consider who should attend it. (Usually the whole team profits from being present.) The agenda should be written, even if it is fairly skeletal, and it should be shaped as a series of action items to the extent possible. Use of action verbs—*plan, develop, decide, determine, identify, recommend, list, prioritize, solve, generate*—to describe agenda items conveys a constructive sense of purpose.

The team leader can get staff input by routinely asking for discussion topics in advance of the meeting, and before sending out the agenda. If the meetings are worthwhile, staff will come prepared to participate.

The actual conduct of the meeting is important. The first order of business is to make certain everyone present is ready to participate. This should mean banning smart phones or requiring them to be in the off position. Team leaders should decide for themselves whether to allow laptop computers to be used for taking notes during the meeting. In larger meetings this is more problematic, since it is fairly easy for staff to shift away from note-taking to emails and web surfing, thereby effectively tuning out the meeting.

After presenting the agenda at the meeting's start, the team leader should ask for other possible agenda items and, as appropriate, add or defer them. The leader may suggest, for example, that a proposed item is likely to require more time to discuss than will be available at this meeting and that a separate meeting at a later date should be devoted to this topic.

As stressed in a previous section, the team leader must draw out contributions from the staff, both because staff members often have valuable views on the topic being considered and because consulting the staff will make them more motivated to implement the result. The team leader needs to be a good listener, ask follow-up questions, promote discussion among the team, summarize or rephrase arguments, and guide the discussion to closure at the right time.

Disagreements among staff members during discussions are a healthy sign. But contributions need to be politely and constructively presented. Challenging statements are a sign of: 1) engagement in the topic and 2) trusting colleagues sufficiently to know that it does not signal a lack of trust (i.e., that a disagreement is unlikely to provoke retribution in some form).[70]

Reporting and information-sharing are important elements in many meetings. The challenge is to focus the contributions from team members to be maximally useful to the team as a whole. The team leader should make clear that reports on project activity should not merely convey information (e.g., "We have done this kind of analysis and the results are …"). Rather, presenters should be challenged to bring out the general points—to concentrate on the lessons from the analysis that are most likely to be useful to other team members.

---

70   Lencioni (2002) provides a very useful discussion on team management. The description differs from many "management books" in that it is mostly devoted to a story of a new manager dealing with a dysfunctional team, including meeting dialogs. The final quarter of the book presents the recommended approach in summary form.

Consider two options for presenting findings from field work. Take, for example, a team that focuses on providing technical assistance to local governments. Two analysts working with a municipality find that the administration with which they are working has decided to bid out contracts for the delivery of certain social services instead of having municipal agencies be the single (monopolistic) delivery agency. Clearly, this would be a major development about which the whole team should be informed, an innovation the team may want to consider promoting with other cities. Phrased in this way, the topic is of strong interest to the team. But had the work been described as a series of meetings with various officials on the general topic of delivering social services, with the innovation left more or less implicit, it would not have been so engaging, or taken in as well.

At the end of the meeting, it is essential for the team leader to quickly review the ground covered. But it is equally important to follow up this general oral statement with a short written statement of conclusions—a page or two is sufficient. (A junior staff member can be assigned to take notes and either prepare a draft for team leader review or just distribute it as drafted.) This written statement reinforces the message from the meeting, creates a clear record of the decisions made, and informs those not at the meeting of the major results. A series of bullet points, which would take only minutes to prepare, is all that is necessary. Unfortunately, few team leaders or senior managers follow this practice, often leading to confusion about exactly what was decided.

People issues. Leaders can get the best from a team when it is positively motivated by its mission and objectives and is pulling together. Achieving and maintaining this happy state is no accident. Box 5.5 lists steps a team leader can take to demonstrate the value of each person's contribution. Putting the rules on this list into action will go a long way to minimizing personnel problems within the team.

This does not remove the team leader's responsibility to be vigilant in watching for morale problems among team members. Common personnel problems (real or perceived) that can undermine a team's cohesion and productivity include:

- grievances between team members
- feelings of powerlessness
- insufficient information-sharing
- dissatisfaction with the allocation of work
- competitive behavior
- anger at decisions
- failure to receive support
- frustration about some past incident
- resentment at a lack of appreciation or recognition.

In many instances these problems will be amply evident to a team leader. Obviously, the problem must be discussed with the person(s) involved and a solution found. Where appropriate, the kind of coaching described earlier can be used. It is a good idea to consult the director of HR about the issue before engaging the staff member in discussion. The HR director is likely to have encountered the problem numerous times and have good advice on how to approach the discussion.

In some cases, the reason for a drop in team productivity will be more difficult to identify. Long-time team members may simply be bored. Keeping the job interesting is a constant challenge for leaders. One way is to assign staff new tasks, perhaps cross-training people within the team on the various team tasks. While there may be initial staff resistance to this because of basic fear of the unknown, the results are often highly positive, giving individual team members renewed interest in their work and the team leader greater flexibility in staffing projects. Similarly, staff can be given tasks that may at first seem beyond their competence, but with proper mentoring can be executed competently. Again, the staffer's self-confidence and job satisfaction will be enhanced. The team leader should be alert to such possibilities and try them out as opportunity permits.

A common failing at many think tanks is to underestimate the level of responsibility that comparatively junior staff can carry. Senior researchers tend to think of junior staff as the people who do the data analysis or literature reviews, when in fact they can often also do other tasks with the aid of some mentoring, such as certain kinds of field work. Such work can include conducting elite interviews, leading focus groups, and organizing and analyzing the qualitative information obtained from the interviews and focus groups.

Even with these efforts, there will occasionally be staff members who are deeply unhappy in their work. In many cases the problems have little to do with their job per se. Common problems are medical disorders (or side effects from medicines taken to treat the disorder), lack of confidence, stress or emotional problems, or family difficulties. When the team leader understands the problem is deeper than s/he can address, the leader should quickly alert senior management and the personnel officer, if there is one. If the staffer needs to take a leave, the organization will want to help the employee return to his/her former role at the think tank. How long and how much assistance is possible will depend on the conditions at the think tank (e.g., whether there is someone else who can take over the responsibilities of the staffer for some time) and, perhaps, the quality of the medical insurance available to the staffer. The way the team leader is perceived to deal with this problem—the degree to which s/he is humane and compassionate—will have a strong impact on team morale more generally.

TAKE AWAYS

Strong Practices

Many think tanks report finding it difficult to attract strong senior researchers; presumably the challenge is even greater for team leaders. Good practice is to devote all necessary resources to a methodical approach. Characteristics of a well-managed think tank in this context follow.

- A comprehensive job description and list of attributes sought in a new team leader is developed, as well as weights for ranking or weighting the factors for importance, for use in assessing candidates.

- New team leaders are supported by their supervisors being clear about the specific tasks they have to discharge (beyond carrying out quality research), unobtrusively monitoring performance carefully in the early months, and, with the think tanks' research director, meeting with them regularly to answer questions and provide guidance.

- Team leaders devote the necessary time to tracking the utilization of available resources on project execution and make adjustments where needed to stay within budgets. Similarly, they analyze the extent of staff coverage for the next 12 months and adjust marketing activities accordingly.

For Funders
Look carefully for:

- *How the research operation is organized.* To be generally informed, ask some basic questions to the research director or executive director about the size of the groups, how team leaders are identified and how hard they are to find, and what team leader attributes the institution views as the most important.

- *How team leader struggles are dealt with.* Follow-up with questions on what new team leaders tend to struggle with and what management does to educate and support them in the early going. Is there any systematic program of support? To go deeply enough, you may have to interview a couple of team leaders on the same points.

- *Appreciate the "research production function."* Unless program officers have a good sense of the time required for various research, survey, policy engagement and related tasks, they are unable to intelligently judge the level of effort required by projects for which they are responsible. One way to develop a handle on this is to sit with a principal investigator or team leader with the budget for an ongoing project and ask about how tight the funding is for various tasks being executed. Probe on why some tasks seem to be so labor intensive. Also ask where higher level management inputs and supervision are charged. Having this type of conversation with different grantees for several projects should provide a solid start to sound judgment on costs and level of effort.

Perhaps to do:
I am not certain there is much of a role for donors, unless they have worked for many years with a particular think tank and have a very strong and open relation with senior management—and a strong understanding of most aspects of its operations.

Box 5.1 Center Director/Team Leader Duties and Responsibilities at the Data Policy Institute (DPI)

1. **Institutional leadership:** Center directors are members of the Data Policy Institute's senior leadership team, contributing to planning and management that advances a shared vision and strategy for the success of the organization as a whole—today and in the future.

2. **Intellectual and substantive leadership:** Center directors are responsible for sustaining and advancing the quality and relevance of DPI's research. Each director is a thought leader in his/her field.

3. **External engagement:** Center directors ensure the center has successful efforts to engage with the full range of audiences for its research and actively participates in new institutional strategies for raising visibility and impact.

4. **Fundraising:** Center directors are responsible for planning and coordinating their centers' fundraising activities so as to maintain a diverse and healthy portfolio of funding sources.

5. **Staff mentoring and recruitment:** Center directors are responsible for building a well-qualified and effective team of researchers and other professionals, so that together the center has the research, policy, communication, and support skills necessary to sustain its success into the future.

6. **Internal management:** Center directors oversee and are accountable for the day-to-day management of project budgets and schedules, internal controls and reporting, and use of institutional resources.

These summary statements are expanded in Annex 5.1.

Box 5.2 Examples of Problems Team Leaders Can Experience

Problems with the Team's Results

- Projects are not completed on time and/or within budget.
- Quality control problems.
- Poor forward planning so team members are under- or overemployed.
- Marketing results are weak.

Unproductive Behaviors from the Team Leader

- Unfairly capitalizes on his/her personal authority to abuse people.
- Overvalues his/her capabilities, has trouble accepting other's views, comes across as arrogant.
- Distrusts others, micromanages, delegates poorly.
- Operates alone and communicates strategies poorly.
- Is enthusiastic one day and indifferent the next.
- Is eager to please and unwilling to challenge authority to support team members.
- Is unwilling to try new things to keep up with changing trends.
- Obsesses about details, is carried away with rules and procedures, and is inflexible.
- Appears to support decisions and then does what s/he wants anyway. Disregards requests but gives no explanation.

Source: Some examples in the lower panel are from Dotlich and Cairo (1999, 96).

Box 5.3 National Priority Issue with Timely Think Tank Input

Housing for Retired Russian Officers

In early October 1997, the highest officials of the Russian government decided it was imperative to address the shortage of housing for retired military officers. Already about 150,000 recently retired officers were living either doubled up with friends or family or in makeshift arrangements. Another 50,000 officers would be retired shortly as part of the structuring of the country's military forces. Neglect had already spawned a new conservative, military-oriented political party that was gaining national prominence. Legitimate grievances would fuel the party's appeal, which would pose a genuine threat to the country's liberal reforms in the next election.

First Deputy Prime Minister Boris Nemstov called up the Institute for Urban Economics (IUE), a local think tank, to draft a program within 15 days. Mr. Nemstov had worked with IUE previously, testing a consumer subsidy scheme for retired officers, when he was governor of Nizhni Novgoord Oblast. He and IUE agreed that this scheme would be the basis for the new program. IUE delivered the draft program on schedule; under it, officers would receive grants covering 80 percent of the purchase price of a unit in the locality where they would reside when they moved into their purchased home, with the subsidy paid through the national savings bank, acting as the government's agent, directly to the seller of the unit. Ten days later the plan for financing the program with minimum public financing was delivered by the Institute. By the end of October 1997, about a month after IUE was asked to help, President Boris Yeltsin had endorsed the concept. The program was subsequently formally created through a government resolution and implemented.

Source: Struyk (1999), p.1.

**Box 5.4 Example of New Policy Issues Discovered and Documented:
Health and Education Spending in Karnataka**

This is a case where the mere gathering and presentation of budget data revealed gaps between a government's promises and its performance. The Centre for Budget and Policy Studies (CBPS) found this in the India state of Karnataka. While the state government had promised increased spending for health and education as a high priority, in fact such spending was not given preference.

In Karnataka transfers from the state (not national) budget provide all district-level funding for health and education. CBPS set out to determine if these transfers varied according to district needs. CBPS began by reviewing spending on health and education in two districts, Chitradurga and Udupi, both having populations greater than 1 million. Districts have little say over health and education spending. Teachers and medical personnel are posted by the state government. Chitradurga is substantially worse off than Udupi on every socioeconomic indicator; so CBPS's hypothesis was that Chitradurga would receive a higher allocation of funds. Analysis of budget data for 2001 – 2007 was undertaken. Their findings went far beyond the hypothesis.

A serious challenge was to figure out how money was spent in these sectors because of the mind-numbing detail in the budgets. Only with the assistance of accountants could the analysts classify expenditures for primary and secondary schools, for capital and recurrent costs, and for wages and other items.

With the data finally organized the basic hypothesis was tested and rejected. Analysts also found that salaries squeezed out all other inputs, making the delivery of high quality services difficult.

But CBPS analysts also found something totally unexpected: real expenditures had been dropping since 2001 on both health and education. This was a period of fast growth in the state economy, and one during which the state government had publicly committed to improving both sectors. This led CBPS to look at spending in these sectors in all districts in the state. Chitradurga and Udupi were not special cases. But CBPS also documented that during the observation period state revenues overall had grown almost three times faster than nominal education expenditures and almost five times faster than health spending. In other words, funds had been allocated to other sectors. For example, subsidies to power companies had surged.

CBPS undertook a communications campaign at both the district and state levels that exposed the facts of the matter and pushed for corrective budget legislation.

Source: Kosack, Tolmie, Griffin (2010), pp. 21-2; the communications campaign is described on pp. 89-91.

Box 5.5 How Team Leaders Can Show that They Value Each Person in a Team

Provide members a worthwhile role by

- giving people meaningful tasks
- confirming that what they do really matters
- delegating fully

Recognize members' efforts by

- showing appreciation when people try hard
- regularly thanking people for their contributions
- acknowledging people's successes

Listen to members carefully by

- giving full attention through active listening
- using responses that show the leader has listened
- encouraging people to say what they think

Show members respect by

- treating each person as important
- accepting that each person has a point of view
- not impugning a person's motives

Discover how people are feeling by

- seeking a personal response
- asking for their instinctive reactions
- paying attention to emotions

Express concern about their welfare by

- showing that the leader cares if people have problems
- offering help in difficult times
- asking how they are getting on

Ensure employees' work is valued by others by

- telling others what the person has done
- offering public praise and recognition

Source: Based on Leigh and Maynard (1995, 121).

CORE OPERATIONS

CHAPTER 6
Quality Control: A Flexible Approach Is Needed

That the quality of a think tank's work is perceived to be above reproach is critical for maintaining the credibility of its reports and recommendations—and perhaps for its very survival. Because many funders' staffers are not in a position to judge the technical quality of a particular product independently, a strong reputation is fundamental to attracting support. Moreover, credibility is key to effectiveness in the policy arena. Court and Young (2008) analyzed 50 case studies of think tanks' efforts to successfully engage policy makers to adopt recommendations from their research findings. They found that the credibility of the recommendations' source was a key factor influencing adoption—and that credibility was built on institutional reputation and the strength of the research for the policy under consideration; recommendations based on pilot project results were particularly forceful.

Pak Asep, the Director of SMERU Research Institute in Indonesia, in a 2013 interview put it this way (Richards, 2013):

> The most important capital for a think tank is its credibility in front of the government, its donors, its other stakeholders, and the public in general. It is enormously important for a think tank to invest in building up its credibility by consistently maintaining the quality of its outputs.

The foregoing point is widely appreciated. There is a significant range of views, however, about the effectiveness of think tank's quality control (QC) regimes and how they should be administered.

- Murray Weidenbaum headed the White House Council of Economic Advisers during Ronald Reagan's presidency and also worked substantially with five of Washington's better known think tanks, ranging from the Brookings Institution to the American Enterprise Institute. In his 2009 book on think tanks he questions the strength of the research reaching policymakers: "The subject of QC deserves much more attention than it has attained in the [American] think tank world" (p. 109).

- At the TTI Exchange 2012, Eric Eboh from the African Institute for Applied Economics in Nigeria, which is associated with five local universities, outlined an extensive process at his Institute for ensuring high quality and relevant research. Projects issue a concept note early on for comment; this is followed by a concept seminar where the research plan is discussed. When the draft report is available, another seminar is held to which outsiders are invited, including officials with responsibility for the issue under analysis. When the comments from this seminar have been incorporated, the report is subject to a rigorous, anonymous review process. Dr. Eboh recognizes this is a time- and resource-consuming process but is confident the results are strong.

- Enrique Mendizabal in his discussion of QC takes a quite different position: "Quality is not always about being 100% right: Inevitably, speed may force some trade-offs in terms of quality. Many of the problems that think tanks will be working on will not be easy to understand or explain. Still they have to engage and communicate. It is no use to tell the public 'come back later when we are done.'" (Mendizabal, 2012)

These perspectives reflect the traditional conflicting pressures of the need for reviews that will ensure a think tank publishes only high quality research findings vs. the need for a quick review process because the report must be delivered on a date specified in a contract, or the issue is very "hot" and the value of the comments highly perishable, among other reasons.

In fact, the pressure on QC systems has risen in recent years because of fundamental changes in the number and type of products generated by think tanks. Today a major report is repurposed into a range of products: a policy brief, a one- or two-page succinct summary, a two-three minute video of an interview with the author that is placed on the think tank's web site, a blog post, and short messages broadcast through social media. Many of the digital products are also produced independently of a major underlying research project and call for a different level of review from those resulting from repurposing.

My theme in this chapter—noted briefly in Chapter 5—is that, given the explosion in the number of products and need for very rapid review for some of them, the standard peer review process must be adjusted to have multiple forms that match the products to be reviewed. Peer review remains essential; but for many products a quicker process is equally essential. And on occasion, a less rigorous one is appropriate compared to the traditional academic standard review. The type of review will depend on the product's visibility and importance to the institute's reputation, the author's or presenter's experience, and whether the research has already been reviewed in the form of other products.

Regrettably, QC too often has only the negative connotation of catching errors. In reality, the process very often results in substantial improvements in analysis and presentation. Indeed, peer review can be a key element in developing research and presentation skills. Experienced writers know this and consciously use the review process to this end. Authors thanking reviewers for their help, in a book's acknowledgements or a journal article's first footnote, really mean it. This is the spirit in which think tank chief executives should introduce and oversee QC regimes. The objective here is to allocate review resources consistent with the cost a substandard product would impose on the think tank.

Exactly how to do this varies with a think tank's particular circumstances. A university-based think tank could, for example, try to take advantage of faculty seminars given by its senior researchers to augment its own quality control process. (See Box 6.1 for a further discussion of this point.)

ELEMENTS OF A PEER REVIEW PROCESS

A peer review process remains a critical element in the overall QC regime and is much discussed.[71] At the same time a comprehensive QC process must assess the full range of product attributes; in other words—explicitly or implicitly—a multi-dimensional concept of quality is necessary. The contents of one such concept are that the product be:

- *Technically rigorous.* The analysis should be factually correct, logically consistent, methodologically sound, grounded in current and historical literature,

- *Policy relevant.* The analysis is placed in the appropriate context, e.g., issues of national concern are cast carefully within existing institutional arrangements and current programs, policy and societal realities. An important element—for the overall review process, not just the formal reviewer—is to be alert to the political ramifications of a work's policy conclusions. Where they are certain to generate political reactions, those overseeing the review of a product should be charged with notifying the executive director of the probable coming controversy so the think tank can prepare itself in advance for the fallout.

- *Written in a way that will be useful to the primary audience.* If World Bank analysts are the primary audience, then the methods used are fully explained and the policy (including program administration) implications detailed. If, on the other hand, the primary audience is the Minister of Health, the principal document is brief and tightly focused on addressing the policy issues, with a short annex briefly summarizing the methods and possibly the analytic results; there may be a separate technical report.

- *Transparent and replicable*—the methods and data used in the research are duly explained in publications, the degree of detail varying with a document's audience and purpose. A more detailed explanation and access to the data are provided in response to reasonable requests. The sponsor of the work is noted in publications so that any potential conflict of interest is disclosed.[72] (This supplements all of the institute's sponsors being published on its website along with the amount each contributed in the most recent year.)

---

71   For example, a set of blogs on the peer review process at think tanks appeared in 2014 on the blog, On Think Tanks. See Ordonez (2014b, 2014c, 2014d, 2014e, 2014f), Ames (2014), Vera (2014) and Romero (2014).

72   Openness on both funding and data sources is becoming standard internationally. For a status report as of spring 2014 and recent trends in think tanks reporting the sources of their funds, see Transparify (2014); also Mendizabal (2014c). Silverstein (2014) provides examples of Washington think tanks with putative conflicts of interest.

Each of the first three dimensions can vary with the particular task at hand, as suggested in the example in the third bullet, above. Depending on the resources available and the audience, a less rigorous than ideal method may be used. When methods of lower rigor and reliability are used—for example, when one is doing a quick, poorly resourced analysis for a local government—the analyst and think tank need to be clear that another result might be obtained from a more sophisticated and data intensive analysis, if the resources were available (e.g., funding, the required data). The point is to be explicit about what was done and why, and to report it in a manner appropriate to the audience, ranging from the editor of a peer-reviewed journal to a local politician.

I now describe a model of the traditional peer review process, most elements of which are still present for at least some products at Stage 3 and a substantial share of Stage 2 think tanks in many countries. The ideal peer review process is formal in the sense that it is mandatory for a certain set of products and is governed by a written policy statement indicating:

1. Range of products subject to review
1. Usual intensity and nature (seminar, internal or external peer review of the draft, a combination of the two) of the review, probably varying for different author/product combinations
2. Person responsible for designating reviewers and review intensity for different products
3. Key criteria to be used in the reviews—high-quality, appropriate methods of analysis, conclusions based on the analysis, clear and effective presentation, policy relevance and related political ramifications, and ensuring that the product corresponds to what was required under a contract or grant agreement
4. Form in which comments are to be provided (e.g., written, oral, in a particular format) differentiated by product type
5. Process for resolving possible disputes between reviewer(s) and author(s)
6. Simple form to be completed that records the name and type of product reviewed and its author(s); kind of review(s) carried out: who did each; who in addition, if anyone, oversaw the review; and signature(s) of the reviewer(s) confirming each did a review.

Worth noting is that "conclusions based on the analysis" in point 4 implies that in the end the conclusions are those of the author (i.e., they are not the institution's official position on the issue). There is no question of authorial independence at true think tanks, but this may not be the case at political party or political ideology think tanks. Where conclusions are those of an institution, it makes sense to be clear on this point ("It is the Center's position…") as the clarity will benefit both supporters and opponents of the position taken.

In reality, many institutions have peer review programs that differ from the approach just outlined. Some are simply less formal: team leaders are held accountable for having products reviewed and no explicit records are kept. Also, organizations may in effect exempt products by the most senior staff from the process—a perilous tactic. Some think tanks may use in-house review seminars in place of product reviews as the method of exercising QC. Such seminars can be very valuable for guiding the project, but they may not adequately safeguard the quality of the final written product.

A Review Program for a New Era

In-depth discussions on QC procedures with several Stage 2 and Stage 3 think tanks make it clear that, even where rigorous formal procedures are codified in an official policy statement, they are often compromised due to the press of time or simply a rational decision on the resources that should be devoted to a particular product.[73] The relevant manager—team leader, higher level manager, or chief executive—typically makes the decisions on review type depending on the importance of the product to the institution's reputation. Thus, the intensity of the review varies with the potential risk to the institution and the experience of the researcher involved.

"Risk" is defined very broadly—to include not only the reputational risk of promulgating technically weak or poorly composed products but also the risk of failure to achieve related institutional goals. Many think tanks want to strengthen their reputation for producing very high quality research, and see publication of articles written by their staffs in scholarly, peer-reviewed journals as a key indicator of quality, as well as a readily accessible indicator that is used by many in the policy world. The fundamental point here is that a think tank may want to devote additional review resources to the work of maturing research staff, so as to improve the odds of their articles being accepted by prestigious journals.

Research and Related Products

Table 6.1 defines product review guidelines in summary form. Review coverage is wide: written products, presentations, and posts on the organization's blogs are all included and each has a separate section in the table. In keeping with the idea of allocating review resources partially on the extent of risk to an institution's reputation of a poor quality product being disseminated, Table 6.1 distinguishes among three levels of risk, or "institutional importance," for written products and presentations. Much greater review expertise and attention is devoted to those where the stakes are highest—for example, a presentation to the minister responsible for an area where the think tank has a major program. The table presents illustrative guidance and defines levels of review resources for only some of the characteristics of each product (i.e., its expected visibility, key audience for the work, author's experience, and extent of prior product review).

---

73   With support from TTI, the Economic and Social Research Foundation of Tanzania has implemented a highly rigorous two-stage QC system for all its "research outputs," including "research reports, articles, working papers, policy briefs, etc." Open questions are whether such an elaborate system: 1) is sustainable without external support and 2) can it meet the demands for quick turn-around reviews needed for timely inputs to policy debates.

Table 6.1 Product Review Guideline Summary

A. Reports, Policy Briefs, Memos to Senior Officials

Institution Importance level	Review method[a]
Institutional importance. Reputation of the organization could be compromised	A genuine expert on the subject from outside the organization or within (but who has not worked on the project) prepares the review and it is read by senior management, as well as research director, and changes subsequently made are shown to the same managers and, if needed, the outside expert.
High importance. Major visibility for the product, particularly complex or risky analysis involved, or conclusions likely to be politically sensitive	Team leader and research director review the report or recruit (internal or external) expert who has not worked on the project. Senior management informed.
More routine report	Team leader manages the review; reviewer likely on staff but, as always, not a member of project team.

a. Degree of rigor may be reduced if the product under review is based on one that has already been through the review process.

B. Presentations

Institutional Importance level	Review method[b]	
	Experienced researcher and presenter	Less experienced staff
Institutional importance. Reputation of the organization could be compromised	Presenter meets with senior management to review conclusions and policy recommendations. A practice presentation is usually appropriate.	Presenter walks through the presentation, likely using Power Point deck, with a senior research and a senior manager with emphasis on conclusions and policy recommendations. Practice presentation is standard.
High importance. Major visibility for the presentation, particularly complex or risky analysis involved, or conclusions likely to be politically sensitive	Presenter meets with senior colleague to review conclusions and policy recommendations	Presenter walks through the presentation, likely using Power Point deck, with senior analyst, emphasizing conclusions and policy recommendations. The senior analyst may ask for a practice presentation.
More routine presentation	None	Presenter meets with senior colleague to review conclusions and policy recommendations

b. Assumes the underlying research has already been reviewed.

C. Postings on the organization's website prepared by research staff

Type of posting	Experienced researcher	Less experienced staff
Blog post	Editorial review—flags issues of too-strong advocacy or possible factual	Content review by senior analyst working in same area and then

	issues to communications leader or research director	editorial review as for the experienced researcher.
Project information/description	Coordinated with communications group; editorial review	Coordinated with communications group; editorial review

D.   Communication's Group Staff-prepared Content

Content type	Reviewer
Descriptions of projects, project findings and related policy development; press releases	Lead researcher; editor
Other content, e.g., event invitations, descriptions of the think tank ("About Us" content) posted on website, etc.	Originator's superior in the communications group or senior management on exceptional basis

Written products. There are multiple ways to execute reviews—written or oral comments on a draft document, comments (verbal or written) on an oral presentation of the research, and combinations of the two. The process adopted by the African Institute for Applied Economics, summarized in this chapter's introduction, is an example of the combination model. A few think tanks, like AIAE, have two rounds of review, one as the research is being initiated and one when draft products are available. Most think tanks focus on draft document review, but a substantial share uses seminars in addition or as the primary review method, as documented in a later section in this chapter.

Those products that are extremely important to the institution's reputation should have the kind of rigorous arm's length assessment typical for academic publications. For more routine reports, a qualified internal staff member who has not worked on the project should be able to do a strong enough job, although small think tanks may have to recruit an external reviewer if there is not a qualified internal analyst. Annex 6.1 contains two reviewer check lists: one to use in assessing analytic reports and the other to use in assessing policy briefs or other documents aimed explicitly at advancing a policy position. Scoring sheets based on these have been used by several projects that worked with think tanks to improve the quality of their policy analyses.[74]

For major reports, time permitting, a wider review procedure could be followed. The Center for Global Development (CDG), a Washington-based think tank, issues a "consultation draft," particularly in cases where it is breaking new ground in proposing a major policy or delivery system shift. As CDG reports:

---

74   See Struyk and Haddaway (2012). The form in Annex 6.1 of this volume offers a good guide of factors for reviewers to consider; the notes on strong and weak examples of each factor (e.g., hypothesis is clearly stated) that follows the factor list can be particularly helpful.

"We circulate them [drafts] widely and think hard about the responses. The feedback helps to tell us whether our ideas are feasible and (perhaps more importantly) whether we have presented the ideas [in] a way that is broadly understood…." MacDonald and Levine (2008), p.5

Many senior researchers are in the position of being able to ask colleagues at other think tanks who work on the same issues to review draft papers for them. Where this is done, these reviews could be made available to the person deciding on the review required for the author's final draft—to reduce the potential risk associated with a less in-depth internal review.

If seminars are the primary form of review, those attending need to include persons knowledgeable about the policy question under analysis and those who are strong analysts. However strong the exchange of ideas during the discussion of the research, it is also highly desirable for major critical remarks to be obtained in writing for use in revising the draft report. (The author will be busy responding to questions and will not be in a position to take notes; even someone else taking summary notes during the exchanges will be challenged to capture all points.) Someone with the technical competence and knowledge of the policy issue being addressed should review the revised document and provide the author comments on it.

Technical rigor is a standard criterion for assessing analytic products. There is, however, a substantial range in the acceptable sophistication of such analyses. Well-trained analysts will seek to do highly sophisticated analysis that may well be publishable in premier international peer-reviewed journals. Getting a few articles published in such places is essentially a passport to a successful career at a first rate national or international university or organization. Success shines a bright light on the think tank as well.

Such creative work should be encouraged by think tank management. At the same time, the virtuosity is often purchased at the price of reduced attention to policy relevance. The policy recommendations in stellar journals tend to be fairly broad, giving little if any attention to the realities of program administration and realistic budget estimates for the solutions authors offer. This lack of detail is acceptable for the journal article but not in program analyses for ministries. In some instances, strong analysts resent having to engage in policy engagement because it reduces the time for research. A result is often some tension between the virtuoso analyst and think tank management if the products developed depart too much from clients' policy needs.

It is possible for whole organizations to move too far in the direction of analytic rigor at the price of relevance to policy makers. A representative of the DIW German think tank, which is funded primarily by the government program described in Chapter 10, in 2011 at an international conference told a revealing story about its experience.[75] A few years earlier, his institute had undergone the external

---

75   The organization is the Dutsches Institut fuer Wirthschaftsforsung and the event was the "KDI

review held every seven years as a condition for receiving government funding. One conclusion was that the institute's research was not sufficiently rigorous. The criticism was taken very seriously by management and the research program reoriented, with the primary indicator of success being the number of staff-authored publications in highly regarded international journals. Within three to four years, the institute had an excellent record for such publications, by far the best among all the premier German economic institutes. At this point its own management and its policy clients came to understand that their work had become distinctly less policy relevant, a problem that was then addressed.

The main point here is that executive directors face a real challenge in balancing the pursuit of technical analytic rigor, a significant level of which is essential for producing reliable research results, with the equally important goal of true policy relevance.

Repurposed documents. An important issue is how much review effort to devote to shorter reports, such as a policy brief or one-pager generated from a major report. For such repurposed documents, it is very important for the reviewer to be familiar with, and understand, the key findings and the methods behind them. This is because the researchers who have written the underlying documents commonly have trouble condensing major studies into these shorter statements, devoting too much space to one point or overly condensing the policy recommendations. Hence, the reviewer should know the work and make sure that: 1) the shorter piece includes a precise statement on the issue covered and a succinct explanation of the methodology used, and 2) the conclusions, especially the policy implications, are well and concisely articulated. Professional editing of these repurposed documents is also advisable.

Review types for both presentations and blog entries are appropriately sensitive to the experience of the analyst involved, with greater attention going to less seasoned analysts. Some review is essential, however, even for the most senior staff.

Presentations. Review depth again depends on the visibility and potential reputational risk to the institution associated with the particular event. For higher visibility events, an experienced researcher should meet briefly with a senior colleague, or even senior management, to review his/her conclusions and policy recommendations. This review should be particularly sensitive as to whether the conclusions are strictly supported by the underlying research and whether they are derived from this project or exist in the broader literature. Clearly political recommendations are to be avoided to maintain the institution's non-partisan standing. A practice presentation is usually appropriate.

Less experienced staff making presentations certainly should make a practice presentation. At a minimum, the staffer should walk through the presentation with a senior colleague reviewer, usually using the Power Point deck as a guide. The reviewer should: 1) comment on the presentation's flow

Conference on the Changing Role of Think Tanks in the Knowledge-Based Society," held on April 28, 2011 in Seoul, Korea.

and if too little or too much information is being provided and 2) focus, of course, on conclusions and recommendations.

My advice is for the presenter, whenever possible, to give a 'dry run' to in-house staff, particularly inviting junior staff and those on the communications team who will work on disseminating this work. The presenter will certainly benefit from the practice, and for the other staff in the audience, it will be an informative seminar that builds their knowledge. The reviewer can have a quiet private conversation afterwards with the presenter about his/her actual presentation—non-logical order of presentation; speaking too quickly; too many "likes," "ahhs," "yanis" (Egyptian Arabic), or other crutch words or expressions; talking to the screen where the slides are shown instead of to the audience; and other distracting habits.

Website and digital products. Blogs and other postings to the website by research staff are included among the products to be reviewed, because reputational risk is present with them just as with other products (Table 6.1, Panel C). I suspect we have all read blog entries where we are disappointed in the shallowness or poor composition of the post; I certainly have. I have also noted consistently poor posting by certain individuals or think tanks and have stopped reading them. To guard against the hurried and low quality postings that turn readers off and can hurt an institution's reputation, some review is essential. As shown in Table 6.1, for experienced researchers an editor should copyedit the draft and also be on the lookout for statements that seem too political given the organization's usual standards. When a statement does seem to be over the line, the editor should take it to the research director or chief executive for a quick check. For less experienced staff, a more experienced researcher should read over the draft before sending it on to the editor. This whole process should take not more than a day. Management's role is to make certain that editors and senior researchers give priority to the modest amount of work involved for a given blog entry.

Research staff–produced web content about projects should also be subject to review. Annex 6.2* contains the communications policy of R4D, the Stage 3 U.S. think tank cosponsoring this book. While the whole document is of interest because of the general communications system it outlines, Section V on posting content to the website is especially relevant. Each research team within R4D has a person designated as responsible for maintaining the team's website presence. Most (all except highly routine) postings require communications group approval.

Products Published Outside the Think Tank
Thus far, my focus has been on products developed by think tank staff or its consultants and issued by it, as well. Considered in this section are two other types of documents: 1) staff work published as books, journal articles, or papers included in books of readings, and 2) postings to blogs on websites other than the think tank's at which the authoring staff work. Authors' institutional affiliations are nearly always listed as part of such publications, which carries inherent reputational risk.

Because the papers included in the first group are all subject to quite rigorous review by the journal or publisher, these should not need an internal review before they are submitted to the relevant editor. A plausible exception may be for less experienced researchers whose credentials the institution particularly wants to improve; in this case, the extra review and revision effort may make the difference between a positive or negative publication decision.

Blog postings on websites not associated with the author's think tank can be much more challenging from a QC perspective. Again, institutional affiliation is typically indicated; and even when it is not, affiliation is easy to determine on the internet. Depending on the intensity of such blogging in a given country, several such draft posts could be offered for review per week at even a mid-sized think tank. Reading these quickly to meet the demands of the give-and-take of many blogs could be too distracting for those asked to be reviewers to be feasible.

Such blogging is simply forbidden by a number of private businesses, to obviate the risks and avoid reviewing candidate postings. But this seems too extreme for think tanks, many of whose staff wish to participate in the interesting and important debates on policies and analytic questions. And it is reasonable for staff to want to participate: 1) by providing valuable input and 2) to become recognized in a certain policy space. The best policy, in my judgment, is to require every post to include a highlighted statement that the views expressed are the personal views of the respective authors and not necessarily those of his/her employer.[76] It is advisable, in any case, for management to strongly encourage staff to have a colleague read a draft before posting.

QC within the Communications Group.

Appropriately, most attention within think tanks is focused on the quality of policy research products. It is nevertheless important for management to keep in mind that many entries on the website and other products are a major component of the think tank's "face to the world." As such, these communications staff–generated statements deserve to be quality controlled.

Part D of Table 6.1 gives some simple guidance for such statements. Two cases are distinguished. The first is website content, press releases, and similar products that contain information on the substance of the policy research. In this case, the lead researcher should review the draft for content accuracy and, thereafter, an editor should review it for presentation. For other writings, the writer's superior in the communications group usually can serve as the reviewer. There may be items, such as statements on the institution's mission or history, where senior management should also be reviewers, as they may be among the few who have full knowledge of the material. For Stage 1 organizations where the communications team has only one staff member, reviewing will likely fall to the executive director or someone on staff that the executive director believes capable of doing such reviews.

---

76   The following website contains numerous policy statements on the use of social media by employees for a wide range of organizations, including nonprofit organizations: http://socialmediagovernance.com/policies.php.

QC Administration for Staff Research Products

Once a review policy is in place, the next critical task is to assign responsibility for deciding what level of review is needed and who should do it, and ensuring it is conducted sufficiently ahead of releasing the document or making the presentation. For a product of significant institutional importance, the responsible person should consult the chief executive about the review, unless the executive director is already taking a proactive interest.

In a small organization (e.g., only three to four staff researchers who are likely augmented with temporary consultants), the chief executive should be responsible for determining the nature of the review for each product, with the only possible exception being if one of the analysts is the formal group leader. As soon as the organization is large enough to have research *teams*, the responsibility should transfer to the team leader.

All analysts and communications staff must fully understand the review process requirements and why it is critical that reviews are done well and on time. As noted in Chapter 3, this should be covered in the on-boarding orientation sessions. The head of communications and the team leaders should make certain they involve newcomers in the review process as soon as it is practical—perhaps as a second reviewer—so new staff can become prepared to participate fully when asked.

Think tanks codify their review practices in several ways. One is a statement that addresses QC only. Another is to include QC procedures as part of a more general statement. Annex 6.3* presents a broad document, the "Research and Publications Policy, Regulations and Guidelines" of the Economic Policy Research Center in Uganda.

A nagging, persistent, and critical problem is ensuring the QC system functions as intended. I have first-hand experience—at both major Stage 2 think tanks in transition countries and Stage 3 think tanks in the U.S.—where the QC system had atrophied over time because senior management had delegated the responsibility to team leaders and invested little in monitoring performance.

The trick to monitoring performance is to identify a common point through which essentially all products must pass prior to release, and to check review status there. For written products, there are two such points at most institutions: the "front office" and the organization's website.

Most think tanks require that all deliverables be officially transmitted by the front office, which is a highly desirable practice in any case for record keeping purposes. In smaller organizations, this means the chief executive's office, in which case someone there must check the deliverable against the contract and record that the report is being submitted. In larger think tanks, a document typically goes to the contracts office for checking and transmission.

Nearly every substantive product is or should be posted on an organization's website. Even in this day of ubiquitous social media messaging, the website remains a think tank's communications flagship.[77] Moreover, website designers catering to think tanks have learned the importance of grouping all the information and products associated with a particular project or program in one place on the site, to facilitate site visitors finding what they are looking for on a topic quickly and easily (i.e., not having to search different pages for different but related products). The best website format is for a substantive summary, which includes the key policy findings, to introduce the product and list the names of the staff who executed the project. "Products" include reports, policy briefs, one- or two-pagers, Power Points from presentations, and links to related videos and to commentary on the think tank's blog.[78]

The key point for here is to ensure the document submitted for transmittal to the client or posting has been reviewed. <u>Note</u>: the responsible official vouches for the review by submitting it.

The Urban Institute (UI), a major Washington, DC think tank, has devised a submission form that captures this assurance and more. UI had nine research centers in 2013 and in general evolves responsibility to its Center Directors, including managing the QC process for that Center's work. The form routes the product first through several stops essential for meeting contract requirements and then on to the communications group, if it can be made public under the relevant contract's terms. The UI form (reproduced as Figure 6.1) merits careful consideration as it embodies ideas potentially worth emulation. It is used for reports and related written products—but not blog entries and videos, which are handled in separate, streamlined processes—and is an on-line form, with response spaces that can be expanded as needed.

---

77   On this point see Georgalakis, (2012) and Scott (2011) p.111.
78   The 2012 redesign of the Institute for Development Studies' website goes most of the way to having this arrangement. www.ids.ac.uk. For a description of the considerations that drove design decisions, see Georgalakis, *op. cit.*

Figure 6.1 Routing Form for Written Products

URBAN INSTITUTE

RESEARCH REVIEW AND RELEASE (R&R) FORM

CONTACT PERSON ROUTING THIS FORM:

ext:

TITLE:		**Comm Use Only**
Author(s):		Pub ID
		By:
Policy Ctr:	Date of document:	No. of Pages:	Date:

FUNDING Prepared with funding under a grant or contract? ☐YES ☐NO

| If yes, Funder: | | Project No.: | | Contract No.: | |

CONFIDENTIAL DATA Does this use confidential data? ☐YES ☐NO

| If yes, Source: | | Release Approval (signature): | |

DOCUMENT STATUS ☐FINAL, Releasable   ☐FINAL, Not Releasable   ☐ DRAFT, Releasable

non-releasable drafts, status or financial reports do not need an R&R - take directly to Contracts

Transmit to Funder? ☐YES ☐NO   If yes, attach transmittal letter for Contracts Office

WEB PUBLISHING Publish to: ☐Urban.org ☐Other UI Site: _____ ☐ NOT FOR WEB

If publishing to the web, indicate these requirements have been completed:

☐ **Light web-ready edit by Publications office** Arrange at least 24 hours in advance with Scott Forrey in Communications _(not required if document was produced by the Publications office or was previously already published elsewhere.)_

☐ **FINAL report PDF and a 100-word or less abstract e-mailed** to RandR@urban.org . Use report title as your subject.

☐ **One copy of the abstract, cover page, and transmittal letter** (if needed) attached to this form

☐ If report was published elsewhere, **copy of e-mail giving UI permission** to post attached

☐ **Topics/tags for the publication selected** on page 2 of this form

SPECIAL INSTRUCTIONS

Author's Signature _____ _Date_ _____

RELEASE VERIFICATION

Center Director	_Center Director verifies that this document has been reviewed for substance and presentation and meets the Institute's quality and review standards._
	Signature Date
Contracts Office _received:_	_Restrictions on UI release:_ ☐none ☐as follows:
Communications	Signature Date

The top two-thirds of the form is completed by the author(s):

- Block 1 gives the basic information on the document and Center submitting it.

- Block 2 captures information needed by the contracts office to identify the project for which the product was produced.

- Block 3 checks on whether confidential (usually survey) data were used in the project; if so, the Institute person who confirms the data have been appropriately used and reported has to sign-off on the form before it can move further in the review process.

- Block 4 (Document Status), importantly, indicates the extent to which the report can be made public (i.e., is it "releasable" and if so, to what extent?). If the report is going to the funder, the Center attaches a draft transmittal letter to be sent by the contracts office.

- Block 5 addresses putting the document up on UI's website. It contains a check list of supporting materials that are required for posting, e.g., a 100-word or shorter abstract. This is also the place where the topics/tags are defined for the document by the Center, selecting up to six of the available topics listed on the second page. These entries govern content placement on the website and are key for the document being found by internet search engines.

- The author's signature under this set of blocks certifies that the information s/he has provided is accurate.

The remainder of the form has three additional verifications:

- The Center Director's signature explicitly signals that the document has been reviewed for substance and presentation.

- At the contracts office, where the completed form goes next, the contract conditions on release are checked. Where restrictions exist, the contracts officer notes them on the form. The form and the various attachments then go to the communications team.

- The communications team logs in receipt of the form and attachments. Because the team has usually been working with the author already on a communications plan for the project, it continues preparations for dissemination, perhaps with adjustments required by various contractual restrictions. The communications team is also responsible for archiving all products.

Any draft documents being sent to a client for comment also require completion of the form. Even though they are, by definition, not to be released or posted on the website (see the statement in italics in the Document Status box), drafts are still transmitted to the client by the contracts office.

The principal virtues of the form are that it clearly assigns responsibilities for QC and meeting contractual obligations, including product transmission to the client, and archiving. It also routes a report to each responsible party. If the process engendered in using the form appears too burdensome, there are many other ways to handle these tasks. Where time is short, for example, the form can be substantially completed in advance of the report's completion; filling in the public release portion of the form can be deferred. The central point is that all of these actions are needed to avoid QC breakdowns, violating contract terms, and losing track of completed reports that may well be sought at a later date.

My objective in reviewing this form in some detail here is not to urge its adoption. Most think tanks have their individual management practices that need to be accommodated in designing such a document flow system. My point is to stress the variety of tasks that need to be done for a successful QC system and give some ideas on how all those essential tasks might be handled.

THINK TANK PRACTICES

Information on QC practices is available from the GDN-15 surveys, in particular the March 2010 monitoring survey,[79] and to a lesser extent from the TTI-48 survey.[80] We do not know if the responses in either survey are based on the institution's policy, its actual practices, or some combination of the two.

Respondents in the GDN survey were asked a series of questions about how the review system at their institutions operates. These questions and the responses to them are summarized in Table 6.2. One think tank said it had no QC system at all and is, therefore, excluded from the tabulations (i.e., the sample size for most panels in the table is 14); there are a couple of panels where one or another think tank did not respond (reducing the sample size accordingly). Surprisingly, only five (38 percent) of the 13 responding think tanks said they have a written review policy (six of the eight without a written policy are Stage 1 organizations). This is a question for which we also have data from the TTI-48 sample. For all 59 observations combined from the two surveys, half said they do have a written quality control policy statement. The low incidence of a written statement suggests that the "system" is informal and may not be very vigorously or consistently enforced.

---

79   Similar questions were asked in a mail-out baseline survey and cross checked with in-person interviews. Given certain inconsistencies in the baseline information, the monitoring data are viewed as more reliable.

80   The following description draws heavily on the report where the GDN-15 results are presented (Struyk, Haddaway, and Damon 2010). One of the TTI surveys included a series of questions on QC. The section inquiring about the frequency of review for specific projects had two possible responses: "always required" and "sometimes required." I decided to show mostly the GDN survey data results for two reasons: 1) the survey had a third response, "never required" (the differentiation between the "sometime" and "never" responses is quite valuable) and 2) the GDN survey has much more information about the review process per se.

Table 6.2 Quality Control Procedures among GDN-15 Think Tanks in 2010[a]

1.Written review process policy (N=13)	% of Think Tanks
Yes	38
No	62
2.Position responsible for making certain reports/presentations are reviewed Multiple responses possible	
Lead researcher for the project	79
Team or department leader supervising the project	64
Central management (they monitor projects and make sure they get into the review process)	21
Other	21
3.Report reviews Multiple responses possible	
Draft report is reviewed by someone outside of the project team	86
Draft report is first reviewed by the author's manager and then sent out	29
Analyst gives a seminar early in the project to get feedback and then the draft report is reviewed when it is ready	43
When analyst has a draft report s/he gives a seminar to get feedback and makes revisions	29
When analyst has a draft report s/he gives a seminar to get feedback and makes revisions, after which it is reviewed by someone external to the project	43
Other	21
4.When experts outside the organization are asked to review a report, do they get paid?	
Yes	79
No	21
5.Is the reviewer required to provide written comments (either a separate statement or comments written on the paper)?	
Yes	100
No	0
6.If the author and the reviewer disagree on an issue concerning the report, which of the following best describes the process for resolving the difference? (N=12)	
Author makes the final decisions	17
Reviewer and author work it out	25
We ask another expert to participate in the discussion with author and reviewer and make a decision if necessary	50
Other	8
7.Does your organization have a form that indicates that a report was reviewed and who did the review?	
Yes, and the reviewer signs it, indicating that he/she completed the reviews	21
Yes	0
No	79
8.Is the reviewer named in the first pages of the report?	
Yes	43

a. Except where indicated the sample size for all entries is 14; one think tank reported that it had no QC system. For those entries with less than 14 responses the actual sample size is reported. Missing values are due to lack of responses by think tanks.

A variety of options were reported by the GDN-15 think tanks for reviewing reports (item 3 in the table). The most common was someone outside the project team serving as the reviewer (86 percent). But 43 percent reported that, at least on some occasions, the author gave a presentation on the report and may have made changes afterwards before the report was handed over for peer review. This suggests an essentially double review process that is quite rigorous. Reviewers were universally required to provide written comments, and procedures were in place in all but one organization for resolving conflicts between an author and his/her reviewer.

Administration of the review system was not as strong. A substantial majority (79 percent) reported that there was no form for recording that a review was done, who did it, or any reviewer signature to establish responsibility. (Only about half the organizations even have the practice of naming reviewers somewhere in a report.) It is important to stress here that formal review forms can be crucial to protecting the institution's' reputation if a serious issue about the work arises—particularly if the issue only emerges when those involved are no longer with the institution. The forms, if stored with the reviewer's comments, can also be valuable input for staff appraisals. About 29 percent of think tanks (item 9) said managers check the reviews as part of a formal annual staff appraisal process (about 65 percent said they have an annual appraisal process in place).

Outside reviewers generally (79 percent of the time) were compensated. The situation for in-house reviews was somewhat different. Importantly, the great majority of think tanks did not have staff fill in timesheets; those working at such institutions were presumably getting paid for reviewing draft reports, on the assumption the reviews were done during working hours. Of the two think tanks that did use time sheet systems, one has a charge code to which review hours can be charged.

An organization is likely to have morale problems, or even senior staff turnover, when a few senior staffers do most of the reviews without any explicit compensation for doing so. They have real opportunity cost and their own projects will generally have priority in their own minds. At a minimum, the time devoted to reviews should be part of their work plans and not just an "add on" duty.

Using the GDN-15 data, analysts constructed a "minimum good practices" index for reviews that focused on three items: how the review was conducted,[81] whether written comments were required, and whether there was a form that records the review was done and is signed by the reviewer. A good program has all three practices in place, but only 13 percent of the GDN think tanks met minimum good practices by this measure. As suggested above, the major problem is the lack of a form the reviewer signs to record the review was done, thereby clarifying the reviewer's partial responsibility for a poor quality report being distributed. This fairly simple administrative matter could easily be implemented.

---

81   All options listed in Table 6.2, item 3 were considered good practice except the analyst giving a seminar and then making revisions, with no further review, and "other."

How frequently are various written products subject to review? Substantial information on this point appears in Table 6.3. Three products have a high incidence of always being reviewed: reports to clients (79 percent of think tanks always review them), books being proposed for publication (92 percent), and documents prepared specially for government officials or MPs (79 percent). More surprising is that while books proposed for publication have a very high review incidence, only about half of these think tanks review proposed journal articles. Presumably senior managers perceive reputational protection from the assurance that a prestigious journal's own review process will prevent poor quality articles from seeing the light of day. But this is not the best outcome for the researchers involved, particularly the younger ones. If a think tank is trying to develop young PhDs into prominent policy analysts, it is in the best interests of the institutions, as well as the researchers, to support these individuals' research careers by ensuring that their journal articles are also carefully reviewed before submission by senior colleagues with significant publications records. Several think tanks admitted that certain product categories are never subject to review at their institution—mostly papers for conferences, press conference materials, and articles for the popular press. Even so, the high review incidence for key products remains impressive.

Table 6.3 Frequency with which Written Products Are Reviewed at GDN-15 Think Tanks, by Product Type[a]

(percentages)

Products Subject to Review (2010)	All		
	Always Required	Sometimes Required	Never Required
Reports to clients	79	14	7
Papers for conference presentation	36	43	21
Papers being submitted to scientific journals	56	22	22
Books being proposed for publication	92	8	0
Articles for the popular press	46	38	15
Documents to be distributed at press conferences	64	21	14
Documents to be distributed at other types of conferences	50	36	14
Policy papers and memos prepared especially for government officials or MPs	79	14	7

a. One organization with <10 FT researchers had no review policy; it is not included in this table. Think tanks also had the option of responding "We do not produce this:" such responses are not included in this table.

The survey also asked about how reviews of presentations were done; respondents could choose multiple answers. Nearly two-thirds of think tanks reported that a supervisor looks through the

Power Point to be used in a presentation; for context, 85 percent reported Power Points being used "nearly all the time" or "most of the time" (Table 6.2, items 10-11). Forty percent said that staff listened to "some" practice presentations. While 29 percent of think tanks reported that practice presentations were made for very important presentations, the most frequent response (64 percent) said that it was up to the presenter as to whether there was a "dry run" (item 12). Two organizations reported that no presentation reviews are done at their institutions, and three said that review methods besides checking Power Point decks or listening to practice presentations were used. Again, these findings confirm substantial review effort among the think tanks represented.

Lastly, in response to a general question (Table 6.2, item 13) about the effectiveness of their QC systems, 36 percent of the 14 respondents said "very well." But all the others said "somewhat well," which seems inconsistent with the details reviewed above. It is possible that while respondents accurately cite review actions taken, they recognize significant issues with the quality of the reviews and the final products issued by their organizations.

Overall, although these data suggest considerable room for improvement in QC regimes, they also highlight real strength in the incidence of review of the most important documents. In countries where think tanks have not distinguished themselves by the technical strength of their research, there is a ready opportunity for those organizations to enhance their reputations in this area through consistent rigorous QC programs.

QUALITY CONTROL SYSTEM CASE STUDIES

I have two case studies for quality control—one for the review of written projects, including blogs, and one for presentation review. Case Study 6.1 for written products was contributed by the Center for the Implementation of Public Policies Promoting Equity and Growth (CIPPEC), in Argentina. This peer review system is carefully structured and tightly administered. A critical strength is that, when needed, a review can be completed in a couple of days (not, of course, counting the time that may be needed for the author(s) to revise the document report in light of the comments received).

Case Study 6.2 on controlling the quality of presentations is from the Bandung Institute for Governance Studies (BIGS), in Indonesia. This case begins with a clear statement of the often-observed weaknesses in presentations, which motivated BIGS to implement the strong review system described here. Because BIGS's presentations often deal with politically sensitive budgetary issues, the system tailors the depth of the review in accordance with the expected audience's composition, particularly whether government officials will be in attendance.

WHAT TO DO WHEN QUALITY CONTROL FAILS

It Does Happen— A Tale of Two Crises
Spring of 2013 witnessed one of the highest-profile exposures of a significant methodological mis-

take in an economic analysis in living memory. Carmen Reinhart and Kenneth Rogoff (CR&KR) published a 2010 paper indicating that national GDP growth slows sharply once government debt levels exceed 90 percent of GDP. This finding was used by some European Union member countries to press for severe austerity programs to reduce the ratio for countries with ratios over 90 percent. This "90 percent rule-of-thumb" was quickly embedded into a new "Euro zone consensus," and several southern European Euro zone countries were forced to implement such programs to obtain loans to stabilize their economies—programs that helped produce highly unpopular mass unemployment and depression-like drops in GDP. But alas, two years later errors were found in the analysis, thereby undermining the whole intellectual base for the austerity program.[82] A media frenzy followed.

CR&KR, though the most conspicuous, are far from alone in making mistakes that get into print. In the U.S., for example, the first few months of 2013 were marked by a fierce debate over immigration reform legislation generally, and specifically about whether "amnesty" should eventually be granted to some aliens who had illegally entered the country years earlier. The debate turned, in part, on the costs involved in adding these people to government-funded assistance programs for which they would qualify—ranging from public education to means-tested welfare benefits—because program eligibility would often come ahead of formal citizenship. On May 6, 2013 a Washington think tank, The Heritage Foundation, which strongly opposed the legislation, published a report by Robert Rector and Jason Richwine (RR&JR) that gave a very high estimate of these incremental costs. At $6.3 trillion for the costs over the lifetime of former unlawful immigrants taken together, their estimate was an order of magnitude higher than any of the many other estimates that had been made.

The general reaction among the expert community was swift and highly negative, viewing the estimates as unrealistically high and politically motivated. An analyst at the Cato Institute, a libertarian Washington think tank, said, "They employed a statistical method that no other economist would use to measure things like this, and on such an important policy issue. And they predictably reached terrible results." Other analysts voiced similar criticisms.[83]

For my purposes here, it is highly instructive to assess how each pair of authors responded to the criticisms leveled against them.

CR&KR went through the analysis that refuted their findings and quickly admitted publicly that they had made a mistake in handling the data; they had omitted some observations that affected the results. But they also defended themselves vigorously by pointing out that the policy implications of the difference between their results and those of the other team of economists were not as extreme as some had suggested (although they were certainly significant for policy purposes).

---

82   Based on "A Seminal Analysis of the Relationship between Debt and Growth Comes Under Attack," *The Economist*, print edition, April 20th 2013. See Wolf (2014, 268-9) for a succinct summary of the importance of this difference in the context of the Eurozone financial crisis.
83   For a discussion of the Heritage study in comparison with several others on these topics, see Enchautegui, Lindner, and Poethig (2013).

The fundamental point is that CR&KR acted responsibly if defensively, and their response was as successful as possible in containing the damage—by working to clarify the best interpretation of their work and the work of their critics taken together.

In sharp contrast, the initial response of RR&JR was total silence. The junior author, Jason Richwine, left the Foundation a few days after the report's release, with no word of explanation as to why, thereby suggesting, perhaps unfairly, that any errors rested with him.[84] The report was still posted on the Foundation's website a month later, still without any note that it was under review. The Foundation essentially opted not to defend its estimate directly but to let it stand as (flawed) ammunition to immigration reform opponents. Finally on June 10, the Foundation posted an Issue Brief on its website that still failed to address its own estimate but attacked a lower cost estimate that was about to be released by the respected Congressional Budget Office (CBO, 2013).

When compared with the generally accepted principles for handling such situations, the Heritage episode is the counter example—what not to do. One can argue that remaining silent is the best course if the analysis really is flawed because the storm will blow over more quickly. Indeed, this is a widely used PR tactic.[85] The problem is that it leaves the think tank's reputation in tatters with all but its core champions.

Good Practice in Crisis Management

Responding to public criticisms of everything from policy research to product defects has developed into a trade termed "crisis management." Box 6.2 outlines four stages that management of a crisis flows through, whether a think tank formally acknowledges them or not;[86] this summary is a guide to widely accepted crisis management practices.

The obvious first step is to understand fully the nature of the criticisms raised—and to appoint a single spokesperson at the institution to take calls and respond to information requests. That spokesperson must be involved in all discussions as long as the issue "remains alive." While criticisms can be fueled by political or professional motivations, the institution must assume (or act as if) they are not. Take the comments at face value until you know they are invalid. Notify your Board and the work's sponsors. As quickly as possible, put out a positive statement saying the institution appreciates the critic raising his/her points and the author and others at the institution will investigate their validity as quickly as possible. Media representatives can be brash and aggressive; your spokesperson cannot respond in kind—keep exchanges perfectly professional.

Sometimes the criticism results from a simple misreading of the analysis or some other cause that

---

84   D. Nakaura, "Study Co-author Leaves Heritage," *The Washington Post,* Saturday May 11, 2013.
85   In the blogosphere the result of vastly more attention being given to a news item resulting from the "defendant" commenting is known as the "Streisand effect," named after the unwanted publicity the actress received when she sued a blogger for posting photos of her estate on line. (Morozov, 2011 120-4).
86   This material is based very loosely on material in Regester and Larkin (2008), principally pp.124-6.

can be expeditiously addressed. Other times the complaint is based on quite sophisticated new analysis, such as in the CR&KR case above. In such cases, substantial additional research and time are needed for the author and institution to completely understand what has happened. Box 6.3 sketches an example of the type of thorough and time consuming process necessary to resolve a QC issue associated with a book I helped edit. The episode also serves as a good example of the lengths to which a think tank will (and should) go to protect is reputation for strong analysis.

Once the facts are clear, the decision must be made on how to proceed. If the allegation of poor quality work is false, the basis for the refutation must be carefully and fully laid out. Depending on the importance of the issue, the chief executive may want to recruit a respected expert from outside the institution to support the findings of the reanalysis. In all cases it is essential to be gracious and to attribute good intentions to the person who challenged the analysis.

If the analysis is flawed, admit it rather than ignore the criticism. If its results were used for actual policy formation, possibly including legislation, apologize. This is standard procedure for major corporations: Cadbury did so in 2007 when its products were found to be instrumental in a salmonella outbreak; Citibank did so in Japan when its private banking license was withdrawn (Regester and Larkin, 2008, pp. 140 and 145-6, respectively). Publish the corrected analysis as quickly as possible or at least issue a statement that you will not use the analysis further in the debate.

Regardless of the outcome, it is crucial to notify your Board—and the work's sponsors—before making a public announcement. Few things are as upsetting for those closely associated with the analysis under examination than to read about its resolution in the newspaper or as a Tweet. And always put a clarifying statement on your website. A permanent statement should be on the website page where the project is described that explains that the presently posted report (with a link to that report) is the corrected one.

TAKE AWAYS

Strong Practices
Characteristics of a well-managed think tank in this context follow.

- A written QC policy is in place and widely promulgated. The guiding principle is that all products get a review consistent with: 1) the product's visibility and importance to the institution's reputation, 2) the experience of the author(s) or presenter(s), and 3) whether the research is based on another product that has already been reviewed.

There are multiple ways to organize a QC system. I describe one approach in the text and include two more as case studies.

- The program is realistic, i.e., embodies sufficient flexibility to handle a range of products with the necessary review rigor, timeliness *and* affordability.

Enforcement of the system adopted is as important as the system's design. Again, ideas for one approach are laid out in the text.

- Compliance with review procedures is nearly universal and enforced by restricting the release of products not explicitly vouched for by a manager as appropriately quality controlled by document review or an equivalent mechanism. Experience shows the best systems to be those where checks are fairly automatic.

- The organization is prepared for QC lapses that result in adverse publicity. A plan has been developed and promulgated to all those who may be involved, including team leader and senior analysts. (Guidelines on how to respond are in the chapter text that give clear direction on the critical first moves—particularly who should be talking with the press.)

For Funders
Look carefully for:

- *The existence of a policy statement on QC and its administration.* Inquiring in detail about a QC program often affords a window on wider management performance and so is doubly useful. Check for comprehensiveness of product coverage and the realism of the standards: two external reviews of every report, for example, is hardly credible.

- *Concrete examples of reviewed products.* To cross-check reality against policy, if a chance presents itself, ask a senior researcher and someone in the communications team about the review process for specific products with which they have been involved.

- *Transparency.* Look at a few publications to see if the work's sponsor is clearly identified. If the report presents analysis using a major data set, check for a statement that the data set can be made available to responsible parties seeking to do a replication analysis.

Perhaps to do:

- Because of the reputational risk inherent in a marginal QC system and the low cost of improvement, consider making a priority of working with grantees to strengthen a weak system, if they show interest. If you are sponsoring research where the QC system is questionable, write into the agreement the type of review to be done.

- Set expectations about high quality products in the initiation of the funding relationship, but also indicate to the executive director your awareness that very rarely poor quality research may be published and that what matters is how management handles the issue in a transparent way. If the quality issue really is a rarity, reassure the executive director that a well-handled incident will not jeopardize funding.

- Encourage think tanks to include the cost of reviews of all products (written and presentations) in their budgets and cheerfully agree to pay for them.

Box 6.1 The Interaction of Academic Department Research Reviews and Those of University-Based Think Tanks

Broadly speaking, university departmental reviews of faculty research are not a particularly valuable asset for university-based think tanks. The closer the relation between a particular department and the think tank, as when all the think tank's senior analysts are members of one department, often economics, can make relations closer.

Seminars by faculty members play a special role in university departments and can interact in a limited way with the quality control procedures of university-located think tanks. The faculty seminars are a primary vehicle for assessing a less senior faculty member's development. The member presents his/her research methods and results at these seminars and is typically subject to very spirited and probing questioning about the work. The research can be significantly improved through a seminar, although this is not its primary purpose. The quality of the draft presented and the presenter's agility in the discussion are highly important for departmental faculty's assessment of the presenter's development.[a] Usually a non-tenured faculty member gives one seminar of this type or perhaps two in an academic year. Senior faculty members also give seminars where the goal is primarily to comment upon the technical quality of the research. The discussion in all seminars can be valuable to a think tank with which the member is affiliated, if the research being presented is being done for the think tank.

In short, the seminars can be thought of as a limited part of a university think tank's quality control process. Importantly, such faculty seminars, where faculty attendance is strongly encouraged, usually cannot be organized by the head of the think tank, nor necessarily on a schedule matching that of a particular project. Organizing the seminars is a departmental prerogative. Naturally, if a think tank's research staff is from a single department, seminar scheduling may well be coordinated with the think tank director.

Generally speaking university departments outsource quality control of faculty research products to journal and book editors, relying on the referees in this process to make valid decisions overall. The faculty member's record in peer reviewed journals is central to promotion decisions. In short, departmental review processes are not well-suited to think tank requirements for comparatively rapid, on-demand research report reviews. Hence, university-located think tanks need quality control procedures much like their unaffiliated counterparts.

a. Faculty seminars at The University of Chicago are regarded as exceptionally productive and rigorous. See van Overtveldt (2007) for a description.

Box 6.2 Four Stages of Crisis Management

1. Awareness. The organization learns that a question about the quality of its work has been raised. It follows the media and other sources, e.g., websites and newsletters of advocacy organizations concerned with the issue, to understand the depth and breadth of the issue. The think tank's chief executive sets up a small group to manage the organization's management of the issue; call this the "crisis group."

   The think tank puts out a statement on its website and social media saying that it is studying the validity of the criticism. A single point of contact for the issue is identified and all staff informed that questions from all sources are to be referred to the spokesperson. If the report or policy brief remains on the website, a statement should be posted saying that questions have been raised about the analysis and are under investigation. The Board of Directors and sponsors of the work are informed of the issue and again when an action plan is developed.

2. Exploration. The specifics of the issue are defined. This may involve contacting the critic directly to learn the details of the analysis s/he has done; this step could include acquiring and reviewing any written document and meeting with the critic. The chief executive decides if the author or someone else should initiate contact. Other steps could include a rigorous review of the researcher's work for possible missteps. The "crisis group" may want to convene a meeting to review the information developed, including an outside expert on the topic at hand to get a third-party opinion.

3. Decision making. Based on the work done in previous steps, the chief executive and the crisis group, possibly with others, meet to determine how to proceed. Options range from (a) issuing a statement saying that (i) the institution stands by the report and giving the reasons why the criticism is not valid or (ii) was improperly stated or reported to (b) withdrawing the report, saying that valid issues were raised and that the analysis will be or has been reworked. The decision is conveyed to the Board of Directors prior to any public announcement.

4. Implementation. The think tank issues a statement on its website and social media outlets as to its conclusion. This may be that a reanalysis will be or has been done. It may be that the report has been withdrawn from circulation, including the website. The report title should still appear on the website with a statement about its status, e.g., it has been withdrawn and the analysis in continuing, and so forth.

   If the think tank stands by its work, the researcher, probably with help from others, prepares a statement on why s/he believes the criticism is unwarranted. In an extreme case, the think tank may engage a third-party expert to prepare the statement to increase its credibility.

   A final statement is issued in a timely way, thus closing the episode if the question is not quickly resolved.

Box 6.3 Checking Analyses Can be Time and Resource Consuming— But Worth It

In the early 1990s authors at The Urban Institute edited a volume of papers on measuring the extent of discrimination in America against African- and Hispanic-Americans in several contexts: renting or purchasing a home, being hired for an entry-level position, and mortgage lending and insurance. The methodology used to establish discrimination was to use the following test: a white man and a black man, both posing as workers with identical resumes, apply independently for the same entry-level job. At the end of the application and perhaps interview process with the firm, the two separately fill out identical forms on how they were treated. Discrimination, if any, is determined by differences in reported treatment.

After the book was printed, but not yet distributed for sale, senior management looked at an advance copy and discovered a potentially embarrassing conflict within it. One of the chapter authors had evaluated the testing methodology in a way that cast doubt on the main findings of the book—and this potential conflict had not been satisfactorily dealt with in the introductory chapter (or, it should be added, flagged by the external reviewers of the book manuscript). The book was immediately embargoed and an outside statistical expert engaged to look into the apparent conflict and try to resolve it. After an intense meeting with all the authors associated with the book, the outside expert went to work. The upshot was that: 1) the contributing author withdrew the chapter that had raised the concern and submitted a new one and 2) the introductory chapter was satisfactorily revised as well.

As is clear from this description, Institute management took the issue very seriously and spent a great deal of time (about a year was added to the book's publication time) and resources (including the considerable sunk cost of destroying the original print run) to make it right.

Case Study 6.1 Implementation of an Efficient Quality Control Process for Written Products

The Center for the Implementation of Public Policies promoting Equity and Growth (CIPPEC) was founded in 2001. Over time, the number of policy programs or areas studied and their associated research production grew. The review process and quality standards varied among different departments.

At this point, the Communication's Director—then in charge of editing and quality assurance of each document published—identified the need to set quality standards for CIPPEC's written products, in part to streamline the process of editing and publishing. Creating a formal process was an opportunity to improve the publications by setting quality standards and introducing design templates to give the production an institutional identity.

Since 2010, CIPPEC has had a publication policy that defines the types of publications the think tank produces; establishes internal processes that must be followed during the planning, writing, and review phases; and determines template designs for each kind of document produced (books, handbooks, guides, working papers and policy briefs, among others).

To ensure implementation of this policy, CIPPEC added a new position within the Communication Division, tasked with supervising and editing the publications. This editor, who oversees the entire production process, with more or less detail depending on the type of publication, is responsible for ensuring institutional consistency. CIPPEC has nine different programs and more than 60 researchers working on different and sometimes overlapping policy areas, and publishes around 50 publications per year. In this context, consistently high quality in policy analysis and recommendations is critical.

The Review Process: Policy Briefs

A key goal of the publication policy is that products are ready in the least time with the best quality. To illustrate the overall process, we use the case of policy briefs as representative of main publications. The separate case of blog postings is discussed below.

One of the features of the quality control process is that it is mainly in-house, but with a significant role of members of the Administrative Board, CIPPEC's highest governance body. In 2010, CIPPEC created the 'Policy Brief Board Committee,' consisting of the five Board members, who read and comment on policy briefs, within 48 hours

if needed, before they are published. The Committee includes people with great experience over a range of areas (communication, policy arena, private sector, etc.) who can provide a rigorous technical review and assess the likely impact that a piece will have on different audiences.

Each year, the Communications Division takes stock of CIPPEC's annual expected production of various types of publications during a series of annual planning meetings. Policy briefs are among the products included in the plan.

1. As the time for writing a brief nears, an internal decision is made that the brief should be written, confirming the plan.
2. With this approval, the investigator writes the policy brief, which is sent to the Publications Coordinator of the Communication Division, who edits it and gives feedback on the content.
3. The researcher then incorporates these corrections and feedback and sends a second version to the Publication Coordinator.
4. The Publication Coordinator reviews this new version and starts the design process.
5. Once it has been formatted according to the template, the Communication Director sends the policy brief to CIPPEC'S Board. Though all Board members receive the document, only the Policy Brief Committee must read it. In cases where a rapid review is needed, they are usually given 48 hours to give their opinion on the piece When the dissemination of the policy brief is not urgent, the Committee has from three to five days to give their comments.
6. When there is critical feedback, the researcher continues to work on his/her piece in response. When the policy brief is expected to attract significant attention from the media and the policy community, the Executive Director might read and comment on it as well. (The Executive Director receives all new policy briefs, although he is not expected to comment on all.) A face to face presentation to the Board is also considered when the policy brief is very important to the organization's reputation.
7. The Communication Division starts the dissemination process.

Results and challenges

This structure has helped CIPPEC speed up the editorial and publication processes. At the beginning, it took time and practice for researchers to adapt themselves to a process that was a little bit cumbersome; but it became easier as each team internalized the purpose of policy briefs, their target audiences, and the writing style.

Another challenge facing the process was timing. CIPPEC realized the process needed to be planned carefully to be efficient. Unexpected events such as sudden political changes can affect the process (making all people involved rush to get the document ready and out quickly). Therefore, the publication policy foresees the possibility of working under pressure and guarantees flexible mechanisms to address quality problems.

The Case of Blogs

In recent years, CIPPEC launched several blogs on different policy issues, such as education and social protection. The relevant policy research area leaders and the Communications Division make the decision on opening these virtual spaces to reach new audiences based on the following criteria: is there capacity, including monitoring, to produce weekly content; is the defined target audience important; and does the policy research area has sufficient resources (mainly related to the number of authors working on the blog). The Communications Division also participates in the design and assembly of sections of the blog.

Although it is not formalized in a document, like the policy briefs' quality control process described, a simple process for editing and publishing blogs' content has been established. It takes into account the speed in which the new blog content needs to be posted. When an author writes a new blog post, s/he has to send it to the Communications Division, which has 48 hours to edit and send it back. If the editor, when reviewing a draft blog, thinks there may be technical issues with the content, s/he is supposed to alert the author to look at the content from the research side. If the Communications Division does not respond within those 48 hours, the author is allowed to publish the original blog post.

Because blog posts are shorter and generally linked to ongoing investigations, the editing process is faster and allows the immediacy a blog requires. Once the post is published, it is automatically sent to all the contacts subscribing to the blog. In addition, the Communications Division coordinates with the authors to disseminate the new content through social network outlets such as Facebook and Twitter.

Leandro Echt and Dolores Arrieta
Center for the Implementation of Public Policies
Promoting Equity and Growth
Buenos Aires, Argentina

Case Study 6.2 Benefits from Pre-event Presentation Reviews, BIGS Indonesia

Background

From attending seminars and conferences I have formed the impression that expositions of some speakers or researchers are too broad, with too many points to make, given the limited time. As a result, the presentation loses focus. This is a form of presentation failure. Reflecting on this, I concluded that my think tank's presentations have a similar problem on occasion.

As an institution working on budget research and advocacy, and often on public expenditures, we frequently have to deliver research results and recommendations on politically sensitive issues. Therefore, we need an appropriate method of presenting research results that recognizes the range of an audience's viewpoints. Another presentation challenge is how to implicitly include information on our institute's vision and mission.

The need for a sharp focus and understanding an audience's perspectives has driven us to run a thorough review process for public presentations on our research results, particularly in seminars, media meetings, and other interactions with the media.

Specific problems to be addressed

The main problems we find are three. First, how to focus the presentation to meet its primary objective. Second, how to make information about our institution well delivered and so improve the audience's appreciation of our research results. Third, how to effectively deliver sensitive and critical research findings to different stakeholders.

A presentation may fail to focus on its primary objective because the researcher wants to announce all the findings on a single occasion. The researcher seems to treat presentations as the one and only chance for an advocacy effort. A presentation, however, is not the end; rather it is part of a campaign and a means of communication and dialog with the primary audience. Unfocused presentations often result in other problems: unclear recommendations for the particular audience and an absence of what may be done in the future to address the issue or implement the recommendations.

Presenting research findings on sensitive and critical issues requires a special approach. Failure to effectively present the findings may be related to the researcher not being attuned to his/her audience's varied interests or not understanding its specific values. Presentations must be tailored for different audiences, for example, the message

to government officials should be different from that to NGOs.

Alternative solutions

There are various options for addressing these problems: providing a guide to the researcher for presentation development, carrying out an internal review of the presentation, and having a review by experts external to the organization (termed an "external review" below).

Review guidelines are a statement of standards for a presentation to be of acceptable quality. The guidelines cover: 1) content: the background, objective, results and others topics that must be included; 2) identification of politically sensitive factors and the most critical points to be made; and 3) guidance on structuring the presentation for the particular audience.

Providing the guidelines is intended to ensure that research findings delivered to the public are carefully structured and ready for consideration by reviewers prior to their delivery. The guidelines allow the researcher and reviewer to assess an exposition from the same perspective, which helps make the review maximally helpful to the researcher in making needed revisions. The guidelines are used in preparing all presentations.

An internal review is carried out by involving peers, senior researchers, or board members. For research on less sensitive issues, an internal review is sufficient. It is conducted through a meeting whose purpose is specifically to review the presentation, prior to outside delivery. Internal reviews are typically used for presentations intended for technical audiences, i.e., those not including public officials or policy makers.

If a project produces findings that deal with sensitive and critical issues, it needs a different type of review, namely review by experts from outside the institute (i.e., experts on the sector addressed by the research and on the methods used). This review is carried out either in the form of a group meeting (workshop) or a separate meeting between experts and the presenter. This type of review helps sharpen or reformulate the message, so the core message is clearly delivered. Also, experts may express different views on the findings and related policy recommendations. These different perspectives tend to enrich and clarify the message.

Challenges

Use of the guidelines can make presentations more effective and appropriately targeted and meeting a minimum standard of conveying the research results very likely. But implementing this approach can encounter obstacles. Despite the guidelines, researchers often make presentations following their own style. This typically occurs because the researcher focuses on research results and pays less attention to presentation standards contained in the guidelines (which call for accenting the policy recommendations and program implementation).

An internal review is easy to organize and is of genuine benefit to less senior research staff, because it can be used as a part of the general mentoring process. The shortcoming, however, is that it may trap the presenter in unfocused discussions among attendees that do not yield a good review.

The external review requires more effort and resources from the organization. Generally it produces a high quality review. The challenge is that the researcher may be discouraged when s/he receives quite pointed comments from the reviewers. Additionally, the researcher may give too much weight to the external review with the result that the original presentation objective is changed.

Benefits
In practice, the guidance just described yields significant results: researchers are more confident when they present their results; the response or reaction of the participants are more focused on the findings; and, the media reporting on the results presented is more consistent with the message delivered.

For researchers, it is sometimes challenging to convey their results when the issue is sensitive, such as the budget issues we study. Through the review process, researchers become more confident when dealing with the audiences or other stakeholders in other settings. Various possibilities on the way an audience will react can be mapped during the review process, so it becomes an arena where researchers practice responding to audiences.

Understanding the perspectives of conference participants is key. In our experience, there are often several different interests among attendees at a forum. Some might be interested in following up an issue based on the content presented. Some might be interested in considering the implications of the information on his/her own organization's mission. There might also be participants who strongly disagree with the analysis or the recommendations. Hence, in the context of future advocacy, mapping the various responses will facilitate the advocacy team's follow up on the report's recommendations. Often, the information from such exchanges helps determine which groups will require greater effort to convince them to support the policy recommendations.

How the media reports the research results and informs and characterizes the presenter's institution is very important. Media can be a "messenger" of the advocacy message, becoming an "ally" in conveying a position. Nevertheless, there have also been occasions when the media has not accurately reported a presentation's key theme. With the advanced review of our presentations, the message becomes clearer and this makes it easier for the media to report findings with greater precision.

Siti Fatimah
Bandung Institute of Governance Studies – BIGS
Bandung, Indonesia

CHAPTER 7
Getting Focused Advice from Your Board

"The role of the Board is to protect and to direct." Michel Kelly Gagnon of the Montreal Economic Institute quoted in Lips (2009)

"Independent think tanks should be governed by an elected or duly appointed governing body that should consist of individuals committed to the mission of the organization and establish its management policies and procedures. Ideally, the governing body should be able to assure that adequate human resources...and financial resources...are available. The governing body should actively monitor the organization's financial and operational performance." Pajas (2011, 14)

The key managerial actors in think tanks are the boards of directors (sometimes called boards of trustees), the president, a management council of senior staff if one exists, and the research team leaders. A board of trustees/directors can be an extraordinarily valuable asset to a private public-policy research institution. But realizing this potential is demanding. Failure to do so can result from such factors as ill-defined roles for the board, a mismatch between its talents and its actual tasks, and the think tank president's failure to work creatively with the board to get the most from members' participation in institutional affairs.

Board productivity can be impaired if the responsibilities for principal managerial decisions are misallocated among the board, the president, and the management council or other boards of senior managers created to advise the president. Key decisions for the institution include, for example, setting the institution's agenda, determining staff compensation, and deciding how to structure the institution's research operations. Of these, only the first typically rests with the board and then only in broad terms. It is important to realize, however, that in many countries the formal distribution of responsibilities is heavily conditioned by laws that mandate particular organizational structures for nonprofit organizations—such structures may not be the most effective for think tanks even though they are the law.

This chapter discusses the structure and potential contributions of boards of directors/trustees (hereafter referred to simply as boards). I address it to the president or executive director (hereafter in this discussion, the president) of think tanks. It outlines methods a president can use to work most effectively with and benefit most from the institution's board, giving thorough treatment to the mechanics of organizing and managing a board. The president's principal objective in such external management dealings should be to focus the board's time advising on key issues in the think tank's development. The next chapter gives ideas on internal management, particularly regarding information flow.

Much of my presentation here concerns the interactions of presidents and the boards of comparatively mature organizations—that is, those 10 or more years old that have been at least a Stage 2 think tank for several years and enjoy low turnover rates for both president and board. The organization's maturity and stability are critical, because they bear fundamentally on how much authority a board will feel it can confidently delegate to the president. The more mature and stable an institution, the more the board can concentrate on "big picture" questions and leave management to the president.

The contents of the guidelines I provide come from four sources: my experience as a board member; interviews with board members of Stage 1 and 2 think tanks as part of due diligence assignments for donors and discussions with senior leaders of many Stage 2 and Stage 3 think tanks; a review of recent books on enhancing board productivity; and, in-depth assessments of three think tanks' operations over the past three years.[87]

GETTING STARTED

The supreme authority for think tanks is its board—the exact title depending on the law and practice of each country. The duties of the board are nearly always clearly stated in the national law governing the formation of nonprofit organizations. At their heart, these duties can be reduced to two: maintaining accountability and safeguarding the public's trust. Responsibility for accountability means ensuring the organization's resources are properly spent—not wasted on excessively expensive offices, travel, and salaries or lost through graft. Think tanks must also maintain the public trust. In most countries, but certainly not all (e.g., Russia), nonprofits acting in the public interest are accorded certain legal advantages, especially tax advantages, compared with for-profit entities. In exchange, they are expected to contribute to the public good. For instance, think tanks should do work that improves public decision making and educates the public on the principal policy issues of the day. The board's task is to ensure the think tank works toward these goals.

Organizational Variations
Stone (2005) has listed boards for five types of organizations that can engage in policy research:

---

87   This experience includes being a member of the board of trustees of the nonprofit Institute for Urban Economics in Moscow (1995–present), the board of directors of the for-profit Metropolitan Research Institute in Budapest (1992–1997), and the board of directors of the for-profit E-A Ratings in Moscow (1997–2001). Also useful was exposure to board responsibilities and activities of the National Council of Family Affairs, operated under royal patronage in Jordan, as part of an evaluation aof the Council's overall operations and similar assignments elsewhere. The books I reviewed include Robinson (2001), Shultz (2001), Carver (1997), Charan (1998), and La Piana (2008).

1. Independent civil society think tank established as a nonprofit organization
2. Policy research institute located in or affiliated with a university
3. Governmentally created or state sponsored think tank
4. Corporate created or business affiliated think tank
5. Political party think tank.

Obviously, those sub-groups have diverse objectives and corresponding governance structures. The best way to get a sense of their differences is to read essays on the structure of think tank communities in individual countries and the specifics of various think tank types within each. (See, for example, Stone, Denham, and Garnet, 1998; McGann and Weaver, 2000; and Stone and Denham, 2004).

My focus is the first type. But even among independent nonprofit think tanks there are significant distinctions to note. Some arise from national laws on the creation and operation of NGOs. In Russia, for example, the management board composed of senior think tank officers constitutes the highest decision making body. No provision in the law is made for an outside board of trustees with oversight responsibility. In some countries, the founders of the organization constitute the equivalent of a board.[88] Government-sponsored think tanks often have different governance structures that more closely resemble an operating arm of a ministry than an independent institution. Even where internal operations are left to the executive director and his/her management team, the board of directors can strongly influence the work undertaken with funds received from the government.

Many think tanks have two kinds of boards: a management board or committee, and a board of directors or trustees. The management board has day-to-day responsibilities for operational issues and is discussed in Chapter 8 (Internal Governance). The board of directors or trustees is more focused on strategy and has the ultimate fiduciary responsibility. This tends to be the standard model.[89] The rest of the chapter assumes the standard model is followed.[90]

---

88   Moncada and Mendizabal (2013) discuss another variation, the membership board. Under this model an assembly is formed of all those individuals who are the associates of the organization, usually its researchers and founding members. The assembly is the highest governing body and periodically meets to choose the executive director and an executive council, either from within the members or from outside. The executive council is more of a management committee than a board in that it has day-to-day responsibilities. See Ordonez (2012) for a good description.

89   Mendizabal (2013a) reports that some think tanks create additional internal committees concerned with management issues of various sorts. He warns against the overlap, confusion, and wasted resources that can result if the tasks of each are not well defined and responsibility within each committee not tightly drawn.

90   In addition, think tanks often elect to form an advisory board of thoughtful and prestigious individuals who provide more technical advice. Members are more heavily drawn from the research and NGO communities and often include a couple of distinguished foreigners. The actual activity level of such boards varies widely, with some meeting never or only one or twice. Advisory boards do not have fiduciary responsibility; so generally they will not be concerned with the institution's audit and related questions. Such boards are not discussed further in this chapter.

Dimensions of the Board's Role

Three aspects of the board's role can be distinguished: legal, functional, and symbolic.[91] The laws that govern the creation of think tanks mandate boards to supervise compliance with certain requirements. Some (e.g., the board meets at least once a year) are fairly routine, but two requirements are more fundamental: the board is responsible for 1) the organization's fiscal integrity and 2) ensuring the organization stay true to its mission (i.e., the purpose for which it was created).

Functional responsibilities of the board vary greatly from think tank to think tank. Indeed, as discussed below, the greatest problem for boards is that their primary tasks are often not clearly defined. A typical list of responsibilities includes ensuring the organization is realizing its mission effectively, hiring the president, evaluating the president's performance, understanding the organization's financial and policy performance, reviewing and approving the organization's strategy, and assisting with fund-raising. But many boards find themselves ensnared in operational details, including having to determine which telephone or computing system to purchase, or how to establish salary ranges for different positions—tasks much better left to management. Often, attention to such details comes at the expense of time to give much more critical advice in determining the institution's main directions.

The symbolic dimension of the board's work is critical. Board members lend the think tank prestige by associating with it, and thus becoming part of its public image. The list of names on the organization's letterhead and website, and in its printed materials, tells a story about the organization's values and strengths.

Board members have a significant advantage over the president and other staff in representing the organization, by carrying an organization's message and expanding its circle of influence. Board members are perceived as having little to gain from promulgating a think tank's good name and, hence, have *prima facie* credibility. Board members can play this ambassadorial role to advance policy positions or raise funds. A key task for the institution's president is to figure out how to motivate board members to take on these active roles.

COMMON BOARD ISSUES AND TASKS

The Board's responsibilities and tasks are spelled out in its bylaws. The bylaws of R4D, reproduced in Annex 7.1*, are representative. As can be seen, the statements are quite broad, leaving the Board with a good deal of leeway in defining its actual role.

Books on creating effective boards of nonprofit organizations are replete with examples of ineffectiveness, wasted time, and lost opportunities. My conversations with think tank presidents about the utility of their institution's boards have also exposed some frustration with presidents'

---

91   This section draws on Robinson (2001, 11–12, 29–40).

178

inability to get more from boards, even though they are made up of creative, dynamic, and successful individuals.

Certain common practices of the board and the structure of board meetings can drain effectiveness. Carver (1997, 9–10) gives some good examples:

- *Short-term bias.* The board concentrates on day-to-day items that could be handled by the staff rather than issues that may have much greater consequences for the organization.

- *Reactive stance.* The board responds to staff initiatives and information rather than asserting leadership (e.g., indicating topics for the meeting's agenda).

- *Reviewing, rehashing, redoing.* The board spends too much time reviewing what staff has already done; this should be a management function.

- *Leaky accountability.* Board members "go around" the president to assign tasks to staff members, making it hard to hold the president responsible for results.

- *Diffuse authority.* The specific responsibilities of the president and board are not well defined, frustrating accountability.

Underlying much of this is the basic problem that boards often get inappropriately involved in management issues. The following is an illustrative list of topics that can siphon attention from more important issues and should not be a major focus of boards (Carver 1997, 75–76).

- *Personnel:* making decisions about job design, hiring, firing, promotion, discipline

- *Compensation:* dealing with issues involving salary ranges, grades, adjustments, incentives, benefits (exceptions include the president's salary, which the board should determine, and those of the most senior staff, which the board should approve)

- *Supply:* making decisions about purchasing, bidding authorization, storage, inventories, salvage.

- *Accounting:* addressing questions of forecasting, budgeting, depositories, controls, investments, retrenchment

- *Facilities:* determining space allocation and requirements, rentals, upkeep, refurbishment

- *Risk management:* actively dealing with insurance, exposures, protective maintenance, and disclaimers

- *Reporting:* ensuring grant reports, tax reporting, law and regulation compliance

- *Communications:* developing policies affecting telephone systems, meetings, postings, mail distribution; digital media usage

- *Management methods:* dealing with internal goal-setting, staffing patterns, team definitions, feedback loops, planning techniques, control methods, participation levels.

Clearly, if a board wades into many of these areas, it will spend most of its time immersed—if not drowning—in details and be at risk of not addressing more strategic issues.

How broad this prohibition on boards keeping out of management issues, however, depends strongly on the size, and relatedly, the age of the think tank and the management experience of its president. The key point is that, as think tanks get larger (and to a lesser extent as they mature), they have the scope to professionalize their management and acquire more management expertise on staff. At newly launched think tanks, in contrast, the president often essentially has no others with relevant experience to whom s/he can turn and must seek board's views on management topics.

The challenge for the president and continuing board members of a recently established think tank is to recognize when to start letting the professional managers take the reins and progressively bring only questions of strategic importance to the board. Usually this is a step-by-step process that requires close cooperation between the president and the board chair. Occasionally, evolving management decisions away from the board is deferred, in which case it can happen more suddenly and sharply with the arrival of a new president or possibly a board chair.

Devolving management responsibility at the right time is, of course, the model. But the problem of a board remaining too involved in internal management issues is surprisingly common, even in Stage 3 think tanks—and this is indeed problematic. The following true story illustrates how such a situation can arise.

> A Stage 3 think tank with a good reputation for being well-managed and having a strong core of professional managers in place went through the normal transition of a president retiring and a new one being selected by the board. The new president, when hit early on with management issues that were novel to him, turned first to one or another board member for advice, which the members willingly gave. After several such episodes two problems emerged: the think tank's management team was miffed because they believed their competence was being questioned since they were not handling problems as they had previously; and the president was getting a continuing stream of questions and advice from board members on management topics, which were consuming a good deal of the president's time and providing no advantage to the institution.

A president has the potential to make the board much more effective, because s/he usually drafts the agenda for board meetings for the board chair's discussion and approval, decides how much background material to provide to members, and when to distribute it. But how can a president best move the board in the right direction?

The following several sections for the most part discuss all boards together, with little differentiation for think tank age or size. In the last section before the "Take Aways" I add remarks for the special case of the board for new think tanks.

FOCUSING THE BOARD

This section first discusses the division of labor between the board and the thank tank's president. The second section addresses the type of information the board should receive to enable it to monitor the organization's condition and achievements.

Who Does What? The Board or Management?

Consultants who work with boards to increase their effectiveness universally decry the kinds of problems just outlined as a clear waste of board members' expertise and experience. Consultants look for ways to promote the idea of focusing the board's energy and intellectual resources on the key tasks of the organization and on long-term planning. In other words, the board of a think tank should concentrate on how well the organization is fulfilling its primary missions of conducting high-quality policy research, influencing policy, and informing policy debates. As to long-run planning, the critical issues are the country's emerging policy agenda, identifying the subset of issues where the institution has or could reasonably develop a comparative advantage, and potential sources of support for the institution's work. The board's advice should deal primarily with these matters. Of course, not all board members are equally qualified to proffer advice on all topics, and the president must guide discussions skillfully to get the most from the board.

The president and the board need to agree on the board's responsibility for providing management advice. As needed, the board can request information and intervene in management issues. Requests for more information are likely to arise from open discussion of principal issues, which will be addressed later. But this should be the exception rather than the rule.

To move a board in this direction, the starting point is to craft a clear statement of the organization's mission. Box 7.1 gives an example of such a statement. It is quite general; once the board accepts it, a set of indicators to measure the think tank's performance should be added. (This is discussed in detail in Chapter 12.)

Regardless of how much responsibility the board delegates to the president and the management team for such tasks, the responsibilities delegated to the president need to be stated explicitly. The intent of codified Executive Limitations is twofold. First, the Limitations prohibit staff practices that the board regards as unethical or too risky. Second, in organizations where full trust has not been established between the president and the board, such Limitations give the president additional guidance on how to execute certain management duties. The board and president both need to understand who is responsible for what. The board is responsible for periodically checking that management is complying with the rules set forth in the Executive Limitations.

Box 7.2 provides an example of two key statements regulating the relations between the board and the president. The "Delegation to the President" outlines the president's powers and responsibilities. The "Communication and Support to the Board" informs the president of his/her obligations to the board. Both could be incorporated into the Board's bylaws.

The "Delegation to the President" ties the delegation of responsibilities to the board-approved mission statement and the Executive Limitations. The statement makes it clear that Executive Limitations can change to shift the allocation of responsibilities between the board and the president. It protects the president from unreasonable requests for information from individual board members. It also makes it clear that the president need only follow decisions of the whole board, not those of individual members or even committees. The statement is crystal clear on the president's operational authority.

The statement on "Communication and Support to the Board" requires the president to provide certain information to the board. This includes the information needed to assess the think tank's progress toward its primary goals and information on any circumstantial changes that could affect the organization's reputation or financial health.

These two statements establish the general rules, but they need to be supported by guidance from the board on the parameters of the president's vested authority. Box 7.3 gives examples of such statements for financial, asset, and staff management. For example, the president has authority to commit the organization to contracts and grants up to $500,000. Beyond this limit, the president must seek board approval. Similarly, the president has wide authority in the personnel area, but decisions on compensation and promotion must be objective and defensible.

The critical point here is that the statements of Executive Limitations define the operating domain of the president vs. the domain retained by the board. There is no reason for the board to enter the president's sphere, especially at the expense of its bigger-picture responsibilities. The board's task is periodically to satisfy itself that the rules it has set forth are being followed. (In the financial and asset protection areas, the annual audit should provide most of the necessary information.) Naturally, the president can seek the board's advice on matters squarely within his/her jurisdiction, and many presidents routinely do so. As long as such interchanges are infrequent and informal, they can build support and confidence.

The foregoing has touched upon the board's fiduciary responsibilities. The documents just reviewed are important because they set limits on the president exposing the organization to excessive risk in key areas. The board's chair and the one or two members with strong financial backgrounds should receive quarterly information on cash flow, expenditures by broad category, profit and loss, and investments—both the nature of the investments and their return. These data make it possible to keep a "finger on the pulse" with little effort. These actions, combined with an annual external audit that will test whether proper procedures are being followed in fund disbursements and other matters, should be sufficient to discharge the board's fiduciary duties responsibly.

The board's own activities are governed by a set of procedures, collected into a by-laws or other statement that covers such topics as:[92]

- Calling board meetings in regular or extraordinary sessions
- Preparing and distributing the meeting agenda
- Monitoring meeting attendance
- Checking quorum and applying voting methods
- Setting methods for contacting members and conducting votes for emergency decision making
- Drafting and approving new policies
- Conducting board elections and filling board vacancies
- Handling a board member's resignation and/or removal from office
- Providing orientation induction for new members
- Organizing board self-assessments
- Preparing and approving minutes of meetings
- Computing board member reimbursements.

A very useful document for developing such a guide, by Marilyn Wyatt and others, is *A Handbook of NGO Governance*; full citation is in the References. (As noted, Annex 7.1* contains an example of these by-laws.)

The Board and the Think Tank's Strategy

A strategy or strategic plan for a think tank is a coordinated set of actions aimed at creating and sustaining a competitive advantage in carrying out its policy research, policy engagement and communications, and possibly other missions.[93] This is the plan that guides the think tank's actions going forward. Obviously, it is highly important for the Board of Directors to provide input on the strategy, approve it, receive information on its implementation, and be involved in making adjustments to it as needed. Options for strategy development are reviewed in the next chapter (Chapter 8). Here I focus on the board's role in the process.

The centrality of a think tank's strategy to its development means that the board should give it full attention when asked to do so. Such attention can come efficiently at two stages: during the strategy's development and monitoring results on an ongoing basis after its adoption.

---

92   From Pajos (2011), p.42.
93   Edited version of the definition given in La Piana (2008), p.31.

During development. On the assumption that a comparatively simple approach is being taken by think tank leaders to strategy development, before the process begins the board should be informed that work on an updated (or first time) strategy is being undertaken and the contents and process should be outlined to them. Thereafter board input could be sought at three points. The first involves reviewing the organization's mission statement if necessary. Such a necessity occurs when major shifts in the organization's activities—a possible major expansion (e.g., beginning to work in other countries or adding a teaching program)—is being considered, sometimes, if rarely, at the board's initiative. Mission clarity is the essential anchor for the whole planning process. If no major change is envisaged, this step can be handled briskly (Selee 2013). The second is when the process is far enough along that candidate direction shifts have been identified (within mission statement parameters) and analyzed. Getting the board's thoughts at this early stage is certainly worthwhile and will pave the way for discussion of the draft plan. The third point for board input is when a draft is available.

At the first session, after an overview from the president, it makes sense to solicit the board's views on likely future developments—including the major policy issues to be addressed over the next few years, potential shifts in funding sources, possible changes in landscape of think tanks and research advocacy organizations, and consultancies working the think tank's space. Then the discussion can turn to possible major initiatives, such as launching a research program in a sharply different area or starting consulting operations internationally, which certainly deserve attention as well.

An advanced strategy draft, incorporating those board comments viewed as valuable by the president, can be presented at a future board meeting for approval. The draft should be supplied to board members 7-10 days ahead of the board meeting to give them plenty of opportunity to read it. If the board meets only semi-annually and the president is anxious to start implementing the new strategy, the final draft could be sent out between regular meetings for a special review "meeting" to be organized in-person or via conference call, depending on board members' locations and preferences. Some boards are willing to hold special meetings and this may be appropriate. But most presidents find their board members do not welcome such *ad hoc* events.

Ongoing involvement. "Major questions" are likely to arise from time to time that will require adjustments to the adopted strategy. In such cases, the president should raise the relevant development with the board at a regular meeting and discuss the challenge and options for addressing it with the board. The president can use this input in making his/her decision and inform the board about it. The written strategy should be amended with any change, so that it remains a useful guide for all managers.

Informing the Board, Tracking Progress

It is standard, as noted, for a think tank's president to present an overview of the organization's status and principal accomplishments at each board meeting, with a more complete accounting once a year. Within this presentation, the president usually flags issues that have developed and explains how they have been addressed or seeks input from the board on how to proceed.

It is very important to provide the board with a limited set of key performance indicators. Shekhar Khan (2012) points out that board members from the business community will be used to reviewing a standard set of financial indicators and will need some coaching to consider a different set of indicators appropriate for judging a think tank's performance—an important topic for new board member orientation.

So what indicators are most useful? Table 7.1 shows the information provided to board members for its 2013 annual meeting by the Institute for Urban Economics in Moscow, a solid Stage 2 think tank. The board of that institution is satisfied with this level of information. Note that it includes a few items that do not always appear among such materials: a copy of the management letter from the audit of its 2012 accounts and the share of payroll accounted for by administrative staff (under financial indicators); examples of instances of policy development where IUE had participated substantially (under policy engagement); and the allocation of staff time among major activities (under staff information). All of this information is presented in a format where the current year's values appear with those for the past several years, facilitating trend analysis.

Table 7.1 Information Provided for the Institute for Urban Economics' 2013 Board of Trustees Meeting

Category	Communications
Financial indicators and information	Total budget and total revenue
	Sources of funds: Major clients and projects
	Data on dynamics of composition of gross turnover for the past five years among three classes of clients, e.g., contracts from foreign organizations
	Percentage distribution of support from Russian clients among three clients types, i.e., federal budget funds, local governments, and NGOs and private firms.
	Share of administrative payroll expenses in total payroll expenses over past five years
	A copy of the management letter from the audit of 2012 accounts
Policy Engagement and Communications	Examples of instances of policy development where IUE had participated substantially
	Number of publications and size of print runs
	Number of items placed on the website
	Ranking among Russian think tanks in terms of website visits
	Several indicators of Facebook activity and ratings
	Number of IUE-related materials in media outlet
	--number of radio/TV interviews
	--citations of work in the media
	--media articles by IUE staff
	--new items featuring IUE
Staff information	Allocation of staff work time among consultancy, education activity (teaching ,etc.), participation in the law development process, research and analysis, dissemination of products, publishing and PR activity.[a]
	Number of staff divided between researchers and administrative personnel over time

a.   These are comprehensive measurements so that, for example, dissemination, publication and PR activity includes research staff time. The value for this figure is 20 percent of all staff time.

Most think tanks track many more indicators as part of routine management practices than they provide to the Board. Indicators for various purposes are thoroughly discussed in Chapter 12.

Some presidents and boards have found it valuable to go a step further than providing indicators of overall performance. For a couple of major projects or work areas the president chooses to discuss with the board, s/he states the goals s/he and the team leader have set for the next year; results are then reported to the board a year later.[94] In effect, this is a report to the board on a priority part of the strategy—but one that is highly focused and gives the board much more information than a general strategy overview could. This approach allows the board to understand more fully the work being done and to provide advice and ideas at this deeper knowledge level.

Board members should be particularly attuned to reports on accomplishments in the policy arena—after all, working to strengthen governmental policymaking is the organization's primary task. Members should not be satisfied only with figures on the various communications activities. Where few policy results are emerging in major research areas, it is reasonable to ask about the nature of challenges encountered, whether they are up to the organizations' aspirations, and to request updates at each board meeting.

The Board Meeting

Obviously, a think tank's president must prepare carefully for each meeting of the board. Two critical tasks must be conducted before the meeting itself: setting the agenda and distributing meeting materials to board members.

Setting the Agenda. Since the agenda should drive the meeting, its items should be thoughtfully considered. A few pointers about formulating the agenda:

- The president usually drafts the agenda, but the board's chair should review it and suggest possible emendations before it is distributed to the rest of the board.

- Discussion at the meeting should be reserved for important points that concern the organization's principal tasks—both reporting on accomplishments and considering future activities—and those dealing with the organization's financial soundness.

- Whenever possible, information on management matters should be provided to the board in the materials sent out before the meeting—but *not* placed as items on the agenda. Although board member can ask about these "information items," they should be clearly relegated to a secondary position.

---

94   The Center for Global Development, a Washington, DC think tank focused on the effectiveness of aid programs for transition and developing countries, uses this technique with its board. MacDonald and Levine (2008).

- Dinner meetings the night before, or a lunch meeting the day of the actual board meetings, can create the fellowship dynamic the board needs to do its job. Informal social occasions are reportedly popular with board members (Shultz 2001, 205). A few senior staff, especially those who will be making presentations, should be invited. Seating should be planned and organized so staff and board members sit next to one another.

Box 7.4 presents a typical agenda for a meeting of a think tank's board of trustees. The first of the three main sections is the report of the Board's chair. At this meeting, the initial section includes discussion of the annual audit report, a topic that must be considered by the full board as well as by the chair.

The second section is devoted to the president's report on the institution's performance in key areas. The information provided should cover at least the indicators of performance agreed upon earlier with the board. The president should also use this opportunity to inform the board about important developments that may affect the organization's financial well-being or influence on policymaking—the so-called "environmental scan."

For example, the election of a new national government (change of party) often has important implications for a think tank. The think tank may have received important contracts from a ministry under the prior government, and the change could diminish the chances of obtaining future work. Equally important, such a changing of the guard may increase or decrease the senior staff's access to key decision makers. Similarly, whenever a major donor or another important source of work for the organization, such as the World Bank, announces a change in its program's direction, that news should be on this part of the meeting agenda. Other items might include announcement of a government austerity program that will likely mean deep cuts in ministry budgets for research and program evaluation, or a major competitor's decision to challenge the think tank on ground where the organization had long enjoyed a clear advantage.

Such information should serve as the basis for board members to contribute intelligence and discuss possible adjustments to the organization's plans.

This is also the place in the agenda for the president to seek guidance, if necessary, on sensitive issues, such as the balance between "opportunism" around policy or funding opportunities and "keeping to the core mission." When is a project too far outside the core work program and mission? Certainly a number of opportunities for consulting work, instead of policy research, fall into this category. Discussions of this type will be more fruitful if key information on the organization's financial situation is provided—especially the specter of an imminent funding shortfall may influence decisions of this type (see Chapter 9).

The final section of the agenda allows two or three senior researchers to present timely or important projects to the board, as described above. Priority goes to the one or two high priority areas that the president said last year would be reported on at this meeting. Immediately after the discussion of the priority report(s) could be a good time for the president to nominate the priority projects for the next year.

Normally, these presentations are crisp (no more than 15 minutes) and well-rehearsed presentations that inform the board of the organization's ongoing work.[95] A good rule of thumb is to allow as much time for discussion by the board as for the presentation itself; board members are senior people used to commanding attention and expressing their views. The president should select the presentation topics partly to capture the board's interest, but also to give board members information they can use in discussions with policymakers.

Distributing materials before the meeting. Any materials management sends to the board should be designed to make the upcoming meeting efficient and productive. Before each meeting, the board should receive background information on substantive agenda issues and information on procedural matters of legal or administrative importance (Charan 1998, 116). These materials should be carefully selected and concise. Sending out too much or poorly prepared materials will defeat the purpose of providing information in advance, because busy board members will not read them (Shultz 2001, chapter 9). Formats and presentations should be kept simple and inviting.

Box 7.5 is the table of contents for materials to send to members before a meeting, based largely on that of a Stage 3 think tank. Although the list is long, no more than about half an hour should be needed to review most of the materials. Many of these are provided only for the board's information and involve topics that will not be discussed at the board meeting unless a member raises a question. These include, for example, reports on personnel and communications and the annotated list of ongoing projects and outstanding proposals (or only the more important ones when the list reaches over 20 or so, with the titles of others listed in an annex). Financial statements and performance indicators are the major exception; they provide essential information for items that should definitely be discussed (see further below).

The background information I have noted as not suitable for the agenda is nonetheless important for the board to have. Consider the list of ongoing projects. If the board has delegated to the president the authority to decide which awards to accept, this list helps the board stay abreast of the institution's work. A board member reviewing the list might see a project on a topic he had thought was outside the work program as discussed with the board, or a project for a client about whom the member has some concern. More positively, a project of genuine interest to a member could be spotted and the member could, over time, become a useful agent for helping advance the

---

95   Charan (1998, 117) suggests using the following three questions as a guide in preparing presentations:

1. What are the two or three insights the board should get from this presentation?
2. What are the two or three issues on which the presenter might benefit from the board's insight?
3. What are the two or three points about which the presenter believes the board should be fully informed?

policy results. The project list affords the member the chance to express his interest.

At the Meeting. The most important part of the meeting—and the biggest block of time—should be devoted to reviewing the institution's performance in its research and policy endeavors and its plans and strategy for the future. For boards that meet once or twice a year, this must be the main topic. For those meeting more frequently, these two items should still dominate the meeting, unless a dramatic development between the semiannual meetings calls for consultation. At least once a year, the board should evaluate the institution's performance, principally in terms of the indicators agreed on with the president. It is the president's task to provide clear information on those indicators for the board's use.

The president's report on accomplishments, difficulties, and future prospects is designed to elicit board members' thoughtful commentary and an exchange of views. Not all members are equally equipped to discuss the "idea industry," but all were selected because they could contribute meaningfully to some aspect the institution's oversight. The task (and responsibility) of the president and board chair is to get the most out of the board.

In summary, most think tanks' decision making authority for the agenda appears to be sensibly divided between the board and senior management. The board exerts important influence (and may even have final authority) on the broad direction of the institution's program.[96] With the general directions set, the president, or in some cases a management council, has the authority to make decisions on individual projects. This authority extends both to projects funded by external grants or contracts and to the institution's own resources.

An already noted, another topic that always demands the board's full attention is the think tank's financial management—a point that can hardly be overemphasized. The board's review is usually centered around the auditor's annual report.[97] It is standard for the board chair and one or two other members to constitute a formal or informal "finance committee." After reviewing the audit report and management letter, the committee will typically be briefed by the auditor in private. The group then reviews the report in detail, discusses the findings, and comes to an agreement on action points prior to the full board meeting.

At the full meeting, the finance committee reviews the auditor's findings for the other members, and announces the committee's conclusions and proposed remedial actions for the president to

---

96   Even in this sphere, however, it is extremely unusual for individual board members or the board as a whole to press an initiative on senior management against its wishes. The board's power lies more in discouraging a new initiative about which it has reservations than in creating one.

97   In the absence of an audit, the board or a committee will have to review the financial statements with great care, and it should appoint a committee to check to ensure that basic controls are in place and are being used. If the board lacks expertise for these tasks, it should engage, at the think tank's expense, a consultant for the purpose and probably seek to add a board member with the required knowledge and expertise.

take where needed—for discussion and approval by the full board. If the audit has identified problems, the board will instruct the president, in writing, to make certain improvements by a stated time. Severe problems with fulfilling the board's requirements may call for more draconian board responses.

Between Meetings. There is general agreement that communication with board members between board meetings is highly desirable (Lips 2009, 7). Members who are reminded of their membership are more likely to work to the organization's benefit. These communications need not be elaborate. Indeed, many think tanks send each board member a physical copy of major new publications including policy briefs. This has a double purpose: it reminds the members of the think tank's work, and, if the publication deals with a policy topic of particular interest to a member, it can better prepare the member to participate in public debates.

In a few cases, think tank presidents send their boards an activities report between board meetings. These reports are typically quarterly letters for think tank boards that meet once or twice a year. Two formats are common. One is a fairly comprehensive report that may run to five or more pages—essentially a newsletter. The other is a shorter, more personal letter, written specifically for each member and signed by the president, with a few highlights of activities on topics in which that board member is known to have an interest.

Perhaps the most important lesson of all, as indicated above: it is imperative that the president inform the board about major problems or positive developments at the organization whenever such events occur. In some cases, the president might be well-advised to seek the counsel of at least the board chair in dealing with the change, whether crisis or windfall.

Operational Matters: Board Structure, Size, Meeting Frequency, New Members
This section covers several practical questions about the structure and composition of the board and the recruitment of new members. It includes discussions of board membership from the perspectives of the think tank and the person being recruited, how to go about identifying and recruiting strong members, and how to introduce new members to the organization and their duties.

Board Structure. A broad trend over the past couple of decades is for both corporate and nonprofit boards to be smaller and to have fewer committees. More work is being done by the full board, and a smaller full board encourages more open discussion and exchange. While the number of board members varies widely, eight to 10 members is viewed as effective; some boards total only five or six members, which reportedly promotes greater exchange among members—both during and outside the board meetings—as well as between the board and the president (Charan 1998, 40–41).

Some information on board size is presented in Table 7.2, based on data for think tanks participating in the TTI and for six Stage 3 U.S. think tanks. The mean board sizes in four of the six regions are in the seven to nine range. The largest among Latin American participant think tanks is 22 and among think tanks in India 24. East Africa favors somewhat larger boards—with a mean of 11 members and a maximum of 29. U.S. boards are the largest of all, with a mean of 17; the Brookings Institute is the largest among the six in this (non-representative) sample with 44 (!) members.

Table 7.2 Size of Boards of Trustees of TTI-48 Think Tanks by Region, 2010, and Six Major U.S. Think Tanks

Region	Mean number of board members
South Asia	9
Latin America	7
India	7
Western Africa	9
Eastern Africa	11
U.S.[a]	17

a. Think tanks included: Heritage Foundation, Cato Institute, Brookings Institution, American Enterprise Institute, Center for Strategic and International Studies, The Urban Institute.

Sources: For TTI data, Moncada and Mendizabal (2013a), U.S. Weidenbaum (2011) and author's website search.

Additional information on TTI-48 boards is given in Table 7.3, this time with the data organized to contrast Stage 1 and Stage 2 think tanks. Rather remarkably, one Stage 2 organization does not have a board. While there is little difference in the overall size of the boards between the two groups, fully one-third of Stage 1 think tanks have small boards (i.e., five or fewer members). Boards of smaller organizations meet about two times less often per year than their larger counterparts, with means of about four vs. six meetings per year. This is somewhat surprising because the executive directors of smaller, younger think tanks, who have fewer specialists in management positions, are thought by many to be more dependent on continuing advice from their boards.

Table 7.3 Characteristics of Boards of Trustees for TTI-48 Think Tanks, 2011

	TTI		
	<=10 FT Researchers	>10 FT Researchers	All
Percent with Board of Directors	100	97	98
Number of Board Members[a]			
1-5	33	17	23
6-10	44	34	38
11-20	17	41	32
More than 20	6	7	6
Mean	9.0	10.7	10.1
Number of Directors that Are Not Staff Members[a]			
0	6	14	11
1-5	33	14	21
6-10	50	38	43
More than 10	11	34	26
Mean	8.1	9.0	8.6
Board Meetings per Year			
0	6	0	2
1-5	78	69	72
6-10	6	17	13
More than 10	11	14	13
Mean	3.8	5.8	5.0
Number of Board Members Usually Attending Meetings,			
Percent answering 75% or higher	61	57	59
Number of think tanks	18	30	48

a. Percent distribution.

Based on studying the employment positions of think tanks' board members, think tanks tend to adopt one of two models in recruiting board members (see Table 7.4). These models are extreme cases; many hybrids exist, but the extreme cases are useful for this illustration.

Table 7.4 Occupations of Persons Recruited to Two Prototypical Boards of Trustees

"Distinguished persons" model	*"Expert advice" model*
• Former ministers, state governors, senior legislators • Renowned social-science academics • Captains of industry and finance • Senior members of the media • Leaders of prominent NGOs, including public interest groups and trade associations	• Former ministers, state governors, senior legislators • Senior members of the media • Leaders of prominent NGOs, including public interest groups and trade associations with interests aligned with those of the think tank

The "distinguished person" model emphasizes attracting prestigious individuals to enhance the institution's image. Of course, the key skills listed above must be present among the overall board. But if the board is larger (e.g., more than eight members), it may include members with a broad range of interests and backgrounds—such as industrialists, financiers, and businesspeople—that have no particular connection to the policymaking community. Although such boards may provide valuable perspectives and advice to the president, such diversity of members may also work against board coherence. In addition, with really large boards, most members will have little opportunity to express themselves during meetings.[98]

In the "expert advice" model, by contrast, the interests of members are more tightly aligned with the research and policy interests of the think tank. These boards are often smaller, to help keep discussions focused and to take maximum advantage of each member's input. Such boards are more likely to be able to give tailored advice to the president on the think tank's strategy and operations. This model is common and valuable among Stage 1 and early Stage 2 think tanks, where executive directors are often frequently seeking advice and guidance. Potential disadvantage are that: 1) boards of this type may become too assertive in giving direction and 2) members may represent a comparatively narrow range of backgrounds and experience.

Perhaps more important than the model chosen are the goals set for the board. The president and chair of the board must determine these. They should also understand that, if necessary, over time they can restructure the board to improve its effectiveness.

On the issue of board sub-committees, the era of nonprofits having a half dozen committees for

---

98   Based on his study of mostly Stage 3 U.S. think tanks, Andrew Selee (2013, 71) gives a strong endorsement to large boards: "Although historically many organizations have had a bias against large boards, there is actually no substitute for having a large and enthusiastic group of board members who are actively engaged with your organization's mission and can help tap resources—financial, political, legal and substantive—beyond the usual reach of staff." The key question is whether think tanks with these large boards can succeed in motivating members to be as active as Selee suggests.

various purposes seems to be a thing of the past. It is now common for nonprofit boards to have a single sub-committee, either an audit committee that concerns itself with financial management issues or an executive committee that deals with these and wider questions.[99] An effective executive committee can ensure that full board meetings are preserved for important issues. For example, the executive committee could be charged with carefully reviewing the audit report and meeting with the auditors; the committee could then summarize the results to the full board and make any necessary recommendations concerning the directions to be given to the president.

Of course, the board will sometimes need to appoint a committee for a particular function. One of the most common temporary committees is that appointed to search for a new president.

A final matter concerns the appointment of a board member as "Ombudsman," i.e., the person whom staff could contact confidentially in the event of wrongdoing on the part of the executive director or other sensitive issues the staffer does not feel safe discussing with management. Informing staff of the existence and function of the Ombudsman would be part of the standard onboarding function. Information on how to contact him/her would be among items in the personnel manual, copies of which are readily available to staff (see Chapter 8 on this). The board would work out and codify how the Ombudsman would proceed if s/he was alerted to a possible incident of misconduct. To my knowledge, designation of Ombudsman is not common but it may well be worthwhile. Selecting a long-serving board member for this post, with broad knowledge and experience with the institution and familiarity with some staff, seems sensible.

How Often to Meet. The vast majority of the boards of Stage 3 think tanks meet only twice a year. There are two reasons for meeting so infrequently. First, because participation as a board member is typically voluntary and unpaid, and because think tanks work hard to attract distinguished persons to serve as members, only a limited time commitment can be expected. Second, over the years, many of these organizations have developed well-established systems for ensuring financial control and research quality, so they require comparatively little board oversight of operations. The twice-a-year norm appears a reasonable standard for such organizations.

Many twice-a-year boards have an Executive Committee that meets quarterly to address matters needing attention before the next full board meeting. As a basis for deciding whether an Executive Committee is needed, the president and board chair can track how often board members are being contacted for input between regular semi-annual meetings to determine if more frequent scheduled

---

99   Alternatively, some boards appoint a treasurer who is assigned primary responsibility for financial oversight. A good treasurer can effectively investigate the reasons for anomalies in the financial reports. On the other hand, with responsibility assigned to a treasurer, other board members often believe they are re-lieved of responsibilities in this area. Moreover, treasurers are not all as diligent in the performance of their duties as is necessary, but the board has little way of knowing whether this is the case. For these reasons, keeping responsibility with the board, either through a committee or as a whole, is desirable (Robinson 2001, 78–80).

meetings with an Executive Committee would be more efficient.

Where the think tank has an internal management board and a separate advisory board, it may be sufficient for the board of directors to meet annually and to focus on the accomplishments of the institution or future direction of the overall program and to check on financial matters.

For younger and smaller institutions, quarterly board meetings may be advisable. The president and board chair could consider using each meeting to focus on a different aspect of the think tank's work and operations. For example, two meetings a year could focus on the most important issue, the institution's progress toward its goals and future directions; the meeting following completion of the audit report (the third meeting) could concentrate on financial management; and the fourth meeting could concentrate on other management issues on which the president wants the board's input. A regular agenda item for one of these meetings should be the division of responsibility between the board and the president: do the Executive Limitations need to be adjusted? When the necessity for comparatively intense board oversight diminishes, the shift to twice-a-year meetings is appropriate.

Recruiting New Members, Replacing Those Facing Term Limits. Even in the corporate world, boards consistently lack an effective process for selecting new members (Nadler 2004, 107). Nonprofits suffer a similar problem.

Boards are self-perpetuating: they select their own members, usually in close consultation with the president. The charters or board by-laws specify how long board members can serve, whether multiple terms are permitted, and the process for replacing them. It is fairly standard for a member to be appointed for a three- to five-year term, with the possibility of being reappointed once or twice. Some organizations make it possible for members to serve even longer by having a separate category of members, such as "life trustees" or "emeritus trustees" who can serve indefinitely. These members are in addition to the regularly appointed members and are less active. Regular members are normally replaced on a staggered basis so that a core of experienced members is always available.

A reasonable argument claims that if a board is working effectively, its composition should not be disturbed. But while the board may be comfortable with its current arrangement and works well with the institution's management, failing to introduce new members regularly is probably a mistake. New members may be the most likely to ask searching questions about performance or to recognize the need for a change in the think tank's agenda, or even of its president. The "life trustee" option allows the board to keep long-serving members as well as add fresh blood.

The following concentrates on whom to recruit. Annex 7.2 expands the discussion to cover what board members typically want to gain from serving on a board, tips on how to recruit new members, and ways to orient new members to the institute and their duties.

All boards seek to attract individuals with strong reputations in their respective fields. But what other qualities should these individuals bring?

To begin, here are a few simple rules on whom *not* to recruit.

- *No conflicts of interest.* A common mistake among think tanks is to ask the director or president of another think tank to serve as a board member. This is counterproductive, because think tanks often compete against one another for funding and in having leading roles in the same policy discussions. Board members have full access to the think tank's future development strategy. Giving such information to a potential competitor is bad business; it also places that board member in an untenable position.

- *No cronies.* Some boards consist largely of friends of the president or of other board members. This makes for enjoyable board meetings but poor management. The presence of cronies also creates the potential for factions to form within the board, complicating the board's oversight tasks and impeding productive discourse.

- *No serving elected officials or civil servants.* The main problem in this case is the appearance, if not the reality, of conflicts of interest. Even if the think tank has no contracts with the government body with whom the member is associated, there can be the expectation that such a member exerts pressure on the institution's behalf outside his own office and that, should the need arise, the institute would have special access to the official to lobby on policy matters in his ministry. A secondary problem is that the presence of such a figure will restrict discussions of anticipated government policy actions and the extent to which the think tank should participate in certain policy areas, because of the risk of offending the official.

- *No sponsors.* Board meetings are meant to be open fora where the institute's current business and future can be openly discussed. Common sense suggests that having a sponsor in the room will fundamentally change the content and type of discussion. I can readily imagine that sensitive business begins being conducted outside board meetings through executive committee meetings or less formal gatherings of a subset of members. It is possible that some sponsors will not understand this and be fairly insistent about participating. Do not give in.

I strongly subscribe to the "four no's" listed above and believe that violating any of them comes with significant negative consequences. That said, I understand that alternative traditions for board membership have evolved across countries. If one is in such a situation, try to minimize the number of board members who "come with baggage" and over time, as members are replaced, work to reduce their incidence among board members.

Each candidate for board membership should be an experienced professional with a strong reputation for integrity, creativity, and thoughtfulness. Beyond this, at least some members should have substantial interest in public policy development, social science research and evaluation, or corporate finance. At the same time, board members should not be "additional staff" in the words of Maureen O'Neil (2012), a former president of IDRC and a member of many boards. In other words, compose the board to bring perspectives to the institution's issues that are different from those of the institution's staff.

In addition, it is important to include someone with a background in working with the media or other form of communications as well as someone with a background in accounting and finance. Boards far too often lack media experience, which deprives the institution of this crucial perspective when new initiatives are discussed. An accounting and finance background is also advantageous to lead the review of audit results and related matters. If either of these skills is missing in the collective board, the board will have difficulty fulfilling all its responsibilities.

Board members should also be able to work well in groups and to be good colleagues: boards are not the place for the *enfant terrible*. One reason nearly all boards are responsible for nominating new members is that current members can vouch for collegiality in the candidates they nominate.

Finally, think tank leaders should at least consider asking a board candidate to make serving on the board one of his top three priorities among board memberships and other tasks beyond his regular job. Many of those best-suited to serve on a board already serve on several boards. Inevitably, serving on many boards reduces the attention one person can give to each. When such a person is recruited to an additional board, expect some missed board meetings and little attention to the institution between meetings. For this reason, asking a potential board member for service on the board to be a priority can send a strong signal about the president's and board chair's expectations. Better for a candidate to decline than to become a member and contribute little.

One more factor enters into the calculus of member selection: diversity. Most boards seek to maintain a diverse representation in terms of several factors, aside from members' professional backgrounds. Such diversity gives the board and president a broad range of viewpoints. The following quotations from CEOs recounted by (Shultz 2001, 128) illustrate this point:

- Any CEO who has 10 or 11 people just like him sitting around the board table will end up essentially talking to himself.

- You add water to water, you get water. It might be drinkable, but it's not joy juice.

- A group of people with the same background, the same experience, is going to come up with a predictable group of solutions to problems—not a good idea in the world we live in. Different points of view yield a wide approach to decision making.

The composition of the board also sends a message to potential sponsors and clients about the organization's philosophy and values. Some foundations may be sensitive to the board's profile.

First among the balancing requirements is political affiliation. Most think tanks strive to be known for producing objective policy recommendations, and few want to appear aligned with a political party. One way to signal nonpartisanship is to include members with various political affiliations on the board. A second balancing factor is gender: given the increasing prominence of women in public life, their inclusion in boards is essentially mandatory. The third is ethnic or regional representation. The specific type of balance in this case depends on local conditions. For example, boards composed exclusively of members from the nation's capital can give the think tank an insular image. Where a country has a few dominant ethnic groups, representing at least most groups through a board member is usually good policy.

Boards spend substantial time recruiting members. They must first determine the qualifications needed, as outline above. Plausible candidates are then vetted within the board. Finally, a candidate is selected and approached.

Assessing the Board

There is no question about the desirability of a board assessing its own work every few years. A penetrating, realistic look at the board's activities can catalyze steps to strengthen its stewardship. But it is a mistake for a board to begin such a process unless it understands the work involved and fully commits to completing it. Robinson (2001, 148–49) outlines the following elements in any serious self-assessment:

- Commitment of the full board to participate
- Committee or small group with an assignment to oversee the review and manage the results
- Clear timetable that specifies when the self-assessment questionnaire will be reviewed by the full board, distributed, and returned
- Time set aside during a regular board meeting or for a special meeting to review the results
- Action plan that addresses the weaknesses the board perceives in its role or structure
- Way to monitor whether the action plan is being realized.

A fairly standard procedure is for the board chair, with help from the president and perhaps certain board members, to prepare a questionnaire raising issues on the board's performance about which there is some concern. (Some typical issues are listed in Box 7.7.) Board members then provide responses, which are analyzed and a summary of responses prepared as the basis for a board discussion. Members can also table additional issues. The discussion may result in changes to the way the board operates.

A number of guides are available to help boards conduct a self-assessment.[100] In the end, whether the board designs its own process or follows someone else's guidelines, questions like those listed

---

100   See, for example, Slesinger (1995) and Holland and Blackmon (2000).

in Box 7.6 will need to be addressed.

Short of a full self-assessment, these questions offer a starting point for the board chair and the think tank's president to assess how well the board is discharging its duties. The board and the president can map out plans to address any obvious problems. The objective, regardless of whether the whole board is involved and whether the changes result from consultations between the chair and the president, is to maximize the contributions made by the talented people serving as board members.

POINTS FOR FOUNDING BOARDS

Boards of new think tanks usually differ from those of more established counterparts in important ways. How different depends significantly on the volume of resources—financial and soft capital in terms of sponsorship—available at launch. Some new think tanks enjoy substantial multiyear support from foundations, aid agencies, or even individual philanthropists, which permits them to start operations appearing quite similar to those of their longer operating counterparts. These new think tanks may well have a certain prestige and panache associated with their funding source that facilitates recruiting for the board of directors and affects the role expected of it.[101]

The comments here are addressed more to boards of think tanks typically being created with few resources by two to six researchers who see a clear need for a new institution to address public policy issues currently being neglected in the policy community. I address three features of founding boards of these nascent organizations that differ significantly from other boards.

Initial board members. Because the new think tank's only assets are its founders, the founders will be challenged to successfully recruit those who are not personally well known to them or who are not passionate about the primary issues the organization plans to address. Board members will also be hard to recruit because their work load will be substantial in the first two to three years as the think tank's structure and the workings and responsibilities of board and the institution are clarified.

Almost always these new boards are small, with three to five members who are strongly committed to the founders' or the think tank's goals. Small boards are useful at start up because of the numerous questions to be addressed and resolved. In recruiting members it is wise for the president and board chair to be clear about the greater-than-usual time commitment that will be involved in serving. Among those recruited, one priority is for someone with substantial business experience who can help address financial and administrative issues. Even with the challenges of recruiting members, the founders still are advised to follow the strictures on certain types of candidates for board membership listed earlier in this chapter. Within the various constraints, the aim is to recruit those

---

101   Broader advice on start-ups in provided in Mendizabal (2014b) and Gutbrod (2013a).

who are well-regarded and well-known in the policy community and beyond.

First tasks. Several fundamental decisions must be made at the outset. On the program side, the think tank's mission must be defined and codified; the president and board members need to be certain they have a common understanding about this. Closely related is to reach a common understanding of the policy research program's initial focus and how it might be broadened over the next two to three years. It is essential for the president to present a clear strategic vision, and justifications for it, to the board when seeking its approval.[102] Presumably there should also be a shared view that the new organization may have to be flexible in pursuing its agenda in the early years, taking on projects on lower priority topics to sustain operations.

On the procedural side, it is crucial to get the board's by-laws in place as well as basic versions of the "Delegation to the President" and similar documents described earlier in this chapter. This will take significant meeting time but will yield very large time savings in the next couple of years, as they provide a basis for deciding a wide range of issues that will come to the board.

How often to meet. The majority of unsponsored start-up think tanks are small, with a few full-time researchers supplemented with consultants and a small (one to two persons) full time administrative team that focuses on daily activities. Under these conditions, the board is often asked for advice on questions that are typically handled by senior administrators in larger think tanks. These fairly numerous issues are in addition to the usual board tasks of overseeing the effectiveness of the institution in the policy arena and monitoring financial management. This heavy workload usually makes bi-monthly or quarterly meetings essential.

Even with the relatively frequent meeting schedule, the president and the board chair must prepare well for each meeting in advance, with an agenda carefully considered and relevant documents distributed in advance, so members can arrive at the meetings ready to tackle the range of issues involved. It is essential to maintain these formalities to demonstrate the importance of the meetings to management and make them more efficient.

As the think tank grows and administrative management becomes more professional, the tasks brought to the board should diminish, as more questions can be resolved by the managers. This will only happen, however, if the president and board chair consciously take action to reduce the board's involvement in administrative issues. As suggested in the early parts of this chapter, this does not always happen; real discipline and team work between the president and board chair are required. As the board's work load and composition shifts, the number of meetings a year may well be reduced. Likewise as the institution grows and gains prestige, changes in the composition and size of the board will likely be appropriate.

---

102   A highly simplified strategic plan as described in Chapter 9 is strongly recommended.

TAKE AWAYS

Strong Practices

Characteristics of a well-managed think tank in this context follow.

- *Board composition.* Members are people of proven capability with a strong interest in public policy who collectively bring a range of perspectives to meetings. The board has a maximum of two scholars. Members include one or two with a background in accounting or finance; also included is someone active in the communications sphere. The board's composition should reflect the think tank nation's diversity.

- *Development strategy.* A basic development strategy is in place, prepared with board input.

The strategy can be in outline form but must be sufficient to signal the board and the institute about the think tank's objectives and general plans for the next few years.

- *Performance indicators.* Such indicators exist and are regularly reported to the board; acceptable indicators monitor major aspects of the strategy implementation as well as more routine developments at the institute.

- *Board meeting focus.* Board meetings focus on oversight and strategic issues, not getting bogged down in managerial detail.

The amount of time the board should spend on management questions legitimately varies with the institution's size and maturity; in all cases it should be a goal for board involvement to be minimized, only assisting the president in special cases where s/he believes s/he needs support.

- *Power distribution between president and board.* In addition to the by-laws governing board operations, it is often useful to have documents in place that state the powers delegated by the board to the president and the duties of the president to the board ("Communications and Support to the Board").

For Funders
Look carefully for:

- *Board size and composition.* It should be sufficiently large and its composition should ensure representation of diverse perspectives. It should include capacity in the key accounting and communications areas.

- *Meeting focus.* The meetings should focus on oversight and strategic issues. Check past agendas; they may suggest disproportionate attention to management questions.

Although the focus should be on large issues, sufficient information should be routinely provided to the board on operations and accomplishments (information that is not usually on meeting agendas).

- *Institutional Strategy.* The think tank should have a written up-to-date strategy, at least in outline form.

Perhaps to do:

Weak boards often have an array of issues, not a single problem. The president and the board chair will also typically be defensive about current practices when questioned. Consequently, board reform will be challenging. Exposure of the president and board chair to strong practices at another think tank in the region may be essential to convincing them that a different model will better serve the institution. If they are not convinced, defer further suggestions for change.

Transition from a weak to a stronger board will require a significant investment. One initiative could be developing a basic strategic plan and putting in place the corresponding system of indicators for management and board use in tracking institutional performance. This investment could be supported in part through an institutional development grant.

Box 7.1 Example of a Board of Directors' Mission Statement for a Think Tank

The Institute for Policy Studies will focus its activities to

- conduct policy research, program evaluations, and pilot projects at a high professional standard, with the objective of contributing the results of this work to the development of public policy

- effectively communicate the results of this work to policymakers and other interested parties, including nongovernmental organizations, political parties, and the public, in ways designed to influence the development of policy positively, and

- conduct seminars, workshops, and courses to contribute to the professional development of public officials, teachers, and researchers and analysts in the area of public policy design, implementation, and training.

Box 7.2 Examples of a "Delegation to the President" and a "Communication and Support for the Board" Statement Issued by a Board

Delegation to the President

All board authority delegated to the staff is delegated through the president. Therefore, all authority and accountability of staff—as far as the board is concerned—is considered the authority and accountability of the president.

As long as the president uses any reasonable interpretation of the board-approved mission statement for the organization and Executive Limitations policies, the president is authorized to establish all further policies, make all decisions, take all actions, establish all practices, and develop all activities.

- The board may change its mission statement and Executive Limitations policies, thereby shifting the boundary between the board's and the president's domains. By doing so, the board changes the latitude given to the president. So long as any particular delegation is in place, the board will respect and support the president's choices.

- Only decisions of the board acting as a body are binding on the president.

- Decisions or instructions of individual board members, officers, or committees are not binding on the president, except in rare circumstances when the board has specifically authorized such exercise of authority.

- In the case of board members or committees requesting information or assistance without board authorization, the president can refuse such requests that are disruptive or require—in the president's judgment—a material amount of staff time or funds.

Communication and Support to the Board

With respect to providing information and counsel to the board, the president may not permit the board to be uninformed. Accordingly, he or she may not

- neglect to submit monitoring information required by the board in a timely, accurate, and understandable fashion.

- let the board be unaware of relevant trends, anticipated negative media coverage, and material external and internal changes, particularly changes in assumptions on which previous board policies were based.

- fail to advise the board if, in the president's opinion, the board is not in compliance with its own policies.

- fail to marshal for the board as many staff and external points of view, issues, and options as needed for making fully informed board choices.

- fail to meet with the board as a whole except when (a) fulfilling individual requests for information or (b) responding to officers or committees duly charged by the board.

- fail to report an actual or anticipated noncompliance with any policy of the board in a timely manner.

Source: Author's edits to material from Carver (1997), chapter 5.

Box 7.3 Examples of Executive Limitations Issued by a Board to the President

Finance Management

With respect to operating in a sound and prudent fiscal manner, the president may not jeopardize the long-term financial strength of the institute. Accordingly, he or she may not:

- cause the institute to incur indebtedness other than short-term loans for routine expenses.

- use advances from the cash reserve fund other than for ordinary operating expenses.

- use restricted contributions for any purpose other than that required by the contribution.

- settle payroll and debts in other than a timely manner.

- allow expenditures to deviate materially from board-stated priorities.

- allow the cash reserve fund to fall below 6 percent of operating expenses.

- sign contract or grant agreements with a value exceeding $500,000 without the explicit approval of the board.

Asset Protection

The president shall not allow assets to be unprotected, inadequately maintained, or unnecessarily risked. Accordingly, the president shall not:

- fail to insure against theft and casualty losses to at least 80 percent of replacement value and against liability losses of board members, staff, or the organization itself in an amount greater than the average for similar organizations.

- allow uninsured personnel to handle funds.

- subject plant and equipment to improper wear and tear or insufficient maintenance.

- unnecessarily expose the organization to claims of liability.

- make any purchase or commit the organization to any expenditure of greater than $50,000. Make any purchase (a) wherein normally prudent protection has not been given against conflict of interest; (b) over $2,000 without having obtained comparative prices and quality.

- fail to protect intellectual property, information, and files from loss or significant damage or unauthorized duplication.

- receive, process, or disburse funds under controls that are insufficient to meet board-appointed auditor standards.

- invest or hold operating capital in insecure investments.

Staff Treatment

The president may not cause or allow conditions that are inhumane, unfair, or undignified. Accordingly, he or she may not:

- discriminate among employees in payment, assignments, or promotion except for reasons that are clearly job-related and have to do with individual performance or qualifications.

- fail to take reasonable steps to protect staff from unsafe or unhealthy conditions.

- withhold from staff a due-process grievance procedure, which should be able to be used without bias.

- fail to acquaint staff with their rights under this policy.

Source: Author's edits to material from Carver (1997), chapter 5.

Box 7.4 Typical Agenda for a Meeting of a Think Tank's Board of Directors

Call to order

Approve minutes of prior meeting

Board Chair's report

- Financial audit results

- Discussion of candidates for board membership

- Report on administrative matters, e.g., organization of the bi-annual assessment of the president's performance

President's report

- State of the institution and institutional performance [references performance indicators]

- Report on administrative matters, if needed

- Issues on which advice is sought

Presentations and discussion

- Progress reports on high priority initiatives

- Briefings on particularly important policy research findings

Box 7.5 Example of Materials Sent to Board of Trustees' Members before a Meeting

1. Agendas for the board meeting
2. Minutes of previous board meeting
3. Financial statements
4. Selected performance indicators
5. Board membership report
6. Funding report
7. Expenditures report
8. Communications report [The Institute in the media, publications, etc.]
9. Personnel report
10. Ongoing projects and submitted proposals [annotated list]
11. Information about trustees
12. Meeting dates for the next year
13. Short biographies of participating staff

Box 7.6 Moderating the Meeting

Two observations about boards at work that the president should keep in mind: first, boards typically work on what is in front of them—no issue is too great or too small; second, boards have no natural breaking mechanism, so they continue to act as they have in the past unless they are nudged off this track (Robinson 2001, 46). These observations should reinforce: 1) the president's central role in defining what comes before the board and 2) the joint role of the president and board chair in guiding the board's discussion to closure when the principal contributions on a topic have been made.[103]

Usually, the board chair runs the meeting. So it is a good idea for the president to meet with the chair prior to the meeting to be sure they agree on their objective for each item on the agenda.

Two pointers for conducting an effective meeting:

Make sure all members get a chance to contribute on significant issues. If some members hang back, the chair should ask one or another for his/her input.

Put everything on the table for all members. In other words, all information and opinions should be presented at the meeting of the full board. Individual board members should not be lobbying the president outside the board meetings; and important issues should not be reserved for a board committee simply because it is more in sympathy with the position of the president or board chair. In the long run, openness is definitely the best policy.

A final word of advice for the president. The information provided to the board at a meeting should meet an important standard: "No surprises." No board wants to be caught unawares or embarrassed by public disclosure of a problem or accomplishment about which board members should have known. If a significant problem threatens the think tank, one of its reports is receiving adverse press, or a major award is expected, the board should know in advance. Such developments, if known, can be reported at the meeting; otherwise as they emerge. A brief email is sufficient. Absent notification, the members will resent the president's decision to withhold the information, even if this is inadvertent. Such resentment can sow the seeds of larger problems. So keep the board informed of significant events—through board meetings or otherwise.

---

103   For a helpful general guide for running meetings, see Rowan (2004).

Box 7.7 Typical Issues and Questions Addressed in a Board Self-Assessment

- *Mission:* Is the mission statement used to guide decisions? Is it current?

- *Board composition and structure:* Is the talent the organization needs represented on the board? Does the committee structure function?

- *Board meetings:* Do meetings focus on the right issues? Does the board have the information it needs to make decisions? Is there adequate time for discussion and debate?

- *Board/staff relations:* Does the board respect the authority of the executive director? Is the evaluation of the executive director useful to the board and to the director?

- *Core activities:* Does the board sufficiently evaluate the think tank's effectiveness in the policy outcomes and in its policy engagement and communications?

- *Finances:* Does the board read and understand the financial reports?

- *Fund-raising:* Does the board understand the plan for resource development? Does the board understand its obligation to help raise funds?

CHAPTER 8
Internal Decision Making and Communications

Internal governance requires senior management to have in place two management practices: an effective decision making process and strong communication within the organization. These two broad operational tasks are central to executing the strategy development and project execution tasks that create an effective environment for research and policy engagement—topics that are treated in later chapters.

If the decision making process is impaired, a think tank's operations will likely be inefficient. Where the president and his key advisers consult insufficiently with other managers and staff, they may lack accurate facts on the actual situation and their policies may lack staff buy-in. Consider the case where the quality control procedures decided upon are highly elaborate and more time consuming than the president and his/her team had anticipated and know about, as they did not monitor implementation. It is almost inevitable that those procedures will soon not be followed as intended. The resulting "work arounds" could easily result in a weak vetting process and actual danger to the institution's reputation.

When information on performance and major decisions is shared, and the views of staff at all levels are taken into account in making decisions—particularly in such areas as benefits and working conditions— organizations run more effectively. A strong flow of information stimulates staff to align their work with new goals or think tank realities, such as when the organization is going through a period of tight finances. Generally, staff adjusts willingly if they: 1) are treated as adults in being kept informed and 2) believe the steps being taken are sensible.

Management guru Peter Drucker stresses this point:

> The most important *do* [among "dos" and "don'ts" for nonprofits] is to build an organization around information and communication instead of around hierarchy. Everybody should be expected to take information responsibility. Everyone needs to learn to ask two questions: What information do I need to do *my* job, from whom, when, how? And: What information do I owe others so that they can do *their* job, in what form and when? (1990, p.115)

In many Stage 1 and 2 think tanks, management believes that, because the head count is fairly small, information on important topics is generally known without management taking explicit action to make this the case. This might be called the "osmosis approach" to information management. The reality almost always is different. Information is power, and not everyone passes along what they know. More, where sharing is not an explicitly encouraged practice, many staffers are not sure what is OK to discuss and what is confidential. And so, for some, information stops with them. At bigger institutes, senior management usually does not embrace the osmosis approach, but it still may not act to ensure that staff is kept well informed.

Information really needs to flow easily and continuously among managers, from management to staff, and from staff to management. The staff-to-management side is the one most often overlooked, which can lead to spectacular misunderstandings. The following is a true story of the perils of not consulting staff that I witnessed:

> Twenty-five years ago, in an era when management sought staff input less systematically and energetically, the president of the Urban Institute took the decision that the think tank of about 250 staff in Washington, DC should relocate to acquire a larger space. The new property was in a semi-suburban area, whereas the current location was in the heart of the city; the new site carried a lower rent and had the advantage of near-by sports facilities. He, the senior vice-president, and the person responsible for administration devoted a great deal of time to finding such a suitable property. The president briefed the board on his plan and obtained its concurrence.

> Only then was the proposed move revealed to the staff. The vehicle was an all staff meeting, with a very large share of the staff jammed into the largest conference room. The president proudly announced his decision. And then all hell broke loose. Staffers were angry at not being consulted about a decision that was going to require major changes in their commute to work. Moreover, the selected semi-suburban location was viewed as: 1) too distant from the Institute's national government clients' offices (increasing the time to visit them and probably therefore the willingness to do so) and 2) creating the wrong image for the *Urban* Institute to flee central Washington. The president was stunned. Over the next week he backtracked. And the move was eventually canceled.

This chapter uses internal communication as its organizing device for discussing decision making and consistent adherence to operational policies and procedures. Such communication can take several forms: meetings among staff, messages or bulletins from management to staff, and a library of documents available to staff that explain the institution's policies and practices.

Basically, the internal communications system needs to provide an efficient flow of information and discussion at three levels:

1. the president with team leaders and the heads of administrative departments,
2. the team leaders and administrative heads with their staffs, and
3. less formally, among administrative staffs.

A special topic is to ensure research and communications staffs have a common understanding of the institution's policy engagement and communications strategy—and the corresponding procedures. Less formal interactions among all staff should be facilitated by senior managers organizing all staff social and work events.

DECISION MAKING AND COMMUNICATION AMONG KEY MANAGERS

Perhaps the greatest difference among think tanks' managerial arrangements is in the degree of formality. Many think tanks have a formally constituted executive committee, composed of key senior staff, that works closely with the president. Often, certain responsibilities are allocated to this committee rather than the president. The workings of the executive committee at the Center for the Implementation of Public Policy Promoting Equity and Growth (CIPPEC) in Argentina offers a strong example, as described in Case Study 8.1. The committee consists of the president and only a few other members and meets weekly for two hours. It takes major decisions on topics ranging from institution building to CIPPEC's external positioning. Decisions are made by vote, although this happens typically by consensus. Summaries of meeting results are sent to lower level managers, who share them with their staffs.

My experience in working with think tanks in various countries is that CIPPEC's model of "shared leadership" is common. But often, the relationship between the president and senior managers is less formal, with the president forming the type of advisory group that best meet his/her needs. A fairly standard model for regular consultation is for the president to meet with team leaders, the Communications Director, and administrative department heads, usually monthly, to discuss mostly administrative issues. (Development of the research agenda and marketing initiatives are handled separately.) Brown-bag lunches over the noon hour are a common venue. In this forum, the president sets the agenda and can discuss significant institution-wide issues with senior staff, although agenda topics can be suggested by others.[104]

Examples of such topics are:

- *The formula for allocating a block of funds among team leaders.* This refers to the institution's policy of giving team leaders a block of funds each year, which they use to pay for team members to attend conferences, have paid time to work on a journal article, and similar expenses.

---

104   Stage 3 think tanks I know that follow this model include the Urban Institute, R4D, and the Center for Global Development, all Washington-based, and the Institute for Urban Economics in Moscow.

- *Quality control.* Is the current system too resource intensive? Is it sufficiently effective?

- *Book publications.* The issue here is that the institution has cooperated with a larger think tank that has its own imprint (i.e., publishes books under its own name). The discussion is about how well this arrangement has worked, with background information provided by the communications director.

- *Salary increases.* In the fall of every year the size of the average percentage salary increase across the institution is discussed, taking into account information on inflation and what other think tanks did last year.

Meetings of the president with managers are more commonly discussions, rather than decision making sessions. The president makes the actual decisions, usually after further consultation with a few key managers whose responsibilities are directly involved. At the monthly meetings, team leaders and administrative department heads express their views, which are expected to be conditioned on what they have heard from and know about their staffs' views and actual circumstances (e.g., how burdensome a significant increase in the employee-paid insurance premium would be). Where staff views are key to a discussion, the president alerts managers at the prior meeting.

Occasionally, special committees are formed for a specific purpose and then are disbanded or lie dormant until needed again. Examples of the latter are the "salary review committee," which is active annually only for a few weeks, to manage the yearly decisions on salary increments for individual staff members; and the "benefits review committee," which every few years considers the whole package of staff benefits—particularly when adjustments are needed because of upward pressure on total research or aggregate costs, or they must compete with think tanks that have added new benefits. Generally, committees should be created sparingly. Each requires major time commitments for all assigned to them. For team leaders and administrative unit heads especially, this entails very high opportunity cost. Almost all matters can be handled at the monthly meetings with the president.

Lastly, the president is likely to set up informal groups to advise him/her on specific topics. These could be restricted to a few senior staff, or include lower level staff as well in cases where s/he wants to be certain to get input from this perspective.

Regardless of the exact form and practices of this high-level management committee, it is the body that oversees the development of internal policies and procedures. The number of such documents that must be developed and maintained by a think tank is surprisingly large; most observers seeing a list of documents—ranging from personnel to finance to communications—find the number stunning. And the committee spends a large share of its time discusses essential changes to existing policies and practices (as discussed later in this chapter).

Because many think tank leaders come from academia, it is worth contrasting the range of responsibilities of a think tank director with those of a university department head or dean. The greatest difference is that the think tank executive director must manage all the overhead functions—acquisition and maintenance of office space, computer systems, public relations operations, tax payments, and retaining legal counsel to deal with various issues, to name a few—whereas few of these tasks are the academic department head's concern. Similarly, most think tanks operate without any regular core funding and therefore must be constantly entrepreneurial in competing for funds. In contrast, academic departments have core funding for faculty and basic administration—although ambitious department chairs and deans raise money to supplement this funding base to be able to expand the department and attract stronger faculty members. At research universities, efforts are also made to garner funds for department-level research, and individual faculty members also seek grants to support their research.

Department heads in the social sciences faculty usually concentrate mainly on personnel issues—hiring and retaining strong faculty members, working hard to ensure the department receives its fair share of university services and resources, and in some cases, raising funds to improve the department's teaching and research. Executive directors of think tanks are, in addition, both running a business (with all the overhead operations) and responsible for their institutions having a positive impact on some areas of the country's public policy. Given the differences between managing an academic department and a think tank, academics becoming think tank directors would do well to embrace the idea that the academic management model has: 1) probably equipped them well in personnel management issues but 2) provided limited experience in confronting the much wider range of think tank responsibilities.

COMMUNICATIONS BETWEEN MANAGERS AND THEIR TEAMS

The monthly staff meeting, at the research team or administrative unit level or for all staff together, is a long-standing tradition within many think tanks because it has proven very valuable. While my focus is on the traditional staff meetings, senior managers may also want to consider other options that are used with some frequency. Organization-wide all staff meetings are almost standard procedure at Stage 1 organizations and common at mid-size ones, with staff counts of 50 or so, as well. Some schedule them more frequently. For example, the Center for the Study of Economies of the Africa in Nigeria finds weekly meetings effective.

Also, many Stage 2 and Stage 3 think tanks now prepare and distribute weekly or bi-weekly internal electronic newsletters to all staff—an easy way to keep people well informed of an institution's accomplishments, routine administrative changes, staff honors, and staff arrivals and departures. Some quite large think tanks with 30+ senior staff have monthly or bi-weekly senior staff meetings to both share information and promote a sense of community.[105]

---

105   The Center for Global Development has bi-weekly senior staff lunches, but they use this forum more like the first level meeting described in the text. They "provide a venue for updates on new and on-going projects, successes and failures in efforts to affect change, and, most important, informal discussion about what the Center should do and how we should do it. Housekeeping announcements, budget discus-

These meetings are really two-way streets. The team leader conveys information from the senior management meeting (described above), usually starting with the "state of the institution" (i.e., how the organization is doing on winning new business or major accomplishments in the policy arena). It is natural to follow this at research team meetings with a similar "state of the team" review—proposals submitted since the last meeting, proposals won and lost, proposals under way, and who the lead is on each. Personnel changes are another important topic, including positions for which candidates are being sought and the like. Many teams have found it useful to keep information on the status of all proposals in on-line spreadsheets that can be accessed by all team members. Other team members cover topics on work produced (outputs) and anticipated developments.

The team leader also uses this as the place to alert the team to the kind of issues being considered by the president and other senior managers. This is the golden opportunity to obtain feedback on matters still very much under discussion. Where the staff's views are really quite different from those voiced at the senior-level meeting with the president, or are quite strongly expressed, the team leader should alert the president. And, of course, this is the forum where the team leader can take care of housekeeping matters on team operations and vet new initiatives and the like. In moderating these meetings, team leaders should heed the advice I give about this in Chapter 5.

There is nothing novel in the system of meetings just outlined. The system has proven effective in sharing important information among think tank staff at all levels, leading to a sense of involvement in the institution's life. Critically, they keep senior management in real contact with the staff in all parts of the organization.

THE SPECIAL CASE OF COORDINATING COMMUNICATIONS ACTIVITIES

This section is about improving internal communication about an organization's priorities and methods for policy engagement. Greater knowledge of a think tank's priority audiences and communications channels, and building these priorities into policy engagement plans, will markedly increase the impact of external communications programs.

When doing assessments of individual think tanks' internal operations, I have often been surprised with the inconsistent responses I received from the head of communications, someone else on the communications team (if there was someone), the executive director, and two or three researchers, when I asked about: 1) the priority audiences for the institution's work, and 2) when the planning for policy engagement and communicating project results are addressed within a project's life cycle (e.g., when the project starts up, who is involved, and so forth). The responses not only differ; they are often highly inconsistent. Sometimes even the executive director and communications manager have different views.

---

sions, and other bureaucratic ephemera are handled by email or in small meetings." (MacDonald and Moss 2014, 6).

To reinforce the inconsistency point, Box 8.1 displays the results of consistency checks for a single think tank on three key elements of communications plans—two dealing with the process of preparing a project level strategy and one on the priority or target audiences for the institution's policy work. The information was collected in fall 2013 and is for an East African think tank. The executive director, three researchers, and the communications director were interviewed separately. Not all questions were asked of all respondent types. Similar information was collected for about a dozen think tanks in the region at about the same time. The results in the table are broadly representative.

The first question inquires about when work on the communications plan begins. The three researchers were unanimous in saying at the proposal writing stage. The communications manager, on the other hand, believed it starts when the research results are available. (Researcher #1 actually gave both responses, although he was asked to select one.) The responses suggest that the communications manager may not be involved in preparing communications plans included in proposals or even know about these earlier plans until s/he gets involved.

The second question asks about how the plan is developed. Here one researcher and the manager say there is a standard plan applied to almost all projects. The other two researchers give two different responses, one saying that not much planning is done, with the project team just following the funder's ideas.

The final question is about priority audiences. Respondents were to list audiences in order of importance. The executive director ranked first "persons who support the organization, many of whom are active in the policy arena." Researcher #3 and the communications manager also included this group, but put it last on their priority lists. The other two researchers omitted them completely. All three researchers and the communications manager put the Executive and Legislative branches and members at the top of the list; the executive director ranked them second. After that, other groups (e.g., CSOs, NGOs, the media) appear in essentially all lists. Only one respondent included donors on the list.

If we take the results of these three questions together, they suggest significant differences among key staff about communications priorities and how communications plans are developed. This and similar evidence indicates that a number of think tanks are failing to promulgate their communication strategies effectively internally. In some cases it may be because the executive director has never made reviewing the communications strategy the central topic of a "president with team leaders and administrative department heads" meeting. Or, such a meeting may have occurred when the institutional-level communications strategy was developed a few years ago but not addressed since, even though there has been significant manager turnover. In some cases, the president/senior managers meeting may have been successful, but the team leaders failed to convey the central messages to their teams.

Whatever the case, every think tank needs staff to work together on PEC to make it maximally effective. My view is that the burden is appropriately placed on the communications director, with the executive director's public support. The communications director should be proactive in both briefing every team on the institution's general PEC strategy and the procedures for its implementation. This should be complemented by the communications director meeting at the beginning of every project with the team leader and the principal analyst (and the executive director if s/he wishes to be involved) to develop the detailed strategy for the specific project. If a communications plan is being included in a project's proposal, the communications director should be an active participant in shaping the proposal's content in this area, to ensure the organization's policies and priorities are being followed. (S/he may also inject new ideas into the planning process.) After a couple instances of hands-on help from the communications director with project strategy development, the principles being followed will be fully understood by the team. The communications director should, however, continue to work with teams on the strategy for each new project, so s/he has a full understanding of the plan's objectives and can contribute to defining implementation methods.

THE POLICY AND PROCEDURES LIBRARY: AN ESSENTIAL MANAGEMENT TOOL

The ready availability of information on policies and procedures provides both transparency and ready answers to a very large share of questions that occur to staff, thereby helping ensure operational consistency and saving large amounts of managers' time that would otherwise be devoted to responding to queries. The library serves as a very important supplement to both briefings to orient new staff and announcements to all staff of changes in policies or procedures.

Developing a comprehensive set of policy and procedure documents is a massive, labor intensive task; and one that most think tanks succeed in accomplishing only after many years of existence. In reality it is forever a work in progress. Often a policy or procedure is formalized only when absolutely necessary, and usually with no overall road map to guide the process.

Nearly as important as producing the policies and procedures is making certain they are widely promulgated. The preferred solution is to have them on line and accessible only to institute staff in a digital special folder. There is a variety of "cloud-based," easy to access storage facilities that could be used to make these documents readily available to staff. Table 8.1 outlines some of the more prominent options. Where use of cloud options or an intranet is not possible or preferred, loose-leaf binders can be used. Several copies need to be placed around the institute so staff can readily see and consult them and do so with some privacy, i.e., without having to visit an administrator's office.

Table 8.1 Options for Sharing Documents Offsite

Several technologies exist to help you store and share documents. These include:

Tool	Pros	Cons
Dropbox	• Easy, fast and intuitive to use—loads as a folder onto desktop and mobile devices and lets you drag-and-drop (allows offline editing) • Effortless synchronization of files • "History" feature allows users to access previous versions of files • Operates without central home at institution • Uses encryption security and allows you to specify which files are private or public	• Base free plan has two GB of storage • Expensive for higher storage • Doesn't easily allow "live collaborating"—you cannot see what changes are being made in real time; changes only noticeable with tracked changes
Google Drive	• Cheaper than Dropbox • Base free plan has five GB of storage • Links to all Google Accounts (Google Docs, Picasa, etc.) • Loads as a folder onto desktop and mobile devices and lets you drag-and-drop • Allows you to see real-time changes being made and to chat with another person as you are making changes	• Not intuitive to use • Mobile experience not good • Offline editing not supported well • Documents often appear with extensions like .gdoc which make them susceptible to opening up in web browser
Microsoft OneDrive	• Base free plan has seven GB of storage • Easy to still use and set up with Hotmail/Outlook mail • Allows offline editing	• Not intuitive to use • More difficult to share files compared to dropbox or Google drive
Box	• Base free plan has 10 GB of storage	• Limitations to file size that can be uploaded • Does not load onto desktop and therefore is web-based only
Amazon Cloud Drive	• Base free plan has five GB of storage	• Not available on mobile devices • No sharing, external linking, or synchronization. Just acts as an external hard drive • Limitations to file size that can be uploaded

Case study 8.2 describes the development and content of CIPPEC's "White Book," which is designed to be a comprehensive set of policy and procedure documents. In addition to covering the array of strictly administrative topics, it includes policy and procedures on CIPPEC's strategic vision, funding sources, and project impact monitoring and evaluation. The summary table of contents (in Annex 8.1) for the White Book is valuable by itself.

TAKE AWAYS

Strong Practices
Characteristics of a well-managed think tank in this context follow.

- Decision making on institutional-level issues is shared among the president and senior managers with an array of responsibilities, to ensure that various viewpoints are considered.

- Critical policy and procedure (P&P) statements are in place and readily available to staff. These include key personnel documents (cited in Chapters 2 and 3 and related annexes), documents on financial management (ranging from practice to prevent fraud to directions on filing travel expenses), quality control policy and procedures, and similar documents.

- An overall list of P&P statements needed by the institution exists and priorities are assigned, so administrative office leaders can efficiently identify which they can next develop when they have the chance to do so.

- Communication within the organization is strong, with the president consulting regularly with senior managers and they, in turn, with their staffs. Upward feedback is relayed regularly at senior manager meetings.

For Funders
Look carefully for:

- Is management shared? Sharing decisions increases staff buy-in to decisions made and institutional ownership by all involved. If sharing is the putative rule, is the process formal or informal? Are meetings among the relevant participants held regularly?

- *P&P statements.* Check the presence of and spot check those P&P statements covering practices to protect your interests as a funder. Foremost are those governing the handling of funds and quality control of various products.

- *P&P statements in areas you may be considering helping the institution improve.* Review P&P statements for the management area of interest to you. Examples are those dealing with staff utilization information (investment in time sheet system) and HR P&P statements on the annual staff review system and performance incentives (investment in staff development).

Perhaps to do:

- To lower the costs of preparing written P&P statements, consider encouraging think tank directors and administrative office leaders to share their development policy and procedures statements with their colleagues at other think tanks, especially when they meet at conferences or less formal meetings to discuss management issues.

- A highly motivated donor or group of donors could commission someone to develop a library of policy and procedure documents covering the full range of management tasks by assembling, reviewing, selecting, and posting statements contributed by think tanks. The library would be on-line and accessible to all, with all documents downloadable in Word format to facilitate their use, adjustments as needed, and adoption.

Box 8.1 Example of Lack of Consistency within a Think Tank on Policy Engagement and Communications Priorities

The tables below show the responses to questions on communications practices within the organization. The executive director, communications manager, and several researchers were asked separately for their views.

When do you develop a communications plan for a project? *Give only one response.*

Responses	Rsch1	Rsch2	Rsch3	Comm
During the proposal writing stage	X	X	X	
At the beginning of the research project				
When we have the research results	X			X
It varies and evolves during the life of the project				
Not much planning is done; we follow what the client wants				

How do you develop the communications plan? *Give only one response.*

Responses	Rsch1	Rsch2	Rsch3	Comm
We have a standard communications plan applied to almost all projects	X			X
We have a package of several communications plans we use, and pick the one that best		X		
We develop a new communications plan for each project				
Not much planning done; we follow what the client wants			X	

What are your think tank's main target groups (by organization type or player and <u>in order of priority</u>)? *(Please add as many as necessary)*:

Target group	Executive Director	Researcher 1	Researcher 2	Researcher 3	Communications Manager
1.	Persons who support the organization; many are active in policy arena	Executive, legislative branches	Executive, legislative branches	Executive branch	Executive, legislative branches
2.	Executive, legislative branches	Civil society, NGOs	Public and media	Parliament	Other think tanks
3.	Media, general public	Media	NGOs, CSOs	Media	CSOs, NGOs
4.	Other think tanks, CSOs	Donors	Private sector	Public	Media
5.				Persons who support the organization	Persons who support the organization

Case Study 8.1 Bodies for internal governance: CIPPEC's Executive Committee

The Center for the Implementation of Public Policies promoting Equity and Growth (CIPPEC) was founded in 2001. Over time, as the organization grew and became more complex in terms of structure and decision making processes, its leaders saw the necessity of designing mechanisms to mitigate the personalization of decision-making. Thus, different governance bodies were built. Most of these bodies' responsibilities are described in CIPPEC's White Book, a volume that documents and formalizes the different internal management processes. (See Case Study 8.2)

Among these internal bodies, one stands out because of its influence on the organization's strategic institutional decisions: the Executive Committee (EC) is responsible for discussing and deciding on strategic institutional issues. On the one hand, it contributes to CIPPEC's external mission, as it pursues a successful corporate strategy to enhance the impact of research on public policy, which is the organization's *raison d'etre*. On the other, it has to deal with strategic internal issues, which include:

- **Institution building.** The EC defines the strategic and operational guidelines of the organization for the implementation of its activities throughout the year; it defines, implements, and evaluates the Annual Work Plan and Budget; and it overseas the work of CIPPEC's different areas to ensure they fulfill their respective objectives.
- **Proposals and projects.** On the one hand, the EC is in charge of allocating proposal preparation to the different policy research areas, based on the proposal's subject alignment with their work, potential complementary of work among different areas, and economic opportunities. On the other hand, the EC is responsible for ensuring institutional, political, and economic/financial suitability of proposals: alignment of projects with institutional strategic agenda, feasibility of implementation and challenges that may arise in the fulfillment of commitments with third parties, economic viability, and impacts on institutional positioning, among other issues. Finally, the EC reviews and enriches the contents of proposals, seeking the highest possible technical standard.
- **Organization policies.** The EC debates and decides on career paths and promotions of staff, schemes for salary increases, allocation and support for scholarships, creation of new research areas within the organization, among others topics. Moreover, the EC is one of the

primary channels for analyzing and dealing with the Administrative Board's requests and decisions.[106]

- **Institution positioning.** The EC decides on and safeguards CIPPEC's reputation when facing high public visibility projects or situations (for instance, when it receives the invitation by other peer organizations to be part of a campaign for or against a certain decision of the government).

Structure and Activities

The EC is composed by three permanent members: the Executive Director, the Communications Director and the Institutional Development (*fund raising*) Director, and three drawn from among the directors of the policy research areas (two of them serve annual terms and one rotates every six months). In addition, the Director of Administration and Project Management may be asked to participate whenever the body discusses legal, budgetary, administrative management, and human resource issues.

This multidisciplinary composition provides the EC with two advantages: 1) it promotes inter-sectorial public policy approaches for the analysis of different projects (especially because the three policy research areas' directors belong to the Social, Economic, and Institutional areas); 2) it ensures the representation of different expertise and knowledge of CIPPEC's strategic and daily work and challenges. In this way, the EC not only enriches the organization's work with different viewpoints, but also ensures the representation of different interests that coexist within the institution.

The Executive Director proposes the agenda for weekly meetings, although other members can suggest topics for discussion. Decisions within the EC are taken by simple majority. However, in the practice, most of the time decisions are by consensus. During meetings, an assistant takes the minutes and subsequently sends a summary to all CIPPEC's directors[107] on the issues discussed.

---

106   The Administrative Board is the highest governance body of the institution, and it is headed by the President of the organization

107   CIPPEC's structure is composed of different areas and programs. Areas are dedicated to institutional issues: Executive Direction, Administration and Project Management, Institutional Development (fund raising), and Communication. Programs are dedicated to research on different policy issues: Education, Health, Social Protection, Economic Devel-

Every week, the Executive Director notifies by email the decisions made by the EC to the body of Directors and Principal Investigators. So the EC is the venue where decisions are made and legitimacy built.

Challenges

Even though the EC is today an effective management vehicle within the organization, some challenges were faced until it reached the deliberative and decision-making effectiveness that was its goal. For instance, in the beginning, the EC served more as a space of legitimation than of deliberation, because its members simply approved decisions they supposed were previously taken by the Executive Director. Over time, as the EC started to be recognized as the main deliberation space within the organization and there was a better understanding of the roles expected for members, another problem emerged: the EC became increasingly transactional, and everything, even relatively minor issues, had to be discussed. It took time to reach the best balance between excessive deliberation and consensus building to enable the proper working of the Committee.

In addition, EC weekly meetings started being seen as a barrier whenever an urgent decision was required e.g., the decision of whether to submit a proposal with a short preparation period. Thus, a more effective mechanism by which the EC was virtually always called to approve or reject a project was created. With this new mechanism, the EC combines a certain rigidity in terms of deliberative routine with flexible mechanisms to speed up the decision making process before situations that require it.

Going Forward

We anticipate that the EC will continue to evolve, although CIPPEC is satisfied with it being a central element of the institution's management. One remaining challenge is related to an intrinsic characteristic of the EC: given its composition and CIPPEC's institutional design, it often happens that members of the EC represent

and defend the interests of the areas they represent, thus generating some kind of corporatization of discussions. The voting mechanism aims to ensure decisions are as objective as possible. However, the proper understanding of the spirit of the EC, as a deliberative space aiming at building consensus, requires that its members understand the privileged position they hold within the institutional structure.

Leandro Echt and Fernando Straface
Center for the Implementation of Public Policies
Promoting Equity and Growth

Buenos Aires, Argentina

opment, Justice, Public Management, Institutions, Local Development, and Influence, Monitoring and Evaluation. Each area and program is led by a Director. The entire body of Directors meets weekly to discuss institutional or political agenda issues.

Case Study 8.2 White Book: An Institutional Investment to Organize and Document Policies and Practices

The Center for the Implementation of Public Policies promoting Equity and Growth (CIPPEC) was founded in 2001. Over time, it grew and became more complex in terms of structure and internal processes. During this process, new situations emerged almost weekly, and while they were individually addressed, the underlying concern was: "Which should be the policy that rules this issue?" Over the years many policies were defined and a body of them accumulated. Thus, the Administrative Board, the highest governance body of the institution, agreed on the need to organize, document, and formalize different organizational processes and practices in a single, comprehensive collection: the White Book. Getting to the decision was a long and arduous process involving different members of the organization and many internal discussions over several years. A substantial institutional investment was required in reviewing processes and practices and systematizing them in the document.

The White Book was initiated under the former Executive Director, who left CIPPEC in 2009. The first draft took so long that when it was ready almost all the processes had already undergone changes. The current Executive Director has continued with the Book's development, updating and consolidating the new version. The first decision was to assign the responsibility for leading its preparation to a specific person who worked closely with the Executive Committee, the body responsible for deciding on strategic institutional issues that ensure the efficient functioning of the organization during that building process.[108] Once the draft Book was ready, some key members of the organization were tasked with thoroughly reviewing one or two chapters and making suggestions for improvements

The White Book
The result is a book organized into 10 chapters, each of which is dedicated to a particular topic. Some of these are: CIPPEC's strategic vision; governance bodies; code of ethics; process for approval; monitoring and evaluation of projects; funding sources and institutional linkage; administration and finance; human resources; and, communications and technology. (The table of contents is in Annex 8.1.)

The White Book serves two main purposes. On the one hand, from a conceptual perspective, it makes explicit

the type of institution CIPPEC wants to be: it reflects its institutional profile by defining a set of policies that structure the organization's work routine. For instance, the White Book states that funds coming from projects supported by Argentine governments cannot exceed 30 percent of the organization's budget, in order to protect its independence.

On the other hand, from a political point of view, the White Book lightens the weight or political cost of making certain decisions. It defines certain policies that otherwise would be subject to individual interpretation. For example, the White Book states that CIPPEC does not endorse any politician or business. So every time CIPPEC is requested to support a stakeholder in his/her public objectives, it is not the Executive Director who needs to reject it: it is institutional policy that does not allow this practice. Moreover, the White Book serves as a background for discussions within the Executive Committee, who meets weekly to decide on strategic institutional issues.

The White Book is for internal use only. Every member of the staff has access to the Book, which is available at CIPPEC's intranet (a virtual space where important institutional information is available for the staff). Moreover, the White Book states that each member has the responsibility to know, respect, and enrich the contents of the Book in order to strengthen the institution and create an environment of conviviality

A Living Document
Important to highlight is that the White Book is a "living" tool: it was built (and continues to be built) from the practices and the different cases the institution has faced daily. This "Common Law" approach gives the organization the possibility of being flexible when change in a certain policy is needed. Every time the Executive Committee identifies the need for a new policy or the necessity of updating an existing one, a formal process is initiated, and the final decision requires the approval of its members. Once the decision is made, the new policy is communicated by the Executive Director to the Directors of the different areas and to the staff by the internal newsletter. Beyond these specific cases, CIPPEC's policy, enunciated in the White Book, suggests a comprehensive annual review of its policies.

An example illustrates how a new policy emerged in a situation when a very important donor asked for a greater

---

108   The Executive Committee is described in Case Study 8.1.

visibility in one of CIPPEC's publications: in particular, it wanted its name to appear on the cover of a book, while the other donors appeared inside. While an appropriate response was given to the donor, the organization generated a new policy ruling on this issue. A similar process took place when the organization identified the need for a publications policy that clearly states which members of the staff were allowed to sign documents or articles in the media.

Being continuously updated, the White Book reaches a very suitable balance between stability and flexibility of policies. While the flexibility gives the book the possibility of being a useful tool over the years, a certain stability generates a favorable environment for discussion when someone identifies the possible need to change a policy or generate a new one.

Because the White Book compiles different kinds of policies, which have different degrees of importance for CIPPEC's mission and performance, different levels of authority are required to make the decision on changes. For instance, those issues related to the institution design require the Administrative Board's approval to be changed. Other issues require the Executive Director's decision and others the Executive Committee approval.

Challenges
As mentioned, developing the White Book was a long and arduous process. Along the way many challenges arose. The main one was the difficulty of reaching the final version, as daily organizational commitments postponed focusing on the Book. In fact, while the final version of the White Book is ready, it still needs to be presented to the Administrative Board for final approval.

Another challenge during the process was defining whether the White Book should be a compendium of key institutional policies that reflect CIPPEC's spirit or a handbook of processes. That dilemma has not yet been fully resolved. The result is a document that addresses not only strategic institutional definitions, but also minor operational issues within specific functional areas.

On another note, there is a need to establish certain content and writing guidelines applicable to all chapters. The current version contains chapters that have very different levels of detail, tone, and structure.

Regarding the White Book's effectiveness, a main challenge concerns its usefulness for the staff. The organization still needs to reflect on an internal communication strategy to ensure knowledge of the Book's contents by each staff member and for it to actually serve as an effective tool for their consultations and daily situations. For instance, the White Book could serve as a primary orientation vehicle for any new member of the staff.

Benefits
The White Book is an important tool for institutional building. Investing time in producing the document provides the organization some advantages: it captures, retains, and makes available over time the institutional memory of an organization with over 13 years of life and a high level of staff turnover; it is a guide for CIPPEC's daily operations, but it also supports our strategic development decisions; it clearly assigns responsibilities to different bodies and positions within the institution; and, it prevents decisions from being the result of individual interpretation, thus promoting objective judgments for sensitive issues.

Leandro Echt and Fernando Straface
Center for the Implementation of Public Policies
Promoting Equity and Growth
Buenos Aires, Argentina

SETTING THE AGENDA

CHAPTER 9
Building a Strategy, Deciding on Innovations

Think tanks, probably more than other types of NGOs, need to renew their agendas fairly frequently for at least three reasons:

- Ensure their work remains relevant to their nation's evolving policy agenda,

- Identify and pursue work on subjects that are not yet a priority for the government or parliament but are or could well become important, and

- Sustain staff retention and morale, by giving key staff the chance to change the focus of their research and policy analysis.

Many of a think tank's agenda adjustments are incremental-to-moderate shifts, but some are major. These larger ones often entail a certain degree of risk and expense and, therefore, need to be especially thoughtfully considered.

Identifying and adopting innovations in a work program often comes about through *strategic planning* (defined below). In its fully developed form, strategic planning yields a formal written product. Developing the plan involves: 1) considering the relevance of the organization's mission statement in light of its current situation and the policy environment and 2) systematically deciding on its new work program. The term I use for significant new directions in an organization's work program is *innovations*. These include new research topics but also major shifts in the type of work carried out—to include, for example, implementing demonstrations of new government programs, taking policy research assignments from governments (when this was not done previously), and launching sizable education programs.[109]

Preparation of a formal strategic plan can certainly be useful and such a plan should be in place. At the same time, it must be flexible—i.e., amenable to fairly rapid adjustments as needed. This chapter concentrates on identifying and assessing new opportunities for a think tank, which can be

---

109   Rochlin and Radovich (2013) list several commonly used definitions of innovation. "Some in the development field use the *Economist* definition: 'new products, business processes or organic changes that create wealth or social welfare,' or 'the fresh thinking that creates value.' Monitor's definition is based on innovation management and is 'about creating and capturing new value in new ways—through products, services, new processes, or business models, new technologies or applications" (p. 200). They also list definitions and examples of four types of innovation: product, process, market, and organizational on p.221.

a key part of a strategy. I favor a comparatively simple strategy development process, because the requirements of preparing a detailed formal strategy can create a high barrier to innovation. Better than developing an elaborate plan and plan document is to spend the limited available resources on generating and assessing ideas for new products the think tank might offer, new clients for some types of analysis or evaluation, or new audiences for its policy findings.

This chapter opens with development of a strategic plan. In some instances, consideration of significant restructuring or mergers with other organizations is part of the process. In the second section I present the limited information I have found on actual think tank practices in strategy development. Information is given both on strategic planning at TTI-48 think tanks and on the implementation of eight innovations, all but one involving ventures other than entering a new research area. This section contains a case study from an Estonian think tank commissioned for this book and an overview of several other Eastern European think tanks' innovations of different types—how they were identified, assessed, and launched; what problems were encountered in the process; and their success.

The next section presents lessons distilled on encouraging innovation in for-profit and nonprofit organizations, which I have refocused for think tanks. The process for encouraging, launching, and assessing innovations is discussed in some detail. As always, "Strong Practices" and "For Funders" conclude the chapter.

THE STRATEGIC PLAN

Most planning exercises focus on expanding into a new policy area, deepening the commitment to an existing one, or acquiring additional clients (both funders and policy clients). The first part of this section explores the development of strategic plans. The second looks briefly at organizational restructuring and merging policy analysis–oriented organizations with other entities. The third discusses development of the institution-level communications plan that complements the strategic plan.

Plan Options

A strategy or strategic plan for a think tank is a coordinated set of actions aimed at creating and sustaining a competitive advantage in carrying out its policy research, policy engagement and communications, and possible other missions. It estimates resource requirements and identifies probable sources of funds.

Andrew Selee (2013a) points out that strategic plans in one way or another need to address five questions. His book's five chapters address each in turn:

1. What does the organization want to achieve? (Its mission)
2. What does the organization do that makes a unique contribution?

3. Who are the organization's key audiences and how does it reach them?
4. What resources does the organization need and how can it develop them?
5. How does the organization evaluate impact and learn from experience?

The first question is fundamental, and the broad answer typically does not shift much from year to year. Therefore, most planning focuses on the other questions. When the mission must be addressed because a change in the institution's mission is afoot, the board must contribute its views from the outset. When the mission is being held constant, strategic planning can go ahead at the staff level, with the board consulted as outlined in Chapter 7.

Several options are available for how developed a strategic plan can be. Some think tanks have a fully developed formal strategy, some have a simplified version—and many have no stated strategy whatsoever, but rely on implicit and oral understandings among an organization's leaders and its board. There are advantages and disadvantages to each approach.

My sense, from discussions with leaders of Stage 3 think tanks, is that many have no written strategy but function with an implicit strategy that enjoys often tacit board endorsement. These organizations believe this informal approach meets their needs. In the past few years I have worked closely with a Stage 1 and a Stage 2 think tank in transition countries that also operate effectively in this way. A couple of examples from U.S. Stage 3 think tanks are illustrative: the Center for Global Development has stated its belief that it does not need a strategy; and, the Urban Institute, founded in 1968, did not seriously consider a strategic plan until 2012.[110]

The option most discussed in the literature is the formal strategy, often developed with consultant assistance; this yields a substantial document. A number of "how to" guides argue for this approach. (See, for example, Allison and Kave, 2005.) It can have the advantage of educating participants during its development about the organization and the market in which it operates; drawing insights and creative planning from staff, board, and consultant participants; and providing thorough documentation of current practices and a detailed plan for future management.[111] But this option has two disadvantages: it requires an organization to devote significant time and other resources, including those of the board, to its development; and, once completed, it is unlikely to be modified for several years.

---

110   CGD's thinking is worth quoting. "…we deliberately don't 'plan' upstream beyond encouraging senior staff members to articulate their major areas of work and expected outputs so that we can match them with funding. Using research to affect policy decisions and development outcomes is rarely linear, and opportunities for impacts almost always hard to predict. Our strategy, so to speak, is to be ready to react to the sudden appearance of a policy window by having a good stock of well-researched ideas and providing our fellows with space to respond." MacDonald and Moss (2014), p.7.
111   Selee (2013a, 17-20) describes such a process undertaken by the Chicago Council on Global Affairs in 2001.

Some have argued, particularly in the past few years, for a simpler strategy and strategy development process for think tanks that requires fewer resources to create and is more amenable to change in light of developments in the policy or political environment. A powerful argument for this approach is that many think tanks operate in environments where significant changes are common (think of major policy interest shifts with the election of a new government), in which case the strategic plan may require corresponding adjustments.[112] The more elaborate the task of plan preparation, the more daunting making formal changes to it will appear—and the less likely the chance of their being made. At the same time, a strategy that is more an outline than a fully developed text and detailed plan has the advantage over the unwritten "implicit strategy" of being a concrete document that helps ensure a common understanding among the staff and between management and the board. It also trumps the formal strategy in being more flexible. My own preference is for this "indicative" or "outline" strategy.

Implementing the Indicative Approach

For organizations that have a research team rather than a "solo star" organization of their research operation (see Chapter 3), I recommend the indicative approach—a kind of bottom-up approach. For some think tanks this less resource intensive approach is a necessity. Weyrauch et al., for example, report that some think tanks they worked with in developing and implementing strong M&E plans for assessing policy influence were unable to pursue the plans because of resource limitations (2013b, 32).

Team leader tasks. Under the indicative approach, each team leader can be tasked to work with his/her team to draft a strategy in outline format for the team's program (e.g., health policy, housing sector reform, or international trade policy). Team leaders as a routine matter should be highly informed about trends in their policy area, likely government initiatives, what the competition is doing, and the trend in funders' interests in the area. It is essential for this exercise that the team leaders discuss potential future sectorial developments and their program's evolving research agenda with potential research users and sponsors, at least at this time if not on a more regular basis. The following, paraphrased from the Politics and Ideas blog (2013a) is instructive:

> The context for the team leaders' agenda definition task is that, in general, the topics pursued depend substantially on two sets of factors: 1) internal factors, including an organization's mission and origins, funding model, particular researchers' interests and experience; and its values, beliefs, and ideology; and 2) external factors, including the historical, political, and cultural context

---

112   Two guides to managing innovation in nonprofit organizations make the same decision, i.e., they do not cover how to prepare a strategic plan: Light (1998) and Dees, Emerson, and Economy (2001). See Bryson (1995) and Covello and Hazelgren (1995) on the preparation of the standard strategic plan. Mendizabal (2013b) argues for a simple plan.

in which the organization operates, windows of opportunity, relations with other stakeholders, and the dynamics or characteristics of demand.

An important goal here is identification of "over the horizon" issues (i.e., those likely to be prominent in one to three years, when the findings of research soon to be undertaken will be available to provide the basis for policy prescriptions). For both the over-the-horizon issues and those that will receive more proximate attention, team leaders should assess where their comparative advantage is likely to be. Andrew Selee (2013a, 34-6) speaks of finding a "unique lane" and identifies four options:

1. Find an issue that no one else is working on (i.e., the first mover advantage).
2. Identify a unique approach to an issue (e.g., developing or exploiting a comparatively un-known data set or introducing simulation results into the discussion).
3. Position the program to make its contribution at a strategic point in the policy cycle (e.g., introduce two additional program design options when the policy discussion is under way but not yet conclusive).
4. Geography (e.g., the case of an organization with field offices around the country or that frequently works with municipalities countrywide or international field offices, which can advance evidence of local problems and opinions more credibly than less far-flung orga-nizations).

The second element—a unique research approach to an issue—reminds one that the time of strategy development is when a team should take stock of the research methods it uses. In particular, does it always turn to the same analytic tools? Should more sophisticated method be used in some projects? Where basic statistical analysis is the norm, would case studies be an effective complement in some instances? What are the staffing and software implications of a planned shift in methods?

Equally essential from the start is a clear statement of the concrete goals for each program—the impacts to which it realistically aspires over the next few years. Even though not all projects undertaken may explicitly contribute to achieving them, the unifying higher level objectives furnish the team with a guiding focus. Such goals are best defined with substantial program staff input (to enhance ownership and understanding) and possibly refined through broader discussions with other programs.

Critically, the team leaders' outlines need to include a concrete statement on how success will be measured; without this rigorous monitoring, measuring change will simply not be possible. Ideally, this statement should be fairly nuanced, essentially tracking the policy development and adoption process, and be designed to record the extent to which the team's work figured in forward progress or not. For large sector-level research-PEC programs that have numerous lines of policy advocacy running simultaneously, often in ways that are interdependent, this will be a complex exercise.

But it can be very rewarding as well to team leaders, because it forces them to work through the probable path policy development will traverse, and helps identify points where the team should be actively engaged with policy makers.

The research team–level draft constitutes a mini strategy and includes identifying emerging policy issues, a market scan, resource requirements, funding sources, and managerial questions.

The standard tools, such as the log frame (also called the programmatic logic model), could be used to help identify the challenges and resource requirements involved in the plan.[113] In structuring the log frame one could imagine a table with one row for each potential new initiative or extension of current work areas and seven columns, as follows:

> Column 1: Initiative name
> Column 2: Achievement oriented goals: short-term policy outcomes; long-term possible impacts
> Column 3: Assumptions, e.g., actions likely to be taken by the government and competitors, and their timing
> Column 4: Activities: including research and demonstration projects, marketing, and policy engagement and communication
> Column 5: Additional and special resource requirements to support the activities
> Column 6: Revenue generation targets
> Column 7: Intended Outputs.

A multi-year perspective is necessary for this exercise. The team leader's planning needs to focus on a program or multi-year project—rather than smaller projects or "quick hits," for which the demand and funding are likely to be comparatively spontaneous.

As discussed further below, the process of establishing goals and developing an explicit monitoring plan can serve as key inputs for preparation of the project-level corresponding policy engagement and communications plan when appropriate.

Tasks at the institution level. Senior management along with the relevant team leaders needs to address the same points for policy topics that cut across the team issue boundaries—to ensure coordination and assign specific questions to the various teams. Additionally, this group needs to address what are sometimes called "major questions," i.e., developments, actual or possible, that would have major implications for the whole organization and very likely result in innovations.

At least three kinds of major questions could require a careful strategic reconsideration, either at a

---

113   Based on La Piana (2008), pp.92-3.

periodic strategy updating or when the specific question arises.[114,115]

1. *New opportunities.* Doubtless, there are many ways to identify such opportunities. One is to exploit a change in government policy that potentially provides possibilities. An example might the think tank's national government deciding to make a fundamental change in the way it supports poor families, shifting from a system of in-kind grants to a conditional cash grant program. Say your think tank has been prominent in the past for its work on a housing allowance program—a means-tested program to assist poor households to pay rents for dwellings meeting minimum quality standards. As such, you have a comparative advantage, not only in the policy space but also in providing expert advice to the relevant ministry on program implementation. Seizing such an opportunity will require shifting resources from another initiative and adding staff with the right expertise—major decisions that need to be made with great care.

Another approach is to assess the potential of current issues for those that align well with the think tank's specific goals. The Center for Global Development (CGD) a few years ago reflected on ingredients that had led to it being frequently successful in addressing issues of aid effectiveness. On selecting new issues (opportunities), it said the following (from Macdonald and Levine 2008, 2-3, emphasis added):

> CGD has been particularly effective at achieving policy change when we select an important problem for which new knowledge, consensus building, and getting attention from new stakeholders or higher-level (potential) champions can make a difference. Selecting the right problem seems self-evident but it is often overlooked. If you deliberately look for problems that can be solved in this manner, you will NOT select a research topic where the goal is merely to increase knowledge or understanding…or to bring visibility to a broad cause. Similarly, you will NOT be selecting a high-profile debate where the entrenched beliefs are so powerful that new knowledge is unlikely to make a difference… *Instead, the "right" type of problem is one that is reasonably neutral, from a political point of view, but clearly important with respect to commonly agreed goals.* Examples from CGD's work include: how to provide debt relief for Nigeria, how to

---

114   These event types are discussed more generally in La Piana, ibid., p.74. In the points below, a few clauses are taken from the La Piana without the insertion of quotation marks.

115   The issues discussed in this section are generally opportunities or challenges that evolve over time and for which the think tank has some time to plan and react. Mendizabal (2014d) has set out a substantial number of possible sudden negative shocks a think tank could experience. He reflects on think tank characteristics associated with more or less risk of experiencing such shocks and the ability to weather these challenging developments.

accelerate R&D for neglected diseases, and how to generate more and better evaluations of development programs.

2. *Competitive challenge.* Such a challenge arises when another organization acts in ways that damage yours, and the damage is great enough to threaten a significant part of your think tank's operations. An example might be that your think tank has, for some years, been carrying out technical assistance projects for a major bilateral donor on rural education improvements. A competitor has recently won two contracts from the same donor for work in this domain. This needs to be addressed, either by strengthening your education team to compete or probably having to deal with the consequences of a permanently smaller level of work in the education sector. One way to compete better is to focus on the area within the education work where you have competence and believe more future work will be required; then build capacity there—in which case your strategy needs to be adjusted to reflect this significant shift.

3. *Business model challenge.* Such a challenge arises when the resources available significantly change. An example might be a think tank noting that it is consistently losing some of its strongest policy analysts. Given the importance of these analysts to the organization's reputation and competiveness, this constitutes a threat to its existence in the present form. In this instance, a thorough and timely review of staff policy—informed by exit interviews and what other think tanks are doing—is in order, particularly concerning staff incentives. It may be that the organization is being out-bid in terms of salaries, but there may be other issues involved, such as the degree of autonomy senior analysts have in selecting the specific projects on which they work and the extent of control they have over their research teams. La Piana (2008) notes that business model challenges often "sneak up" on organizations, reaching an acute stage by the time they are addressed.

Of course, issues like these could emerge at the team-prepared mini-strategy level as well as at the institution planning level. In each of these cases, an organization's management needs to work through possible solutions and develop a plan for addressing the issue at hand. Note that "major questions" of this type that are on the horizon but not yet at an acute stage should be addressed in any regular strategy update, by senior management adding them to the plans drafted by the team leaders.

In the course of a recent updating of its strategy, the Center for the Study of the Economies of Africa in Nigeria decided to add the pervasive issue of income inequality to its work program. Initial tasks defined included understanding a rigorous definition of poverty and learning how informed policymakers were of the extent of poverty and of inequality in the country.

At this point in developing the strategic plan, senior managers and team leaders need to work together to meld the mini strategies and institution-level ideas into a single coherent plan. Trade-offs are very likely to be necessary among work areas in allocating resources to staffing and other areas, e.g., IT.

One communications element also needs to be addressed within the strategic plan's development—the level of internal financial resources to be allocated to communications. Funds are required for overall institution-level communications, including website development and maintenance (discussed later) and unfunded project-level communications.

Worth noting is that communications operations' resource requirements have increased substantially in recent years, as the volume of products generated by think tanks has expanded and the volume of digital products and social media participation has exploded. Often funders are uninterested in funding such activities—in which case they must be funded from overhead accounts. The greater the share of internal funds devoted to these activities, of course, the lower the share of a fixed overhead pool available for discretionary research and improvement of working conditions.

These and other resource allocation decisions should flow from a *full review of future administrative requirements*, some of which may not have been identified and addressed so far in the process. Heads of administrative service areas can outline for senior management the implications of the draft plans for their service activities.

Resources check. So far, my discussion of the planning process has focused on the policy agenda. It is often useful, in addition, for senior managers and team managers to take an alternative approach within strategic plan development. This is to assessing potential funding sources—in other words, to predicate the work program on funding that is fairly likely to be available. This approach can highlight certain programs being suggested by team leaders as unlikely to be funded, and thus help keep the planning realistic. The institutional decision may still be to go forward with work on an issue for which funding is suspect. But given the probable dearth of finance, a slower entry into the area may be the wise strategy.

The Corresponding Communications Strategy

An institution-level communications strategy should be closely related to the think tank's strategic plan, and it is typically developed or amended shortly after a new strategic plan is adopted. While executive directors seemingly support this position nearly universally, my experience based on information from many think tanks is that these plans frequently are not in fact produced. What are such plans and why are they worth developing?

Institution-level strategies differ fundamentally from the more familiar project-level plans, which focus on getting policy research results into the hands of opinion leaders and government and parliamentary decision makers, so the analysis positively influences policy outcomes. (Highlights of the project-level plans are described in Chapter 5 in the subsection on "Project Execution" under the "Team Leader Tasks" heading.) As stated earlier, in strategy development each team identifies goals for each major research area and development of the corresponding plan for monitoring the impacts of policy engagement and communications. These are the key ingredients for project-level communications plans' structuring when the projects are launched.

Institution-level communication strategies have the goal of creating a positive institutional image that will facilitate project-level policy engagement and communications campaigns. Think tanks have adopted such strategies with varying contents and thrusts, although some key elements are fairly constant. Some want the strategy to be related to additional objectives, such as knowledge management (European Centre for Development Policy Management 2013). Some base their plans explicitly on a SWOT analysis (Center for Economic Research 2011). And some of these plans are really hybrids, covering both a high-level strategy and outlines of project-level plans.

Based on conversations with communications directors at strong think tanks and reviewing several institution-level strategies, my view is that the best institution communications strategy focuses primarily on establishing a positive image in the policy and supporter marketplaces, both generally and in specific markets carefully selected because of their importance for realizing the communications goals.

The main components of such a strategy are shown in Box 9.1. The first element is its goals. These are typically stated in general terms, such as: "increased leadership visibility and recognition to strengthen our profile among target stakeholders and donors, thereby enhancing our influence and reach." More specific goals can be stated in greater detail, as the following (edited) list from an annual strategy statement indicates:

- *Public awareness*: Secure public knowledge and understanding of the organization's strategic objectives.

- *Brand and reputation*: Support management of the brand and reputation by enhancing external stakeholder perception of us as a credible and responsive organization; this will in turn strengthen supporter and donor perception and engagement.

- *Visibility*: Increase visibility and raise awareness of our strategic vision to reduce poverty throughout the country, positioning us as an expert opinion/thought leader on development issues.

- *Empowering staff*: Mentor staff to speak about the organization, its core strengths and impact.

- *Recruitment*: Greater visibility will help us build a world-class team by enhancing influence among specific stakeholder groups.

Goal setting is followed by three closely interrelated activities: defining the broad approach, the target audiences and narrative about the organization to be communicated to each audience (steps 2-4 in the box).

Formulation of a list of "key messages" about the organization (step 4) is a critical element. These are based on the institution's principles and its record, i.e., its concrete accomplishments. The accomplishments list is organized to relate its specific strengths to various targeted stakeholders among officials and donors, i.e., there are multiple lists tailored for different audiences.

Finally, in step 5 specific activity objectives and tasks are assembled in an actionable program. Increased institutional visibility (within step 5) is one of the specific activity objectives. Among the elements that might be included here is "executive positioning"—senior researchers and the executive director working with the communications team to identify and take advantage of opportunities where high priority stakeholders are to make presentations or be available for informal discussion about the think tank's accomplishments and capabilities. Other elements include exploiting traditional and social media and the organization's web site to garner attention, particularly with messages that highlight actual successes of its own work in improving program administration and persons' lives.

Branding is another highly important element. This ranges from the prosaic—consistency in using the logo and standard formats in reports and publications—to the critical, for example, senior policy experts that are on the institution's staff and only the institution's staff. It is here that the exclusivity concerns raised in Chapter 3 are critical; an organization gets no brand payoff if a star analyst is essentially a freelancer who in fact works for multiple organizations.

As suggested, one objective of the institution-level communication plan is to create an ambience of trust and receptivity in the policy research space to an institution's results, its recommendations, and its staff.

Restructuring and Mergers

In addition to changes to a think tank's work program and sponsors, two other forms of innovation deserve mention. One is restructuring the organization—including creation of new sister organizations—to achieve significant improvements in productivity, policy relevance, mission clarification, or in response to government policies regarding NGO operations. A second involves mergers, which occasionally occur between previously independent think tanks. Both are clearly matters to be addressed during a strategy formulation exercise, since they have fundamental effects on many administrative issues (even if the policy research agendas are not strongly affected).

We hear little about major internal reorganizations designed to drive down costs and make a think tank more efficient and competitive. This lack of information likely results from the fact that such changes are wholly internal events. Nevertheless, one can imagine the kinds of changes that could be made. For example, a think tank that had organized its work along thematic lines (e.g., health policy, local government finance, social assistance) may decide that this arrangement is inefficient, because each thematic group—though all require the same types of expertise in technical assistance projects, evaluations, and econometric analyses—is too small to possess true expertise in each technical area. As long as each thematic group is siloed, some work will be poorly done by non-experts, some staff will not be fully employed, and some staff will be frustrated by not being able to work on their preferred assignments. Reorganizing by type of technical expertise combined with much smaller thematic (subject matter) teams could address these problems—with the technical experts working for the thematic teams as needed.

Another example is a think tank where team leaders are responsible for designing the PEC program for each of their projects—informing the communications team what it needs to do to implement their plan. Some team leaders may consult effectively with the communications team in structuring the design; but others may not. Shifting to a joint team leader–communications team design responsibility is likely to improve the PEC process overall.

Think tanks create subsidiary institutions with some frequency to clarify the distinct tasks of both organizations to funders, policy makers, and the public. As discussed in Chapter 10, for example, it is often useful to create a for-profit sister organization when a think tank enters the consultancy market. Another reason for a split off is to clarify focused advocacy work from more rigorous policy analysis. In 2008, for example, PATTIRO (Pusat Telaah dan Informasi Regional) in Indonesia was a strong advocacy organization using an evidence-based approach. It had been successful using this approach in the policy arena and with sponsors, in part because of its 10 or so regional offices that advocated locally. At this time, however, it saw the possibility of making complementary contributions through the more rigorous kind of research think tanks carry out. PATTIRO's management was concerned that its established clients might be confused with the addition of this new line of work within PATTIRO. So a think tank, PATTIRO Institute—later renamed Article 33—was created to execute the more rigorous research and survey projects. (Article 33 refers to the article in the 1945 Indonesian constitution setting the basic principles for management of natural resources—the primary focus of Article 33's research, along with social issues.)

RAOs with service delivery or professional development primary missions, in particular, are well advised to carefully assess the gains in administrative efficiency and mission clarification that could result from lodging the research and policy advocacy operations in a separate legal entity (one that would remain very close to the main NGO). The Ethiopian Economics Association, for example, was created as a professional association in 1991. In 2000, when it formed its research wing, the Ethiopian Economic Policy Research Institute, it elected to form it as a separate legal entity and subsidiary to the Association.

A number of countries have NGO laws that are quite intrusive for think tanks. Important examples include laws that prohibit NGOs from accessing public funding or engaging in any "profit-making" activity. Some restrict allowed funding sources; others have instituted very extensive (and costly) reporting requirements; and there are cases where board qualifications are restrictive. Moreover, NGOs in certain countries enjoy no tax privileges. In such situations, many thank tanks have created for-profit subsidiaries through which they channel all their work (except what comes from foundations that can only fund nonprofit organizations). The for-profit's mission is the same as the nonprofit's and profits generated are devoted to unfunded research and communications activities.

Another form of restructuring is elimination of research on a topic heretofore significant at the institution. Some policy issues have a kind of natural life cycle, in part because major improvements in sector policy are realized that increase the opportunity cost of further investment in the government's and the parliament's time. Correspondingly fewer resources for policy analysis flow for additional analysis. Think tanks that traditionally had core programs for the sector at issue will either close them or cut the activity and staff levels sharply—hoping that the skills of staff members thus released will be valuable in addressing other policy issues.

Although such strategies sound straightforward in principle, the reality is that many think tanks find such cutting very difficult because of their tradition of having a strong team in the area affected. Strategy developers need to foster open and honest discussions about marginal areas, and senior managers to make the necessary decisions after consulting with the board. Noncore programs with shorter histories focused on topics with little active interest from the policy community, and few expectations of future interest, will generally be the easier ones to close out.

The root cause for most mergers is financial pressure: to cut costs, gain market share, and/or offer sponsors a broader array of capabilities. This pressure was especially acute in Eastern Europe from the late 1990s on, as international foundation support for the economic and political transition in the region fell and think tanks that had relied upon such funding were forced to retrench and consider fundamental adjustments. To be fair, much of this funding was eventually replaced with European Union (EU) contracts and grants for accession countries; but there was a several-year funding gap and the fact that EU's policy research interests differ from those of the foundations that had supplied the previous funding caused substantial dislocations, nevertheless.

Two forms among the several possible adjustments (La Piana 1997) seem particularly relevant here. One is back-office consolidation, under which the costs of core administration functions are shared among a group of think tanks, while each think tank maintains its own identity. Example functions include accounting, copying, public relations, IT support, secretarial services, and in some cases, even research assistance. While appealing in theory, however, such "back office" mergers seldom actually occur.

More common is the merger of near-equals, or the effective acquisition of one think tank by another. There is a growing literature on these processes for nonprofit organizations that gives pointers on what leaders of a think tank might expect in such a process. A common theme is that few mergers are carefully analyzed from a business perspective as part of the preparation. The greatest problem in achieving agreement to merge is the relative status of the two organizations— and their leaders—after the merger.

Mergers seem to more often occur between a think tank and a survey firm or between a think tank and a training organization than between two think tanks. But little is known about how successful such mergers actually are.

Two final points: 1) Where NGO mergers have been hurried, post-merger staff morale problems are common; and 2) key ingredients for success are good leadership and honest, open communication between an organization's leadership and its staff. [116]

Plan Benefits

A strategic plan bestows the obvious and extremely valuable benefit of clarity about the think tank's direction. By providing a cogent statement of policy research priorities, the strategy powerfully counteracts the tendency for a think tank to become caught up in chasing funding opportunities—rather than working to create them. If the strategy is properly promulgated, staff has a strong sense of mission and the tasks to be done.

Jeremy Avins (2013), whose group has assisted think tanks with fund raising, argues that strategic plans are also a valuable fund raising resource.

> Those [think tanks] that have good strategies (including monitoring and evaluation) are more likely to make donors comfortable with the idea of core and multi-year funding by: 1) giving the funder a clear sense of what it means in practice to support an organization *as a whole*; and 2) showing the funder that the think tank is thoughtful about achieving the most with its resources.

What available data say about think tanks' actual practices is my next discussion topic.

WHAT THINK TANKS DO

Information for the TTI-48 on Strategy Development

We are fortunate to have data on strategy development practices of the TTI-48 think tanks, as presented in Table 9.1. Note that this information was gathered in 2009 when partner think tanks had just joined. TTI requires participating organizations to have a strategic plan in place. The information is about strategy development prior to think tanks responding to the TTI requirement.

---

116   For more on these points, see, for example, LaPiana (1997), McMurtry, Netting, and Kettner (1991), Singer and Yankey (1991), and Wernet and Jones (1992).

Table 9.1 Strategic Planning Practices of the TTI-48 Think Tanks
(percent distributions)

	TTI		
	=<10 FT Researchers	>10 FT Researchers	All
How often do you conduct a strategic planning process? (2009)			
Annually	22	23	23
Every 1 to 2 years	17	20	19
Less often than every 2 years	28	20	23
No fixed schedule but we do conduct a strategic planning process	22	37	31
We do not conduct strategic planning	11	0	4
What was the result of the last strategic planning process? (2009)			
A formal strategy statement	81	57	65
It was quite an informal process and after our discussions we generally followed our conclusions/recommendations	19	43	35
It was an informal process and we are not following the conclusions/recommendations	0	0	0
We do not conduct strategic planning	0	0	0
What kinds of persons and organizations did you consult in the planning process? (2009)			
Senior national government officials	69	60	63
Mid-level national officials	44	47	46
Senior sub-national government officials	38	33	35
Mid-level sub-national government officials	25	10	15
Business leaders	63	43	50
Think tank leaders	56	53	54
Advocacy-NGO leaders	56	70	65
Members of parliament	25	40	35
Members of the media	50	33	39
University professors	63	73	70
Other donors/development partners	69	70	70
Number of think tanks	18	30	48

Nearly all these think tanks reported preparing a strategy at least periodically. Forty-two percent reported preparing a strategy at least every two years, while the balance seems to have no particular schedule for strategy development or prepared a plan less often than each two years. As noted above, comparatively infrequent strategy development may be perfectly justified under certain circumstances. I assume that those reporting annual strategy development are engaged in limited updating in light of various changes and challenges.

For two-thirds of those who do develop a strategy, the result is a written document. Somewhat surprisingly, the incidence of a written document, rather than an understanding of priorities and plans among the participants, is much higher among the smaller think tanks than among their larger counterparts—81 percent versus 57 percent. It is possible that the larger (and more established) institutions excluded basic strategy statements and outlines and selected the "informal process" response because the pre-coded response ("a formal strategy statement") was taken to mean a more elaborate document than they had prepared.

Perhaps the most interesting information in the table is on the range of persons consulted in some way for preparing the plan. More than half of these think tanks reported consulting persons in six types of position: senior national government officials, business leaders, think tank leaders, advocacy NGO leaders, university professors, and donors and development partners. A substantial degree of outreach and effort is clear from this list. Also worth noting is that fully two-thirds said they had engaged consultants to assist with the "organizational development process."

The fact that considerable resources are invested in strategy development by these institutions is impressive and an encouraging sign of capable leadership.

Case Studies of Different Innovation Types

This section reviews the experience of think tanks that introduced innovations to their work programs. I first describe a single innovation that added a major new policy area, which is the subject of a Case Study commissioned for this book. I then describe another seven, which were all in the form of adding a non-policy research area, such as consulting services to governments of countries undergoing economic transition. The lessons from all eight in terms of the challenges faced and the benefits from undertaking them are highly instructive.

Adding training as a major activity complementing a research program. Case Study 9.1 summarizes how Praxis, located in Tallinn (Estonia), decided to pursue establishing a robust training program that built on and complemented its research activities. The idea evolved internally and gradually. There were (and are) challenges, but the Praxis Academy is proving financially viable and rewarding to staff who participate.

Selected initiatives in Eastern Europe and Russia. Examples of innovations actually undertaken are hard to identify and document. This section discusses seven innovations adopted by four think tanks in the mid-1990s in Eastern Europe and Russia, which I learned about in the course of previous field work with these think tanks: the Center for the Study of Democracy (CSD) in Sofia, the Institute for Urban Economics (IUE) in Moscow, the Center for Democracy and

Free Enterprise (CDFE) in Prague, and the Center for Social and Economic Research (CASE) in Warsaw. I chose them as particularly entrepreneurial examples of developing new lines of work—including commercial activities similar to those of consulting firms—and in tapping the business community for in-kind donations in the form of seminars or other products of direct interest to this community. Specifically, the seven innovations were:

1. Founding a radio station with high news and public service content
2. Starting a marketing survey operation
3. Launching the first credit rating agency in the country
4. Beginning to offer consulting services to municipalities on economic development
5. Initiating training for corporation staff
6. Starting consulting services on economic development in Central Asian countries
7. Creating a program under which corporations sponsor some high interest projects.

Only the fourth case can be thought of as introducing an additional research area to the think tank's program.

I identified the organizations through interviewing their leaders for an earlier study and through consultations with people knowledgeable about think tanks in the region. It is worth emphasizing that those who nominated think tanks consistently cited the same institutions, and the list was short—suggesting that such entrepreneurialism is far from common. Only four institutes beyond the four included here were recommended, of which three did not agree to participate and the fourth was not available for a visit. The information is based on my semi-structured interviews of institute leadership in 1998 and 1999 and a review of annual reports, web sites, and other materials. Details on the innovations implemented, how they came about, the motivation for undertaking them, and their challenges and rewards are in Annex 9.1.[117] Here I give my conclusions about the overall experience.

These case studies clearly illustrate that it is possible for think tanks to go beyond the traditional funding sources to sustain and expand their operations. Indeed, my examples make it look almost easy. As related in the interviews, identification and analysis of potential opportunities was not overly demanding, nor was the set of actions needed to launch the activity. All four think tanks reported remarkably few problems with management, institutional identification, or staff morale from adding the new, more commercially oriented activities—probably in part because they were young, flexible, and dynamic organizations. All four were under the threat of declining donor support—giving them a strong impetus to search for more opportunities to expand into new types of work areas.

---

117   The author's sense is that in at least two of these cases the heads of the think tanks did not want to give away what they viewed as commercial secrets.

Can other think tanks count on such a smooth experience? Probably not. The general record of NGOs in the United States that try to generate funds for their core missions through for-profit operations, for example, is not strong (Foster and Bradach 2005).

Two important factors must be taken into account in using these examples as typical of think tanks' ability to emulate these examples. First, all four think tanks included in this analysis were careful to build on existing strengths—the innovations were in areas where their existing competence and reputation gave them a running start. Working in an area close to an existing competence increased their ability to judge the potential demand for a new service. It also minimized start-up costs, as staff could continue to work on the traditional tasks while the demand for the think tank's new services increased. For an innovation further from the core competence, one or two new experts would have had to have been hired, and they would have charged most of their time to program development (i.e., overhead).

Second, these four groups were all entrepreneurial institutions whose leaders had good market instincts, could realistically assess possibilities, and had demonstrated the willingness to take the initiative when opportunity appeared. Indeed, they had all founded think tanks near the beginning of the Eastern European transition from Soviet domination. This package of characteristics is rare. In some cases, these institutions also had a culture and a system in place to encourage staff to think creatively and to propose ideas beyond the current work program. It is these qualities that caused the organizations to be consistently recommended as innovative organizations when I sought examples of organizations launching creative new programs.

An important question is whether the seven innovations described actually proved successful. At a minimum, success is indicated by whether the programs I review are still part of the relevant think tank's program. I was able to determine the December 2013 status of five of the seven (see Table A9.4). Four of the five were clear successes: three are still operational within the think tank and one was sold profitably to an international firm.

The one unsuccessful innovation was establishment of a radio station in Sofia by CSD. Over time, increased competition shrank its market share and the station was sold. On the basis of this experience, CSD's executive director draws the conclusion that major new undertakings should be closely related to a think tank's core competencies.

STIMULATING INNOVATION

The business community is characterized by a constant struggle to produce new products and services for clients. Since the 1990s, the U.S. nonprofit sector has been under similar pressure, forcing NGOs to rethink the services they provide and how they provide them—including the incorporation of more fee-generating activities.[118] This is an era of increasing competition both

---

118   See, for example, Bullen et al. (1997) and Burlingame and Ilchman (1996), Davis (1997) and Maxwell (1996).

among NGOs for support from foundations, and between NGOs and for-profit firms for the role of delivery agents for social services to local governments. Nonprofits found it necessary in the early going to think and organize themselves more like businesses (Letts, Ryan, and Grossman 1999; Light 1998).

A principal challenge these NGOs—and think tanks specifically—face is to develop an environment and practice of innovation. Students of innovation in NGOs in the United States say unequivocally that most guidance available to nonprofits focuses on how single acts of innovation were created and implemented—not on creating an environment that fosters innovations again and again (Letts et al. 1999, 73; Light 1998, 7). Indeed, Letts and colleagues state categorically that there are no good general concepts to guide nonprofits in program development (1999, 74). At the same time, experts in the field are calling for "the relentless pursuit of opportunity" (Kitzi 2001, 44).

In the following two sections, I build on the broader experience of nonprofit organizations. The first addresses key factors in a think tank's working environment that are conducive to generating innovations. The second provides key points for identifying, assessing, and piloting promising innovations. My accent is on principles rather than on detailed planning, although key calculations and steps are identified.

Creating a Conducive Environment

Any of the half-dozen actions discussed briefly below can create conditions conducive to staff thinking about new directions for the organization.

A flat, informal organization is the most effective. Those studying innovation have observed that the more hierarchical layers there are between staff and senior management, the more likely that management will not learn about many good ideas. The corresponding lesson is to keep the organization "thin" (i.e., with few layers). In the same vein, the more responsibility is pushed downward in an organization, the more likely that lower-level staff will have access to, and a working relationship with, management and believe themselves important to the entity's success. In larger think tanks, if responsibility is concentrated on the team leader—rather than on a combination of team leader and subordinate project leaders—project leaders are likely to have less contact with management and be less comfortable advancing ideas. A concomitant point is that greater informality in an organization increases the odds that a staffer will directly approach management with innovative ideas.

The reality is that most think tanks are small enough that they do not have multiple layers of managers separating a project leader from the director of the organization. But even a single layer, if not properly managed, can create a barrier to good ideas flowing upward.

Staff diversity is helpful. Put simply, the decision process will typically be stronger when people with different backgrounds and views are involved: what may appear a good idea to a group with academic backgrounds may strike someone from the business community or with a local government background as much less sound. If a think tank has a fairly homogeneous staff, e.g., heavily dominated by PhD economists, inviting trusted advisors with other perspectives to discuss possible innovations is certainly worthwhile.

Internal turbulence can stimulate change. Sometimes a jolt is necessary to induce staff to think creatively; otherwise, they tend to focus on what they have been doing and on marginal changes to the current agenda. Internal turbulence, in the form of the departure of a key staff member or a bleak funding outlook, can push staff to think beyond their normal boundaries. Of course, the key question is how much turbulence is too much. Beyond a certain point, shocks and uncertainty can make the staff dysfunctional. A telltale sign of too much disruption is staff huddled in groups talking about their possible futures rather than doing their regular jobs.

Low internal barriers help staff exchange ideas. Think tanks with as few as 10 full-time researchers are likely to have separate teams for addressing different policy topics. Managerially this can certainly make sense. But if these units become isolated islands, the organization can lose the ideas that result from the interaction of teams working on different subjects and for different clients. One technique used by a number of think tanks to prevent this is to have seminars devoted to ongoing projects that are attended by staff from all groups. This informs everyone about the substance of ongoing projects and provides a base for further interactions. Another technique is to hold regular joint meetings of senior managers and team leaders to exchange notes on projects and institutional questions, as suggested in Chapter 8.

Internal resources are needed to launch possible innovations. If staff knows there are funds available to support development of an innovative concept, they are much more likely to advance it for discussion. Two distinct elements are involved here. First, the funds must actually exist. Many think tanks fund initial work on an innovation from a pool of fee income (essentially profit) and funds from overhead, through a line item designated for "institutional development" or similar purposes (Letts et al. 1999 73). Second, the staff has to know that the institution does actually use such funds to develop or pilot-test innovations. Senior management can make this clear by financing the development of an innovation from time to time. Even in a large organization (50 staff members or more), most will know the source of the funds financing any new activity.

Innovation is continuous. Staff will understand that proposing new projects and alternative directions for the organization is encouraged if there are clear indicators to this effect. If the think tank has an annual retreat of senior staff to consider current operations and the future of the organization—including possible innovations in the work program—and inputs are widely solicited for the retreat, staff will be encouraged to be creative and expansive in their thinking. But it is wrong for management to signal that ideas are welcome only at specific times. Opportunities seldom wait. Other "markers" to indicate that staff can contribute to the store of fresh ideas are certainly possible, especially if management supports some of those offered. This ongoing process is in sharp contrast with the one-big-initiative model, in which a significant change of direction is adopted once, and then the organization goes back to business as usual.

The Process of Innovation[119]

The process of innovation can be divided into three phases: calling for ideas, assessing alternatives, and piloting the strongest candidates. These are unlikely to be clean, discrete phases, and there will probably be overlap, both for phases of a single innovation and between successive innovations. In other words, although I divide this process into distinct and rather formal steps for ease of presentation, the reality will almost certainly be much more informal. The key point is to consider how a candidate innovation fairs against the various criteria I lay out. The process outlined here would ideally be launched so decisions about new initiatives would be made in the context of overall strategy development. But it is important for the door to be always open for staff to advance new ideas.

Calling for ideas. Staff must understand the welcome mat is out for ideas. If a retreat for team leaders and management is planned, team leaders should solicit and discuss ideas from their groups. They should understand that the retreat will be more productive if at least some people arrive with well-articulated ideas, but first musings should also be on the agenda. Instead of a retreat, one of the monthly meetings among the president and managers could be devoted to this topic once a year or so.

It is essential for the think tank's director to provide early guidance for the type of ideas sought. If the topic of the discussion is to identify significantly new directions for the organization that have a good prospect of external support, it is not appropriate to present research topics only marginally different from those already being addressed.

Those advancing innovative ideas should be asked to consider seven questions in testing their thinking, and be ready to discuss their thinking on each. The list is similar to those for the overall strategy presented above in the "Plan Options" section, but focuses more sharply on points especially relevant to assessing an innovation. Since the questions are demanding, it may make sense to develop more complete and informed answers in several steps, i.e., devote progressively more resources as an idea receives stronger support.[120]

1. What is the need—problem definition and scope? Is it expanding? What are the root causes? What needs to be done to refine and address the specific policy issues (type of work:

119   This section draws generally on Bacon and Butler (1998) and Kitzi (2001).
120   Development of this list benefited from the presentation by Claudia Juech, "Opportunity Identification and Assessment at the Rockefeller Foundation," on October 31, 2013 at the Results for Development Institute, Washington, D.C.

analytic studies, consulting services, on-site technical assistance, training, software)? Is this likely to be a single engagement or really a new work area?

2. What is the basis for the competitive opening—is there an unmet need no one has previously identified or is in a position to address? Are we likely to get "first mover" advantages of recognition and niche domination if we move quickly?

3. What is the basis for the think tank's competitive advantage? Is it superior analysis (including simulation modeling, etc.), lower cost, better outreach and marketing capabilities than other providers, greater potential for continuous innovations (e.g., being able to provide cutting-edge technical assistance to local governments in a particular sector by transferring best practices among them)?

4. Does the organization have the expertise to pursue this opportunity? If not, is it likely that the expertise can be acquired at a reasonable cost?

5. Does the organization have the capacity to support the initiative (e.g., classroom space, the computer hardware and software for creation of a sophisticated web site)?

6. Who are the likely supporters and, of these, who are the likely funders? Can this issue be viewed as part of a larger problem currently being addressed to some degree at the institution, to which support for the new problem could be linked?

7. Are there likely to be substantive early findings to clarify the urgency or scope of the problem in a way that can be used to generate financial support?

Assessing alternatives. The greatest emphasis must clearly be placed on assessing the market for the innovation. A formal business plan can be produced, and it may help to map out expected costs and revenues (see Covello and Hazelgren 1995). But determining the probable market is the key task. Think tank staffs typically have little experience in assessing markets. Put simply, for the kind of services think tanks offer, they need to canvass such potential clients as:

- Major donor organizations, for technical studies and technical assistance projects

- Local governments, for technical assistance with certain policy and management reforms and training events

- National governments, for policy analysis and possibly program evaluations (assuming the government is purchasing policy research services)

- Trade associations and their members (banks, municipalities, hospitals), for training courses and possibly technical assistance.

Besides speaking directly with clients, staff can get ideas about potential demand from other sources—including: 1) presentations at conferences and 2) the direction of change set by the national government (e.g., more responsibilities assigned to local governments could mean an expanded market in technical assistance and training to these entities). Note that monitoring what the competition is doing can also be valuable in stimulating thinking in new directions. Determining the extent of the market is time-consuming, demanding work, but think tanks shy away from it at their own peril.

Where initiatives are further from their "home markets," such as creation of a country's first credit rating agency by one of the CEE think tanks, contracting for expert advice may make sense.

Think tanks face a particular challenge in analyzing the potential demand for services, because the client for the services is often not the entity providing the funding. For example, a bilateral donor may fund technical assistance to local governments, but the governments are the direct client for the services. In such cases, think tanks must try to identify programs that will better serve the interests of both local clients and funder. In some cases, a think tank can advance ideas to a donor, based on market research with beneficiaries of new projects. In all cases, it is critical that the source of effective demand be clearly identified when innovations are being assessed. Identifying the assistance local governments need is insufficient if the donor-client is not convinced.

At the point where an innovation candidate looks fairly promising, it is important for the executive director to have an initial discussion about the initiative with the board chair; after all, significant resources are to be committed. The key point is that the board chair agrees the initiative: 1) is within the organization's mandate, 2) is consistent with broad institutional development, and 3) has a reasonable chance of success given the information then available. In brief, the executive director is seeking permission to devote more resources to further development, usually with a promise to return to the board before shifting to the operation or launch stage.

An example of a Stage 1 think tank identifying and exploiting a genuine opportunity follows:

> The Foundation "Liberal Academy Tbilisi" (LAT) in Tbilisi, Georgia was established in December 2006 by former Economic Stability Initiative analyst Ketevan Tsikhelashvili. For two and a half years, LAT worked with young leaders and policy/opinion-makers through educational seminars, issue-based conferences, workshops, and expert meetings. In 2009 LAT decided to try to launch a separate analytical component (the European Initiative) to complement its capacity building and educational activities and encourage a well-informed public discourse on a range of policy issues involving Georgia-European Issues (EU). One objective was for the Initiative to "translate" Europe to local stakeholders who work on the EU integration process and to the wider public. At this time, Georgia's president had made clear the very high priority he assigned to Georgia pursuing its candidacy for successfully closer relations with the Union.
>
> Ms. Tsikhelashvili assessed various funding possibilities and adjusted the specifics of the proposed work program to match a particular donor's. The timing of her initiative was perfect. The European Initiative-Liberal Academy Tbilisi (EI-LAT) received a three-year institutional development grant from the Think Tank Fund (TTF) in November 2009. At the time of

the application the Initiative existed only on paper, but it soon surged to life. To expand the resources available, she applied successfully to "open RFPs," where the applicant selects its own topic. Funding also came from EU-supported programs. Projects on EU-Georgian relations were carried out on topics such as visa restrictions to Georgians compared with other Eastern non-EU members and Georgian-EU trade issues. (Struyk 2013)

Piloting promising innovations. A think tank will typically decide to pursue one or perhaps two innovations in a year, reflecting the presence of two kinds of constraints: limited financial resources for discretionary spending and limited staff capacity to launch and manage the initiatives.

Once the think tank's leadership has decided to implement an innovation, plans are usually made to pilot it by developing the new offering sufficiently to test the market.[121] At this stage, a draft budget should be prepared to include costs for the following range of expenses:

- *Developing the new product, such as a training course or the expertise that can be applied in the new area.* This may entail hiring a new expert and making a one- or two-year commitment to that person.

- *Carrying out one or more applications in the new work areas, to develop greater expertise and to establish a track record for use in further marketing.* A think tank may need to find cooperating clients and carry out a trial application of the new service (e.g., working with a bank to develop its mortgage lending program, helping a municipality develop its economic development plan, or offering a training program for NGOs). Alternatively, it may need to finance the writing and publication of the initial issues of a new magazine aimed at a broad policy audience. Whatever the case, the initial experience may need to be subsidized.

- *Developing and executing a carefully conceived marketing program tightly targeted on the specific client group(s).* This could include producing print materials, such as brochures, but might also involve allowing staff to participate in conferences where the new offering could be announced. The marketing campaign would be timed to follow the development stage and, where appropriate, the pilot stage, so this experience could be used as a qualification.

At this point it is critical to define the total resources that can be devoted to piloting the innovation and the timing of their availability: how much will be available each month for the first six months and quarterly thereafter during the trial period? Some iteration between the draft budget for the pilot and the funds available may be necessary.

---

121   I do not discuss in detail the mechanics of actually implementing the innovation. Nickerson (2007) covers this (although in a business handbook format).

Three ideas for minimizing the cash outlays are listed below:

- *Phase in the implementation, funding only one or two stages at a time.* Allocate cash on a stage-by-stage basis as the milestones are reached. Only lay out more cash if completed prior stages yield promising results.

- *Convert fixed costs into variable costs.* Instead of hiring the new experts needed for the program, try to engage them as part-time consultants during the early phases. An organization establishing an extensive training program could rent space for classes as needed, instead of acquiring a larger office and classroom space.

- *Look for excess capacity and underused resources.* Can staff from an area where work is light be reassigned to help develop the innovation? Can the public relations specialist work on the marketing campaign instead of hiring outside resources? (For more, see Dees 2001a).

Even after the general plan for implementation is developed, a number of further preparatory steps can increase the odds of success. The major tasks remaining include the following:

> *Get board approval.* All the information is now at hand on the actual innovation: the results of the market analysis, how to launch it, and what the launch will cost. The board chair's earlier go-ahead is sufficient to go this far but now general approval is appropriate. Some board members may have ideas for improvement and these should be taken under advisement. As discussed in Chapter 6, the board should be kept away from operational questions, such as which staff should participate. But board offers to help promote the new activity should be greeted warmly and very carefully considered—they should be consistent with the overall plans and not change them, unless the offered actions are unambiguous enhancements. If a board meeting is not already conveniently scheduled, the executive director should decide, with the board chair, if a special meeting is required or if informal consultation would provide sufficient board input.

> *Define performance targets for the testing period—usually one to two years.* Setting targets forces everyone to be explicit about their expectations for the innovation. These goals should be set out in terms that are as concrete as possible. Obviously, the expectations should be determined in light of the resources being devoted to launching the innovation.

> *Create a calendar of activities necessary for achieving the goals.* This is the monthly "to do" list. Again, be explicit about: 1) the schedule for each

component, 2) relations among components, and 3) who is responsible for each can save resources and frustration during the pilot phase.

Write down the assumptions behind the definition of the pilot's success and identify the most crucial ones. For example, the most crucial assumption in an innovative technical assistance program designed to foster economic development in municipalities might be the rate at which the municipalities contract for this service *after the new approach has been demonstrated in two cities and a subsequent marketing campaign fielded.* What if the assumed rate is too optimistic? How large a margin of error can be tolerated without the innovation being a failure? If more realistic assumptions render the margin of error too thin, the decision to go forward may need to be reconsidered.

Design the venture with explicit milestones that reflect the points at which the most crucial assumptions will be tested. The milestones should cover the development stages for the product or service and should track the interest, orders, and cash generated by the innovation at various points in time.

Include "permission to fail" in the plan. A think tank must be prepared to admit there is insufficient demand for the new product or service when this is the case—and to do so in a timely way. It is important for the staff to know that advancing an innovation that ultimately fails is not necessarily a demerit on the person's standing within the organization. If innovations were assessed in the thorough manner outlined above, then the failure— like a success—would have a "thousand fathers." Senior management ultimately makes the decision and bears the responsibility, but there is little gain in assigning blame.

It is profitable, however, to try to understand which assumptions were wrong and how the review process failed. The answer may be that only limited useful information was available on the point. But it may be that the organization did not conduct enough market research—an area that could be improved in the future. The value of such careful, systematic, ex post reviews is difficult to overstate.[122]

It is also important to assess whether the critical condition that led to failure of the innovation is likely to change in the near future or could be changed with a different promotional approach. While the odds are generally against this, there may be reason to allocate modest additional investment to keep the innovation alive or to make a different promotional campaign.[123]

---

122   Darling, Parry, and Mooore (2005) include a good discussion of how to conduct ex post reviews.
123   Rochlin and Radovich (2013, 208-9) give a useful list of issues that an *ex post* evaluation can address.

In the end, innovation may be essential for most think tanks for reasons stated at the opening of this chapter. They will adjust with greater agility if they consciously foster innovations through an orderly process containing the elements outlined in this chapter.

TAKE AWAYS

Strong Practices
Characteristics of a well-managed think tank in this context follow.

- A basic strategy covering the planned research program, target audiences, and funding plans along with corresponding improvements in the organization's communications and administrative activities exists and is at least summarized in writing.

- Team leaders are key participants in the strategy development process, defining emerging policy issues, corresponding projects, resources needed to execute them and effectively communicate the results, and probable funding opportunities. Senior management leads a process to address cross-cutting issues and to define and investigate new opportunities, administrative requirements, and funding sources for these initiatives.

- RAOs with a substantial in-house policy research and engagement program from time to time carefully consider transforming the program into a sister organization (separate legal entity) to improve management—through its having administrative operations (e.g., personnel and communications) tailored to its specific mission—and to clarify the strong primary service or member enhancement mission of the main organization.

- Senior management encourages discussion of innovations at all times but particularly when strategy development is under way.

- A process for developing candidate innovations rated as highly promising is in place: modest funds are set aside for support and a simple but effective protocol defined for assessing progress (milestones defined and measured).

For Funders
Look carefully for:

- *A written strategy statement.* Fairly often the statement will be one or two pages of key points; but sometimes it will not have been committed to paper. More important than the degree of formality is the thoughtfulness and extent of over-the-horizon thinking reflected in the content. These points may only become clear in conversations with the executive director or board members. Try to get an understanding of the degree to which it affects the choice of projects undertaken and on whom and how policy research results are targeted.

Perhaps to do:

It is natural for funders to define policy questions in which they are strongly interested. Sometimes these are issues actively discussed in their own country or in others where they are active. At the same time, think tanks have agendas of their own. On occasion the funder and think tank agendas correspond closely, often not. Many think tanks make major investments to thoughtfully develop their strategic plans, which are geared to addressing priority issues. Funders should consider options like the following to support partners' work on these topics:

- Setting some share of its policy research funds aside for competitive "open calls," where think tanks present proposals for policy questions they understand to be of significant importance for their country.

- For a think tank with which the funder has an established relationship, a share of its support could be earmarked for priority research as defined by the think tank. In a number of cases, such funding would permit a think tank to undertake a genuine innovation in its policy research program.

- Be open to supporting promising innovations that have been rigorously defined and have a realistic plan for piloting.

Box 9.1 Simplified Outline for an Institution-level Communications Strategy

	Step	Examples/Comments
1	Define organization-level communications goals	Increased leadership visibility and recognition to strengthen our profile among *target* stakeholders and donors, thereby enhancing the perception that we are *(option examples)*: --A thought leader on the delivery of health services in Sub-Saharan Africa --The leading think tank on minority group education issues in countries with multiple significant groups --The leading technical assistance contractor for international agencies.[a]
2	Approach—broad statement of actions as related to goals	Examples for policy issue leadership --Produce internationally recognized economic analysis *[two tasks: producing high quality analysis and taking actions for it to be recognized]* --Use this position to compete for program funding and influence.
3	Define target audiences	Based on goals and approach. Essential to be precise because resources are limited. Examples include: a country's policy elite for a specific issue; a set of 2-3 international foundations active in a policy area; implementing NGOs created by public-private partnerships, such as the Global Partnership for Social Accountability.
4	Delineate key messages—narrative about the institution to be marketed	Priority messages are likely to differ by audience. The most successful tend to be vignettes on successful engagements, especially those featuring concrete improvements in peoples' lives or significant improvements in the administrative efficiency of services delivery.
5	Detail specific strategic activity objectives and related actions	Examples of objectives: --Increased institutional visibility --Strengthening the institutional brand Corresponding activity examples: --Participation at strategically selected conferences --Production of stronger analytical work and evidence that it is recognized to be of high quality and valid.
6	Track results of actions defined in prior step	

a. Additional sub-goal examples are listed in the text.

Case Study 9.1 Founding of Praxis Academy as the Training Arm of Praxis in Estonia

Praxis was established in 2000, and in the early years an institutional grant from OSI supported us as follows: in 2000 – 90 percent; in 2002 – 55 percent; in 2005 – 30 percent of annual turnover. OSI's grant ended in 2007. So we knew from the very beginning that we must look for additional sources of funding and become self-sufficient. Also, it was important to maintain autonomy from the government. By the end of 2008, Praxis had become the largest independent think-tank in Estonia, conducting high-quality policy analysis and research. It had five thematic programs (education, health, economy, labor and social affairs, civil society and governance), a staff of 15, two offices (Tallinn and Tartu) and an annual turnover of 612,950 euros. We were serving as a catalyst for political and economic reforms in Estonia. In 2010, we took another important step – we hired an outreach person to bridge the gap between academia and policy-making, by communicating our research to diverse audiences to increase our impact. Ever since, outreach has been built into our policy analysis and projects from their preparatory phases.

Still, we were facing two challenges. First, we were looking for additional ways to increase our impact and to see our policy recommendations and ideas used in decision-making. For example, rather than yet again conclude that interest groups need to be more engaged in policy-making, we were exploring ways to empower the public sector to improve its engagement practices. Second, we were looking to gain additional value from our research and earn independent income using in new ways the knowledge generated through our analytical work.

At the same time, public sector organizations were turning to us for advice and support. Our research was of high quality, but the actual implementation was challenging policy makers from the ministries. Initially, they asked for policy analysis, then for analysis-related consultations, and finally for trainings.

From one side, we experienced growing recognition of our work and from the other side, we expanded our thinking of how to utilize and recycle our knowledge. If there is a demand, and there are not many others who could fill this gap, why not tackle the opportunity to build up training and consulting capacity in addition to the existing analytical competence and expand the ways we work as an independent think-tank?

The birth and essence of Praxis Academy

After discussion among the staff and the Supervisory Board of Praxis, the managing board of Praxis decided to launch Praxis Academy in June 2011 as a new unit inside Praxis; a program director and a project manager were hired.

Initially, most of the time of the director and the managing board was focused on defining the vision and mission of the Academy, its expected role and competitive advantage, its position inside Praxis, and its public image. The Academy was a serious decision also financially – about 15,000 euros were spent as initial investment to elaborate the conceptual side, prepare the first trainings, and introduce our new role to potential partners. At first, there were some occasional trainings, but in January 2012 Academy started its first larger training project for civil society organizations (CSOs) on charitable giving. A year before, Praxis analysts had completed research on the same topic, so the training was a logical and valuable step to take.

From its birth, Praxis Academy has been a center for training and development to offer expertise for good governance and handling complicated policy challenges in Estonia and abroad. Our main services are training and development activities for civil servants, civil society leaders, politicians, and researchers. Praxis Academy's work is building on research, knowledge, and reform experience of the experts from Praxis, Estonia and other countries. Our work is supported by applied research, with the main focus on better, open, and accountable policy-making. The Academy does not work on issues not related to our programmatic work; we consider every potential project carefully to ensure we have relevant understanding, knowledge, and experience on the topic. Activities organized by Praxis Academy have enabled us to disseminate knowledge of our research in novel ways, build better contacts with our target groups, develop and expand the competencies of our analytical staff, and generate income in order to maintain independence.

Measuring Performance: the work of Praxis Academy in 2013

- In 2013, we implemented 81 training/development days and on average, 20 people attended each training. About two-thirds of the trainings were carried out by Praxis' own experts (9 people) and the remaining third by external experienced trainers. Our own people are empowered to disseminate their analytical work; external trainers have been proud to be associated with Praxis Academy and look forward to working with us in the future.
- The trainings differ from each other: some are

repetitions of the same training 10-15 times (e.g., impact assessment, public engagement) and some are different trainings but with the same target group (e.g., three trainings for 20 Georgian CSOs). Repeated trainings show that we have pin-pointed important topics that interest many people.

- Our clients return to us, asking Praxis Academy to design and conduct tailor-made trainings, development programs, or seminars to meet the specific needs and requests of their staffs.
- We use feedback forms to evaluate our trainings (on a 4-point scale, 4 being the highest and 1 the lowest score), and all our trainings and trainers have been rated between 3.75-4—a very high score.
- During its two and a half years of life (as of the end of 2013) Praxis Academy has become one of the biggest programs in Praxis, in terms of the contribution to its annual overhead—which is covering the think-tank's administrative and general personnel costs (25 percent of the total in 2012 and 21 percent in 2013). The Academy's annual turnover as a percent of the Praxis total increased from 12 percent in 2012 to around 17 percent in 2013.
- We have also worked in Georgia, Montenegro, and Latvia, and hosted study-visits to groups from China, Mongolia, and Vietnam. Our goal is to have 50 percent of our activities abroad, but that is still a long way ahead.

Challenges and the future

We have a few challenges to work on:

- **Cross-organizational work:** to ensure that all our programs have at least two topics they are ready to provide trainings on, in order to reuse their expertise. Historically, Praxis has been a center for policy analysis; and such new activities as training, consulting, and direct empowerment of different target groups need time and constant effort to succeed. Not all analysts are well-suited and wish to be trainers. But those who have taken these new roles have enjoyed the experience and cite its value for their professional development. So the challenge is about balancing the analytical and training work.
- **International work:** to increase the Academy's level of activity working abroad. The main challenge is that our experts are mainly working and living in Estonia and are not ready to spend a lot of time abroad. Also, we are still young and we need to build up our experience and reputation for international work. We wish to extend our network beyond the current countries, and we

have worked and built a solid network of think-tanks from the Baltic Sea countries in order to advance topics that affect us all (e.g., health, migration, labor market).

- **Opening market and generating income:** to test new steps in enlarging the potential clients of our trainings. In 2012, we conducted an open summer school on quantitative methods of assessment that was very popular. Other than that, we have responded to the bids from the clients. Open-enrolment trainings besides the current pre-ordered group-trainings are something we must assess.

During the recent strategy renewal process of Praxis, we confirmed the importance and role of Praxis Academy in Praxis. Knowledge brokering is as important as research itself, and if we want to be a successful and influential think-tank, we need to get out and put that knowledge into good use for those we are trying to engage and influence.

Annika Uudelepp & Kristina Mänd
Praxis
Tallinn, Estonia

Chapter 10
Pluses and Minuses of Government Funding

When a government agency spends money on policy research, it is usually because it needs the information and analysis for policy or program development or improvement. Yes, there are exceptions, most notably during the era of the Soviet Union and today in a few of the Central Asia successor states, where institutes grind out seldom read studies in compliance with an annual plan. But otherwise, where the agency-client is interested in the findings, the think tank that produces them has a head-start in influencing the direction of the ultimate policy decision, both through its research findings and as a continuing trusted advisor. For a think tank, government support also can be an important source of funding diversification.

Nevertheless, the decision on whether to work for the government is very often a difficult and complex one for think tanks—such as justified concerns about an actual or perceived loss of independence, perceived interference in the research, and loss of control over the institution's research agenda. This chapter considers government support for policy research from several angles, starting with a review of think tanks' current revenue sources. Hiring think tanks is then explored from the government's perspective. After reviewing arguments for and against working for the government from the think tank's perspective, I give some thoughts on framing the actual up or down decision and advice on ways to be competitive in this market for those deciding to enter it or already participating in it. Overall, I seek to encourage think tanks not to dismiss accepting (or competing for) government funding without thoroughly exploring, not only the downsides of doing so, but also the potentially positive aspects.

Think tanks' heavy dependence on financing from international organizations is ample evidence that they need little help understanding this market. The government market, in contrast, often seems poorly understood, although in many countries working on government contracts holds substantial promise as a revenue source and as a way to enhance policy engagement.[124]

---

124   A general resource of all types of NGO fundraising (both to reach various target audiences and for using a range of methods) is The Resource Alliance—http://www.resource-alliance.org/. See particularly the material in the site's Knowledge Hub. CIPPEC is currently well-advanced in developing an on-line course, "Re-thinking Your Funding Model," which will be specifically tailored to think tanks and builds on its experience in mentoring think tanks on this topic.

THINK TANK REVENUE SOURCES—DEPENDENCY ON THE INTERNATIONAL COMMUNITY

A common view is that support to think tanks from domestic foundations and other philanthropies is meager in developing and transition countries. This leaves many such think tanks heavily dependent upon international foundations, multilateral aid agencies, and bilateral aid programs.[125] The figures in Table 10.1 for the GDN-15 and TTI-48 think tanks support this idea. They show that these think tanks received over 70 percent of their funds from international sources, with smaller organizations being slightly more dependent than larger ones. Table 10.2 provides further information on the importance of this type of support. Two-thirds of all think tanks and almost 80 percent of Stage 1 organizations derive over 70 percent of their revenue from these sources. Such dependence is, indeed, heavy.

Table 10.1 Revenue Sources for the GDN-15 and TTI-48 Think Tanks[a]

Percent distributions

Source	<=10 FT researchers	>10 FT researchers	All
International organizations	78	69	72
Contracts from domestic government agencies	8	7	7
Contracts from domestic for-profit firms	2	3	2
Grants from domestic foundations and other nonprofit organizations	5	10	8
Other (publications, course fees, dues)	5	11	11

a. Data are from the 2010 and 2011 surveys for GDN and TTI, respectively.

Table 10.2 Revenue from International Sources for GDN-15 and TTI-48 Think Tanks[a]

Percent distributions

	<10 FT Researchers	>=10 FT Researchers	All
Under 10%	4	3	3
11% - 30%	4	11	8
31% - 50%	13	14	14
51% - 70%	0	14	8
Over 70%	78	58	66

a. Data are from the 2010 and 2011 surveys for GDN and TTI, respectively.

---

125   On the utility of various funding sources to think tanks in a specific context see, for example, Richards (2013a) and Moncada (2013).

As anticipated, grant funding from domestic foundations and other NGOs is very limited, accounting for only 8 percent of revenues on average. Contracts from government agencies account on average for 7 percent of all funding. Contracts with domestic for-profit firms yield negligible income on average (Table 10.1).

The funding patterns just reviewed point to four funding-related issues that think tank leaders must manage. While these are discussed further below, some initial comment helps set the stage. The first issue is vulnerability to an unexpected decline in funding available from one or more international sources. Even among U.S. think tanks, which usually have diversified funding sources, substantial instability in overall revenues is evident. Between 2011 and 2012, Hans Gutbrod (2013a) has documented revenue changes of *under* 10 percent for only 8 of 20 major think tanks. But seven of the 20 had revenue changes *greater than* 25 percent. Some of this is presumably due to the vagaries of payments around the end of a fiscal year, but real changes are certainly involved as well.

Generally, funding source diversification offers some protection against very large funding swings. Most think tanks in transition and developing countries are highly dependent on international funders but they may be well-diversified within this particular source. Even so, building up another category of support to account regularly for 15-20 percent of total revenues typically offers significant help in cushioning annual funding variations.

The second issue is lack of control over the topics on which a think tank works. An important question concerns the extent to which think tanks are receiving unrestricted funds for projects and institutional development grants. If they have significant funding from such sources to pursue their primary research missions and institutional development, accepting government and other contracts for other work will be less constraining.

Information on this point is also available from the GDN-15 and TTI-48 surveys. About half of these think tanks combined had at least 15 percent of their project funding from unrestricted funds, with no particular variation by think tank size. In other words, there is some, though limited, unrestricted project money available. For many of these think tanks the inability to find project funding consistent with their planned research programs means real difficulty in executing them. While government funding will usually be restricted, it nevertheless can help think tanks "buy time" in retaining research staff until they can align funding with their priority research themes. Moreover, as noted, they will be working on issues important to governments.

A third, and related, issue concerns the incidence of institutional development grants among think tanks. Among GDN-15 think tanks in 2011, two-thirds received major funding of this type, with *all* Stage 1 think tanks receiving it. Although this question was not asked in the TTI survey, TTI participating think tanks typically have grants from the program equivalent to about 25 percent of their expenditures, a substantial share of which goes to institutional development. (Larger organizations receive a smaller percentage.)

The final funding-related issue is the short-term nature of the great majority of project funding, i.e., a year or less. Obviously, this vastly complicates executing larger projects—those requiring before-and-after surveys, for example, or those whose research sequencing makes compression into a 9-12 month execution period nearly or actually impossible. Only foundations and some bilateral organizations generally support projects with lives of two to three years or more.

GOVERNMENTS AS SUPPORTERS OF POLICY RESEARCH

This section covers several distinct topics on government agencies outsourcing policy research. I begin by exploring agencies' motivation to do so. I then discuss the model under which support is in the form of substantial budget support to a small number of government affiliated but still independent think tanks. I turn in the last section to the more common model of contracting out specific surveys, studies, and analyses. The chapter ends, as usual, with 'Take Aways' and 'For Funders.'

Why Outsource?

Five reasons for a government agency to contract out for research and evaluation studies come readily to mind.

1. *Staff constraints*. It is doubtful that a government ministry will ever be permitted to hire the volume of staff it would need to meet the reasonable requests for research and program evaluation made by the minister and assistant ministers, plus requests from the prime minister's office. Given this reality, hiring additional resources from outside the agency is a necessity.

2. *Staff Mix*. It is rare that government agencies are able to attract the necessary mix of economists, policy analysts, statisticians, sampling and survey experts, and others to serve as civil servants.

3. *Flexibility*. Practically every agency operates a range of programs. The typical range of research and evaluation projects calls for diverse skills and backgrounds to address the issues of these different programs efficiently and accurately. It makes no sense for the agency to have such a large staff when the need for a specific skill set is episodic. A particular program, for example, may need an impact evaluation once every several years. Hence, contracting out is more efficient than building up an agency's in-house staff.

4. *Having advice available when needed*. Government agencies in some countries may have believed, or do believe, that private sector support would be insufficient to sustain high quality think tanks whose advice they badly want. They may have also have wanted, or do want, to be certain they can get advice very quickly when it is urgently needed, without going through a contracting process. Hence, they want to provide support to sustain capacity.

5. *Need for longer-term advice*. When providing long-term support, governments are looking for deeper, more thoughtful analysis in a sector, ranging from identification of new issues to development of sharply different options for addressing long-standing problems. Therefore, it sets up think tanks or provides substantial long-term budget support to a few institutions.

Under the socialist system, most ministries had research institutes attached to them, and some countries continue this practice today. In the Soviet system, the ministry and the institute would negotiate a work plan annually, and funds to execute the plan would be allocated from the central budget (not typically the ministry's). In other words, there was a tradition of contracting out for research in the Eastern Europe-Commonwealth of Independent States (CIS) region. What has changed in these countries is that the work is now often (although not always) allocated competitively, and managers probably have a stronger interest in the timeliness and usefulness of the analysis produced.

In many transition and developing countries today, public universities have in-house think tanks that enjoy substantial government funding. Through government representatives on their Boards and other channels, ministries' priorities are conveyed to these organizations. Governments in these countries also often heavily support a few free-standing think tanks.

But do not think the model of major general or budget funding to think tanks by government agencies has been used only in socialist or transition countries. The Urban Institute in Washington, DC, for example, received generous budget support from the housing ministry for 10 years before this type of support was discontinued by mutual agreement. The Institute was created in the last months of 1968, at the end of the administration of President Lyndon Johnson. Major U.S. cities had experienced serious rioting in 1967-1968 due to a toxic combination of race relation issues, poor services to inner city neighborhoods (including education), and disproportionately high Viet Nam war casualties to African Americans. Johnson created the Institute because he feared the incoming administration would devote too few resources to understanding the problems of cities as a basis for better public policy to address their problems.

Examples of think tanks in Africa with government founders and substantial, consistent general support include the Ethiopian Development Research Institute and the Economic Policy Research Center in Uganda.

Budget Support

As Goran Buldioski (2013) points out, core and institutional support, from donors or governments, usually has three components:

1. *Sustainability*—funds that partially underwrite the grantees' payroll, administrative, technical, and core expenses;
2. *Development*—funds spent on developing capacity of employees and improvements in the organizations' research infrastructure, plus communication capacity, management practices, and governance;
3. *Seed funding*—funds spent directly on policy research, often on topics that are not yet attractive to other donors or that the grantee prefers to pilot carefully or design further before scaling it up and applying to project-based donors.

Many national governments provide very substantial budget support to a wide range of think tanks, although there is no inventory of them as far as I know. And the support they provide usually includes all three of the components I have listed. I now focus on budget support provided in two quite different countries: the Federal Republic of Germany and the Republic of Korea (South Korea). I follow this with a brief description of government think tank support in Uzbekistan—quite a different case because of the political environment.[126]

Germany and South Korea. In both Germany and South Korea, the original motivation for creating such think tanks was to provide support for strong analytic work on issues of national concern at a time when the only analysis available was from university professors and aid agencies. (To my knowledge there are no cases of existing institutions having been selected for budget support of this type.) In Germany, support was more general than for think tanks *per se*. Funding is provided jointly by federal and state governments to a range of about 80 organizations, among which are six that focus on economic policy research. In Korea, the first government-supported think tank, the Korean Development Institute, was created in 1971 to fill a gap in the analytic basis for economic decision making. Today there are 23 budget-supported think tanks in Korea, each with a particular topical interest (e.g., health, real estate). Both countries have added think tanks in the past decade, indicating that the contributions of such think tanks remain highly valued.

The key characteristics of the arrangements under which these think tanks operate are quite similar and can be readily summarized:

Independence. In both countries, the council managing support of these think tanks is housed in the office of the prime minister (i.e., not under the direct oversight of a particular ministry). Government input comes in three forms:

- a review of the annual work plan (see below);
- a minority of the members of each think tank's Board being government representatives (e.g., 6 of 15, mostly from ministries relevant to the think tank's work) who tend to vote together—giving them quite a strong influence;
- external reviews of the quality and policy utility of the think tank's work (see below).

In case of a conflict between the government representatives and the think tank, the council (in the prime minister's office, as noted) would mediate.

---

126   Several sources were used in preparing this section. For Germany, I used the general description in Thunert (2004) and a presentation by and communications and discussions with Rolf Ketzler at one of the six supported economic institutes, DWI (Deutsche Institut fuer Wirtschaftsforschrung). For Korea, I worked at KDI in the late 1970s and visited there for a conference in 2011. KDI staff also provided written responses to questions. Observations on Uzbekistan are based on interviews conducted with think tanks there in early 2012.

Agenda setting. Each year a think tank drafts a work plan to the council that names the topics to be analyzed and outputs to be produced, based on consultations with the relevant ministries and private sector entities (in both business and civil society). The council itself reviews the plan and asks for comments. Eventually an agreed-upon plan is produced.

Dissemination. Although government agencies are their primary clients, these think tanks are expected to communicate their findings widely and to engage actively with civil society organizations in the policy development process. The quality of policy engagement is one of the areas on which they are evaluated.

Oversight and quality control. The funded think tanks are subject to external reviews that examine the technical quality of the work produced and its usefulness in the policy process—as judged by government agencies, businesses, and civil society. Review panels consist of well-respected persons outside government with knowledge of the sector on which the think tank works. In Germany, these reviews occur every seven years; in Korea they are annual. The review results are taken very seriously by the think tanks, because funding can be reduced in the case of consistently poor performance. A passing mark is required for continued funding.

Funding. Government-supported think tanks in both countries are encouraged to take contracts and grants from other funders. There is a strong belief by the think tanks and government that being responsive to external demand and possibly working on a broader array of topics are both useful experiences for the think tank. National government funding is determined annually based on proposed plans. Budgets are first approved by the council in the prime minister's office, and then the funds are voted by the parliaments. In reality, government funding is fairly constant over time in real terms. In Germany, the national budget support accounts for 65-70 percent of the total budget. In Korea, the proportion is somewhat higher on average.

Overall, the system seems to work well in both countries. Critically, there is strong good will on all sides, ensuring that the think tanks work independently and quality standards for their work are high. The external reviews are competently conducted and the results taken seriously by all. The think tanks themselves try to identify work that involves emerging policy issues as well as long-standing problems.

Uzbekistan. Not surprisingly, such strong results do not emerge everywhere a national government provides substantial budget support to think tanks. Uzbekistan is widely rated as governed by an authoritarian regime. The government expects organizations it supports to follow official policies and generally is not looking for contrarian advice. A couple of indicators of how six think tanks operating in that country nearly exclusively with government funding follow, based on interviews with senior officials and checking the websites of those of the six that have them:

- In determining their research agenda, four of the six consulted only government. Of the other two, one consulted international counterparts and faculty at a local university focused on international issues; the other, an economic think tank, discussed ideas with other think tanks and international donors.

- There are marked differences in the interest among these six think tanks in communicating results beyond their immediate government clients. Three have no website. One has a website but no reports are posted on it. One, the Center for Economic Research, displays a few—only those produced with international donor support. And one, the Center for Political Studies, displays all its reports; this institute addresses international questions and its chairman is the Uzbekistan president's daughter.

Overall, only two really appear to have the same motivations and objectives as most think tanks, although they are cautious in pursuing them. The one fully private think tank, the Center for Economic Development, in contrast, displays a strong desire to produce rigorous, policy-relevant research and to use that research objectively to improve government policies.

Contracting Out

It is much more common for government agencies to acquire policy research services by contracting for them as needed, rather than providing budget support to a set of think tanks. This section explores how such contracting is organized. The different arrangements are more or less favorable in winning work to strong technical proposals vs. "insider" relationships.

First and foremost, outsourcing requires money—that is, the agency's budget must have the necessary funds in its budget to spend for this purpose. Most countries have an explicit line item in an agency's budget for "research and evaluation" or something similar. Where this is not the case—and there are countries in Eastern Europe, for example, today without explicit line items—the agency is forced to divert funds from the delivery of services to fund outsourced work (if it is permitted by laws governing such spending), clearly a problematic situation.

Beyond money, outsourcing for research and evaluation requires the agency to be organized for this function. Table 10.3 illustrates three typical structures agencies adopt for this kind of contracting out.

Table 10.3 Ways Government Agencies Are Organized for Contracting Out

Model	Program office	Centralized research office in the agency	Procurement office in the agency
A	Secondary	Primary	Broad oversight
B	Shared	NA	Shared
C	Exclusive[a]	NA	Broad oversight

NA = not applicable
[a] Typically on small contracts—that is, those below a maximum amount set in the national procurement regulations

Model A is found in many western countries, but not often in transitional and developing countries. The main player is a special office responsible for policy development and research that reports directly to the minister. In this model, the policy development function is centralized rather than assigned to the assistant minister responsible for a particular program area. The model places the small number of policy experts in the ministry in the same office, which facilitates their work. It also addresses the reality that the policy development workload in a single program area varies sharply over time. When the policy staff is dispersed by program office, the staff in one office can be overwhelmed while that in the next office is underused. The Model A arrangement also collects in one place those staff with expertise in research, writing terms of reference, and conducting competitions.

The centralized office in Model A consults with the program offices to develop its annual research and evaluation agenda. Program office staff reviews terms of reference for a project being contracted and participates in the panels that score proposals from contractors for projects relevant to the office; but the process is controlled and managed by the central research office. The agency's procurement or contracts office monitors the competitions, negotiates contracts with help from the research office, and signs them.

Model B depicts the common arrangement in the Eastern Europe-CIS region and perhaps elsewhere. Responsibilities are shared between the program office and the procurement office. There is no centralized research and policy development office in Model B. Tasks within the contracting process (as described in the next section) are shared between the two.

Model C, where the program office has full responsibility, coexists with Model B in most agencies. Usually, an office can use this arrangement only when the value of the contract is below a maximum amount—an amount specified in the national procurement regulations. In principle, Model C should be used rarely. The reality appears rather different, with many offices using this model routinely to avoid the administrative complications that come with Model B. Within Model C, in some countries the program office can simply select a firm without competitive bidding for small value contracts.[127] For amounts above the limit on the non-competition contracts and below the threshold for a full competition (when Model B must be used), the program office runs a limited competition—meaning typically at least three firms must submit a bid. The flexibility afforded program offices by these rules affects how think tanks market themselves to agencies with whom they want to work, as described later.

The three models engender sharply different opportunities for freedom of action by program offices. The absence of constraints can lead to unhealthy practices in deciding who receives contracts. Many think tanks, when confronted with such bias against them, simply stop competing.

---

127   In Hungary in 2005, an office could negotiate a contract with a single contractor if the contract value was under HUF 2 million (~$10,000); the maximum contract amount for limited competitions was HUF 10 million; both maximum amounts are exclusive of the applicable value-added tax.

Annex 10.1 provides an overview of the tasks government agencies must execute well to contract out successfully for policy research. Understanding these tasks is useful for think tanks that seek to compete for work with the agency in question.

CHALLENGES AND BENEFITS OF BEING A GOVERNMENT POLICY RESEARCH CONTRACTOR

Deciding to work under government contracts, especially for think tanks just beginning such relationships, will raise a host of issues for think tank management to consider and to discuss with the staff. A review of the factors discussed below will suggest that pursuing government work could have complex repercussions within an organization that need to be considered carefully in making the decision to do so. The list of considerations should be useful for assessing other possible relationships, e.g., working closely with a political party.

This section focuses on possible negatives and positives to contractual relations with government agencies, i.e., it does not treat a think tank becoming a budget-supported organization similar to the German and Korean think tanks discussed above. Traditionally budget-supported think tanks were founded with this status: very few existing think tanks apply to become a budget-dependent organization. It is worth noting, however, that in some African countries a hybrid model appears to be emerging: a national government selects a few existing think tanks it believes are playing a positive role in the public policy arena and provides them with consistent unconstrained funding. One reported example is le Centre d'Etudes, de Documentation et de Recherche Economiques et Sociales (CEDRES) support from the government of Burkina Faso.

Challenges
Lack of independence, confused identity. By far the greatest worry of think tanks that have not worked previously with government agencies is that their policy independence will be limited. Even when the right to publish materials based on work done under contract is present, there is still some question of whether the think tank consultant is engaging in some self-censorship to ensure continuing good relations with the client. And, inevitably, the clients themselves are nervous about what the consultant may release and in what form. The following example is instructive.

In February 2013 I met with a Deputy Minister of a Georgian Ministry, who had formerly been a senior researcher at a local think tank. A new government had just been elected in November, with Bidzina Ivanishvili the new prime minister. In the course of our discussion, the Deputy Minister said he was encouraging international foundations and bilateral donors to support more policy research on particular issues faced by the ministry. I asked why his ministry did not set aside funds to commission its own research. His response was that no one would believe a think tank would, under a contract, produce recommendations that were truly independent of the ministry. As a consequence, think tanks, worried about their reputation for independence, would not accept such contracts.

Another common concern arises in countries where the procurement process is often corrupt. The think tanks' worry here is that even if they win a competition strictly on the basis of their proposals, the common view will be that they must have paid a bribe to receive the contract. The reality may be a more complex mixture of honest and corrupt procurements, where the honest ones are likely to be cases where the results are of high importance to the ministry.

It is unclear in how many countries such concerns exist, although they are a force to be addressed. But in many, many countries, think tanks clearly are able to accept government grants and contracts while still retaining their policy independence and integrity. (It is also the case that agencies often want solid, objective research, even if the contractor pays a bribe to get the work.)

Okechukwu Ibeanu has written a thoughtful review of conditions in Nigeria since the country's return to civilian rule in 1999. He concludes that the likelihood of government agencies trying to influence a think tank's findings varies with the institution's reputation, type of issue addressed, and methodologies used. Ibeanu finds it useful to distinguish among three cases (Ibeanu 2008, paraphrased):

- Think tanks with a track record of independence, access to internal or corporate funding, and a professional approach—particularly those producing high-quality output or work that fills a special niche—are unlikely to curtail any criticism implied by their findings, in spite of their position as clients of the government.

- The more technical the focus of a think tank's work, the less likely it is that government will interfere and/or that the institution will moderate any legitimate criticism.

- Think tanks focusing on material of a political or ideological nature are more vulnerable than others; the more political the content, the more likely it is that government will interfere and that the institution will be forced to modify its criticism when present.

The lessons here have validity beyond Nigeria. Independence (and credibility) can be fostered by a think tank's consistent record of taking policy positions squarely based on its research. The more politically charged the research topic or policy prescriptions, the greater the tendency of government agencies to attempt to influence the think tank's reports and publications.[128]

My experience also indicates several practical steps a think tank can take in managing relations with a government agency it has a contract with that will result in few "crises" about what the think tank disseminates. One is to study the provisions of draft contracts regarding use and ownership of information collected in the project and the contractor's rights to disseminate findings. I have found over the years that both government contract officers and those at multi-lateral organizations have

---

128   Additional background on the historical factors at work in Nigeria and elsewhere in sub-Saharan Africa can be found in Kimenyi and Data (2011).

been quite open to making adjustments to relax the very stringent limiting language in boilerplate contracts. With specific regard to dissemination, two often acceptable provisions are that the contractor: 1) can disseminate findings, but not until the final report is accepted or 60 days after its submission whichever comes first, and 2) must provide the agency a copy of all publications one or two weeks before they are issued—for information purposes, not review.

Two more points on contract provisions are important. First, you may be a subcontractor to a prime contractor that has the contract with the government or other client. Quite often, "flow through provisions" are included in subcontracts (i.e., articles in the prime contract that apply to subcontractors). Such provisions are usually cited by reference and not actually listed in the subcontractor's contract. It is wise to ask if they deal with intellectual property rights or publications provisions and, if so, ask to review them before signing the contract. These clauses can be very restrictive, even if those explicitly stated in the subcontract are not.

The second point is that severe restrictions on the intellectual property content of the work and publication rights are a common feature in contracts issued—not only by government agencies, but by many multilateral agencies, bi-lateral donors, foundations, and even think tanks. To my knowledge, no source is currently available for think tanks to use in tailoring alternative formulations with varying degrees of stringency. Thus, each think tank is forced to learn by doing in trying various formulations with clients over time.[129]

Because a think tank's working life with a particular agency will likely last a number of years, the think tank has a strong incentive to maintain positive relations with it. The golden rule for a successful relationship is the same *no surprises* rule I allude to earlier in the book. No minister or even program officer wants to learn from a local news show or tweet about a think tank's release of a report, or the content of the think tank expert's testimony about their agency before a parliamentary committee. Notifying the agency of releases and events, sharing the report or other content in advance, and even inviting agency staff participation are well-appreciated courtesies and often add credibility to events. Such notifications afford the agency staff time to prepare articulate, factual responses to criticisms rather than being caught unawares.

A relevant facet of managing the start-up of work with government agencies is that some traditional funders may be concerned about the potential effects on a think tank's mission when it begins to take government contracts or receive substantial budget support. They may, for example, be concerned that information collected in projects they support will be made available in an unauthorized way to government sponsors. A tailored letter/email sent in advance to the project officer at each funder can effectively alleviate such misgivings.

Some think tanks have found it advantageous to set up wholly owned for-profit subsidiaries for

---

129   Additional commentary on contract provisions is in Mendizabal (2014a).

executing projects for government agencies or the business community. Typically, the subsidiary has the same overhead structure as the nonprofit parent organization, with the addition of an explicit fee (profit). The subsidiary frequently is given a different name, to avoid confusion among clients and sponsors about which part of the organization is working on which projects.

Creating a separate entity may be an especially good idea for RAOs embedded in a service-provider NGO, to minimize confusion about its mission and place in the larger organization.

Agenda-setting and lack of focus. Consultants, almost by definition, are responding to the perceived needs of their clients. Because clients are setting their own agendas, the greater the share of a firm's work based on consulting rather than its own agenda, the more reactive the firm will be overall and the weaker its ability to set its own agenda.

In the United States, for example, major think tanks that receive a substantial share of their income from U.S. government contracts (such as RAND and the Urban Institute) maintain control over a significant portion of their agenda, by obtaining funds from foundations and state governments to pursue topics that may not be on the federal agenda at the moment. The difficulty this model presents for think tanks in many other parts of the world is that the volume of funds from foundations may not be sufficient to permit a critical level of self-determined projects. That said, the potential of contractors to influence future government agency research agendas through their work with agency staff (rather than the other way round) can be considerable.

Similar focus issues arise with international funding from foundations, bi-lateral funders, and the major multi-lateral agencies. (See the initial section under the Rewards section, below, for further discussion.)

Restricted use of data and publications. In consulting for government agencies and, increasingly, in work for donors, there are sharp restrictions on consultants' rights to use data assembled or reports produced during the consultancy, for any purpose besides those of direct interest to the client. Such restrictions correspondingly limit the work of consulting think tanks in the policy process.

Think tanks with contracts with government agencies deal with this problem, in the countries where it occurs, in two ways. First, they work hard at negotiating publication and use-of-data clauses in their contracts, so their rights in these areas are preserved. Sometimes this involves giving the client exclusive use of the data for a longer period than the 60 days mentioned above— often three to six months. In other cases, the clients secure the right to receive an advance copy of any publication dealing with the project and comment on it within a specified period, but they cannot block publication. The second way to deal with this problem is for a think tank to simply refuse to accept contracts with some classes of restrictions. In the U.S., one of the requirements for think tanks to maintain their nonprofit tax status is that all the work done by such organizations be broadly for the public good—meaning it can be shared openly with the public; proprietary research and consulting is inconsistent with this requirement.

The same lessons are applicable to work for International Finance Institutions (IFIs), such as the World Bank. I have been involved in a dozen or more projects where publication and data clauses were renegotiated—after winning a competition but before signing a contract—with government agencies and IFIs, with little fanfare, to give the think tank more use rights.

Conflict of cultures within the think tank. Think tank staff dedicated to the public purposes and freedom of expression for which a think tank was created can be seriously disturbed if the institution decides to take on for-profit work.[130] Charges of incompatibility of objectives, operational styles, and "corporate behavior" are all likely to be raised.

Very often, the consultant-think tank is not familiar with a client's specific needs or operations before being contracted, which means an intense start-up phase for many projects. Hence, team leaders and staff may be unenthusiastic about initiating such contracts.

Restive clients or sponsors. An institution's traditional sponsors may not agree with the arguments for a think tank taking on consulting work for government agencies. At an extreme they could even withdraw their support. This, in my experience, is extremely unusual. Most foundation executives appreciate both the need for a steady stream of revenue and the fact that work directly with government gives researchers a distinct advantage in the policy process.

Management challenges. While think tank directors must have good management instincts to run a successful firm, their instincts alone are frequently insufficient to guide the enterprise when the scale of operations expands significantly—particularly when the number of projects under way simultaneously, and the number of separate sponsors, rise. Moreover, the nature of the contractual conditions often differs by project, as do reporting requirements. In short, establishing a consulting practice with government agencies often requires further development of management and financial systems, and the size of the task can easily be underestimated.

Benefits of Being a Government Contractor

The foregoing recitation of the difficulties think tanks face when taking on consulting assignments sounds formidable. These problems, however, are balanced significantly by certain positives from doing such work—gains that go far beyond increased revenues.

Relevance and visibility. There is broad agreement that think tanks working on issues of high priority to government agencies or to senior parliamentarians have a better chance of having their work noticed and used than those working on less prominent issues. Martin's (2013) statistical analysis with data for TTI participants shows a significant positive relationship between the share of a think tank's revenue from government contracts and the strength of its being positively viewed in the local policy community. The following, somewhat extreme example, makes the point vividly

---

130   This problem and the next two are discussed in Davies (1997, 33-44).

about relevance to local policy issues:

> Bosnia Herzegovina, in the early years of its redevelopment after its war with Serbia through 2003, offers a fine example of donors utterly crowding out local analysis—which had never really moved to the private sector (from government institutes because the war with Serbia followed the break-up of Yugoslavia so closely). After the Dayton Agreement, the UN Office of the High Representative and various international agencies (bi- and multi-lateral) working with the government defined the policy agenda and carried out the related research—sometimes inviting local firms and nascent think tanks to do parts of the survey and analysis tasks. Draft laws, ready for approval, were submitted for largely rubber-stamp action by the government and parliament.
>
> In 2003, when the international community began to withdraw from its nearly total dominance of policy making, a three-year think tank mentoring project was initiated with the support of USAID. At the beginning of the project, the project team asked think tank leaders for policy research topics it could support. They had almost no ideas. They had been so restricted to being contractors (supporting the UNDP, the World Bank, and others) and to doing surveys and technical analyses in support of the UN's policy agenda, that they were not really thinking critically about identifying the major policy issues confronting the country. In short, these think tanks were both crowded out and debilitated.
>
> Some think tanks were invited by the USAID contractor to carry out a policy research project. Each had to define a policy issue of interest to a government agency and was required to have a senior government "sponsor" for the project, i.e., someone who said they would use the analysis to promote change if it were done.
>
> At the beginning of the project, policymakers were interviewed by those involved with the mentoring project about the extent to which they used materials developed by think tanks. Most did not even recognize the names of the main think tanks. Three years later, another survey by the same group documented that the situation had changed very sharply, because think tanks had been delivering results regarding issues on the government's and the parliament's agenda. In short, relevance to the local policy agenda accounted for much of the fundamental shift in officials' attitudes over the period. (Struyk et al., 2007)

A second example comes from the spring 2014 interviews I did with a dozen executive directors of South Asian think tanks.[131] Three said they discounted their bids to certain government agencies to win contracts, so they would have the insider advantage in working on policy issues with ministry officials.

The point in the present context is that a think tank's refusal to compete for project funding is particularly unfortunate when its core policy interests coincide with the government's. Because foundations and other international players have their own agendas, support from these sources is generally not readily available for many of the government's priority policy topics. In other words, local and donor agendas may have limited overlap. Heavy reliance of donor funding (and working on that agenda) is likely to reduce a think tank's visibility and relevance to local policymakers.[132] While executing government policy research projects under contract increases think tanks' relevance and visibility, it does not provide them the freedom to work on high priority issues on their own country's agendas.

Broader base of experience for policy development. Many government consultancies require researchers to delve more deeply into the operational details of a public program than they would do in their regular research. For example, the agency responsible for an income-targeted food subsidy program wants to better understand why participation rates are low. One hypothesis is that applicants face time-consuming and intrusive procedures at front line intake offices. A think tank wins a contract to investigate the situation because of its prior work on program design, including developing materials for income-testing. To carry out the new assignment, it must learn and document in detail the various steps in the intake process at front-line offices and then survey applicants, both successful and not, about their experience at a sample of intake offices. This is highly specific analysis. But the experience gained will be invaluable, even if as only general background, in working with the relevant ministry or the parliament on means-testing procedures more generally.

Funding diversification. Heavy dependence on international agencies, particularly foundations and bi-lateral programs, is risky. Earlier I note that about two-thirds of sample GDN and TTI think tanks' funds are coming from the international sources. Typically, foundations and bi-lateral donors see their missions in terms of providing a time-limited catalyst to their grantees to achieve a major policy objective, and at the same time, to help recipients solidify their position in a country's policy arena. Foundations conscientiously work to avoid a think tank or NGO becoming dependent on them for funding over protracted periods.

The international finance institutions (e.g., World Bank, UNDP) are less concerned about dependency than are foundations, because they contract with think tanks for a project and are generally clear about having an arm's length relationship with its contractors. Governments have no "de-

---

131   These circumstances for these interviews are sketched in Chapter 1.
132   See Ordonez (2013) for commentary on the tension between local policy agendas and donors'.

pendency" concerns. Indeed, they often prefer to work with contractors they know to be reliable in producing good work on the schedule specified in a contract. In terms of funding likely to be available year-after-year, government contracts are attractive.

In this environment, diversification to include government contracts and grants for a meaningful funding share can often be sensible for think tanks.

Improved efficiency. Some think tanks work predominantly for a restricted set of clients in the foundation world. Foundations tend to favor work on the cutting edge of policy development—work where some risk of low return is present. Moreover, for at least some of these projects, the work schedule is not very intense. The contrast with the work regime involved in government consulting is stark. First, services are typically provided to government agencies on quite tight schedules. An opportunity or problem has been defined, and the organization must act quickly to address it.

A second difference between work for foundations and government agencies concerns the difference between work done under grants vs. contracts. Contracts are more specific about products, deadlines, and reporting. In addition, competition is generally keener for these contracts, because for-profit as well as nonprofit entities compete. So, think tanks that work under contract to government agencies or private businesses, as well as donors, are exposed to a different and in some ways more demanding work regime than those working exclusively for foundations. Several think tank directors I interviewed for an earlier think tank study made this point about consulting work, and they saw the result on the efficiency of their overall operations as positive (Struyk 1999).

Support for overhead functions. From a financial perspective, consulting contracts are usually viewed positively because they keep the professional staff engaged on reasonably interesting and policy-important projects. But there is a second important financial dimension. By raising the overall revenue base of the firm, consulting income reduces the firm's overhead rates. For example, operation of the website, an overhead item, is now amortized over a larger revenue base, driving down the cost of communications services associated with each hour of staff time. True, the existence of more projects is likely to result in more pages needed on the website, but for many overhead items the increases are less than proportional. Thus, over a reasonable range of expansion, a greater volume of work results in lower overhead costs per hour of professional labor—provided, of course, that the array of overhead services remains constant.

A think tank can elect to take advantage of this "dividend" in two general ways: overhead rates can be reduced, making the firm more price-competitive for acquiring additional work, or new overhead services can be added. For example, as the firm expands it can hire a public relations officer without undermining its competitive position.

Improved visibility and marketing possibilities. By expanding the range of topics and clients with which the think tank works, consultancies should lead to greater exposure of the organization's capabilities to new market segments. Being associated with major government reforms is particularly attractive to sponsors interested in change.

MAKING THE DECISION

There are actually two decisions involved here. The first is whether to pursue work from the government at all; the second is the decision on whether to compete for a specific project.

The general decision depends on how the think tank's senior management and board of trustees weigh the various factors just discussed. Importantly, it must be understood that some general investments will be necessary to pursue government work beyond the cost of preparing proposals. Contract provisions and reporting requirements will differ from those of foundations and other funders; staff will have to master these details; software may be needed to efficiently discharge the reporting requirements. These are not costs that must all be incurred at the outset, but they will impose a significant burden over the first year or two.

On the question of whether to pursue a particular opportunity, including government contracts, Lykke Andersen (2012) sets out six criteria for deciding whether to take on a consulting project, regardless of the funding source, to support a long-term research agenda.[133]

1. *Synergies with other projects.* Make sure new projects complement ongoing projects and fit well with your long-term research agenda.
2. *Publication potential.* Avoid projects that result in confidential reports. Instead, aim for projects that dedicate at least 10 percent of the budget to publication and dissemination. You want your work to be known and contribute to the global knowledge pool.
3. *Relationship building.* Prioritize large projects involving many different institutions rather than individual desk work. This is more complicated; but it is an excellent way of building relationships and trust with policy makers and key stakeholders, a necessary condition for achieving real impact on real people someday.
4. *Project duration.* Choose projects of at least 6-12 months duration; short consulting projects tend to disrupt the long-term research agenda because they always tend to become the most urgent, even if they are not the most important.
5. *Knowledge transfer.* Choose international, collaborative projects where you will learn new research tools from cutting-edge researchers abroad.
6. *Financing.* Choose only projects that pay the full cost. There is no need to subsidize development banks or government agencies.

---

133   The list of items is slightly paraphrased from Andersen (2012). Similar commentary is provided by Arellano (2014).

To these I would add one more—*intellectual property rights*. These need to include use of data and other material gathered by the project, in both prime and subcontracts if both are involved.

The greater the extent that the proposed project matches these criteria, the more desirable it is to pursue. Of course, a potentially important factor can be how badly the institution needs the funding to sustain its overall operations; at certain points, you can expect this to override nearly all other considerations.

Annex 10.2 discusses how think tanks who decide to compete for government contracts can be competitive in doing so.

WHEN GOVERNMENT AGENCIES DO NOT HAVE RESEARCH BUDGETS

Remarkable as it may seem in this era of the "new public management," when outsourcing by governments for all kinds of goods and services is commonplace, some countries have not enabled government agencies to contract out routinely for research and program evaluations. Bosnia and Herzegovina is one such example.[134] Azerbaijan and Georgia are others.[135] In these countries, the little contracting out that is done is financed by funds taken from other budget lines, usually those that fund actual program operations. Occasionally, agencies rely on separately funded research institutes.

The question of interest here is: what can think tanks do in such cases to promote legislation that would create a line item for research in government agency budgets? Based on observing think tanks and certain donors lobbying for the creation of agency research budgets in Bosnia, I think three ingredients are necessary for progress on this front.

The first is to demonstrate the utility of using research in the policy process. The idea is to identify examples of research conducted by local think tanks with funding from international foundations or from international donors (such as the World Bank or UNDP) that played an important role in informing the government and the parliament on a particular policy issue. Examples may differ for the government and the parliament. Several examples are better than one or two. And they should be examples where the use of the information was quite visible, i.e., cited in the press and by officials on TV and radio shows. These cases are evidence for the government and parliament that policy research can play an important role in developing the country's policies and programs.

The second ingredient is a united effort by local think tanks and research-advocacy organizations

---

134   In 2004, with assistance from the European Union, the Bosnia and Herzegovina government created the Economic Policy Planning Unit in the office of the prime minister, with the tasks of monitoring implementation of the country's midterm development strategy and conducting timely policy research. This was the only formally funded research in the government at that time, although some agencies found funds from non-dedicated sources to finance some studies. My understanding is that this pilot project did not succeed in convincing the government and parliament to establish a policy research line item in the budgets.

135   Based on interviews with ministry officials in both countries.

to lobby key government ministers—perhaps ultimately even the prime minister—and members of parliament, to enact the necessary legislation and to appropriate at least small funding amounts for the new research line item. Getting cooperation among think tanks may be difficult. The adjective best describing their relations with each other is probably "competitive" rather than "collegial." Although such an attitude is understandable, this is one case where the common good has to prevail to make progress. Combined local think tanks, possibly partnering with advocacy NGOs, have the necessary contacts with government and parliamentary leaders. With cooperation in hand, the way forward is execution of a carefully drawn lobbying plan, under which two or three think tank leaders together visit the key political leaders and make the case for funding research.

The basic argument to make in this situation is clear: there are concrete examples where research has served an important role in improving legislation or program implementation; it is only available now if the funding is external, which is only present on a hit-or-miss basis for issues that are a local priority; to improve national policymaking and program administration, agencies should be able to fund their own research. It also may be useful to fortify this argument with an example from a neighboring country that explicitly funds research in agency budgets. Enlisting carefully targeted support from heads of the local representative offices of the international donors should also be helpful.

The final ingredient is the capacity of government agencies to administer research programs professionally. The tasks involved, which are outlined in Annex 10.1, are formidable. The civil servants managing the program need not be highly experienced social science researchers. But they must have training, and probably advanced degrees, in the social sciences to be able to draft terms of references, critically review proposals submitted, and rigorously monitor contractor performance. Few ministries without significant in-house policy development offices have persons on staff with such credentials to execute these functions, although most countries have a surfeit of unemployed university graduates with the relevant degrees. Hence, a team with such credentials must eventually be recruited, initially perhaps five or six in number, and located in a new office for policy development and research. In addition to commissioning external research, this team would also provide ongoing policy development support to the minister and assistant ministers responsible for administering major programs. (Because of the ministry staff costs for running an external research program, the program costs are substantially higher than just the funds paid to contractors.)

The head of this department is the critical player. S/he has to understand both research and, to some extent, business—so that both: (1) the effectiveness of the team and organizational structure of proposed teams and (2) the reasonableness of budgets submitted can be intelligently assessed. S/he will also have a major mentoring job to train staff in the various functions of an office dedicated to contracting for policy research.

In some countries, the government has opted to begin to provide support for policy development to ministries by creating a centralized facility for this purpose. Egypt, for example, has the centralized Information and Decision Support Center of the Cabinet of the Government of Egypt (IDSC), a government survey operation and think tank with a staff of 700. The Center carries out assignments for the cabinet, but also is fully involved in assessing and preparing policy initiatives that involve multiple ministries. The individual ministries handle narrower initiatives internally, but generally do not have well-developed policy shops. IDSC hires individual consultants to lend expertise and additional resources to the execution of its projects. It does not, however, contract with firms for whole projects.

Altogether, it is a highly challenging task to convince a government and parliament of the value of enhancing ministries' policy development capacity through appropriations for additional staff and for contracting for research from think tanks and other vendors. Nevertheless, my impression is that most middle-income countries are well along the path to developing such capacity.

TAKE AWAYS

Strong Practices
Characteristics of a well-managed think tank in this context follow.

- Working for government agencies is given full consideration because of the rewards this can bring in terms of analysis of important policy issues, close contact with officials who have at least some responsibility for the issue under analysis, and diversification of funding sources.

If you have heard government agencies are hard to work with—in the sense of trying to "steer" results or restricting contractors' use of findings or data collected in a project—try to get first-hand information. Ask to see the standard contract used by the agency and, if there are problematic provisions, inquire as to whether key points are negotiable on a case-by-case basis. In other words, learn the facts before dismissing what may be a valuable source of revenue and policy influence.

- An open and comprehensive approach is taken to assessing the possible effects on the organization of working with government agencies, if government agencies' contract provisions are at least minimally acceptable.

Perhaps agree to compete for a few contracts and assess the experience. The worst decision is to compete without giving your full effort; half-efforts nearly always fail—which gives those opposing work with the agencies the chance to say the process is biased against you—when this may well not be correct.

- Whether to bid on projects is decided on the basis of six objective factors: the synergies of the new projects with your work program, publication potential for the results, the project's probable contribution to relationship building, whether the work period is sufficiently long for the tasks to be done without severely disrupting other work, the extent of knowledge likely to be gained, and the sufficiency of the revenue for the work to be done.

For Funders
Look carefully for:

- *Think tank independence.* If working for government raises concerns about the think tank's independence in undertaking such projects, ask the executive director about several key points: whether the government changed the institution's or others' findings or asked them to do so, whether the institution has been permitted to publish the results without undue restrictions, and whether the institution has been able to use the data gathered in projects for other purposes (including policy participation and readily given permission to use, if agency permission is required).

- *Existence of policy research departments within government agencies.* If the think tank you are working with does not receive funding from government agencies, determine if national ministries have dedicated policy research departments and, if so, if they contract out for policy studies and surveys. Be aware, for example, that in some countries contracting for policy research is consolidated in the office of the prime minister.

Perhaps to do:

- If national government ministries are not supporting significant policy research programs, consider working with other donors to lobby senior national government officials to initiate such programs, including contracting out in some form. Agencies contracting for policy research are very likely to improve the decision making knowledge base. You could offer to engage a local organization to monitor the effects of the new funding stream.

- Because many think tanks have very limited opportunities to compete for policy research grants where they can select the topic or where multi-year funding is provided, consider focusing your grants to fill these voids—assuming the case is effectively made for the topic and the analysis time-frame.

- Consider, alone or with other funders, supporting the development and promulgation of model contract clauses on intellectual property ownership and publication rights of varying stringency that think tanks could draw upon in their negotiations with clients. These would be particularly effective in cases where model clauses could be cited that had actually been accepted by funders.

FINANCIAL
AND PERFORMANCE
ACCOUNTABILITY

CHAPTER 11
Accountability and Sustainability
with Jeffrey P. Telgarsky

Once a think tank has the technical research competencies and policy engagement skills to be competitive in the market for ideas and policies, being able to compete successfully for the available limited funding requires the organization to demonstrate two additional qualities:

- Full understanding of its costs, for example, the composition of the all-in cost of an hour's time of a senior researcher, including direct compensation; fringe benefits, such as health insurance and paid vacation time; and the costs of supporting his/her work that are not billed directly to clients, such as the services of the human resources, accounting, and contracts offices; and,

- Control of and accountability for the organization's use of sponsor funding.

Full cost understanding is necessary to link research the organization intends to carry out with the funding available from a sponsor. An organization that consistently underestimates the real costs of carrying out an assignment will soon either: 1) deplete its own resources or 2) find that sponsors are reluctant to continue supporting work that is incomplete or requires additional funding.

Spending control and accountability are necessary to demonstrate to sponsors that the funds provided were used for the purposes intended. Sponsors provide varying latitude in the use of research funds (for example, grants often allow more discretion on the part of the recipient than do contracts). But most sponsors require an accounting of the expenditures made with their funds. More generally, to be efficient in its operations, a think tank has to know in some detail how the funds available are spent, to avoid relatively bloated senior management or accounting operations, for instance.

Despite the importance of these aspects of financial management to think tank sustainability, as think tanks develop into more substantial organizations, understanding and accounting for costs frequently pose problems for both the organizations themselves and their sponsors.[136] Systematic data are lacking on think tanks' actual practices in this sphere but here are some hints:

---

136   Some funders prefer fixed price contracts that usually do not require cost reporting.

- At a 2011 Cairo workshop on think tank management organized by the Information and Decision Support Center of the Cabinet of the Government of Egypt, I asked the 71 participants from 40 organizations, mostly from Gulf counties, how many of those organizations had a time-sheet system in place for monitoring labor devoted to projects and managerial tasks. The answer was: 2!!

- Among the 15 think tanks in the GDN mentoring program in 2010, the answer was the same: 2!!

- When I interviewed a prestigious Russian think tank about its management practices a few years ago, I asked if it had a time sheet system. The response: 'No.' Knowing the organization received generous support from USAID, I asked how they met USAID's requirement that completed time sheets and back-up invoices be submitted. The response: 'We create them if they are needed.'

Lack of systems for tracking expenses reflects the way most think tanks were created and how they developed over time. Outside highly industrialized countries, think tanks often start in one of two ways: 1) as a small group of professionals, often around a single strong technical leader; or 2) as an organization supported mainly by a single sponsor. In both cases, the systems of financial management usually adopted do not readily respond to the two qualities identified above.

In the first case, the organization often operates ad hoc—staff are not salaried (or only paid nominal salaries) but paid on a project basis (much like consultants) when funding is available; fixed costs (for items such as rent, utilities, and administration) are allocated to projects unsystematically; business development costs are either unpaid by the organization (through staff providing unpaid labor) or improperly financed from project funds; and record keeping varies with the requirements of each project.

In the second case, the other extreme often prevails—the organization's financial management is geared to meeting the requirements of the sponsor, not the organization. In such circumstances, sponsor funding often does not cover many of the fixed costs of the organization, leading to underestimation of the real cost of developing and carrying out work for other sponsors.

As a think tank develops from these initial stages into a mature organization, several situations naturally occur:

- Greater formality in staffing arrangements (payment of fixed salaries, payment of employee-related taxes and social insurance contributions, provision of paid leave, provision of support for staff training and professional development);

- More substantial fixed costs related to facilities (rent, utilities, equipment, and maintenance) and administration for the organization (personnel administration, meeting legal requirements for taxation and registration, internal organizational management); and

- Higher costs for business development (staff time for collecting information on new funding opportunities and writing proposals) and fund-raising. (I use 'fund-raising' here to mean funds solicited by the think tank for its own unrestricted use, as compared to 'business development,' which is used here to mean the solicitation of funds for specific research project activities.)

These changes result in the organization incurring costs that either are not attributable to specific research projects or can only be attributed to specific projects with great administrative difficulty. Such costs are typically referred to as *fringe benefits* when they relate to costs associated with staff and as *overhead* for the cost of facilities, administration, and business development and fund-raising. All these costs taken together, typically referred to as *indirect costs,* are vital inputs to an organization's long-term sustainability. Without proper accounting for such costs, the following difficulties can be expected:

- If the organization cannot offer a competitive package of compensation and benefits, it will be difficult to retain and motivate staff.

- Without adequate facilities and equipment, staff will not be able to conduct their research efficiently and effectively.

- Without training and opportunities for professional development, staff will not maintain a level of technical knowledge necessary to remain competitive.

- Without funds to support business development and fund-raising, the organization will be unable to continue obtaining new project work necessary to provide continuing support to the organization and its researchers.

Simply put, the full cost of a research project rightfully includes a share of the overall non–project specific costs needed to operate the organization as a sustainable going concern. Knowing the full cost of a research project sets a baseline for financial analysis of the project (from within the organization) and provides a basis for requesting reimbursement from sponsors for the full costs of carrying out the research project.

The balance of this chapter addresses four topics. First, I describe a program for tracking costs (i.e., to permit management to understand how funds raised are actually spent). Second, I turn to indirect cost rates, beginning with the serious issue created by funders setting arbitrary limits on the rates they will pay. Third, I detail development of an indirect rate, beginning with the concept and concluding with a step-by-step example. Finally, I address the external financial audit. As an organization develops and its level of support from sponsor organizations increases so, too, does the argument for having an annual external audit. Boards welcome such audits, because their information is so helpful in discharging the Board's fiduciary responsibilities.

TRACKING COSTS

Without a system for tracking expenditures, think tank managers are essentially flying blind. They are ignorant, for example, about how much is spent on an individual proposal effort, or on all proposals during the year. Spending $5,000 to win a $10,000 award is clearly unsustainable, but a think tank may occasionally be doing so. In a similar vein, managers only have the most general sense of the resources actually being spent to execute a project. Some think tanks control project costs by simply giving everyone on a project a fixed payment for the tasks assigned. That may control cost overruns, but researchers may be devoting a large number of uncompensated hours to the complete the project well—which will certainly encourage them eventually to look for a position at better funded and managed competitors. Expenditures on projects, proposals, and overhead charges (such as human resources and general management) need to be known. Likewise, accurately monitoring spending on communications is essential—with costs paid for by projects and costs charged to overhead being carefully differentiated and recorded in separate accounts.

Staff Costs

Because labor is such a large share of think tank spending—around 70 percent, typically—it makes sense to address time sheets first. The first step to controlling time charges to a project is for the team leader to prepare a careful plan for executing the project that budgets specific time allocations for each person who is to work on it. Equally important, the tasks the person is to do and the amount of time available must be clearly communicated to each staff member. Thereafter, control is a matter of monitoring staff time charges and comparing them with progress on the tasks.

Tables 11.1 to 11.3 illustrate the time management or timekeeping system at the Institute for Urban Economics in Moscow. Table 11.1 is a simplified version of the time sheet staff fills in. This is the form completed by one person for one week. Staff members are encouraged to do this daily, so that the charging is accurate. Time charged to specific projects and proposals, sick leave, annual leave, paid holidays, training, and overhead functions is all recorded on this form.

Table 11.1 Time Sheet Example

Name: Dima Gofman

Pay period ending: September 10, 2013

Project number	Project name	M	T	W	TH	F	Total
10468-702-04	USAID task 3	8	4	4			16
20069-000-00	Perm municipal			4	8	8	20
999-001	Paid time off		4				4
Total		8	8	8	8	8	40

Just filling out this form each day makes staff aware of how much time they are spending on a project and, at least implicitly, to compare the hours remaining against the tasks yet undone. Research staff who have done essentially all tasks assigned to them and have time remaining are more likely to ask the team leader if s/he has another assignment than if there were no formal time monitoring. The senior vice president of a major U.S. think tank who has also worked abroad told me that s/he is convinced that a time sheet system increases productivity, because staff are more conscious of their output being judged against time expended on projects.

Tables 11.2 and 11.3 illustrate how the information contained in the time sheets, once aggregated, is used by managers, most importantly the team leader. Each table is an excerpt from a larger monthly report. The report illustrated in Table 11.2 is organized by project number (column 2) and shows the hours charged for everyone who has charged time to the project. The project-based report is designed for team leaders and management to use in assessing time utilization for a particular project. The report excerpted in Table 11.3 is organized by staff member, showing time charged to each project for which a staff member is budgeted to charge time as well as otherwise charged time. The final line for each staff member shows the totals for all projects to which this person can charge time. It is intended to help the team leader understand how much coverage (billable hours) his/her team members have and the fund-raising effort required in the near term—information the executive director uses to forecast possible capacity constraints or funding shortfalls.

Table 11.2 Control Table for Staff Time Charges: Project Based, August 2013

Employee	Project	Total hours spent	Hours spent last month	Hours in the budget	Balance
Gasyak, Vladimir	10468-702-04	4	4	346	342
Gofman, Dima	10468-702-04	448	32	778	330
Khamova, Lena	10468-702-04	145	7	346	201
Molchanov, Andrei	10468-702-04	88	0	259	171
Puzanov, Sasha	10468-702-04	60	0	86	26
Rumiantsev, Igor	10468-702-04	366	32	518	152
Sedova, Lena	10468-702-04	89	4	173	84
Tolstova, Ira	10468-702-04	11	0	173	162
Zadonsky, Georgy	10468-702-04	596	24	1123	527
Total	**10468-702-04**	**1,807**	**103**	**3,802**	**1,995**
Anopochkin, Volodia	50039-000-00	76	10	90	14
Belozerskaya, Lena	50039-000-00	56	2	192	136
Elagina, Elena	50039-000-00	456	88	2079	1623
Golenkova, Galina	50039-000-00	4	2	96	92
Levina, Liza	50039-000-00	16	4	96	80
Makhova, Lena	50039-000-00	30	15	96	66
Tolstova, Ira	50039-000-00	18	10	48	30
Yashanin, Victor	50039-000-00	20	5	96	76
Zykova, Tatiana	50039-000-00	48	8	192	144
Total	**50039-000-00**	**724**	**144**	**2,985**	**2,261**

Source: Institute for Urban Economics

Table 11.3 Control Table for Staff Time Charges: Staff-Based, August 2013

Employee	Project	Total hours spent	Hours spent last month	Hours in the budget	Balance
Khakhalin, Andrei	10468-501-00	48	0	86	38
	10468-503-00	176	28	346	170
	10468-505-01	732	40	950	218
	10468-703-04	40	8	69	29
	10468-802-04	64	32	69	5
	10468-807-04	223	16	864	641
	20279-000-00	40	16	40	0
	50029-000-00	209	16	208	−1
	OVH-019-10	16	8	16	0
	OVH-019-23	8	4	8	0
Total		**1,556**	**168**	**2,656**	**1,100**
Kutakova, Tatiana	10468-300-00	242	22	259	17
	10468-300-01	1304	96	1382	78
	10468-704-04	48	24	173	125
	20019-000-00	4	4	4	0
	20069-000-00	136	16	136	0
	20279-000-00	24	0	40	16
	OVH-018-30	8	4	12	4
	OVH-019-01	8	2	4	−4
Total		**1,774**	**168**	**2,010**	**236**

Source: Institute for Urban Economics.

It is worthwhile to look at these reports carefully, both of which report for August 2013. The "hours in budget" column shows the number of hours allocated to a staff member to charge to a project. Normally, this would come from the budget prepared to determine the cost of executing the project. The column labeled "total hours spent" shows the number of hours used through August. The column labeled "balance" shows the hours remaining for the staff member to use. So, in Table 11.3, the first row for Andrei Khakhalin shows that he was initially allocated 86 hours for project 10478-501-00, has used 48 hours through July, and has 38 hours remaining to charge to the project. If the team leader changes the allocation of time among staff working on the project, s/he informs the staff person responsible for maintaining these records. Obviously hours charged that exceed the number allocated raises a red flag; the team leader needs to look into why this has happened, because s/he will have to change other allocations to compensate.

The system is updated monthly on the basis of the previous month's time sheets, is straightforward, and eliminates uncertainty. Even so, installing such a system can appear a bit overwhelming. It is certainly not necessary for a think tank to have computer-prepared reports such as those shown, but such programs certainly save accounting staff time. The key point is for team leaders to have some form of records to allocate their resources effectively and avoid overrunning project budgets.

Stage 1 organizations can probably operate a system manually with spreadsheets. For others, there are two options. One is to develop one's own program. A program for the basic tracking function should not be a very large undertaking; but managers are soon likely to want more comprehensive reports. Instead of developing your own program, the second option is to outsource. Automated payroll systems with a wide range of comprehensiveness and complexity are commonly available from local or international software vendors or through the internet—both as locally installed software or secure cloud-based system—and are often well-customized to local tax and regulatory requirements. Staff log on to the vendor's system to fill in their time sheets daily. The vendor provides reports in a range of formats.

Other Direct Costs

Most think tanks do a much better job recording and allocating other direct costs than staff charges to individual projects. These costs include such items as project-related travel; purchase of data sets, books, and journal articles for a project; long-distance and international telephone calls; expenses associated with holding a conference; and other significant charges easily identified as incurred for a project.

Consolidated Reports

Keeping a sharp eye on research staff utilization is clearly a major step to overall project cost control. However, the team leader often is not kept informed of charges besides those being made to the project—such as communication group staff time or the final cost of a conference held by his/her project. It is essential for team leaders (and higher managers) to have timely, comprehensive reports on each project's cost performance. Table 11.4 contains a template of a comprehensive summary project cost-to-date report.[137] Importantly, all fringe and overhead charges are added to direct costs to yield "fully-loaded" cost-to-date figures for staff costs. This summary table enables the team leader and principal investigator to know the actual resources remaining in the budget to complete the project. If the team leader questions the extent of spending in one of the summary account lines, s/he can ask for more information from the accountant or accounting team.

137   This is a simplified version of the format used by NORC at the University of Chicago, a Stage 3 think tank.

Table 11.4 Template for Project Cost Status Report

Summary Project Status Report
Month: August 2013
(financial figures in dollars)

Project	6718	Contract value fee	$5,000
Project name	Mortgage finance	Contract value cost	$700,000
Client	AHML	Contract value total	$705,000
Contract number	VN 7444	Funded value total	$250,000
Project manager	S. Sivaev		

Account	Expenditures			
	Prior years actual	Current month actual	Year to date actual	Contract to date actual
Regular staff – on-site				
Regular staff – off-site				
Temporary staff				
Total staff cost				
Consultants				
Travel & related expenses				
Long distance tel/internet				
Reproduction				
Postage & delivery				
Subcontractors				
Other ODCs				
Unbillable/unallowed				
Total direct costs				
Fringe-regular staff				
Fringe-temp staff				
Overhead—onsite				
Overhead—offsite				
Total indirect costs				
Total expenses				

More senior managers can review both the individual project reports and aggregate monthly data on overall performance for "red flag issues." This is absolutely critical information to enable troubled projects to be caught before they get too far off track—something that can happen to experienced as well as novice team leaders. I worked at a large think tank where the president of the institution actually met regularly with managers whose projects were in danger of running over budget to discuss the nature of the problem and possible solutions. A key element in team leaders' annual performance reports should be their success as financial managers. Clearly, none of this can be done is the absence of the type of information discussed here.

AN INCONVENIENT TRUTH: SPONSORS' TREATMENT OF INDIRECT COSTS

Despite the importance of indirect costs to think tanks' vitality and sustainability, sponsors are often reluctant to pay for these costs. From the narrower perspective of the supporter of a particular piece of research with limited funds, the sponsor naturally wishes to limit its support only to costs that can be most directly related to the research project. However, even taking a broader view of the sponsor as a supporter—not only of the research but also of the think tank carrying out the research—the question naturally arises: in the long run, is all of this indirect cost necessary for the think tank to carry out this work? Given limited funds, the sponsor desires the greatest result for a given investment and, therefore, wishes to be assured that indirect costs are being limited to those reasonably necessary for the think tank to continue to survive and develop.

Sponsors, being the ones with the funding, obviously have the upper hand here. One response on their part is imposition of limitations on the amounts of indirect cost they will pay. However, as is more fully discussed below, the definition of what constitutes an indirect cost is subject to interpretation—depending on the nature of the organization, the activities it carries out, and the administrative ease or difficulty of allocating costs to individual projects. The issue is further complicated by the methods available for charging indirect costs to projects, which can validly use different bases of direct project costs over which indirect costs can be fairly allocated (usually expressed as a percentage of the base direct project costs). Thus, any limitation on indirect cost that seeks to describe an overhead rate of 30 percent as "too high" runs the danger of inadvertently penalizing organizations whose cost structures do not match those implied by the rate limitation.

Many funders want to both avoid spending time assessing the reasonableness of an organization's indirect costs and focus their spending on the topic in which they are interested. Their solution is to set an arbitrary and often low indirect rate they will pay. As this practice has become common, many think tanks increasingly find themselves with no funding for vital administrative tasks and institutional development. There is no alternative funder, however beneficent, who will pay unallowed overhead costs.

This problem is often compounded by strict rules against the think tank transferring expenses between budget lines (e.g., less research staff time vs. more on a planned event). Frequently, shifts among hours allocated to staff are prohibited without explicit permission from the financial officer at the donor institution. These officers are said on occasion to make it clear that they do not want to entertain such requests. The result is that approved budgets are cast in concrete, and all parties pretend they are meaningful when they are not.

The following true incident indicates the actual situation:

> In winter 2013, a consultant who wishes not to be named, visited a think tank in the Caucasus for a week, in part to assess its management practices. He had an extended conversation with the financial manager. To the consultant's delight he was told that there was a time sheet system in place. But when actual practices were described further, the story was much less encouraging. The financial manager generates time sheets for each staff member for each project. Each time sheet accords with what is in the grant agreement budget, regardless of what actually happened during the period. The consultant asked about what is done if the project spends more on an event or some other project activity than budgeted. The response: they only report what is in the budget because funders get really upset when they have to deal with deviations from the plan. In other words, the cost tracking system consists of "Potemkin" accounts. Essentially, there is no system. Funds *are* moved between budget lines as needed. Some of the revenue received does in fact go to pay for computers, general communications activities, and other things not included in the funder-approved budgets but essential for basic operations and development.

Donors who provide core support (unrestricted funds that can be used for institutional development and research projects) are aware that their funds are being diverted in part to cover overhead expenses associated with communications, computers, and other needs for which think tanks have no other funding. Goran Buldioski, director of the Open Society Foundation's Think Tank Fund, which provides core funding, says it plainly: "…fellow donors who award project funding have been 'free riding' on our support" (2013).

In sum, the administrative convenience of arbitrary indirect cost rates and rigid budget allocations causes many think tanks to be dishonest and to have weaker financial administration than is appropriate. But in the interviews with Executive Directors (EDs) at South Asian think tanks, introduced in chapter 1, when I inquired about respondents' experience with sponsors' policies on overhead rates, I found that almost no donor is open to a full analysis of a proposed overhead rate's composition—costs treated as direct and indirect charges, item-by-item reasonableness, and overall cost composition implications. Among projects with international foundations, EDs rated about 40 percent as having strictly nonnegotiable rates and 50 percent as being willing to negotiate *marginal* changes. The parallel figures for multi-laterals and bi-lateral aid agencies, respectively, are 55 and 40 percent and 20 and 80 percent, respectively. At best, the overhead rate policies of international foundations are essentially no better from the EDs' perspective than those of other types of funders.

In this circumstance, why should a think tank devote resources to developing a credible indirect cost rate? One reason is that some funders will pay the actual indirect rates proposed by a think tank, if they are defensible, both overall and on a line-item basis. USAID pays reasonable indirect charges. It also delegates to its prime (generally U.S.) contractors, the responsibility for assessing local firms' indirect cost rates and paying them, perhaps negotiated to a different level that is judged defensible. (Prime contractors often do substantial mentoring in the course of arriving at a mutually agreeable rate with subcontractors.) The U.S. Congress in 2011 mandated that a larger share of USAID's spending should go to local firms. So the possible award pool is increasing in a number of countries. Additionally, there is informal evidence that some funders' attitudes are changing. Certainly discussions among funders on the topic are ongoing.

INDIRECT COSTS

This section discusses how to develop an indirect cost rate. I begin by laying out basic principles and then illustrate with a concrete example how such a rate is constructed.

Defining Indirect Costs

Within any think tank, all costs can be divided into two different types: direct and indirect. Direct costs are unambiguously attributable to a specific research project. For example, the cost of carrying out a survey to collect data for research on low-income households can clearly and easily be related to that particular research project.

Indirect costs are not easily identifiable with a specific research project, but are (as described above) necessary to the operation of the research project or, more generally, to the organization carrying out the project. These costs are shared among projects and, in some cases, among functions within the organization (direct research, management and general administration, and business development and/or fund-raising). Costs are typically classified as indirect when either of two conditions is met (or both): 1) the costs benefit the entire organization and all projects carried out by the organization; or 2) the costs are attributable to specific projects, but the administrative cost of tracking and allocating these costs to individual projects outweighs the benefit of doing so.

An example of the first case is the cost of a personnel director who handles recruiting, develops and implements personnel policies, and ensures compliance with employment law. These necessary services are benefit the organization as a whole. An example of the second case is the cost for local telephone service, which is difficult to attribute to individual projects, because either the costs are typically not tied to the number of calls, or the calls are not itemized in invoices from the telephone company. Thus, allocating local telephone charges would require maintaining logs to list the number and duration of calls and then distributing the costs across the logged calls. Since the cost of local telephone service is small (relative to total costs) and the cost (in staff time) of creating such logs is significant, allocating such costs as an indirect cost across all projects is a sensible solution.

While there is general agreement on the division between direct and indirect costs, however, the specifics of what sponsors view as valid (or "allowable") in each category vary widely. Annex 11.1 provides an example of differences in allocations used by two U.S. national government agencies—illustrating that there are no widely accepted hard-and-fast rules for allocating cost items between the two categories.

Since this lack of standard practices means there are no "standard" indirect cost rates against which an organization can evaluate its own indirect cost rates, it makes sense for think tanks confronted with clients who resent paying indirect costs to allocate a relatively high share of their costs as direct.

Examples of items that may be in indirect costs but can plausibly be moved to direct costs if deemed advisable include the following:

> *Computing costs.* Such costs include the computers themselves as well as related servers and other hardware (appropriately amortized), software commonly used (including Microsoft Office Suite), basic statistical programs (e.g., SPSS), and computer support staff time for addressing computer users' problems and system programming and maintenance. Because essentially all staff members work constantly with computers, the cost can be charged directly on an hourly basis for all staff hours worked, excluding a few staff (such as drivers and coffee boys) whose jobs defined them as never using computers for their work. The hourly rate is computed as the sum of the projected annual costs divided by the number of staff hours. There is one more step, however. Staff using computers whose time is devoted to indirect functions must still have this hourly charge allocated to the relevant indirect cost account, to ensure consistency in how the cost is allocated across all users.

> *Certain communications expenses.* Project budgets seldom include explicitly the costs of social media activities and website postings associated with a specific project. These costs (almost completely staff salaries and related overheads) can be easily computed and included as direct costs. (Add up communication staff time taken at each step in developing a project announcement for the website, posting reports, preparing and sending social media messages multiplied by the planned volume of each; also compute the cost of tracking and reporting the volume of "hits" and related tasks.)

> *Time of draft report reviewers.* Some think tanks view quality control as an institutional responsibility and fund it from general rather than project-specific funds. This need not be the case, however. An alternative is inclusion

in project budgets, under the staff heading, a direct line item for reviewers' time.

Careful thought is likely to reveal additional costs that can reasonably be moved from indirect to direct charges. In every case, full documentation and justification for each cost item must be available to provide to sponsors upon request, and budget submissions should clearly state that such documentation is available.

THE INDIRECT COST RATE

Once an organization has identified what to include in its indirect costs, the next step is to develop a method for distributing or allocating these costs across its activities (since these indirect costs are defined as providing some benefit to all the organization's activities). Although there are several methods for allocating indirect costs, I focus here on the most common: developing an indirect cost rate proportionately across an organization's activities or projects. (The alternative, the so-called case-by-case method, is outlined in Annex 11.1, although we think its disadvantages outweigh its strengths.)

To do this, after an organization has divided its costs into direct vs. indirect costs, the indirect costs are aggregated into a *pool*. A share of the pool is then allocated to project cost, usually in proportion to the ratio of indirect costs (the numerator in the ratio) to direct costs (either total direct cost or a component [such as direct labor expense] of total direct cost; the denominator in the ratio is known as the *base*).[138]

Selection of an appropriate allocation method and direct cost base for an indirect cost rate should be based upon the commonality of indirect costs to all direct cost expenditures. For most organizations, there will be a strong correlation between indirect costs (which tend to be heavily weighted toward administrative labor and support costs and facilities costs) and direct labor costs. In most cases, therefore, a direct labor cost base will produce an equitable distribution of indirect costs. However, where the ratio of direct labor to total direct costs varies significantly from project to project (for

---

138   The base can be set in various ways (for example, number of hours expended by project staff, number of persons working on or served by a project, size of the facilities used for each project, or other methods that have a logical basis related to the nature of the activity or project), although most organizations use direct labor cost or total direct costs as the base. There simply is no single "right" way to calculate an indirect cost rate to determine what costs to include as indirect costs, or how much is "fair." Under U.S. federal government guidelines, allowable direct costs range from 3 to 70 percent, varying from agency to agency.

Many funding organizations seem to operate from the perspective that a lower overhead rate is better, but this *does not necessarily imply a more efficient organization*. For example, imagine a single organization implementing multiple projects where each project has its own accounting staff, purchases its own supplies, and has all of its own equipment. Such an organization would have no indirect costs at all, but it would clearly be less efficient than if the projects shared accounting costs, supplies, and equipment.

example, where projects have widely differing costs for travel, consultants, subcontracts, or other direct costs), total direct cost is more appropriate as a base.

In the balance of this chapter, I look in more detail at how to develop an indirect cost rate.

INDIRECT COST RATE CALCULATION AND DOCUMENTATION

To support a proposed indirect cost rate, an organization should develop a set of documentation it can provide to funders. This documentation typically includes the information outlined below. Sample documents for an Example Organization (EO) are shown as exhibits.

Organizational information. This should include the following:

- ○ Information on the structure of the organization that describes the duties and/or responsibilities of all units that make up the organization;
- ○ Financial data, such as financial statements (audited if appropriate), budgets, or other accounting reports, upon which the proposed indirect cost rate is based;
- ○ If the proposed indirect cost rate is recognized by other funders, a list of contracts or grants, giving details on funders, value, period of performance, and any indirect cost limitations.

> *Cost policy statement.* The cost policy statement (CPS) states explicitly which costs the organization will charge directly and which costs it will charge indirectly. An example of a CPS for the EO is shown in Annex 11.2.

> *Statement of salaries and benefits.* This document should contain the estimated/actual costs of personnel salaries and fringe benefits. Personnel fringe benefits typically divide into two types: 1) those that are statutorily determined (such as social insurance contributions, unemployment insurance premiums, payroll taxes, and other required employer contributions or leave allowances [holidays or sick leave] on behalf of employees and other personnel); and 2) fringe benefits determined by the organization (such as annual leave, non-salary compensation [for example, performance bonuses], or health/life insurance). Organization-determined fringe benefits are usually evaluated by funders as part of the determination of the reasonableness of total compensation to personnel. A sample statement of salaries and fringe benefits for the EO is shown in Table 11.5.

Table 11.5 Example Institute Statement of Salaries and Fringe Benefits

	Total annual salary	Leave component of salary[a]	Non-leave component of salary[b]
Salaries			
Executive director	$ 60,000	$ 9,231	$ 50,769
Technical staff (5 @ $40,000 each)	200,000	30,769	169,231
Financial manager	30,000	4,615	25,385
Administrative assistant	20,000	3,077	16,923
	$ 310,000	$ 47,692	$ 262,308
Fringe benefits			*Fringe benefits cost*
Social/health insurance (employer contribution)	15.00% of total salaries		$ 46,500
Retirement fund (employer contribution)	5.00% of total salaries		15,500
Annual leave, holidays, sick leave (40 days/year)	15.38% of total salaries		47,692
			$ 109,692
Fringe benefits rate[c]			41.818%

[a] Leave component of salary equals 15.385 percent of total annual salary (i.e., 40 leave days divided by 260 paid days per year). These costs are paid as part of fringe benefits and are not considered part of salaries for the purposes of calculating fringe benefit and indirect cost rates.

[b] Non-leave component of salary equals 84.615 percent of total annual salary (i.e., 220 non-leave work days divided by 260 paid days per year).

[c] The fringe benefits rate is calculated by dividing the fringe benefits cost by the non-leave component of salaries ($109,692/$262,308 = 41.818%).

Statement of labor allocation and total costs. A sample labor allocation and total costs statement for the EO is shown in Table 11.6. This statement, when used to support a provisional indirect cost rate, is based on the EO's planned budget. When a final indirect cost rate is being calculated, actual costs should be used in this statement.

Table 11.6 Example Institute Statement of Labor Allocation and Total Costs

			Column A	Column B		Column C		Column D		Column E = B + C + D = A	
				Indirect Costs		Direct Project Costs		Excluded/ Unallowable		Reconciliation	
			Total Costs	% Share	Cost	% Share	Cost	% Share	Cost	% Share	Cost
Salaries (labor cost, non-leave component only)											
Executive director			$50,769	75.00%	$38,077	25.00%	$12,692	0.00%	$ -	100.00%	$50,769
Technical staff (5 @ $40,000 each)			169,231	10.00%	16,923	90.00%	152,308	0.00%	-	100.00%	169,231
Financial manager			25,385	100.00%	25,385	0.00%	-	0.00%	-	100.00%	25,385
Administrative assistant			16,923	100.00%	16,923	0.00%		0.00%		100.00%	16,923
			$262,308	37.097%	$97,308	62.903%	$165,000	0.00%	$ -		$262,308
Fringe benefits	41.82%	Non-leave salaries	$109,692	41.818%	$40,692	41.818%	$69,000	41.818%	$ -		$109,692
Non-labor indirect costs											
Rent, utilities, cleaning	$2,500	/month	$30,000			$30,000					$30,000
Office supplies	300	/month	3,600			3,600					3,600
Local telephone/long distance telephone/fax	200	/month	2,400			2,400					2,400
Postage, courier, delivery	200	/month	2,400			2,400					2,400
Copying	200	/month	2,400			2,400					2,400
Computer support, Internet	500	/month	6,000			6,000					6,000
Lease of equipment	250	/month	3,000			3,000					3,000
Depreciation of capital equipment owned	20.00%	equipment value	5,000			5,000					5,000
Staff training			4,000			4,000					4,000
Business development			6,000			6,000					6,000
Board of trustee expenses			2,000			2,000					2,000
Insurance			3,000			3,000					3,000

[a] The cost of equipment purchases and major renovations (and in some cases [but not in this example], subcontract costs) may vary considerably from project to project, thus causing the indirect costs to be allocated in a disproportionate amount to the benefit derived. Therefore, such costs are typically excluded from the base when a total direct cost base is being used. Bad debts and entertainment are typical examples of unallowable costs.

The sample statement reflects the estimated/actual direct salary costs (net of the portion of salary paid through fringe benefits) expended on either direct or indirect activities. The percentage of time per position should be spread under the appropriate cost category, making sure that 100 percent is allocated in total for each position. The statement also shows (in conformance with the CPS) which costs are allocated as indirect, direct, or excluded/unallowable.[139] The sum of these cost categories must match the total costs of the organization.

Indirect cost rate calculation. Table 11.7 shows the calculation of two different types of indirect cost rates: Method 1 one uses direct labor

---

139   The organization must maintain a time sheet system for documenting how salary expenses are incurred across indirect and direct cost activities and across projects for personnel whose time is charged to more than one cost activity or project.

as the direct cost base, Method 2 uses total direct cost as the base. The calculation of the indirect cost rate is done by: 1) classifying total cost for the base period (usually the organization's fiscal year) as either direct or indirect (as shown in the statement of labor and total costs), and 2) dividing the total allowable indirect costs by an equitable distribution base (as discussed above).

Table 11.7 Example Institute Statement of Indirect Costs and Rate Calculation

Method 1—Base: Direct Labor Cost (Including Fringe Benefits)	
Indirect costs (from Table 11.6)	$ 210,800
Cost base (from Table 11.6)	
Direct cost labor	$ 165,000
Fringe benefits (41.818% of direct cost labor)	69,000
Total cost base	$ 234,000
Indirect cost rate (indirect costs / total cost base)	90.085%
Reconciliation with total cost (from Table 11.6)	
Direct cost labor	$ 165,000
Fringe benefits (41.818% of direct cost labor)	69,000
Indirect costs (at 90.085% of direct salaries and fringe benefits)	210,800
Other direct costs	45,200
Unallowable costs	3,000
Excluded costs	7,000
Total cost	$ 500,000
Method 2—Base: Total Direct Cost	
Indirect costs (from Table 11.6)	$ 210,800
Cost base (from Table 11.6)	
Direct cost labor	$ 165,000
Fringe benefits (41.818% of direct cost labor)	$ 69,000
Other direct costs	$ 45,200
Unallowable costs[a]	3,000
Total cost base	$ 282,200
Indirect cost rate (indirect costs/total cost base)	74.699%
Reconciliation with total cost (from Table 11.6)	
Direct cost labor	$ 165,000
Fringe benefits (41.818% of direct cost labor)	69,000
Indirect costs (at 74.699% of total direct cost)	210,800
Other direct costs	45,200
Unallowable costs[a]	3,000
Excluded costs	7,000
Total cost	$ 500,000

[a] Unallowable costs are included in the cost base if they represent activities for which indirect costs are properly allocable.

The result of this process is an indirect cost rate, which is used to distribute indirect costs to individual projects funded by contracts or grants and for unallowable costs that benefit from indirect cost activities. The rate is expressed (in percent) as the ratio of the total amount of allowable indirect costs (the numerator) to the base selected (the denominator).

Note that, despite the total amount of indirect cost being the same in each calculation, the rate varies depending on the choice of the direct cost base. Thus, the lower rate is not "better" than the higher rate; the different rates simply reflect the distribution of the indirect cost pool over different direct cost bases. It is important for a think tank to understand the cost base being used by most of its clients. Wherever possible, think tanks should push for a broader base; this results in a lower nominal indirect rate, which will be more palatable to funders.

CASE STUDY: INSTITUTE FOR URBAN ECONOMICS, MOSCOW

The Institute for Urban Economics (IUE) was an "early adapter" of developing a rigorously derived indirect cost rate. As Case Study 11.1 illustrates, the modest effort involved has been well worth it over the years, in terms of having it accepted by an array of donors in budget negotiations. The case study includes one table detailing the structure of its indirect cost rates and another displaying for one month the generation of revenue assigned to each indirect cost line item and the overall total versus actual expenditure on each item in the same month. The list of overhead items may be instructive.

The case study also illustrates the value of accurately knowing the composition of overhead costs. When IUE had a major funding shortfall and needed to make sharp cuts to overhead to sustain operations, knowledge of how much was being spent on each overhead category gave management the ability to make informed decisions on where to cut and how deeply.

FINANCIAL AUDITS

An audit is a process to test and assess the completeness and accuracy of an organization's financial information (typically a set of financial statements). It is usually conducted annually by an outside accountant who meets the prevailing professional standard; in the United States, this would be a certified public accountant. While nonprofit organizations such as think tanks are often required by law to obtain an audit if their level of activity exceeds a certain threshold, the organization can and should use the audit also as a management tool. As an organization matures and its financial structure becomes more complex through the use of indirect cost recovery mechanisms, audits provide assurance to both the organization and its sponsors that the organization's financial management is sound and the financial information it presents accurately portrays its operation at the corporate and project level. In particular, the audit can identify some of the common indirect cost problems discussed below and suggest measures for correcting such problems and avoiding them in the future.

Audit Content

The main objectives of an audit should be to assess the following:

- *Adequacy of the organization's system of internal control over financial transactions.* Internal controls are essential for ensuring the accountability of the organization to sponsors, government regulators, and the public—a think tank offering public policy prescriptions has to adhere to the highest levels of legal compliance and ethical behavior to maintain its credibility. In general, sound internal controls provide for procedures that ensure the organization's resources (cash, equipment, property, or other assets) are used solely for authorized purposes and the responsibility for the documentation and approval of these uses is divided (so that it does not rest with a single person in the organization). Although this division may not be completely feasible in a small organization, some measure of internal control may still be established by carefully planning the assignment of responsibility and having frequent management review of transactions.

- *Financial records accurately reflect the operation of the organization.* An audit will review financial records and supporting documentation to ensure all significant financial conditions are accurately reflected in the organization's financial information. The audit will also typically review a sample of transactions to ensure there is proper supporting documentation for the transaction and it was correctly entered into the financial management system. But an audit does not typically guarantee that all transactions are properly documented or correctly entered into the financial management system. In other words, a successful audit should not be interpreted as proof there are no such problems.

- *Proper authority for expenditures and projects.* Both organizational documentation (such as actions approved by the board of directors or organizational policies and procedures) and contracts/grant agreements with sponsors will be reviewed in an audit to ensure expenditures are consistent with the requirements of those authorizations. In particular, the audit should confirm that expenditures have complied with any restrictions or specific requirement included as a condition of any contract or grant.

- *Existence of recorded assets.* The existence and verification of the organization's assets—such as bank balances, accounts receivable, and physical assets such as equipment, real property, securities and other investments—will be included in an audit.

- *Timely reporting and payment of public obligations.* Finally, an audit will review the filing of required reports to government regulators and the payment of public obligations (such as license fees, corporate, sales, value-added taxes, and payroll and other personnel-related taxes) to ensure these are paid accurately and on time.

In carrying out the above reviews, the auditors should pay particular attention to the allocation of indirect costs to their appropriate internal financial management accounts in conformance with the organization's cost policy statement. Where problems are identified (such as the common ones listed after the next section), the auditors and management should work together to identify improvements to financial management systems and internal controls to prevent future occurrences.

Auditor Selection

What should you look for in assessing auditor candidates? The choice of an auditor is usually informed by several criteria, each of which the organization has to assess against its particular circumstances:

- *Qualifications and experience.* Because of differences between for-profit and nonprofit accounting, an auditor with experience with similar corporate entities—particularly those doing similar kinds of work—is likely to better understand the issues and concerns of the organization than one whose experience is further removed. This criterion needs to be evaluated both at the firm level and with respect to the individual staff assigned to do the audit; good results are more likely when well-qualified and experienced audit teams remain intact and have continuity with the organization's audits over time.

- *Quality control systems.* The auditor's record with respect to restatements or corrections to previously issued audit reports, disciplinary action by regulatory authorities or remedies imposed by the courts as a result of legal proceedings, and policies and procedures with respect to internal oversight, should be examined to ensure the auditor has a proven system of delivering accurate and thorough audits.

- *Conflicts of interest.* The auditor should be free of any conflicts of interest with respect to the organization being audited (such as an auditor's existing business relationships with members of the organization's board of trustees or funders of the organization's projects).

- *Resources.* The auditor must be able to provide the necessary staff and technological resources to meet the organization's schedule for completing the audit (particularly where the audit is required to meet a statutory or regulatory requirement). Additionally, the organization and the auditor should share a clear understanding of what resources will be required from the organization to assist the auditor.

- *Other services.* The auditor may be able to help the organization with other services that take advantage of the auditor's detailed knowledge of the organization—which might include assistance in filing tax returns or monitoring regulatory requirements and assisting with compliance. However, the organization must be aware that certain services, such as bookkeeping or asset appraisal, are potential conflicts of interest with the audit function.

- *References.* References should be obtained (preferably from clients that are similar to the organization in non-profit status and, if possible, type of work) to help assess all the above criteria, as well as to judge more subjective factor—such as the auditor's communication skills, flexibility in understanding the specific requirements of the organization, and ability to make the auditing process work smoothly.

- *Fees.* Fees represent a particularly difficult criterion to evaluate. On rare occasions, some audit firms may offer pro bono or discounted fees for nonprofits; but in most cases, the organization will have to balance the services offered by the auditor with their costs. In particular, low fees may not be a bargain; they may be a sign the auditor does not fully understand the work required, lacks the experienced resources and so takes longer to produce the audit, expects the organization to do much of the work to prepare for the audit, or is deliberately underbidding the work in the first year, with significantly higher fees to follow later (when it will be more costly for the organization to switch auditors). The auditor should be able to provide a proposed fee and agreement with sufficient detail to allow the organization to evaluate the level of auditor staff commitment and the specific products to be provided. (For example, will the auditor merely carry out a review of the financial statements prepared by the organization? Or will it provide a written management letter that reviews the organizations financial management policies and procedures, identifies internal control weaknesses, and suggests remedies?)

It is not cost-effective for an organization to constantly be changing auditors or to receive an audit that is poorly done or does not meet the organization's needs. All the above criteria need to be weighed to balance all costs and benefits of the audit in assessing the suitability of a particular auditor.

Common Problems Found in Think Tank Audits
This section presents examples of the more common problems related to indirect costs disclosed by audits of nonprofit organizations.

Timekeeping systems. Labor costs, whether charged directly to grants and contracts or to the indirect cost pool, must be based on accurate time records reflecting the actual activities of personnel. These time records must account for all activity of the personnel. The most common problems are either failure to use a timekeeping system to track personnel activity or using a timekeeping system solely for the purpose of calculating payroll (i.e., only to record time and attendance of personnel, but not their activities).

Additionally, an auditor is very likely to find fault with the kind of "Potemkin accounts" we discussed earlier that result from arbitrary time sheet entries.

Consistent treatment and specific identification of costs. Costs must be treated consistently on all an organization's projects. Typical problems with this include directly charging particular projects with costs specifically identifiable with other projects, or charging costs that were not treated consistently with other costs incurred for the same purpose in similar circumstance.

Costs of "unallowable activities." If unallowable costs are improperly charged as indirect costs, two problems result. First, inclusion of unallowable costs in the indirect cost pool overstates the amount of indirect cost, resulting in an indirect cost rate higher than appropriate for the recovery of allowable indirect cost. Second, because not all such costs were directly charged to the "unallowable activities" cost category, an appropriate share of indirect costs was not allocated to these unallowable activities. As a result, direct cost projects are allocated a disproportionate share of the organization's indirect costs.

Even if an organization's own activities or certain direct cost projects funded under contracts or grants provide for little or no reimbursement of indirect costs, the full share of indirect costs must be allocated to such own activities and contracts or grants (i.e., indirect costs cannot be unfairly shifted to projects with no restrictions on indirect cost payment).

Allocation of Credits. Credits generated through project activities, such as fees for conferences held for the benefit of a specific project, must be credited to that specific project. Similarly, applicable credits to indirect costs, such as subletting rental space included in the indirect cost pool, must be credited to the indirect cost pool.

Indirect cost allocation base. The direct cost base must allocate indirect costs to all direct cost projects equitably. To ensure that objective is met, organizations must continuously evaluate whether the direct cost base is disproportionately distributing indirect costs among projects. For example, an organization may have chosen a direct labor cost base because the organization originally had projects with similar shares of labor and other direct costs. If the organization undertakes a new, very large project (relative to the total activity of the organization) that has a much larger share of other direct costs compared to direct labor, a switch to a total cost base may be appropriate to allocate the organization's indirect costs more equitably.

Inter-organizational transfers and related-party transactions. Supplies and services acquired from affiliates, related parties, and organizations under common control must be based on the actual costs of the organizations providing the supplies and services. The "costs" of supplies and services from these related organizations must not include profit or other mark-ups added by the related organization.

Unsupported costs. To be allowable, all direct and indirect costs must be adequately supported by source documentation that clearly shows the purposes of, and circumstances under which, the cost was incurred. For example, canceled checks, bank transfer records, or credit card receipts alone are insufficient as cost documentation, because they do not establish the purpose of the expense, they simply record the payment of funds. Adequate supporting cost documentation should record the purpose and circumstances of the expense. For example, the supporting documentation for a travel expense should identify the expense incurred, by whom and when, and the project/activity for which the travel was undertaken (to determine whether it is a direct/indirect and/or allowable/ unallowable cost).

TAKE AWAYS

Strong Practices

Characteristics of a well-managed think tank in this context follow.

- A comprehensive time management (time sheet) system is used.

There are two reasons for its use. First, it is necessary to provide funders with an accurate accounting of the expenditure of their funds. Second, this information gives management the information necessary for the efficient use of resources (are proposal development funds being well-used across the organization?) and provides team leaders the data to manage the allocation of staff time efficiently at the project level (why is the assembly of secondary data taking so much staff time?).

- All significant non–direct labor expenses associated with individual projects are allocated to each. This includes expenditures on such prominent items as events, publications, some types of communications, and travel.
- A defensible indirect rate is in place. It is reviewed for accuracy every 3-4 years to confirm its size and the distribution of included costs.

Knowing what indirect costs are and how they are structured permits think tank leaders to better manage them. There are also signs that more donors in the future may move to pay actual, reasonable overhead costs. Knowing the composition of your indirect rate is a key management tool for controlling costs on a line item basis, and for reallocating them as necessary within a given overall indirect rate once it is established.

- As many budget line items as possible appear under direct costs to minimize the magnitude of the indirect rate. The organization is prepared to detail to funders the basis for their indirect cost calculation.
- There is an annual external audit of accounts.

Funders may well ask to see audits, particularly as part of their due diligence for large grants. Board members should especially champion annual audits, because they often have fiduciary responsibility under national NGO laws. Malfeasance apart, it is important to ensure costs and revenues are being appropriately allocated in the accounts and necessary safeguards are in place and working.

For Funders
Look carefully for:

- *A timekeeping System.* Every organization should have a timekeeping system in place for reasons outlined above. Make certain the hours recorded are actual hours worked on each project and not just those that correspond to what is shown in the financial proposal.

- *The cost rate*. Check the presence of a defensible indirect cost rate, if your organization is willing to consider actual indirect rates rather than setting one arbitrarily for grantees.

Perhaps to do:

- Funders' use of maximum, often unrealistically low, arbitrarily set indirect rates in grant programs drives grantees to set up accounting systems to produce costs reports consistent with grant budgets. Sometimes the low rates are accompanied with formal or informal strictures against changes in budget line items. Hence, grantees' cost reports may have little to do with actual spending. These distorted accounting systems yield little useful information for institutional management.

  To address this, consider two course of action.

  1. *Limit restrictions on budget alterations to major changes (e.g., changes of over 30 percent in a budget line)*. Changes over the established threshold could still require grant officer approval, which should be readily granted if the reason for the adjustment is reasonable to the program or technical officer.
  2. *Very carefully assess the case for paying grantees' actual indirect rates, where the organization can justify its proposed rates*. Reviewing indirect rates is a challenging task and one where funder staff often serves as a mentor in development of a realistic rate. This is a time-consuming and patience-demanding task, but well worth it.

- Consider banding together with other donors to review proposed indirect cost rates (and correct them through negotiation if necessary) and then certify rates as technically correct. Such a rate, certified by any participating donor using the same standards, would be accepted by all participating donors in contracting with a think tank with such a rate. Thus, the certification burden would be shared among many donors. Donors could select a common outside vender to do the reviews where they do not have the capacity to do them.

Case Study 11.1 Implementation of a strong procedure for computing indirect cost rate, Institute for Urban Economics

The introduction for this chapter listed several natural transitions at think tanks that occur as they develop from small start-ups into mature organizations. In this case study I use the example of the Institute for Urban Economics (IUE), a Moscow-based think tank founded in 1995, to review the structure of an *indirect cost rate* of a mature organization. The sample structure and calculation of *the indirect costs rate as practiced by IUE* are given in Table CS 11.1.1 (at the end of this statement).

In the course of IUE's rapid growth, its founders realized their projects had multiplied faster than their ability to coordinate and manage them. As a result, the Institute fell short of fulfilling its potential. Therefore, priority was assigned to institutional development for achieving better integration and coordination, building the administrative and technical infrastructure needed to manage its operations, and securing financial sustainability. The main challenge was to overcome narrow, exclusively project-oriented attitudes.

Development and Use of the Indirect Cost Rate

As a part of this strategy the IUE adopted an *indirect cost rate* structure in which indirect costs encompassed everything from strategic planning and staff training to computer system upgrades. In the example, tables that follow indirect costs include office rent and overhead (OVH) which refer to all indirect costs or fixed expenses of operating a business that are not directly related to any particular project.

In the process of financial planning, IUE management takes the provisional indirect cost rate[140] determined by using its estimate of essential indirect spending in the coming year and calculating the corresponding rate as a percentage of direct labor charges. For making prompt decisions at any later stage, the leadership needs to know the deviation of the actual rates, both overall and for each of the line items shown in Table CS 11.1.1, from the corresponding provisional rates over the accounting period (as a rule, it is a month or a quarter). To enable leadership to make a comparative analysis of the

foregoing indirect cost rates, it is provided with a report on the spending on overheads on a line item basis over the reporting period, on an accrual basis from the beginning of the financial year.

The indirect cost structure constitutes an integral part of the financial policy as well as the budget for the forthcoming financial year, including provisional indirect cost rates. It is approved by management but can be modified by management decision if necessary.

A sample report prepared in accordance with the financial policy and the approved budget structure is given in Table CS 11.1.1. Under the budgeting procedures practiced by the IUE, calculation of target levels of indirect costs requires use of different provisional rates, i.e. 92.8 percent for employees and 28.9 percent for consultants. In other words, indirect costs are equivalent to 92.8 percent of the cost of staff labor, for example.

The reasons for the differences in the rates for staff and consultants are evident in the table. For example, overhead funds are needed to pay for vacation time for employees (direct labor—DL) but not for consultants. So this charge is excluded for consultants.

Calculation of target levels is also made separately for grants and commercial projects. Such an approach allows analyzing overhead shares of commercial and non-commercial sources of funding in covering of overall indirect costs.[141]

Table CS 11.1. 2 illustrates the case where there are some budget variations in the number of line items. For example, the item Legal fees was overspent by $ 1940.85. At the same time, for the item Office management we can see a non-spent amount of $1,735.29. Analysis of these variations plays an important role in a budget preparation, including calculation of a provisional indirect costs rate for the forthcoming financial year.

Advantages of using an indirect rate structure

The strong procedure for computing indirect costs rate plays a critical role for a think tank's vitality and sustainability. On the one hand, it provides management with a tool for identifying and tracing costs to the sustainability of the organization. On the other hand, it permits the think tank to furnish a clear and comprehensive statement

---

140   In the process of budgeting for the next financial year, the provisional indirect cost rates for each item of the indirect cost structure are calculated on the basis of forecast direct labor and/or other direct costs. After approval of the budget the relevant indirect cost rates shall apply to budgeting of particular grants as well as commercial projects

---

141   Provisional rates of indirect costs applied to grants and commercial projects are identical.

of indirect cost recovery policies to sponsors which addresses their concern that they pay only for a fair share of the organization's necessary costs.

A critical question is how to derive an indirect cost rate that will stand up to close examination. IUE followed the procedure for computing an overhead rate that is required for contracts on the projects financed from the U.S. federal government budget. The Institute then successfully passed a special audit that confirmed the accuracy and fairness to all clients of its procedure. On this basis it was able to conclude a Negotiated Indirect Cost Rate Agreement (NICRA), which confirms the overhead rates for this particular organization. Furthermore, possession of a verified procedure for computing indirect costs rate has helped the Institute work with other sponsors, because it can be easily transformed into other presentation forms accepted by these sponsors.

Therefore, within the framework of such an agreement, an organization will be able to include in the project cost estimate not only direct expenses, but also indirect costs. This will enable it to focus on the following activities, highly important for its institutional development: business development (staff's time spent on collecting information on new funding opportunities and writing proposals), staff development, and fundraising. Additional activities include those that contribute to the general strengthening of sustainability, such as preparation and publication of annual reports, financial audits, litigation, and general management.

In addition, the presence of a strong procedure for computing indirect costs will enable a think tank's leadership to make prompt decisions if financing is reduced and, thus, to ensure the viability of the organization in times of crisis. For example, the IUE experienced certain financial difficulties due to the drastic cuts in financing provided by USAID—from 55 percent of revenue in 2011, to 5 percent in 2013, and to zero in 2014.

It took time for the IUE to adjust to the new situation. However, use of the strong procedure for computing the indirect costs rate enabled senior management to make correct decisions during the transition period regarding the cutting some overheads (e.g., proposal costs, staff development, fund-raising, administrative costs) to save the organization as a whole.

In the process of developing the indirect costs system described above, IUE used its solid experience in working on projects funded by different sponsors. IUE's experience in using its indirect costs system over a period of 15 years confirms that such a system can make a positive

impact on the organization's sustainability. First and foremost, it helped preserve the organization in times when it suffered from lack of contracts to employ all its staff members (those with uncovered time could work on institutional development projects). For another thing, IUE set activities financed from overheads in the proposal development line for fund-raising, the search for new contracts, and participation in tenders. Finally, capacity for staff development led to improvement in the overall competence and quality of IUE's personnel.

In sum, our experience suggests that application of a strong procedure for computing indirect costs is likely to make a strong positive impact on an organization's overall management and contribute to financial efficiency. On the cost side, development of such system costs several person months and its annual maintenance expenses amount to approximately two person months. The resulting financial effect far outweighs all incurred expenditures.

Galina Golenkova and Alexander Puzanov
Institute for Urban Economics
Moscow, Russia

Table CS 11.1.1 Computation of Indirect Costs Rates

Indirect Cost Element	Units/Base	Units/Rate, USD	Base for Indirect Cost Rate	Percent of Base (DL or DL+Consult)	Applicable to	
					On-Site Employees	Off-Site Consultant
1	2	3	5	6	7	8
Office Rental	12 sq. meters/pers.	132	DL+Consult	56.7%	56.7%	0.0%
OVERHEAD:						
Vacation, Holidays & Sick (HVS)	from Payroll	VHS	DL	25.6%	26.6%	14.8%
Office Management	from Payroll	Admin	DL+Consult	23.4%	22.4%	
Proposal & Institutional Develop	from Payroll	Prop&InstDev	DL Only	13.0%	13.0%	
Staff Development	from Payroll	StafDev	DL Only	4.88%	4.9%	
Computer Support	from Payroll, plus $600/mon	Computer Sup	DL Only	3.43%	3.4%	
Depreciation		10/FTE/month	DL Only	1.26%	1.3%	
Property Tax		100/month	DL Only	1.14%	1.1%	
Bank Charges		90/month	DL+Consult	0.75%	0.7%	2.0%
Auditing			DL+Consult	2.76%	2.8%	3.1%
Legal Fees	1 wk/month lawyer	650/month	DL+Consult	1.66%	1.7%	1.1%
Office Insurance		900/year	DL Only	0.95%	1.0%	
Maintenance		10/FTE/month	DL Only	1.26%	1.3%	
Office Supplies		20/FTE/month	DL+Consult	2.15%	2.2%	3.5%
Photocopy/Books/Journals/Library		20/FTE/month	DL+Consult	2.15%	2.2%	2.1%
Local Phone,Internet, E-Mail		10/FTE/month	DL+Consult	1.08%	1.1%	2.1%
Postage/Delivery		5/FTE/month	DL+Consult	0.54%	0.5%	0.5%
Annual Report		2000/year	DL Only	1.91%	1.9%	
Board Meetings	2 meeting/yr	1000/year	DL Only	0.95%	1.0%	
Auto-Related Expenses (Auto)	from Payroll	Auto	DL Only	3.43%	3.43%	
Miscellaneous		5/FTE/month	DL+Consult	0.54%	0.5%	0.5%
SUBTOTAL					92.8%	29.8%

Table CS 11.1.2 Total Expenditures

Total Expenditures for January 01, 2xxx -December 31, 2xxx

	Budget		Total amount (Grants)			Total amount (Other projects)			Total amount (all projects)	USD Total	
	employees	consultants	empl	consult	Total	empl	consult	Total		expenses paid	DIFF
Salary	56.7%		680,992.00	67,491.62	748,483.62	126,131.37	25,514.27	151,645.64	900,129.26		
Office Rental			386,122.46			71,516.49			457,638.95	454,723.00	2,915.95
Overhead											
Vacation, Holidays & Sick	25.6%		173,993.46		173,993.46	32,226.57		32,226.57	206,220.02	205,388.79	831.23
Office Management	23.4%	14.8%	159,352.13	10,015.76	169,367.89	29,514.74	3,786.32	33,301.06	202,668.94	200,933.65	1,735.29
Proposal and Instit Development	13.0%		88,776.18		88,776.18	16,442.87		16,442.87	105,219.05	105,132.00	87.05
Staff Development	4.9%		33,206.79		33,206.79	6,150.47		6,150.47	39,367.25	38,211.56	1,145.69
Depreciation	1.3%		8,573.70		8,573.70	1,588.00		1,588.00	10,161.70	10,068.23	103.46
Property Tax	1.1%		7,794.27		7,794.27	1,443.63		1,443.63	9,237.91	8,663.74	584.17
Bank Charges	0.7%	2.0%	5,077.65	1,316.09	6,393.73	940.47	497.53	1,438.00	7,831.73	7,575.90	255.83
Auditing	2.8%	3.1%	18,806.09	2,098.99	20,905.08	3,483.21	793.49	4,276.70	25,181.79	24,960.63	221.16
Legal Fees	1.7%	1.1%	11,283.66	742.41	12,026.06	2,089.93	280.66	2,370.58	14,396.65	16,337.50	-1,940.85
Office Insurance	1.0%		6,495.23		6,495.23	1,203.03		1,203.03	7,698.26	4,144.05	3,554.21
Maintenance	1.3%		8,573.70		8,573.70	1,588.00		1,588.00	10,161.70	12,931.30	-2,769.60
Office Supplies	2.2%	3.5%	14,668.75	2,362.21	17,030.96	2,716.90	893.00	3,609.90	20,640.86	19,093.16	1,547.70
Photocopy/Books/Jour/Library	2.2%	2.1%	14,668.75	1,430.82	16,099.58	2,716.90	540.90	3,257.81	19,357.38	19,915.19	-557.81
Local Phone,Internet, & E-Mail	1.1%	2.1%	7,334.38	1,430.82	8,765.20	1,358.45	540.90	1,899.35	10,664.55	11,490.02	-826.47
Postage/Delivery	0.5%	0.5%	3,667.19	357.71	4,024.89	679.23	135.23	814.45	4,839.35	4,409.16	430.19
Computer Support	3.4%		23,153.73		23,153.73	4,288.47		4,288.47	27,442.19	28,281.14	-838.95
Annual Report	1.9%		12,990.46		12,990.46	2,406.05		2,406.05	15,396.51	14,892.00	504.51
Board Meetings	1.0%		6,495.23		6,495.23	1,203.03		1,203.03	7,698.26	8,522.00	-823.74
Auto-Related Expenses	3.4%		23,382.82		23,382.82	4,330.90		4,330.90	27,713.72	26,769.80	953.92
Miscellaneous	0.5%	0.5%	3,667.19	337.46	4,004.65	679.23	127.57	806.80	4,811.44	5,653.90	-842.46
TOTAL	92.8%	29.8%	631961.35	20092.26	652063.61	117050.06	7695.60	124645.65	776,699.26	773,343.73	3,355.54

CHAPTER 12
Monitoring Performance

Beginning around 2010, think tanks' interest in being able to link their research clearly to policy outcomes increased sharply. This is due in part to publication of several strong analyses of the research-to-policy process.[142] It is also related to funders pressing for better documentation of policy relevance and impact to justify their organizations continuing think tank support programs.

In April 2013, Enrique Mendizabal (2013c) reported the key points from the workshop, "Monitoring and Evaluation for Performance Impact," held in Lima, Peru. Conference attendees were from think tanks participating in the TTI. Monitoring and evaluation (M&E) in this context differs from the standard assessment of government programs. Rather, it is the self-assessment of a think tank's effectiveness in influencing policy in its country. The workshop's focus is consistent with the surge in the desire to measure effectiveness. The report contains several striking points:

1. Many of the think tanks present have made large investments in developing indicators and generating the data to populate them. "Most had a person (or more) dedicated to M&E."
2. M&E results are related explicitly to multiyear strategic plans.
3. Despite these substantial efforts, some frustration was expressed at not being able to establish a clear link between the think tank's analyses and recommendations and policy impacts.
4. At the same time, several think tanks present had not yet developed formal M&E programs.

While tracking policy performance is certainly important, it is remarkable that so little parallel interest has emerged in assessing the many aspects of think tank operations—including meeting the financial and reporting expectations of its funders, invoicing clients and collecting receivables in a timely manner, limiting staff turnover to reasonable levels, and operating accounting and HR functions without excessive staff. In short, the level of resources a think tank has from a given budget to generate research findings and use them in policy engagement depends on administrative efficiency: fewer funds are available for research and policy engagement the more are being consumed in administrative operations.

A think tank's leadership needs timely information on how *all* the various parts of the organization are working. Without such information, managers have trouble leading, because they are more often responding to events than anticipating them. For example, an emerging cash shortage crisis

---

142   See particularly Carden (2009), Court and Young (2006), Lavis et al. (2003), Woelk et al. (2009) and Struyk and Haddaway (2011).

could have been prevented with timely information on cash flows and projected staff-utilization rates. A great deal of senior managers' time can be consumed dealing with such crises—an obvious drain on an organization's effectiveness.

In the past 20-plus years, for-profit firms have taken a much broader view than simply looking at profits and shareholder value. Increasingly client-oriented, many firms have begun monitoring client satisfaction because that is what substantially drives financial results. Kaplan and Norton (1992) led this movement with their publications on the "balanced scorecard" approach. Think tanks need to take a similarly broad approach to monitoring their activities. That said, the differences between think tank missions and those of other types of nonprofits and for-profit firms become starkly evident when the information relevant for top managers at think tanks is compared to what their counterparts at other organization types need.

This chapter sets forth several kinds of monitoring information think tanks should regularly assemble and use. I first define the broad areas to be monitored. Subsequent sections then describe the specific indicators for which data should be collected. I devote substantial space to monitoring the research-to-policy area and illustrate with a specific program. Annex 12.1 contains additional examples of the kinds of report formats managers can use in their work.

I focus on a monitoring program appropriate for a fairly large (50+) staff with specialists in such functions as personnel and public relations. Smaller think tanks (and those in special circumstances, such as being embedded in a university) can select the indicators best suited to their needs and the management information that should be collected for those needs. Because even moderately comprehensive monitoring appears rather limited among think tanks in transitional and developing countries, generally—and among mid-sized and smaller ones, in particular—I used the practices of Stage 3 think tanks and a few Stage 2 think tanks in preparing this chapter.

Such basic financial indicators as cash flow, reserve position, and return on investments are discussed only in passing. Many texts on basic finance and accounting are readily available for this. Additionally, some donors, including USAID, have guidance materials on financial operations that are strong on controls, cost allocation, and expenditure monitoring.

Four further introductory points are in order.

1. *Information must be channeled to the right person at the right time, who may not always be the organization's president or chief operating officer.* As an initial step toward allocating performance indicator reports, managers should decide who is in the best position to exploit specific information items to improve the organization's work. These targeted people should receive the information and act on it, or in some cases, jointly decide with senior management on actions to take as problems and opportunities are identified. It may well be, for example, that team leaders are the key players in policy engagement—that they are the ones who often have the critical contacts in government and the parliament and are in

the best position to advise senior staff how to be policy-proactive. If so, they should be on the distribution list for the regular report on communication activities.

Care must be taken not to overwhelm senior managers with information. Often, it will be sufficient for the head of communications or chief accountant (as examples) to have the indicators more often than the executive director. An institute's leader expects these managers, at least implicitly, to systematically track their office's efficiency. Complete information on an operational area can be provided to the leadership for semi-annual reviews or for board meeting preparation. Specific developments, with supporting indicator information, can be brought to the chief executive's attention as necessary.

2. *Indicators provided to management must comprehensively cover the institution's activities and be in a useful format.* In 2010, for example, when the Institute for Urban Economics (IUE) was suffering a downturn in revenues, it needed to cut overhead expenses. Because of the complexity of Russian government reporting requirements and documentation for contractual transactions—for example, formal acts of acceptance from the client for each deliverable must be submitted by IUE for signature, ultimately obtained from the client, and kept on file for inspection—accounting departments are larger per dollar of revenue than in most other countries. IUE's president had the sense that its accounting department was overstaffed given the current number of open contracts and number of staff. She wanted to see workload indicators for the accounting team for the past several years, standardized by the number of accounting staff, to have a realistic idea of the present workload in the relevant context. These indicators were not available at that time and would have been difficult to prepare for prior years. Hence, decision making had to be done in a vacuum.

3. *Generating information for senior managers and giving it to them in a usable form does* not *mean that elegant, comprehensive reports are required.* A negative example: at the U.S. housing ministry at the end of the 1970s, every month big loose-leaf binders of statistical tables on all important aspects of ministry performance were presented to the minister and her principal staff. These 300-page binders contained highly useful information for managers responsible for expenditures of $10 billion a year, but required an enormous amount of staff time to assemble. A less elegant presentation and moderately less content would have saved 20-30 percent of the total effort.

Even management at large Stage 3 think tanks get some monitoring information piecemeal. Managers collate the data informally as they address specific questions. In short, rather than becoming fixated on presentation formats and the preparation of consolidated, exhaustive reports, it is better to focus on generating fewer, reliable indicators that cost-effectively convey meaningful information to managers on a timely basis.

4. *Most indicators are best interpreted in comparison with earlier values for the same indicators.* The tables in this chapter list useful indicators and who in the organization is usually

likely to have the data to construct the indicator. The tables in Annex 12.1, in contrast, are in formats that are more useful for actually presenting the information.

WHAT TO MONITOR: THE BIG PICTURE

A truly successful monitoring system provides senior management, and those to whom they have delegated significant responsibility, with relevant, timely information on key elements of the think tank's operations. Widely adopted in the private sector in the last 20 years and often labeled "the balanced scorecard," this approach insists that, to excel, the company should score well in all key operations—whether inventory control, customer satisfaction, product innovation, or profitable investment of cash reserves.[143]

A similar logic applies to think tanks. What is the point of running a financially solid operation if it does not advance the organization's research results in the policy process? In particular, without investing in staff and initiating innovative research, the institution may see its creativity and policy prowess decline.

The logic of the "balanced scorecard" suggests five critical areas or activities senior managers at think tanks should monitor. Each also represents a way to measure a think tank's performance.

- *The public policy perspective*—success in communicating research results to and engaging policymakers, other stakeholders, and the public, and in informing the public on key issues of the day. (This was the topic of the M&E conference described at the opening of this chapter.)

- *The funder perspective*—success in meeting the expectations of donors who sponsor policy work and of those contracting with the organization for research, pilot projects, and evaluations.

- *The internal business perspective*—success in *efficiently* conducting research, communications activities, and support functions.

- *The innovation and learning perspective*--success in enhancing the skill level and mix of the staff and in defining important policy projects to pursue.

- *The financial perspective*—success in raising funds to support the research and policy engagement program and properly managing the organization's resources.

The *public policy perspective* is special to think tanks and not one routinely used by business, i.e., such indicators are not part of businesses balanced score cards. Many think tank funders care less about the think tank's primary missions of constructively influencing policy and informing the public than about the direct research results. For example, a ministry may commission a program evaluation from a think tank to determine the reasons for the low participation rate in a welfare program. The think tank may want to insert the results of the evaluation into policy discussions

---

143   See Kaplan and Norton (1992) for a full explanation.

more generally, even though the ministry staff commissioning the work sees enriching the debate as peripheral to its task of program improvement. Generally, the interests of foundations and think tanks are more tightly aligned than those of other clients and think tanks.

Table 12.1 gives examples of performance indicators for each of the five perspectives. The range of items listed suggests the breadth of the topics on which senior management needs to be kept informed. With a narrower approach, problems are more likely to develop and fester. Again, the objective is to identify an incipient problem and address it before it becomes a major challenge for the organization as a whole.

Table 12.1 A Balanced Think Tank Information Scheme, Illustrative Indicators

Perspective	Example indicators
Public policy perspective	No. of visits to the web site; no. of documents downloaded No. of blogs moderated; no of posts and no. of comments on posts No. of conferences and seminars at which staff are presenters No. of policy briefs produced and distributed to policymakers No. of articles by staff in newspapers or popular magazines No. of policy memos requested by officials
Funder perspective	No. of projects not completed on time Distribution of evaluation scores for workshops and training events offered Average no. of publications sold per publication; and numbers downloaded per publication Trend in participation in fee-based courses No. of contracts/grants from established funders; average contract value No. of contracts/grants from new funders; average contract value
Internal business perspective	No. of projects over budget and dollar amount as percentage of project budgets Staff utilization rate (% time charged to billable projects) Revenue: realization to date as percent of target Proposal spending: funds used versus projected spending Cost/proposal; percent of proposals won
Innovation and learning perspective	No. of staff trained for new roles and broad staff development No. of new staff hired with special skills to work on innovative topics or strengthen teams No. of pilot projects under way; success compared with benchmarks
Financial perspective	Cash flow Year-on-year revenue growth Rate of return on liquid assets Receivables: total and by aging

Most think tanks probably monitor many of the activities I list using indicators similar to those shown. Often, however, staff provides individual pieces of information in response to specific, ad hoc requests from the president. This can be a mistake. Some critical information must be generated and used regularly; the few most critical items need to be tracked monthly, although quarterly or even annually may be sufficient for information on other functions and areas of performance.

In the following discussion of useful indicators, note that some indicators provide useful information on more than one perspective. As noted, I do not address compiling indicators on financial conditions, since there are many sources available for these.

PUBLIC POLICY PERSPECTIVE

The public policy perspective concerns the think tank's service in the community—in terms of constructive participation in policy development and informing citizens about the key public issues that affect them. This section first presents a set of serviceable indicators and then maps out their role in an internal analysis of a think tank's policy effectiveness.

Indicators

Determining a think tank's success in influencing policy or informing the public is a formidable challenge. There is scholarly literature on this topic and some case studies on the importance of different types of organizations and individuals in shaping a particular policy outcome. But monitoring impact through what are in effect case studies is time consuming and expensive; alternatives, such as interviewing key policymakers, require setting up the interviews on a regular basis, and there is no guarantee policymakers will be absolutely candid.

The more economical and probably better approach is to use indicators that record activities aimed at exerting policy influence and educating the public—that is, *outputs*. Unquestionably, these indicators provide very limited information on impacts. But they do have value. At a minimum, an organization doing little or nothing to get its policy research results used will be made starkly aware of this fact. Using indicators to assess the mix of communication activities may also prove very useful. For example, senior management may have decided that issuing short "policy briefs" to a well-targeted mailing list of policymakers is the best way to influence policy outcomes. If so, a glance at a chart showing the number of policy briefs issued over the past six months would reveal the extent to which this tool is being used.

But management can, with only limited additional cost, go well beyond outputs to *intermediate outcomes*. As the phrase indicates, these are not final outcomes (i.e., policy change), but they do document that the output has at a minimum reached its target or the first step in the process of affecting policy. For conferences, it is not simply that conferences were held but how many people attended them; not just that reports were placed on the website, but how many people downloaded them; not just that articles were published in international refereed journals, but the number of times they were cited in other publications. Such intermediate outcome indicators are extraordinarily useful in alerting management to where practices need to be changed to make them more effective in initiating a process of policy influence.

Table 12.2 lists multiple indicators for monitoring a think tank's operations from the public policy perspective. There are two sets of columns: one for outputs and the other for intermediate outcomes.

Table 12.2 Performance Indicators for Public-Policy Perspective [a]

Outputs			Intermediate Outcomes		
Indicator	**Current period**	**Last period**	**Indicator**	**Current period**	**Last period**
Events [b]			*Events*		
Number events held			Number of people attending events		
Number of persons registering					
Number of dropouts (registered non-attendees)					
Number of high priority attendees invited			Number of high priority attendees		
			Feedback surveys completed at events		
			Scores from surveys at events		
Number of webinars			Number of webinar visitors		
Number of videos offered			Number of people watching the videos		
Number of presentations made by staff at events not sponsored by the organization					
Publications [b,c]			*Publications* [b,c]		
Number of publications issued in past 6 months [a,b]			Number of publications sold		
Number of publications issued in past 6 months out of print [b,c]			Number of physical copies distributed free of charge		
			Number of publications downloaded without charge [b,c]		
			Clicks of "print" button		
			Clicks of "share" button		
No. of articles in international peer-reviewed journals during the reporting period			Citation tracking of articles published in the past 3 years		
No. of articles in national peer-reviewed journals during the reporting period			Citation tracking of articles published in the past 3 years		
Newsletter			*Newsletter*		
Number and type of recipients			New subscribers		
			Number unsubscribed		
			Number of click-throughs from items		
			Number forwarding the newsletter		
			Social media mentions		
Website			*Website*		
No. of visitors to the site			No. of items downloaded		

No. of pages viewed					
Split of web entrances[f]					
			Clicks of "share" button on home page		
Search engine positioning for 6-10 topics;[e] mean position in the list (e.g., 1st, 2nd...)			Social network mentions of site as a whole		
On-line participants			On-line participants		
			No. of likes on Facebook		
			No. of followers on Twitter		
			No. signed up for email newsletter		
--Blogs			--Blogs		
Split of web entrances					
No. of posts on your blogs			No. of subscribers to your blogs		
			No. of views		
			Webpage views		
			Comments on blogs		
Number of posts by staff on other relevant blogs					
Search engine positioning					
Media releases			Media releases		
Contacts on media release list					
No. of releases					
			Follow-up calls or email queries from media contacted		
			Subscribers to news feeds		
Appearances			Appearances		
No. of TV appearances			Average viewership of programs		
Share on topics where institute does research			Average viewership of programs		
No. of radio appearances			Average viewership of programs		
Share on topics where institute does research			Average viewership of programs		
Print media exposure/PR			Print media exposure		
No. of newspaper and magazine articles by staff			Average readership of publications		
No. of op-ed pieces placed			Average readership of publications		
			No. of calls from reports and editors to staff		
No. of newspaper and magazine articles where think tank is mentioned			Average readership of publications		

No. of press conferences held			No. of media stories and blog posts on subject of press conferences		
			Touches[d]		
			Number of touches		

a. **Important:** The entries for an output and an outcome in the same row are related, i.e., the outcome entry is for the output in the row. Empty cells indicate the nonalignment of one type of indicator with the other (output vs. outcome).

b. Could disaggregate by type

c. Could disaggregate by topic

d. Policy research and communications staff count of their contacts with NGO, government, and legislative staff that include phone calls (made and received), meetings, e-mail conversations, and requests for information. This excludes notices of events and other mass mailings from an organization or individual. Idea from MacDonald and Levine (2008), p.16.

e. Where an organization's information appears on the list of sources provided in response to a query to a search engine. Position is influenced by the key words used in post.

f. Search engine, email, other sites.

Source: Many of the table entries are from R. Scott (2012a), which also presents a more complete discussion of monitoring communications activities and information sources for media use data, e.g. search engine positioning.

It is worthwhile to examine a few of the table entries in some detail.

- *Events.* It is, of course, useful to know how many events were held during the reporting period, but the complementary information on number of attendees is essential. Naturally, this figure needs to be interpreted with information on the event type (i.e., were some designed for only a few participants?). Hence, disaggregation by meeting type is useful. A key meeting outcome is whether the "right" stakeholders attended. The table has entries for the number invited and the number who actually attended. A low participation rate obviously points to the wisdom of a stronger effort to attract these potential participants, such as in-person phone calls the day before the event. Attendance by "high priority" persons is an important intermediate outcome.

- *Peer reviewed journal articles authored by the staff.* This is an important indicator of the quality of research being produced and the effort expended in getting worthy work published. The intermediate outcome, the number of times articles published by staff in the past three years have been cited in other articles and books, is also very informative— indicating the extent to which the research is part of the dialogue on the issues researched, at least in academia and think tanks. An observation period longer than the reporting period (quarterly or semi-annual) is essential, since it takes time for published articles to be absorbed by the research community.

- *Website.* One output of particular interest is "search engine positioning" achieved for major areas of the institute's work (i.e., where in the list of sources the institution is positioned among the results of a search). Rankings are very sensitive to the key words used on the research items page on the website, and the communications group can strongly affect the ranking of an institution's reports and blog entries.

- *Touches.* This is a useful metric (last item in table under outcomes) used by the Center for Global Development. It is the count tabulated by the policy research team and communications staff of their contacts with NGOs, government, and legislative staff—which include phone calls (made and received), meetings, email conversations, and requests for information. Essentially, it is a strong signal of the extent to which staff is really active in the policy community. Disaggregation by touch type is advisable, because a meeting with an official is potentially much more effective that sending an email (that might not have been answered).

A key question is which of these information types senior management needs to see regularly. Practice suggests a limited amount. Generally, public relations specialists (lodged in the communications team) are charged with insuring information of this type is generated, and they use their judgment about which information to forward to senior management. Strong press coverage ("applause") of the institution's work always interests the boss. So does information indicating worrisome or very positive trends or critical one-time events. The PR staffer will use the information assembled to prepare the semi-annual report and data for management "retreats." Often an essay with separate short sections summarizing developments and trends, based on the indicators, tells senior management more than a table of figures.

My preference would be that senior management, including team leaders, see essentially all data items in the table quarterly. There is a great deal of information presented that alerts them to the effectiveness of the institute's practices.

AN M&E PROGRAM FOR POLICY ENGAGEMENT IMPACTS

Monitoring performance in the policy arena can be conducted at two levels. The first, concentrated on policy engagement, is ongoing and draws on information internal to the organization, supplemented by input from external sources on policy developments and the organization's role in them. The second level focuses on external perceptions of the organization's broad performance in the *policy community*. Given the greater resources needed to take measurements in the policy community, it is done much less frequently than ongoing monitoring. This section and the next discuss these two types of monitoring in turn.

An effective program for documenting a think tank's performance in having its research successfully influence policy decisions could have two components. The first is the kind of information displayed in Table 12.2. This table differs from the others presented in this chapter, as noted, because it includes both outputs and intermediate outcomes—for example, not just the number of events held, but also the number attendees overall and the number of high priority attendees; not just the number of articles published in newspapers and magazines, but the outlets' circulation as well. These figures give at least an idea of how many people were exposed to an institution's work. (Selee reports that "output measures are particularly valuable for funders, who often like to have statistics on what an organization is doing. Indeed, for most programs within think tanks, reports to funders often drive the tracking of inputs and outputs." (2013, 89-90).)

Especially useful is to array these indicators over time, to assess performance trends more readily. Close analysis of the relation between outputs and intermediate outcomes is important. If the think tank is holding more events of the same type but attendance is dwindling, for example, that is a red flag.

The second component is the tracking of actual policy developments in areas where the think tank has made significant contributions. Obviously, there is usually but little contemporary correspondence between current policy engagement reflected in the indicators in Table 12.2 and developments on the targeted policies. This is because it often takes several years before real action is seen as a policy initiative works its way up slowly through the bureaucracy.[144] For a change requiring parliamentary approval, the path would be something like the following: in the responsible ministry the policy change passes from the division director, to the office director, to the deputy minister, to the minister; and then to the ministry of finance; then up its chain of command and on to the office of the president (which may have several levels); then on to parliament and through the committees of both houses; and then finally to each of the full chambers for action. Obviously, this is a highly time consuming process for all but the most urgent business. Quicker action is possible when the ministry has the power to make the change, as for many administrative regulations.

There are many approaches to trying to measure a think tank's influence in policy development, ranging from the comparatively simple to those that involve a series of studies and significant resources.[145] I favor a comparatively straightforward approach. This is because of my sense that: 1) most think tanks now do very little explicitly in tracking policy effects, and therefore, 2) the benefits from implementing a basic approach need to be evident before they will invest in more

---

144   Salee (2013, 7) reports that Fred Bergsten, founding president of the Petersen Institute and a person very experienced in moving policy ideas forward in international finance, has said it requires "ten years from inception of an idea to implementation of an idea."

145   An overview of issues involved is presented in Politics and Ideas (2013b) and in Summer et al. (2009). Weyrauch, D'Agostino, and Richards (2011) have prepared a handbook on organizing a comprehensive research-to-policy M&E program. CIPPEC in Argentina has also produced a very useful set of toolkits on carrying out these analyses. Hovland (2007) provides an overview of methods for evaluating an institution's performance; a more recent review is in Tsui, Hearn and Young (2014). On two specific tools, i.e., "Most Significant Change" and "Outcome Mapping," see Davies and Dart (2005) and Earl, Carden, and Smutylo (2001), respectively. Also see Alcazar et al. (2012) for three case studies of approaches to tracking impacts.

elaborate approaches. This is consistent with expert opinion, which argues for starting with simple measurements (Weyrauch, 2013b).

It is also consistent with information in a diagnostic of the communications programs of a dozen East African think tanks noted in Chapter 8. The diagnostic gathered information on the indicators (listed in a somewhat simplified version of Table 12.2) being used at each think tank. Nearly all of those think tanks used only a minority of these indicators. With routine monitoring so limited, pressing for sophisticated M&E programs seems inadvisable.

My basic approach to tracking the policy developments flowing from a think tank's research and policy engagement is to rely on team leaders. They are best positioned to keep track of developments, as they are deeply involved on a daily basis on actions in their specialty sphere. As stated in Chapter 9, it is extremely important for team leaders *at the start* of a project or program to define indicators of success, for both intermediate and ultimate results.

A simple way for team leaders to organize the information is to keep a log on developments for each topic where the team had made an important contribution—checking with contacts every calendar quarter if nothing obvious had happened during the period. This implies that, as part of a project or strategic plan development, the team leaders have worked through a theory of change, identified whom should be influenced, and indicators of effects.

The link between policy engagement activities and ultimate outcomes would be clearer if the indicators in Table 12.2 were compiled by major topical research area—for example, a think tank's research programs. Such a breakdown might, in any case, motivate team leaders whose teams were doing relatively little in the way of outreach to and interaction with stakeholders to be more energetic in advancing their recommendations.

As just outlined, a comprehensive program takes a good deal of resources. Few think tanks can really devote this kind of attention to tracking policy developments possibly associated with their research, although some Latin American think tanks are doing so, as reported by Mendizabal. An alternative is to focus the tracking of policy developments on a small number of high profile initiatives where the think tank has made major investments. This is the explicit policy of the Center for Global Development, and I believe, of many Stage 3 think tanks (McDonald and Levine 2008, 14-6).

In summary, a sensible program consists of the following steps. Develop the kind of information in Table 12.2, because it will help manage policy engagement effectively and provides good data on efforts being made. Supplement this with actively tracking the policy developments associated with a small number of major initiatives taken by the think tank. Ask team leaders to report policy developments for lower priority initiatives as they learn about them, but not to invest much in generating the information. This information together should provide a think tank, and its Board, with a strong basis for assessing its progress.

A Broader View of Think Tank Effectiveness

I now shift my focus beyond individual project or program success in policy development to a wider assessment of the think tank as effective, or as a "good citizen," in the policy community. Does it tend to work on issues of high priority to the country, in part identifying such issues by being a good listener to a range of stakeholders? Does it partner well with relevant organizations, particularly civil society organizations? Is it an effective communicator broadly defined? Assessment at this level relates to how well the think tank is defining and executing its institutional-level communications strategy (i.e., generating visibility, building a strong brand, and communicating its mission well).

To generate information on this performance level it is necessary to consult the policy community—in short, to conduct semi-structured-to-structured conversations with a reasonable sampling of community members. In developing the assessment plan, four questions need to be addressed: 1) what to discuss, 2) whom to interview and how many, 3) how to gather the information (in-person, mail-out survey, etc.), and 4) who should ask the questions.

What to discuss? I think the Policy Community Survey (PCS) fielded by NORC at the University of Chicago in evaluating the effectiveness of the Global Development Network's technical assistance program is a good source of ideas. (The GDN project is sketched in Chapter 1; other NORC surveys for the project are the source of the data for the GDN-15 think tanks presented in various chapters. TTI later fielded a survey very similar to the PCS.)

This survey consists of four principal blocks, besides basic information on the respondent, that obtain information on the respondent's views about:

1. Information sources used in learning about or addressing policy issues
2. Extent of the use of research and analysis in policymaking by government officials and MPs
3. Openness of government and parliament to accepting analysis and recommendations from organizations like this think tank
4. Regarding the specific think tank,
   a. general questions on effectiveness
   b. strength in certain policy areas
   c. the degree to which it focuses on priority policy issues
   d. ratings of various types of publications and communications, including events.

The full questionnaire is in Annex 12.2,* but a good idea of the kinds of questions asked about effectiveness is given by the battery of questions in Table 12.3. One can argue about the value of specific questions developed for the particular evaluation, but this gives one a good sense of the breadth of topics covered. In any case, the questionnaire may prove to be a useful starting point.

Table 12.3 A Question Set on a Think Tank's Effectiveness from the Policy Community Survey[146]

Question	Very much	Somewhat	Not much	Not at all	Don't know
1.Are the organization's policy recommendations helpful?					
2.Is the organization a valuable source of research, including data and statistics?					
3.Does the organization's work positively impact public policy or administration?					
4.Does the organization have an impact in holding the government accountable for public expenditure quality, i.e., efficient and honest use of public resources?					
5.Does the organization have an influence on the budget making process in terms of openness, quality or equity of budget choices?					
6.Does the organization effectively partner with other domestic civil society organizations or NGOs in developing analyses or working for change?					
7.Does the organization effectively partner with international civil society organizations or private sector entities?					
8.Does the organization operate transparently and openly?					

Whom to interview and how many interviews are needed? Here one has to address both the types of respondents and the overall number to include. Regarding interviewees, one wants naturally to cover government officials and senior members of parliament. One should select positions and individuals active in the policy process broadly defined—including, for example, certain "special assistants" or "advisors" to ministers who are actually key advisors. If subnational officials are important players, include them. Leaders or staff at advocacy and non-advocacy NGOs often are important in the process, sometimes indirectly as opinion leaders. Certain academics are relevant. And, of course, key media people are to be included, ranging from print editors, to TV producers, to prominent bloggers in the relevant policy spaces.[147] One does not want to be too mechanical in

---

146   The full questionnaire is in Annex 12.2*.
147   Question A.1 in the PCS (see Annex 12.2*) has a basic listing of possible interviewees.

making these selections. There are certainly individuals active in the policy process with whom think tank leaders and senior researchers have good relationships and who are likely to be open in their remarks. They should certainly be included.

With respect to numbers, based on my own experience leading the GDN evaluation analysis, using the PCS data, and talking with several think tank communications directors who have carried out such surveys, 30-40 completed interviews are necessary to provide a sufficient number of responses to identify clear response patterns and to permit small sample statistical tests.

How to gather the information? The standard four options are in-person interviews, telephone interviews mail out survey forms, and an on-line survey. Response rates will be highest and the information most informative with the in-person option. The information is "better" because respondents often not only respond to a direct ratings question like those shown in Table 12.3, but also comment on the reason for the particular response. Many senior officials will not fill in a form, hard copy or otherwise, and dislike phone interviews. There will be some interviewees with whom some in the think tank want to establish a relationship; this could be a chance to have the initial interaction. For less senior government officials and media members, a mail out or on-line survey will likely work. In sum, if the budget is available, use the in-person interview. In any case, persistent follow-up is essential for a good response rate.

Larger sample sizes are, of course, desirable to permit greater statistical accuracy. But interviews can be costly, especially when most are conducted in-person, and arranging interview appointments is complicated and time consuming.

Who should ask the questions (for in-person interviews)? Many of these interviews can be done by mid-level staff, after training on what each question is really after and the kind of supplementary notes to take. It is probably evident that wherever someone in the think tank has a good working relationship, having that person do the interview may be the right course. That said, in assigning interviewers one needs to consider whether having that person ask the questions may result in the respondent being less than fully forthcoming. Because of such concerns and because it was an internal evaluation, when organizing the in-person GDN interviews, NORC recommended to participating think tanks responsible for the in-person interviews that the interviewer not be their employee, but rather a consultant hired for the task.

Broad assessments of the type discussed here are not often undertaken on a routine basis, in part because of their expense. The Results for Development Institute undertook one after about three years of activity, to understand how the institute was perceived in several communities. The information was extremely useful. In-person interviews of stakeholders form a common part of in-depth evaluations of think tank performance. After its first five years of existence, for example, the Center for Global Development's funders commissioned a wide-ranging in-depth evaluation that included over 150 in-person interviews with key stakeholders (and generated 1,259 responses to an email audience survey) (Bumgarner et al. 2006). The Think Tank Fund's evaluations of the productivity of its institutional development grants regularly include a small scale stakeholder survey with in-person interviews. The Think Tank Initiative has also undertaken PCSs in all the countries where it supports a think tank. In short, experience with such policy community surveys indicates that the results have been generally useful to the think tanks involved.

FUNDER/CLIENT PERSPECTIVE

This perspective considers the institution as viewed by its primary funders, in addition to its research quality and policy engagement (covered in Table 12.2).[148] Funders are the foundations providing grants or the aid agencies and government bodies letting contracts. The indicators shown in Table 12.4 focus on a few basic elements of performance.

---

148   Sample tables in Annex 12.1 show possible report formats.

Table 12.4 Performance Indicators from the Funder Perspective[a]

Indicator	*Possible source[b]*
Project work	
No. of reports not delivered to clients on time as percentage of all reports delivered	Team leaders
No. of projects with cost overruns, (a) total, (b) no. of times additional funds were received from the sponsor, (c) no. of times additional funds were requested and refused; and (d) no. where overrun was funded internally	Head of finance
Client satisfaction	
No. of contracts/grants in past 12 months from established clients as percentage of all contracts/grants. Total number of contracts/grants	Head of finance
Feedback on pay-to-attend courses developed with or partially supported by funders	
Seminar on municipal budgeting Date course offered Mean student evaluation score % of scores < 3.5[c] No. of attendees	Training program manager
Certified Mortgage Lender course Date course offered Mean student evaluation score % of scores < 3.5 No. of attendees	Training program manager
Course on municipal economic development Date course offered Mean student evaluation score % of scores < 3.5 No. of attendees	Training program manager
Transparency • Think tank's rating for transparency in its funding sources computed using the Tranparify 5-star rating protocol[d]	

a. These supplement the indicators in Table 11.2.
b. Person who should send information for preparing the indicator and report.
c. On a scale from 1 to 5, with 5 indicating the highest level of student satisfaction.
d. This is described in Transparify (2014); a slightly easier to compute 5-star system is presented in Mendizabal (2014c).

The first two indicators under "project work" speak directly to an institution's core performance on research projects: Are the reports being submitted on time and are project costs to the client staying within the budget? Barring extraordinary circumstances, delivering reports late or asking clients for additional funds to finish the defined tasks are the mortal sins of the research business. The only thing worse is to submit technically weak or sloppy analysis and recommendations.

The indicators under the "client satisfaction" heading measure satisfaction as reflected in client behavior. The entries assume the organization offers training courses on a pay-to-attend basis. Each of these needs to be interpreted with care.

- *Funder satisfaction.* A clear sign of doing high-quality and relevant policy research is when sponsors return to fund new projects at the same think tank. A caveat here, though, is that a substantial share of all foundations has a policy forbidding continued grant funding for any think tank. So two or three grants in succession may be possible, but then no more until several years have passed. For this reason, it makes sense to track "repeat sales" separately for grants and for contracts.

- *Seminar/training evaluation scores.* Participation should be influenced by the quality of the offerings. The trend over time is as important as the absolute level. But the usefulness of comparing average scores can be diluted by changes over time in the topics covered and the composition of the faculty. So it is best to track these results course by course.

- *Trend in attendance of fee-based courses.* This "market test" indicator is fairly accurate because it tracks each course separately. But in interpreting it, one must remember that the market for a particular course may become saturated or the topic no longer relevant. An example of saturation is teaching a course for mortgage bankers in a central Asian republic where mortgage lending volume is low. Once the current bankers responsible for such loans were taught, there was little demand. An example of reduced relevance is teaching a course on preparing annual municipal budgets in a central European country; once most municipalities had participated, demand fell. Training can then be done on the job at the municipalities, and city finance officials are ready for more advanced courses.

The final indicator in the table, *transparency,* measures the extent to which the think tank openly reports on its sources of funds. The donor community, led from early 2014 to some extent by the blog "Transparify," embraced the idea that think tanks should report the sources of their funds, for individual projects and overall. The early focus is on think tank websites listing support from all funders, whether grants or contracts, and made by firms, agencies, or individuals. Knowledge of revenue sources will help the public judge whether a think tank's position on a particular issue may be influenced by a funder with vested interests in the issue. (Similarly, reports, articles, and Power Points should indicate who financed these products to alert audiences to possible conflicts of interest.)

Many donors care about this and will be looking at grantees' reporting and using this as one factor in deciding whether to work with an organization—which is the reason this indicator is included in those for the "funder perspective." Annual reporting with the specific methodology indicated seems appropriate.

The specific indicator in Table 12.4 is the one developed by Transparify (2014). This or another widely accepted indicator should be computed based on the information actually presented on a think tank's website and possibly its annual report. Other indicators for the same purpose were already being created in early summer 2014, (e.g., Mendizabal 2014c). Because this is a new area, further developments are likely, of which think tank directors will want to be aware.

The indicators in Table 12.4 can help senior managers better understand relations with funders. Even so, these same managers must still speak directly to key funders about how well the institution is performing on a particular project and in communicating its results generally. Managers will likely want to augment these indicators with others suited to their specific operations.

INTERNAL BUSINESS PERSPECTIVE

These indicators focus on the relation between inputs and outputs, including such items as the percentage of a project's budget spent to date in relation to the project time elapsed, and the average revenue won through proposal writing compared with the cost of writing proposals. The indicators listed in Table 12.5 give senior managers an idea of the efficiency of a half-dozen areas of the think tank's operations. (Sample Tables 3 to 7 in Annex 12.1 are formats for reporting some of these indicators.) Because labor constitutes such a large percentage of total think tank expenses, the indicators often use the ratio of a given output (e.g., contracts under management, number of articles placed in newspapers) to the number of staff assigned to the function.

Table 12.5 Performance Indicators from the Internal Business Perspective

Indicator	*Frequency*[a]	*Possible source*[b]
A. Basics		
1. Project expenditure overview—spending on each project, comparing expenditures to date as percent of total budget versus percent of work period used	M	Accounting dept.
2. Fundraising results: funds acquired vs. quarterly or annual goals	M	Accounting dept.
3. Pipeline by team: contract revenue unspent/loaded team labor costs	Q	Accounting dept.
4. Staff utilization by team over the past three months[c]	Q	Accounting dept.
5. Projected staff utilization for the next quarter	Q	Team leaders
6. Overhead rate line items (YTD) versus targets	Q	Accounting dept.
B. Proposals and development		
7. Proposal funds utilization versus projected spending over the year	Q	Accounting dept.
8. Proposal efficiency analysis by team and overall	Q	Accounting dept.
• Proposals won versus total proposals (both by number and by expenditures on proposal development)		
• Average cost/proposal		
• Value of grants and contracts won/proposal funds spent		
9. Program development funds utilization (by initiative) by team—spending, comparing percent expenditures of total allocated funds versus percent of total development time used	Q	Accounting dept.

C. Human resources		
10. Total staff/human resources (HR) staff	S	HR dept.
11. No. of new hires/HR staff	S	HR dept.
12. No. of new staff HR asked to recruit/HR staff	S	HR dept.
13. No. of departing staff/HR staff	S	HR dept.
14. No. of health insurance claims process per HR staff[d]	S	HR dept.
15. Time take to fill vacant positions by position type	S	HR dept.
D. Accounting/finance		
16. No. of projects unbilled more than 60 days after the end of the billing period	M	Accounting dept.
17. No. of projects and amount of funds for which cash advances were not applied for on time[e]	M	Accounting dept.
18. Vol. of receivables by age of debt	M	Accounting dept.
19. No. of projects under way by type of sponsor,[f] total and per accounting staff	Q	Accounting dept.
20. No. of projects closed, total and per accounting staff	Q	Accounting dept.
21. No. of staff business trips, total and per accounting staff[g]	S	Accounting dept.
22. No. of budgets for proposals prepared, total and per accounting staff	S	Accounting dept.
E. Contract management		
23. No. of contracts and grants under management, total and per contract staff	S	Contracts office
24. No. of new contracts and grants, total and per contract staff	S	Contracts office
25. No. of contracts closed, total and per contract staff	S	Contracts office
26. No. of subcontracts originated, total and per contract staff	S	Contracts office
27. No. of subcontracts closed, total and per contract staff	S	Contracts office
28. Dollar volume of open contracts	S	Contracts office
29. Mean dollar size of open contracts	S	Contracts office

[a] M = monthly, Q = quarterly, S = semiannually.

[b] Source of information for preparing the indicator and report.

[c] Percent time billed to projects vs. overhead accounts.

[d] This is an example of a routine task an HR department be assigned; others tasks could be included as well.

[e] Population of projects includes only those for which such advances are possible.

[f] The desegregation by type of sponsor is useful when grants or contracts from a particular sponsor take much more time to administer than others.

[g] In some countries, such as Russia, per diem payments above a very low minimum are counted as income to the traveler. This extra income must be recorded and taxes assessed, which is a significant burden at a think tank with a high volume of travel.

An additional column in this table shows how often management should review each indicator. The very few requiring a monthly check are those used to monitor key aspects of the institution's financial effectiveness—that is, production of research within budget and fund-raising. Most indicators in the table need to be reviewed only semiannually. If a concern is spotted, reporting frequency can be increased.

Panels A and B of the table focus on the status and efficiency of the research operation, including proposal writing and program development.[149] While many indicators in these panels are self-

---

149   As noted in the introduction to this chapter, many indicators of financial condition have been deliberately omitted, since they are available elsewhere. One not included in the table that could be a priority

explanatory, the following deserve comment.

A.3 *Pipeline by team: contracted revenue unspent/loaded team labor costs.* This is a rough indicator of the extent of a team's future coverage. Its utility is limited because the work in hand may be spread out over a short or long period. If it is a long period, the amount may not be sufficient to cover all current staff for the whole period. Consider the following example: the loaded team cost is $20,000 per month, and the team has the following contracted funds remaining to be spent:

Contract	Amount of funds remaining	No. of months remaining in the contracts	Average funds available per month
1	$50,000	5	$10,000
2	150,000	36	4,200
3	50,000	12	4,200
Average			18,400

In this example, if the team spends the funds evenly over the contracted periods, there will be a shortfall of about $1,600 in the first month. Of course, this problem could be met in the short run by accelerating work on the first contract (with five months remaining) to make up the shortfall. But there are probably hard limits to the amount of work that can be front-loaded. The example illustrates why this indicator needs to be interpreted with caution.

A.4 *Staff utilization over the past three months.* If staff regularly charges significant time to overhead accounts, it may signal that the team has coverage problems. When a report points in this direction, management should follow up with the team leader. Possibly, overhead funds are being used just to cover the time of an underemployed analyst. A decision should be made whether this is a good investment of such funds, which in part depends on how soon additional funding is expected. It could also be that the overhead charges are justified, for example, by a lot of proposal writing.

A.5 *Projected staff utilization over the next quarter.* While a standard form can be useful in guiding the discussion, senior management should meet with each team leader about the team's prospects. Some information is hard to convey in writing. For example, team leaders often have had conversations with sponsors that give them fairly good ideas about the potential for fund-raising with them. When the team appears to be heading for a period of excess demand for its work, how to acquire the additional resources to meet this peak load needs to be discussed.

B.7 *Proposal funds utilization versus projected spending over the year.* Most think tanks experience a regular seasonal pattern in fund-raising. Think tanks with significant work

item is a quarterly comparison of overhead spending on a line-item basis with the projections for the year.

for government agencies often find that a large share of the contracting—and therefore a good deal of all proposal writing—is done near the end of the government's fiscal year. The projected spending on proposal writing should be based on this experience, so senior managers understand how to correctly interpret figures on the rate of spending of proposal development funds.

Panels C through E address the volume of services provided and (crudely) the staff efficiency of several types of support operations: human resources, accounting/finance, and contract management. The goal is to provide senior managers with meaningful indicators on workload and productivity. Most indicators measure productivity by output per staff member. In computing staff members, use full-time equivalents (FTEs). In other words, if three people each devote about half their time to personnel matters, the FTE value is 1.5; this is the value to use in constructing the indicators.[150]

> *Panel C. Human resources.* Generally speaking, new hires and separations take more staff time than do continuing employees. As a result, job turnover and staff growth drive the workload. But the ratio of total employees to the number of human resources employees is also a useful measure, because the HR workload for health insurance, leave monitoring, performance assessment, and salary administration increases with staff size.

> *Panel D. Accounting/finance, other indicators.* For most of these measures, it is useful to see both the total workload as well as that per accounting staff member. Not shown here are indicators related to the number and complexity of filings for various taxes and contributions to social funds, since the level of effort for these filings should be fairly constant over time. If not, then adding indicators to capture this particular type of labor expenditure is appropriate.

> *D.16 – D.19.* These indicators on accounts receivable are the most important elements in the accounting/finance block. Failure to collect amounts due from clients on time can damage an organization's financial health. Even worse is being delinquent in billing clients. Strong senior management attention and oversight is essential.

> *Panel E. Contract management.* The contract manager generally expends greater effort when a new contract is won and when a contract is closed out than during the performance period. Hence, these indicators focus on new contracts and close outs. Similarly, when

---

150   Another tool for understanding the efficiency of internal operations is activity-based costing, (i.e., determining the full cost of each activity). This can be very demanding, because the costs of many activities are scattered across various parts of the organization, and creating an operating system to track these elements and assemble them into the costs of discrete activities is both complex and expensive. For this reason, the approach is not recommended in general for think tanks. Some examples of such costing are in Chapter 5. Also see, for example, Ness and Cucuzza (1995).

the think tank subcontracts with another organization, the substantial effort needed must also be monitored. Still, ongoing contracts have certain basic activities:

- ○ transmitting reports to clients
- ○ requesting permission to place subcontracts
- ○ documenting that specified procedures were followed in selecting a subcontractor
- ○ dealing with changes in scopes of work, key personnel, and other terms.

For this reason, tracking the total number of contracts under management is also useful. Larger contracts usually entail somewhat more work for routine reporting; indicators E28 and E29 provide some sense of developments in this area when data are tracked over time.

The information for preparing the indicators listed in the table comes from many sources. It may make sense for staff in the chief accountant's office to compute the indicators to insure consistency and timeliness.

While the indicators in the table are certainly useful, they are far from sufficient by themselves. Experienced managers offer four general pieces of advice on how to develop additional information for judging operational efficiency:

1. *Compare your operations with those of similar organizations.* In Washington, D.C., a group of chief financial officers for several large think tanks meets regularly to discuss operational issues. They share information without divulging corporate secrets (such as their overhead rates). If possible, the chief financial officers in other cities and countries could try to have similar conversations about, for example, the number of staff used in the various support functions and their wages or salaries.

2. *Listen to the "internal clients."* Senior management should take to heart staff complaints about such things as slowness in getting reimbursed for travel expenses, staff-reported complaints from clients about billing delays, lack of support from the PR team in placing articles in newspapers, delays in getting critical action on contractual matters from the contracts manager, or unrealistic time required by the director of research for proposal review when response periods are very tight.

3. *Do not staff based on peak periods.* There is a seasonal rhythm for nearly all support functions. The accounting staff will be especially pressed when the think tank's fiscal year ends and various tax filings are due. The contract manager will be deluged at the end of the government's fiscal year if new contracts must get executed urgently. Those in charge of these activities would prefer a staff large enough to make it through these peak periods without undue stress. But this approach leads to overstaffing during the balance of the year. Senior managers simply must place staff complaints in the context of each department's seasonal

workload, and remember that complaints during the peak load season may have a different meaning and call for a different response from those aired during a slacker time.

4. *Monitor trends.* For many of the indicators in panels C through E, the absolute values are difficult to interpret. Is 65 employees per human resource staff member, for example, a realistic figure? Alone, this number may be hard to interpret, but it is very clear that a rise from 65 to 97 per HR staff member over two years means that the HR staff is much busier now than it was two years ago. Whether more staff is essential is less clear in light of how the total number of tasks done by the team has evolved—including the extent to which tasks have been automated or outsourced. A big change in the reported number will, appropriately, generate the request for an explanation from senior management.

INNOVATION AND LEARNING PERSPECTIVE

These indicators are designed to give senior managers information on how well the organization is working to renew itself, principally through strengthening the quality of the staff, but also through forays into new fields or work with new groups of clients. The key here is the trends, but an annual review of developments should be able to spot highlights.

Many think tanks have line items in their overhead cost schedule for staff training and forms of institutional development, such as starting work on new topics and launching pilot projects. To judge whether funds are being used optimally, senior managers should be informed whether the funds available for the year were expended (items 8 and 10 in Table 12.6).

Table 12.6 Performance Indicators from the Innovation and Learning Perspective

Indicator	*Possible source[a]*
Training	
1. No. and share of staff that received training for new roles/products	Staff dept. and team leaders
2. Total no. of trainings	
3. No. and share of staff that received general training to improve professional qualifications: total and separately for research and support staffs	Staff dept.
4. No. of staff trained in donor-sponsored events	
5. No. of donor-sponsored events in which staff participated	
6. Overhead staff training spending/total staff	
7. Overhead staff training spending/staff trained with these funds[b]	Accounting dept.
8. Percent of overhead staff training funds spent	
Staff improvement	
9. No. of new staff hired with special skills to work on innovative topics or strengthen teams: total no. of new staff hired	Team leaders
Innovation	
10. Percent of overhead funds allocated for institutional development expended for innovative programs	Accounting dept.[c]
11. No. of pilot projects under implementation	
12. For pilot projects under way, success compared with benchmarks	Team leaders managing the pilot projects

[a] Source of information for preparing the indicator and report.
[b] Excludes those trained through donor programs, for example, without charge.
[c] The accounting department will only have this information if it is informed, when the accounts for such activities are set up, that the activity falls into this class.

The training indicators track the number and share of the staff that received training during the year from any source—whether the think tank itself or various donors. It is useful to separate out training activities sponsored to improve individuals' qualifications for new tasks (e.g., improving their skills in econometrics or preparing them for work on a new topic such as health economics).

Keep in mind that think tanks often find it more effective to hire a new person with the needed skills than to try to retrain someone already on staff in the new topic. Again, it is useful to keep track of such hiring decisions to understand the extent to which the organization is adjusting to new demands (item 6 in table 12.6).

Finally, Table 12.6 includes three basic indicators on the use of institutional support funds (last panel in table, indicators 10-12). Indicator 10 is simply the share of funds dedicated to this purpose available from overhead charges that were expended in the report period on developing innovative programs. In other words, to what extent did the organization use the available resources for this purpose last year? Indicator 11 is simply the number of pilot projects testing innovations that are presently being implemented.

Lastly, indicator 12 is the number of innovations under implementation that are meeting the success benchmarks defined for them. It is doubtful that the success of pilot projects can be boiled down to a few figures. Therefore, an explicit comparison with stated milestones is important (indicator

12). Senior management will need to meet with the relevant team leader to explore progress. Good indicators of positive developments are success in implementing the pilot project as designed (using milestones defined at that time) and the interest of potential sponsors in the new topic. Actual funding received is an additional solid indicator that the work is perceived to have merit.

How One Think Tank Tracks Performance

Setting up a comprehensive system is a major undertaking. Case Study 12.1 describes how the Center for the Implementation of Public Policies Promoting Equity and Growth (CIPPEC) in Buenos Aires has undertaken this task. The emphasis is on the tasks necessary to organize and construct a system. The CIPPEC system was just coming on line as this book was written, but the introduction had advanced far enough that the main challenges to staff acceptance could be identified.

Final Thoughts

Many indicators have been presented for tracking institutional performance at think tanks. Very few think tanks generate such a comprehensive set of indicators, and even fewer compile them into reports for the institution's leadership. But many think tanks do have informal systems that go a long way toward meeting this need. Informality is fine, as long as the monitoring is getting done.

Naturally, each think tank is different. Leaders at each organization should identify operational areas for which they already have good information vs. those for which they do not. Then they should weigh the potential benefits from generating or collating additional information for the "under-monitored areas" against the costs. Such deliberations should probably include input from the most important managers.

If these managers think more or better information is needed, the next step is to consider the options for generating that information on a regular basis and deciding who should receive it. The indicators listed in this chapter's tables and the sample tables shown in Annex 12.1 provide ideas on the most relevant information to develop.

It is hard to overstate the necessity for think tanks to have monitoring systems that cover all critical aspects of their operations, as defined in the five perspectives discussed above. With only a little imagination one can define an array of developments that—if left undetected for too long—could impair the institution's operations or even threaten its existence. The benefits of monitoring are large and palpable, if hard always to quantify.

TAKE AWAYS

Strong Practices

Characteristics of a well-managed think tank in this context follow.

- A think tank with 50+ staff has a process in place to track performance in all five domains discussed—public policy, funder, internal business, innovation and learning, and financial perspectives.

Compiling 80 to 90 percent of the indicators seems a reasonable goal, as long as coverage in all domains is significant. Even smaller think tanks with fewer resources need to be tracking half or more of the indicators across all five domains.

- Smaller think tanks monitor their most important performance areas through a modest number of well-defined and carefully selected indicators.

- The think tank is concerned with its policy engagement performance. An effective program requiring a sensible level of resources is in place: 1) to compile many of the indicators on performance from the public policy perspective (Table 12.2) and 2) to have team leaders track policy developments in areas where the institution has carried out significant policy research and been engaged in getting the results used in the policy development process.

For Funders
Look carefully for:

Performance indicators for a few example areas. Trying to inventory the full set of performance indicators a think tank is tracking would require a good deal of effort. It is quite possible the think tank itself has not thought of some of the information it collects (as part of its monitoring system) and uses as "performance indicators" and would provide an incomplete listing if asked for one. My suggestion is to ask about one or two areas, using the tables in this chapter as a kind of check list to prompt (if necessary) the executive director or COO for some items they might be overlooking.

Areas that could be given preference in exploring current practices are given in the following listing, which assumes the funder staff has a good sense of "think tank-funder" relations from actual experience.

- Top priority goes to the indicators for the "public policy perspective"; after all, these address success in fulfilling the think tank's mission. Table 12.2 has an extensive list of indicators. All think tanks are expected to have good information on outputs; the real test comes with the corresponding intermediate outcome indicators.

- The second priority goes to monitoring topics covered under the "internal business perspective." One could ask, for example, how senior management keeps track of the work load and productivity of the accounting/finance team (block D in Table 12.5), an area that is often neglected. If tracking is weak there, explore other areas in the table.

- A third area that should be of clear importance to senior management is how the experience in competing for projects requiring proposals is tracked and assessed (i.e., what specific indicators are compiled and how they are used). (Items 7 and 8, block B, Table 12.5.)

Perhaps to do:

Weak performance and financial tracking systems are a genuine danger to a think tank. At a minimum, this means senior management is being surprised with problems needing immediate attention. The ongoing costs of producing the information and reporting it to senior management should be quite modest. The impediment is the start-up cost. This also could be fairly modest, because most of the data items needed to generate the indicators should already be in project and administrative records. Effort would be needed to make the data easily accessible and to develop and initially populate the digital table shells for the reports to management. Partially supporting development of the "performance information system" would be one-time cost with significant payoff, as long as the executive director is clearly convinced of the value of such a system.

Case study 12.1 Establishment of a Comprehensive Set of Indicators to Track the Organization's Performance in a Range of Areas

The Center for the Implementation of Public Policies promoting Equity and Growth (CIPPEC) was founded in 2001. Since its foundation, its budget has increased more than 100 times, and projects now average 100 per year and generate more than 70 percent of total income. Other income comes from: individual donors, companies, governments and international cooperation.

This increasing complexity made the available tools for tracking projects activities and budget matters outdated: they did not allow generation of timely information or appropriate reporting to governance bodies or external stakeholders. In particular, the fact that this institutional growth was not accompanied by a strengthening of internal management procedures caused the following problems: tasks that could be carried out but were not; excessive dependency on certain staff who had knowledge of the specifics of the administrative practices; inefficient processes that persisted; common duplication and inefficiency of labor; too much information scattered in various places and very poorly integrated; the risk of making mistakes higher due to the unavailability of the relevant data; and available information underutilized.

After some time, CIPPEC decided to address this problem by including an upgrade of management processes as a priority in its Triennial Plan for 2011-2014, allocating resources to update and improve the management system. It is important to highlight that the Administrative Board was involved throughout the decision-making process. The objective was to increase CIPPEC's productivity and the quality of internal processes and, as a consequence, strengthen effectiveness in the policy arena.

System development
After the decision, a market survey was carried out to identify different options available. The main two options were to contract for: (a) an already packaged system or (b) an open-source tool. However, neither of these alternatives met CIPPEC's specific requirements as a think tank. Most of the systems were developed for private profit-making companies and their marketing activities, not with think tanks' or nonprofit organizations' management issues in mind. Moreover, customizing already packaged systems required a significant investment in consulting services.

Finally, CIPPEC decided to develop its own new management system customized to CIPPEC needs and characteristics. The first task was then to search for possible suppliers. A short list of companies was developed and presented to the Administrative Board. Once the company was selected, CIPPEC's Administration and Project Management Department and the Influence, Monitoring and Evaluation Program started to work jointly with the software company to design and develop the new tool. For this purpose, a development by modules was scheduled: Project Management, Publications, Management of Income without specific allocation (mainly from companies and individual donors), Management of the Economic and Financial Budget, and Interfaces with the existing accounting system.

The main advantage of this tailored option was that it considered all the particular characteristics of CIPPEC's work and allowed scaling and adapting its functionality in the future. Moreover, this option allowed CIPPEC to have an in house–hosted system and also enabled integration with the existing accounting system. Beyond these advantages, development of the tailored management system required a very good preparatory analysis of current processes, to avoid replicating their weaknesses. This required a large time commitment in the design stage.

Gains and Challenges
The new software adds greater efficiency to the processes, generates reliable information, and avoids duplication of tasks. In short, it allows more effective and efficient resource use. It is a comprehensive system that involves all processes related to project management, such as design, approval, implementation, and monitoring. It also covers budget management and contracts approval, and supports report generation, including performance indicators management—thus contributing to a more evidence-based decision making process.

Some of the accomplishments to date can be illustrated with performance indicators:

Module	Indicator
Publications	No. of books published No. of policy briefs published
Management of the Economic and Financial Budget	Net result (annual) Accumulated result (current year plus previous years) Percent of all funds coming from international cooperation over total of funds Percent of all funds coming from projects with governments over total of funds Percent of all funds coming from individuals over total of funds, Percent of savings in projects' direct costs (approved/executed), Projects' implementation rate (the average percent of funds expended of all ongoing projects)
Project Management performance	Rate of completed products over planned products (such as publications and events)

At the same time, CIPPEC has some organizational features that will help while managing the change and educating staff on the new system: existence of consolidated organizational processes and routines, appropriate functional distribution among institutional areas (Executive Director, Administration and Project Management Department, Communication Department, Fund Raising Department) and a solid governance performance among others.

Looking ahead

Pending activities to be carried out during first quarter of 2014 to conclude the roll out include: implementation of the second pilot of the new system with a new selected group, defining the security scheme (permissions and users), training the users (all staff), and launching the final implementation. The new system is expected to be fully operational in late 2014. As needed, the system's design permits the addition of other modules in the future.

Leandro Echt and Romina Wuckzaryk
Center for the Implementation of Public Policies
Promoting Equity and Growth
Buenos Aires, Argentina

Even though the new management system is currently being tested by only a selected group of users within the organization, some challenges have arisen. The major one is managing the change (and the resistance to it). It is well documented that successful implementation of an information system is measured by the support of the people who use it. Furthermore, benefits are progressive and are consolidated in the medium term. Other challenges include design of an effective internal communication strategy and prioritization and allocation of time and resources by the Institutional and the Policy Research Areas for training and adoption.

REFERENCES[151]

Ahiadeke, C. 2013. "Stories of Change-From the Institute of Statistical, Social and Economic Research (ISSER) at the University of Ghana." Ottawa: International Development Research Centre, Think Tank Initiative, Stories of Change Series.

Alcazar, L., M. Balarin, D. Weerakoon, and E. Eboh. 2012. *Learning to Monitor Think Tanks Impact: Three Experiences from Africa, Asia and Latin America.* Lima, Peru: GRADE Report to the Think Tank Initiative, http://www.thinktankinitiative.org/sites/default/files/Learning%20to%20monitor%20think%20tanks%20impact%20final%20report%20july%202012.pdf

Allen, T., and G. Henn. 2007. *The Organization and Architecture of Innovation: Managing the Flow of Technology.* Oxford: Elsevier.

Allison, M., and J. Kave. 2005. *Strategic Planning for Non Profit Organizations: A Practical Guide and Workbook.* Hoboken, NJ: John Wiley, 2nd edition.

Andersen, L. 2012. "Can Consultancies Sustain a Long-Term Research Strategy in Developing Countries?" Posting on "On Think Tanks," www.onthinktanks.org, October 1. Ordonez, A. 2014c.

Ames, P. 2014, "(Re)Creating a Culture of Peer Review." *On Think Tanks.* www.onthinktanks.org, July 2.

Areliano, A. 2014. "How to Improve Your Capacity to Write Proposals: Grupo FARO's Committee for Project Approval." *Politics & Ideas*, February 10. http://www.politicsandideas.org/?p=1510

Avins, J. 2013. "Strategy is a Fundraising Necessity, Not a Luxury." Posting on "On Think Tanks," www.onthinktanks.org, November 26.

Bacon, F.R., Jr., and T.W. Butler, Jr. 1998. *Achieving Planned Innovation: A Proven System for Creating Successful New Products and Services.* New York: Free Press.

Ban, C., S.R. Faerman, and N.M. Riccucci. 1992. "Productivity and the Personnel Process." In *Public Productivity Handbook*, edited by M. Holzer (401–23). San Francisco: Jossey-Bass.

---

151   References include works cited in the paper and a few additional items found particularly useful.

Bardach, E. 1984. "The Dissemination of Policy Research to Policymakers." *Knowledge: Creation, Diffusion, and Utilization* 6(2): 125–44.

Benequista, N. 2014. "Communication Off the Map: Three Principles for Policy Influence in Emerging Democracies." *Politics & Ideas*, August 19. http://www.politicsandideas.org/?p=1853 Nancy Birdsall, N. 2012. "Successful Policy Engagement." TTI EX 2012. http://www.youtube.com/watch?v=fSePtWWTEWY

Birdsall, N. 2013. Comments at the book launch for *The Governor's Solution: How Alaska's Oil Dividend Could Work in Iraq and Other Oil-Rich Countries.* Event at the Center for Global Development, Washington, DC, January 23, 2013.

Bowsher, J.E. 1998. *Revolutionizing Workforce Performance: A Systems Approach to Mastery*. San Francisco: Jossey-Boss, Pfeiffer.

Bracken, D., and D. Rose. 2011. "When Does 360-Degree Feedback Create Behavior Change? And How Would We Know When It Does?" *Journal of Business and Psychology,* vol.26, no.2, pp. 183-92.

Bruckner, S. 1996. "Policy Research Centers in Russia: Tottering Toward an Uncertain Future." *NIRA Review* (summer): 32–36.

Bruckner, T. 2014. "Are Think Tanks Turning into Lobbyists?" *Transparify*, March 12, 2014.

Bryson, J.M. 1995. *Strategic Planning for Public and Nonprofit Organizations*. San Francisco: Jossey-Bass.

Buldioski, G. 2013. "Supporting Think Tank Series: From Core and Institutional Support to Organizational Development Grants." Posting on "On Think Tanks," www.onthinktanks.org, June 3.

Buldioski, G. 2012. "Capacity Building for Think Tanks." Goran's Policy. November 26. http://goranspolicy.com/capacity-building-for-think-tanks/?utm_source=feedburner&utm_medium=email&utm_campaign=Feed%3A+goranspolicy+%28Goran%27s+policy%29.

Buldioski, G. 2012. "The Peculiar Use of Training Activities as Vehicles for Policy Research Uptakes in Serbia." Posted on *Goran's Musings*, www.goranspolicy.com, August 28.

Buldioski, G. 2010a. "Marriage of a Think Tank and a Consultancy Firm: A warning from Slovakia." Posted on *Goran's Musings*, www.goranspolicy.com, September 30.

Buldioski, G. 2010b. "Defining Think Tanks." Posted on *Goran's Musings,* www.goranspolicy. com, November 10.

Bullen, P., S. Lawrence, P. Schwenke, A. Williamson, and S. Williamson. 1997. *Nonprofits in Busine$$.* Surry Hills, NSW, Australia: WorkVentures, Ltd.

Bunkder, K.A., K.E. Kram, and S. Ting. 2002. "The Young and the Clueless." *Harvard Business Review*, December: 81–87.

Bumgarner, R., D. Hattaway, G. Lamb, J. McGann, and H. Wise. 2006. *Center for Global Development: Evaluation of Impact.* Washington, DC: Arabella Philanthropic Investment Advisors, processed. Accessible in 2012 on the CDG website, www.cgdev.org.

Burlingame, D.F., and W.F. Ilchman, eds. 1996. *Alternative Revenue Sources: Prospects, Requirements, and Concerns for Nonprofits*. San Francisco: Jossey-Bass.

Carden, F. 2009. *Knowledge to Policy: Making the Most of Development Research.* Los Angeles: Sage Publications.

Carver, J. 1997. *Boards That Make a Difference: A New Design for Leadership in Nonprofit and Public Organizations.* 2nd ed. San Francisco: Jossey-Bass.

Center for Economic Research [Baku]. 2011. "Communications Strategy for 2011-2012." http://erc.az/az/index.php?option=com_content&view=article&id=199:communications-strategy-for-2011-12&catid=66:projects-and-activities-&Itemid=91.

Center for International Private Enterprise (CIPE). 1998. *Financial Management Handbook.* Washington, DC: CIPE.

Charan, R. 1998. *Boards at Work: How Corporate Boards Create Competitive Advantage*. San Francisco: Jossey-Bass.

Charan, R., S. Drotter, and J. Noel. 2001. *The Leadership Pipeline.* San Francisco: Jossey-Bass.

CIPE. See Center for International Private Enterprise.

Colvin, K., J. Champaign, A. Liu, Q. Zhou, C. Fredericks, and D. Pritchard. 2014. "Learning in an Introductory Physics MOOC: All Cohorts Learn Equally, Including an On-Campus Class," *International Review of Research in Open and Distance Learning*, vol.14, no.4. http://www.irrodl.org/index.php/irrodl/article/view/1902

Conger, J.A., and B. Benjamin. 1999. *Building Leaders: How Successful Companies Develop the Next Generation*. San Francisco: Jossey-Bass.

Congressional Budget Office [CBO]. 2013. *Congressional Budget Office Cost Estimate: S.744, Border Security, Economic Opportunity, and the Immigration Modernization Act*. Washington, DC: CBO, June 18.

Corwin, R.G., and K.S. Louis. 1982 "Organization Barriers to the Utilization of Research." *Administrative Sciences Quarterly* 27: 623–40.

Court, J. and J. Young. 2006. "Bridging Research and Policy: Insights from 50 Case Studies," *Evidence and Policy*, vol.2, no.4, pp.439-62.

Covello, J.A., and B.J. Hazelgren. 1995. *The Complete Book of Business Plans*. Naperville, IL: Sourcebooks.

Crutchfield, L.R., and J. M. Grant. 2008. *Forces for Good: The Six Practices of High-Impact Nonprofits*. San Francisco: Jossey-Boss.

Darling, M., C. Parry, and J. Moore. 2005. "Learning in the Thick of It." *Harvard Business Review*, July-August: 84–92.

Davies, Lee. 1997. "The NGO-Business Hybrid: Is the Private Sector the Answer?" Washington, DC: The Johns Hopkins University, Nitze School of Advanced International Studies.

Davies, R. and J. Dar t. 2005. *The 'Most Significant Change' (MSC) Technique; A Guide to Its Use*. www.mande.co.uk/docs/MSCGuide.pdf.

Dees, J.G. 2001a. "Mobilizing Resources." In *Enterprising Nonprofits: A Toolkit for Social Entrepreneurs*, edited by J.G. Dees, J. Emerson, and P. Economy (63–102). New York: John Wiley & Sons.

———. 2001b. "Mastering the Art of Innovation." In *Enterprising Nonprofits: A Toolkit for Social Entrepreneurs*, edited by J.G. Dees, J. Emerson, and P. Economy (161–98). New York: John Wiley & Sons.

Dees, J.G., J. Emerson, and P. Economy, eds. 2001. *Enterprising Nonprofits: A Toolkit for Social Entrepreneurs*. New York: John Wiley & Sons.

Dibble, S. 1999. *Keeping Your Valuable Employees: Retention Strategies for Your Organization's Most Important Resource*. New York: John Wiley & Sons.

Dixit, A. 2012. "A Reflection on the Contribution of Research in the Framing of Local Adaption Plan to Climate Change in Nepal." Ottawa: International Development Research Centre, Think Tank Initiative, Stories of Change Series.

Dolowitz, D., and D. Marsh. 1996. "Who Learns from Whom: A Review of the Policy Transfer Literature." *Political Studies* 44: 343–57.

Dotlich, D.L., and P.C. Cairo. 1999. *Action Coaching*. San Francisco: Jossey-Bass.

Drucker, P. 1990. *Managing the Nonprofit Organization*. New York: Harper.

Dunn, E., and M. Norton. 2013. *Happy Money: The Science of Smarter Spending*. New York: Simon & Schuster.

Earl, S., F. Carden and T. Smutylo. 2001. *Outcome Mapping: Building Learning and Reflection into Development Programs*. Ottawa: International Development Research Centre (IDRC).
www.idrc.ca/en/ev-9330-201-1-DO_TOPIC.html.

Eboh, E. 2012. "Sustaining Quality in Economic Policy Research." Presentation at the TTI Exchange 2012. https://www.youtube.com/watch?v=IqltstqzrL8

Echt, L. 2012. "How to Employ, Retain and Motivate Staff." Posting on "On Think Tanks," www.onthinktanks.org, May 18.

Echt, L. 2014. "The Challenges Facing Southern Researchers in the Arab World." Posting on Politics and Ideas. September 18, http://www.politicsandideas.org/?p=1966.

Economic and Social Research Center [Tanzania]. 2012. "IDRC – TTI Success Stories." Ottawa: International Development Research Centre, Think Tank Initiative, Stories of Change Series.

Economic Research Center [Baku]. 2011. "Economic Research Center - Communications Strategy for 2011-2012." http://erc.az/az/index.php?option=com_content&view=article&id=199:communications-strategy-for-2011-12&catid=66:projects-and-activities-&Itemid=91. Site visited on November 6, 2013.

Enchautegui, M.E., S. Lindner, and E. Poethig. 2013. *Understanding the Economic and Fiscal Impacts of Immigration Reform: A guide to Current Studies and Possible Expansions*. Washington, DC: Urban Institute. http://www.urban.org/UploadedPDF/412944-Understanding-the-Economic-and-Fiscal-Impacts-of-Immigration-Reform.pdf. Site visited November 9, 2013.

European Centre for Development Policy Management. 2012. "ECPDM's Knowledge and Communications Strategy 2012-2016." http://www.ecdpm.org/Web_ECDPM/Web/Content/Navigation.nsf/index2?readform&http://www.ecdpm.org/Web_ECDPM/Web/Content/Content.nsf/80ba021853007405c1256c790053145c/82467adc9075fd16c1257512003f10cf. Site visited on November 6, 2013.

Feulner, E.J. 1985. "Ideas, Think-Tanks and Governments." *Quadrant*, November: 22–6.

Fix, M., and R. Struyk (eds.) 1993. *Clear and Convincing Evidence: Measurement of Discrimination in America.* Washington, DC: Urban Institute Press.

Foster, W., and J. Bradach. 2005. "Should Nonprofits Seek Profits?" *Harvard Business Review*, February: 92–100.

Fox, C.J. 1991. "Employee Performance Appraisal: The Keystone Made of Clay." In *Public Personnel Management: Current Concerns, Future Challenges*, edited by C. Ban and N. Riccorci (58–71). New York: Longman.

Freedom House. 1999. *Think Tanks in Central and Eastern Europe: A Comprehensive Directory.* Budapest: Freedom House.

Garrett, J.L., and Y. Islam. 1998. *Policy Research and the Policy Process: Do the Twain Ever Meet?* Gatekeeper Series no. 5A74. Stockholm: IIED.

Georgalakis, J. 2012. "Is It Wrong to Herald the Death of the Institutional Website?" Posting on "On Think Tanks," www.onthinktanks.org, December 10.

Glen, R.M. 1990. "Performance Appraisal: An Unnerving Yet Useful Process." *Public Personnel Management* 19(1): 1–10.

Graham, P. 2009. "Maker's Schedule, Manager's Schedule." http://www.paulgraham.com/makersschedule.html

Greenberg, D., D. Linksz, and M. Mandell. 2003. *Social Experimentation and Public Policymaking.* Washington, DC: Urban Institute Press.

Gutbrod, H. 2013a. "Advice to Think Tank Startup: Do Not Do It Alone. Posting on "On Think Tanks," www.onthinktanks.org, Feb 4.

Gutbrod, H. 2013b. "How Did Lead US Think Tanks Fare in 2012? Analysis by Numbers. Posting on "On Think Tanks," www.onthinktanks.org, September 13.

Hall, P. 1990. "Policy Paradigms, Experts and the State: The Case of Macro-economic Policy Making in Britain." In *Social Scientists, Policy and the State*, edited by S. Brooks and A.-G. Gagnon. New York: Praeger.

Hayes, J. 2005. "Feedback about Think Tanks – Report on the Findings." Washington, DC: Stratalys Research. E-mail communication.

Heath, C., and D. Heath. 2013. *Decisive.* New York: Random House.

Heneman, R.L. 2001. *Business-Driven Compensation Policies.* New York: American Management Association.

Herzberg, F. 1987. "One More Time: How Do You Motivate Employees?" *Harvard Business Review* (September–October): 109–20.

Heskett, J.L. 1987. "Lesson in the Service Sector." *Harvard Business Review* (March–April): 118–26.

Holland, T.P., and M. Blackmon. 2000. *Measuring Board Effectiveness: A Tool for Strengthening Your Board.* Washington, DC: National Center for Nonprofit Boards.

Hovland, I. 2007. "Making a Difference: M&E of Policy Research." London: Overseas Development Institute, Working Paper 281.

Huberman, M. 1994. "Research Utilization: The State of the Art." *Knowledge and Policy: The International Journal of Knowledge Transfer and Utilization* 7(4): 13–33.

Hulme, D., and M. Edwards. 2013. *NGOs States and Donors: Too Close for Comfort?* New York: Palgrave Macmillan Press.

Ibeanu, O. 2008. "Payment and Independence: Does a Client Relationship with Government Inhibit 'Think Tank' Criticism?" Cape Town: South African Institute of International Affairs Governance and APRM Programme, Occasional Paper No.15.

Institute for Public Policy. 2007. "Think Tank's Sustainability—Models of Overhead Expenses Calculation and Their Effective Use." Bucharest: author, processed, draft.

Institute of Dalit Studies [IIDS]. 2013. "Collaborative Research, Knowledge Exploration and Wider Use of Research Outcome through 'Community of Researchers'." Ottawa: International Development Research Centre, Think Tank Initiative, Stories of Change Series.

International Committee of Medical Journal Editors [ICMJE]. 2013. "Ethical Considerations in Conduct and Reporting of Research: Authorship and Contributionship." http://www.icmje.org/ethical_1author.html

International Development Research Centre (IDRC). 2013. *Enabling Success, 2011-2012 Think Tank Initiative Annual Report.* Ottawa: IDRC.

Johnson, E. 2000. "Think Tanks in Sub-Saharan Africa." In *Think Tanks & Civil Societies*, edited by J.G. McGann and R.K. Weaver (465–90). New Brunswick, NJ: Transaction Publishers.

Jones, S. 2013. *Georgia: A Political History Since Independence.* London: I.B. Tauris.

Kaplan, R.S., and D.P. Norton. 1992. "The Balanced Scorecard—Measures that Drive Performance." *Harvard Business Review*, January–February.

Karatnycky, A., A. Motyl, and B. Shor. 1997. *Nations in Transit 1997.* New Brunswick, NJ: Transaction Publishers.

Karel, F. 2000. "Getting the Word Out: A Foundation Memoir and Personal Journey." In *To Improve Health and Health Care: The Robert Wood Johnson Anthology*, edited by S.L. Isaccs and J.R. Knickman (23–51). Princeton, NJ: The Robert Wood Johnson Foundation.

Kellerman, B. 2004. "Leadership, Warts and All." *Harvard Business Review*, January: 40–45.

Kerr, S. 2003. "The Best-Laid Plans Incentive Plans." *Harvard Business Review*, January: 27–33.

Kimenyi, M.S., and A. Datta. 2011. "Think Tanks in Sub-Saharan Africa: How the Political Landscape Has Influenced Their Origins. London: Overseas Development Institute. http://www.docs.mak.ac.ug/sites/default/files/7527.pdf

Kingdon, J. 1984. *Agendas, Alternatives and Public Policies.* Boston: Little Brown & Co.

Kingsley, T. 1993. "Ideas for Managing a Japanese Think Tank." In *A Japanese Think Tank: Exploring Alternative Models*, edited by R. Struyk, M. Ueno, and T Suzuki (appendix D). Washington, DC: The Urban Institute.

Kitzi, J. 2001. "Recognizing and Assessing New Opportunities." In *Enterprising Nonprofits: A Toolkit for Social Entrepreneurs*, edited by J.G. Dees, J. Emerson, and P. Economy (43–62). New York: John Wiley & Sons.

Khan, S. 2012. "Enhancing Organizational Governance." TTI EX 2012. https://www.youtube.com/watch?v=slpd_cHawdo&feature=plcp

Kosack, S., C. Tolmie, C. Griffin. 2010. *From the Ground Up: Improving Government Performance with Independent Monitoring Organizations.* Washington, DC: Brookings Institution.

Kotler, P. 2000. *Marketing Management.* 10th ed. Upper Saddle River, NJ: Prentice Hall.

Kucharczyk, J. and P. Kazmierkiewicz. 2007. "Learning from the Experience of Western European Think Tanks: A Study in Think Tank Management." Warsaw: Institute of Public Affairs.

Kulasabanathan, R. 2012. How to Attract and Nurture Quality Researchers. TTI EX 2012. https://www.youtube.com/watch?v=7LW6tLEMuXo

Langsford, J.W., and K.L. Brownsey, eds. 1992. *Think Tanks and Governance in the Asia-Pacific Region.* Halifax, Nova Scotia: Institute for Research on Public Policy.

La Piana, D. 1997. *Beyond Collaboration: Strategic Restructuring of Nonprofit Organizations.* Washington, DC: National Center for Nonprofit Boards.

La Piana, D. 2008. *The Nonprofit Strategy Revolution: Real-Time Strategic Planning in a Rapid-Respond World.* St. Paul, MN: Fieldstone Alliance.

Lavis, J., D. Robertson, J. Woosdie, C. McLeod, and J. Abelson. 2003. "How Can Research Organizations More Effectively Transfer Research Knowledge to Decision Makers?" *The Milbank Quarterly*, vol.8, no.2, pp.221-248.

Ledford, G.E. Jr. 1995. "Designing Nimble Reward Systems." *Compensation and Benefits Review* (July–August): 46–54.

Lee, C. 1996. "Performance Appraisal." *Training* 33(5): 44–59.

Lee, U. 2005. "Estonia's Policy Analysis Industry Grows Up." *Local Governance Brief*, spring-summer: 37–38.

Leigh, A., and M. Maynard. 1995. *Leading Your Team: How to Involve and Inspire Teams.* London: Nicholas Brealey Publishing.

Lencioni, P. 2002. *The Five Dysfunctions of a Team.* San Francisco: Jossey-Bass.

Letts, C.W., W.P. Ryan, and A. Grossman. 1999. *High Performance Nonprofit Organizations: Managing Upstream for Greater Impact.* New York: John Wiley & Sons.

Liebovitz, H., and L. Wherry. 2004. "Research to Practice: Evaluating *Assessing the New Federalism* Dissemination Activities." *Assessing the New Federalism* Discussion Paper 04-02. Washington, DC: The Urban Institute.

Light, P.C. 1998. *Sustaining Innovation: Creating Nonprofit and Government Organizations that Innovate Naturally.* San Francisco: Jossey-Bass.

Light, P. 2000. *Making Nonprofits Work: A Report on the Tides of Nonprofit Management Reform.* Washington, DC: Brookings Institution Press.

Liner, B., H. Hatry, E. Vinson, R. Allen, P. Dusenbury, S. Bryant, and R. Snell. 2001. *Making Results-Based State Government Work.* Washington, DC: The Urban Institute.

Lips, B. 2009. "Developing a High-Achieving Board of Directors: A Primer on Think Tank Governance." Washington, DC: Atlas Network.

Lomas, J. 1993. "Diffusion, Dissemination, and Implementation: Who Should Do What?" *Annals New York Academy of Sciences*, pp. 226–37.

Lovitt, J. 2011. *How to Win Respect and Influence Policymakers: Principles for Effective Quality Controls in the Work of Independent Think Tanks.* Prague: Policy Association for an Open Society.

MacDonald, L., and R. Levine. 2008. "Learning While Doing: A 12-Step Program for Policy Change." Washington, DC: Center for Global Development Essay.

MacDonald, L., and T. Moss. 2014. "Building a Think-and-Do Tank: A Dozen Lessons from the First Dozen Years of the Center for Global Development." Washington, DC: Center for Global Development Essay.

Majeska, K. 2001. "Understanding and Attracting Your 'Customer'." In *Enterprising Nonprofits: A Toolkit for Social Entrepreneurs*, edited by J.G. Dees, J. Emerson, and P. Economy (199–250). New York: John Wiley & Sons.

Martin, P. 2013. "How Do Policy Actors Assess Southern Think Tanks? Insight into Factors Affecting the Perceptions of Performance in Policy Communities. Ottawa: International Development Research Centre, Think Tank Initiative. http://www.thinktankinitiative.org/sites/default/files/How%20do%20policy%20actors%20assess%20Southern%20think%20tanks_PMartin.pdf

Maxwell, M.M. 1996. "New Ventures in a Nonprofit Environment." In *Alternative Revenue Sources: Prospects, Requirements and Concerns for Nonprofits*, edited by D.F. Burlingame and W.F. Ilchman. San Francisco: Jossey-Bass.

McAdams, J.L., and E.J. Hawk. 1994. *Organizational Performance and Rewards*. Scottsdale, AZ: American Compensation Association.

McGann, J.G. 2013. *2012 Global Go to Think Tanks Report and Policy Advice*. Philadelphia: University of Pennsylvania, International Relations Program.

McGann, J.G., and E.C. Johnson. 2005. *Comparative Think Tanks, Politics and Public Policy*. Cheltenham, U.K.: Edward Elgar.

McGann, J. and R. Kent Weaver, (eds). 2000. *Think Tanks and Civil Societies: Catalysts for Ideas and Actions*. New Brunswick, NJ and London: Transaction Press.

McGann, J. 1999. "Think Tanks: Catalysts for Ideas in Action—An International Survey." Philadelphia: Foreign Policy Research Institute.

McMurtry, S.L., F.E. Netting, and P.M. Kettner. 1991. "How Nonprofits Adapt to a Stringent Environment," *Nonprofit Management & Leadership* 1(3): 235–52.

Medvetz, T. 2012. *Think Tanks in America*. Chicago: University of Chicago Press.

Mendizabal, E. 2011. "The Onthinktanks Interview: Simon Maxwell (Part 2)." Posting on "On Think Tanks," www.onthinktanks.org, September 7

Mendizabal, E. 2012. "Quality Control: Who Should Be Involved?" Posting on "On Think Tanks," www.onthinktanks.org, October 8.

Mendizabal, E. 2013a. "Governance Dilemmas and How to Avoid Them." Posting on "On Think Tanks," www.onthinktanks.org, February 6.

Mendizabal, E. 2013b. "Strategic Plans: A Simple Version." Posting on "On Think Tanks," www.onthinktanks.org, April 19.

Mendizabal, E. 2013c. "Monitoring and Evaluation: Lessons from Latin American Think Tanks." Posting on "On Think Tanks," www.onthinktanks.org, June 24.

Mendizabal, E. 2013d. "For-profit Think Tanks and Implications for Funders." Posting on "On Think Tanks," www.onthinktanks.org, October 3.

Mendizabal, E. 2013e. "New Office for CGD: Food for Thought." Posting on "On Think Tanks," www.onthinktanks.org, November 9.

Mendizabal, E. 2014a. "Fair is Fair: On Contracts and Sub-contracts." Posting on "On Think Tanks," www.onthinktanks.org, February 24.

Mendizabal, E. 2014b. "Setting up a Think Tank: Step-by-Step."." Posting on "On Think Tanks," www.onthinktanks.org, May 5.

Mendizabal, E. 2014c. "A Quick and Dirty 'Transparify-like' Assessment of TTI Think Tanks." Posting on "On Think Tanks," www.onthinktanks.org, May 12.

Mendizabal, E. 2014d. "Think Tanks Stress Test." Posting on "On Think Tanks," www.onthinktanks.org, September 19.

Mensa, J. 2012. How to Attract and Nurture Quality Researchers. TTI EX 2012. https://www.youtube.com/watch?v=8n1xGe2bC-Y

Moncada, A. 2013. "The Woes of Domestic Philanthropy in Developing Countries." www.onthinktanks.org, February 8.

Moncada, A., and E. Mendizabal. 2013. "Think Tank Boards: Composition and Practices." www.onthinktanks.org, March 25.

Morariu, J. 2011. "EPE TIG Week: Johanna Morariu on an Evaluation Approach for an Environmental Think Tank & Advocacy Organization." *AEA365 | A Tip-a-Day by and for Evaluators.* http://aea365.org/blog/?p=3341

Morozov, E. 2011. *The Net Delusion: The Dark Side of Internet Freedom.* New York: Public Affairs.

Morse, K., and R. Struyk. 2005. *Policy Analysis for Effective Development: Strengthening Transition Economies.* Boulder, CO: Lynne Rienner Publishers.

Morse, K., M. Pinegina, C. Romanik, M. Shapiro, and R. Struyk. 2002. "In-Service Training in Public Policy for Russian Local Government Civil Servants and Advocacy NGO Staff." Report to the Institute for Urban Economics. Washington, DC: The Urban Institute.

Nadler, D.A. 2004. "Building Better Boards." *Harvard Business Review*, May: 102–11.

Nalbantian, H.R., and A. Szostak. 2004. "How Fleet Bank Fought Employee Flight." *Harvard Business Review*, April: 116–25.

Ness, J.A., and T.C. Cucuzza. 1995. "Tapping the Full Potential of ABC." *Harvard Business Review*, July–August.

Nicholson, N. 2003. "How to Motivate Your Problem People." *Harvard Business Review*, January: 57–65.

Nickerson, J. 2014. *Leading Change from the Middle.* Washington: Brookings Institution Press.

Ofori-Mensah, M. 2012. How to Attract and Nurture Quality Researchers. TTI EX 2012. https://www.youtube.com/watch?v=ff6XVJ6mLYc&feature=plcp&noredirect=1

O'Neil, M. 2012. "Enhancing Organizational Governance." TTI EX 2012. https://www.youtube.com/watch?v=z00ZuRIqNiA&feature=plcp

Ordonez, A. 2014f. "Lessons from Peer Reviewing Among Think Tanks." *On Think Tanks.* www.onthinktanks.org, July 7.

Ordonez, A. 2014e. "Perspectives on the Peer Review Pilot." *On Think Tanks.* www.onthinktanks.org, July 6.

Ordonez, A. 2014d. "Is Research from Think Tanks Really Different?" *On Think Tanks.* www.onthinktanks.org, www.onthinktanks.org, June 25.

Ordonez, A. 2014c. "What are Peer Review Systems?" *On Think Tanks.* www.onthinktanks.org, June 23.

Ordonez, A. 2014b. "Peer Review: Experimenting with Think Tanks." *On Think Tanks.* www.onthinktanks.org, June 16.

Ordonez, A. 2014a. "Researchers habits: unlocking the potential for impact?" Politics & Ideas, April 22. http://www.politicsandideas.org/?p=1632

Ordonez, A. 2013. "Why is Changing Donor-driven Research Agendas So Hard?" *Politics & Ideas*, November 22. http://www.politicsandideas.org/?p=1390

Ordonez, C. 2012. "Enhancing Organizational Governance." TTI EX 2012. https://www.youtube.com/watch?v=6k5i8UeJKfM&feature=plcp

Pajas, P.P. 2011. *Thinking Ethically! A Think-tank Code of Good Governance.* Prague: Policy Association for an Open Society.

Pautz, H. 2011. "Revisiting the Think Tank Phenomenon," *Public Policy and Administration*, vol. 26, pp.419-35.

Perry, J.L., D. Mesch, and L. Paarlberg. 2006. "Motivating Employees in a New Governance Era: The Performance Paradigm Revisited," *Public Administration Review,* July/August, 505-14.

Perry, J.L. 1991. "Linking Pay to Performance: The Controversy Continues." In *Public Personnel Management: Current Concerns, Future Challenges*, edited by C. Ban and N. Riccorci. New York: Longman, 73–86.

Platt, J. 1987. "Research Dissemination: A Case Study." *The Quarterly Journal of Social Affairs* 3(3): 181–98.

Politics & Ideas. 2013a. "Research Agenda and Production." http://www.politicsandideas.org/ideas-by-a-new-think-net/topic-guide-research-and-policy/topic-guide-research-agenda-and-production/ Accessed on September 12, 2013.

Politics & Ideas. 2013b. "The monitoring and evaluation of research influence and impact." http://www.politicsandideas.org/ideas-by-a-new-think-net/topic-guide-research-and-policy/topic-guide-the-monitoring-and-evaluation-of-research-influence-and-impact/ Accessed on September 20, 2013.

Quigley, K.F.F. 1997. *For Democracy's Sake: Foundations and Democracy Assistance in Central Europe.* Washington, DC: The Woodrow Wilson Center Press.

Rabin, J., C.E. Teasley III, A. Finkle, and L.F. Carter. 1985. *Personnel: Managing Human Resources in the Public Sector.* San Diego: Harcourt Brace Jovanovich.

Rees, F. 2001. *How to Lead Work Teams.* San Francisco: Jossey-Bass, Pfeiffer.

Regester, M., and J. Larkin. 2008. *Risk Issues and Crisis Management in Public Relations: A Casebook of Best Practices.* Philadelphia: Kogan Page.

Richards, C. 2013. "The Onthinktanks Interview: Dr. Pak Asep." Posting on "On Think Tanks," www.onthinktanks.org, April 24.

Richards, C. 2013a. "The Onthinktanks Interview: Sandra Polonia Rios on Brazilian Funding Models." www.onthinktanks.org, February 20.

Rich, A. 2001. "U.S. Think Tanks and the Intersection of Ideology, Advocacy, and Influence." *NIRA Review* 8(1): 54–59.

Richman, B., and R. Struyk. 2002. "Local Administration of Social Assistance Programs in Russia." *International Journal of Public Administration.* 25(6): 773–804.

Robinson, M.K. 2001. *Nonprofit Boards that Work: The End of One-Size-Fits All Governance.* New York: John Wiley & Sons.

Rochlin, S. and S. Radovich. 2013. "Evaluating Innovation," in S.I. Donaldson, T. Azaam, and R.F. Conner (eds.) *Emerging Practices in International Development Evaluation.* Charlotte, NC: Information Age Publishing, Inc.

Rothwell, W.J., and H.C. Kazanas. 1994. *Improving On-the-Job Training.* San Francisco: Jossey-Bass.

Romero, A. 2014. "The Donor Perspective: Why Support a Peer Review System." *On Think Tanks.* June 18.

Rowan, J. 2004. *Facilitating Meetings & Chairing Discussions.* Cork, Ireland: NUBooks.

Saywell, D., and A. Cotton. 1999. *Spreading the Word: Practical Guidelines for Research Dissemination Strategies.* Leicestershire, UK: Loughborough University. Available at www.lboro.ac.uk/wedc/publications.

Scott, D.M. 2011. *The New Rules of Social Marketing & PR.* Hoboken, NJ: John Wiley & Sons.

Scott, N. 2012a. "Responding to Digital Disruption of Traditional Communications: Three Planks to the ODI Strategy." Posting on "On Think Tanks," www.onthinktanks.org October 3.

Scott, N. 2012. "A Pragmatic Guide to Monitoring and Evaluating Research Communications Using Digital Tools." Posting on "On Think Tanks," www.onthinktanks.org January 6.

Selee, A. 2013a. *What Should Think Tanks Do? A Strategic Guide to Policy Impact.* Stanford, CA: Stanford University Press.

Selee, A. 2013 b. "Thinking About Think Tanks: What Are They and What Do They Do? Interview at the Woodrow Wilson International Center for Scholars, December 20. http://www.wilson-center.org/article/thinking-about-think-tanks-what-are-they-and-what-do-they-do?mkt_tok=3Rk-MMJWWfF9wsRoluq7IZKXonjHpfsX96O8kT%2Frn28M3109ad%2BrmPBy72oUFWp8na-%2BqWCgseOrQ8kl0BV82jSc0WrqY%3D

Shultz, S.F. 2001. *The Board Book: Making Your Corporate Board a Strategic Force in Your Company's Success*. New York: American Management Association.

Silverstein, K. 2014. *Pay-to-Play Think Tanks: Institutional Corruption and the Industry of Ideas*. https://docs.google.com/file/d/0B5MMPY9ZYoG1ajB5TjRhRnVCZ2M/edit?pli=1

Simons, R. 2005. "Defining High-Performance Jobs." *Harvard Business Review*, July–August: 55–62.

Singer, M.I., and J.A. Yankey. 1991. "Organizational Metamorphosis: A Study of Eighteen Nonprofit Mergers, Acquisitions, and Consolidations." *Nonprofit Management & Leadership* 1(4): 357–69.

Slesinger, L.H. 1995. *Self-Assessment for Nonprofit Governing Boards*. Washington, DC: Center for Nonprofit Boards.

Smith, J.S. 1991. *The Idea Brokers: Think Tanks and the Rise of the New Policy Elite*. New York: The Free Press.

Stanton, T. 2012. *Why Some Firms Thrive While Others Fail: Governance and Management Lessons from the Crisis*. London and New York: Oxford University Press, 2012.

Stapleton, B. 1983. "Disseminating Social Services Research." *Research, Policy and Planning*, 1(2): 14–17.

Stone, D. 2005. "Think Tanks and Policy Advice in Countries in Transition." http://www.adbi.org/book/2005/12/01/1686.policy.research.vietnam/think.tanks.and.policy.advice.in.countries.in.transition/

Stone, D. 2000. "Think-tank Transnationalization and Non-profit Analysis, Advice and Advocacy, "*Global Policy,* vol.14, no.2, pp.153-72.

Stone, D. 2000a. "Non-Governmental Policy Transfer: The Strategies of Independent Policy Institutes." *Governance: An International Journal of Policy and Administration* 13(1): 45–62.

Stone, D., with S. Maxwell and M. Keating. 2001. "Bridging Research and Policy." Paper presented at an International Workshop, Coventry, UK.

Stone, D., and A. Denham (eds.) 2004. *Think –tank Traditions: Policy Research and the Politics of Ideas*. Manchester University Press: Manchester.

Stone, D., A. Denham, and M. Garnett. 1998. *Think Tanks across Nations: A Comparative Approach.* Manchester: Manchester University Press.

Stone, M.M., B. Bigelow, and W. Crittenden. 1999. "Research on Strategic Management in Non-profit Organizations: Synthesis, Analysis, and Future Directions." *Administration & Society* 31(3): 378–423.

Studwell, J. 2013. *How Asia Works: Success and Failure in the World's Most Dynamic Region.* New York: Grove Press.
Struyk, R. 1993. "Learning from the U.S. and European Experience." In *A Japanese Think Tank: Exploring Alternative Models*, edited by R. Struyk, M. Ueno, and T. Suzuki (31–55). Washington, DC: The Urban Institute.

Struyk, R. 1999. *Reconstructive Critics: Think Tanks in Post–Soviet Bloc Democracies.* Washington, DC: Urban Institute Press.

Struyk, R. 2006. *Managing Think Tanks*, 2nd edition. Budapest and Washington: The Open Society Institute and Urban Institute Press. http://r4d.org/sites/resultsfordevelopment.org/files/Managing%20Think%20Tanks%20(Second%20edition)_0.pdf

Struyk, R. 2013. "Evaluation of the Think Tank's Fund's Grant to the European Initiative Liberal Academy Tbilisi for the 2009-2012 Period." Budapest: Report Submitted to the Open Society Think Tank Fund, only available from the Fund.

Struyk, R., M. Damon, and S. Haddaway. 2009. *Evaluation of the 'Strengthening Institutions to Improve Public Expenditure Accountability' Project: Baseline Report.* Bethesda, MD. NORC at the University of Chicago, Report to the Global Development Network. http://www.gdn.int/html/page2.php?MID=3&SID=24&SSID=5&SCID=6

Struyk, R., S. Haddaway, and M. Damon. 2010. *Evaluation of the 'Strengthening Institutions to Improve Public Expenditure Accountability' Project: Monitoring Report.* Bethesda, MD. NORC at the University of Chicago, Report to the Global Development Network. http://www.gdn.int/html/page2.php?MID=3&SID=24&SSID=5&SCID=6

Struyk, R. and S. Haddaway. 2011. "What Makes a Successful Policy Research Organization in Transition and Developing Countries?" *Nonprofit Policy Forum, Vol.2, Issue 1, Article 4.*

Struyk, R. and S. Haddaway. 2012. "Mentoring Policy Research Organizations: Project Evaluation Results," *Voluntas*, Vol.23, pp. 636-60.

Struyk, R., K. Kohagen, and C. Miller. 2007. "Were Bosnian Policy Research Organizations More Effective in 2006 than in 2003? Did Technical Assistance Play a Role? *Public Administration and Development*, vo. 27, pp.426-38

Struyk, R., M. Ueno, and T. Suzuki. 1993. *A Japanese Think Tank: Exploring Alternative Models*. Washington, DC: The Urban Institute.

Summer, A. N. Ishmael-Perkins, and J. Lindstrom. 2009. "Making Science of Influencing: Assessing the Impact of Development Research." Brighton: Institute of Development Studies, University of Sussex.

Sundquist, J.L. 1978. "Research Brokerage: The Weak Link." In *Knowledge and Policy: The Uncertain Connection,* edited by L.E. Lynn. Washington, DC: National Academy of Sciences. Telgarsky, J., and M. Ueno, eds. 1996. *Think Tanks in a Democratic Society: An Alternative Voice.* Washington, DC: The Urban Institute.

Think Tank Fund, Open Society Foundation. 2012. "Core Survey Highlights-Final." Budapest: author, processed.

Think Tank Initiative. 2013. "PEC [Policy Engagement and Communications] Lessons Learned from Francophone Africa." http://www.thinktankinitiative.org/content/pec-lessons-learned-francophone-africa.

Thurnet. M. 2004. "Think Tanks in Germany," in D. Stone and A. Denhem (eds.) *Think Tank Traditions: Policy Research and the Politics of Ideas.* Manchester: Manchester University Press, pp.71-88.

Toegel, G., and J. Conger. 2003. "360-Degree Assessment: Time for Reinvention," *Academy of Management Learning and Education*, vol.2, no.3, pp.297-311.

Transparify. 2014. "How Transparent are Think Tanks about Who Funds Them?" http://static.squarespace.com/static/52e1f399e4b06a94c0cdaa41/t/536a108ee4b0e77a5729562c/1399459982820/How%20Transparent%20are%20Think%20Tanks%20(Transparify%2007May2014).pdf

Tschirbart, M. 1996. "Maintaining Legitimacy and Reputation through Impression Management." In *Alternative Revenue Sources: Prospects, Requirements and Concerns for Nonprofits*, edited by D.F. Burlingame and W.F. Ilchman (75–86). San Francisco: Jossey-Bass.

Tsui, J., S. Hearn, and J. Young. 2014. *Monitoring and Evaluation of Policy Influence and Advocacy.* London: Overseas Development Institute, Working Paper 395. http://www.odi.org/publications/8265-gates-monitoring-evaluating-advocacy

van Overtveldt, J. 2009. *The Chicago School: How the University of Chicago Assembled the Thinkers Who Revolutionized Economics and Business.* Evanston, IL: B2 Books, Agate Publishing.

Vera, H. 2014. "Peer Review and the Training of Young Researchers" *On Think Tanks.* www.on-thinktanks.org, June 30.

Wernet, S.P., and S.A. Jones. 1992. "Merger and Acquisition Activity Between Nonprofit Social Service Organizations: A Case Study." *Nonprofit and Voluntary Sector Quarterly* 21(4): 367–80.

Weyrauch, V. 2013a. *Lessons Learned on Promoting Better Links Between Research and Policy in Latin America.* Buenos Aires: CIPPEC, processed.

Weyrauch, V. 2013b. "M&E: How Can we Enhance Its Perceived Value?" *Politics & Ideas.* Nov. 1, 2013. http://www.politicsandideas.org/?p=1248. Accessed on Nov. 1, 2013

Weyrauch, V., J. D'Agostino, and C. Richards. 2011. *Learners, Practitioners and Teachers: Handbook on Monitoring, Evaluating and Managing Knowledge for Policy Influence.* Buenos Aires: CIPPEC. http://www.cippec.org/documents/10179/60576/M+Sociedad+Civil%2C%20 Learners%2C%20practitioners+and+teachers%2C%202010.pdf/0995404d-10ab-4e42-ba03-f0122514e765

Wheeler, T.L., and J.D. Hunger. 2000. *Strategic Management and Business Policy.* 7th ed. Upper Saddle River, NJ: Prentice Hall.

Weidenbaum, M. 2009. *The Competition of Ideas: The World of the Washington Think Tanks.* News Brunswick, NJ: Transactions Publishers.

Whitty, B. 2008. "Stretched in All Directions: The Demands, Pulls and Pressures on Policy Research Organizations." London: One World Trust.

Wilson, T. 1994. *Innovative Reward Systems for the Changing Workplace.* New York: McGraw-Hill.

Woelk, G., K. Daniels, J. Cliff, S. Lewin, E. Sevene, B. Fernandes, A. Mariano, S. Matinhure, A. Oxman, J. Lavis, and C.S. Lundborg. 2009. "Translating Research into Policy: Lessons Learned from Eclampsia Treatment and Malaria Control in Three Southern African Countries," *Health Research Policy and Systems,* Vol.7, no.3, pp.1-14.

Wolf., M. 2014. *The Shifts and Shocks: What We've Learned—and Have Still to Learn—from the Financial Crisis.* New York: Penguin Press.

WonkComms. 2013. EVENT: Wonkcomms teams and skill sets: what does the future hold? December 10. http://wonkcomms.net/2013/12/10/event-wonkcomms-teams-and-skill-sets-what-does-the-future-hold/. Accessed December 13, 2013.

Wyatt, M. and The Central and Eastern Europe Working Group on Non Profit Governance. 2004. *A Handbook of NGO Governance*. Budapest: European Center for Not-for-Profit Law. http://www.ecnl.org/dindocuments/18_Governance%20Handbook.pdf.

Young, J., V. Hauck, and P. Engle. 2013. *Final Report of the External Evaluation of the Think Tank Initiative*. http://www.ecdpm.org/Web_ECDPM/Web/Content/Navigation.nsf/index2?readform&http://www.ecdpm.org/Web_ECDPM/Web/Content/Content.nsf/0/4F796B695A372376C-1257BEF0028E8CA?OpenDocument

Young, D., and L.M. Salamon. 2002. "Commercialization, Social Ventures, and For-Profit Competition." In *The State of Nonprofit America*, edited by L.M. Salamon (423–46). Washington, DC: Brookings Institution Press.

ABOUT THE AUTHOR

Raymond Struyk is a Senior Fellow at Results for Development Institute and economist with significant experience in developing and transition countries. As a resident advisor he has led housing and housing finance development projects in Indonesia (2 years), Russia (7), Hungary (2), an Eastern Europe regional project based in Frankfurt (3) and Egypt (1). Until 2012 he was a Senior Fellow at the NORC at the University of Chicago, where he worked on strengthening housing finance, program evaluation, and the institutional development of think tanks. He joined NORC in 2007 after 30 years at the Urban Institute (where he founded its international program in 1981) and three years as the Department of Housing and Urban Development's Deputy Assistant Secretary for Research and Evaluation during the Carter Administration.

Dr. Struyk helped create think tanks in Hungary and Russia and has worked in detail with a dozen more on management, communications, and research issues. Among his publications concerning think tanks are *Reconstructive Critics: Think Tanks in Post-Soviet Bloc Democracies* (Urban Institute Press, 1999); and, *Managing Think Tanks* (Open Society Institute and Urban Institute, 2nd ed., 2006) and a dozen journal articles.

Dr. Struyk holds a PhD in Economics from Washington University in St. Louis and has published widely on housing, housing finance, and evaluation topics.

Improving Think Tank Management:
Practical Guidance for Think Tanks, Research Advocacy NGOs, and Their Funders

ANNEXES

Table of Contents

*Annexes listed with an asterisk are available for download on
http://r4d.org/improving-think-tank-management*

ANNEX 1.1 EXAMPLE OF A LOCAL PROGRAM FOR MANAGEMENT IMPROVEMENT: THE THINK TANK CAPACITY BUILDING PROGRAM IN BAKU

Context

The Economic Research Centre (ERC) is a policy research oriented think tank established through the initiative of three young economists in 1999. ERC's mission is to contribute to formulation of economic and social policies of the government through research and exchange of ideas. At that time, involvement of citizens in state governance, control over spending of public assets, transparency, and accountability of state agencies were alarming issues. There was a scarcity of in-depth research in all sectors of economy; the budget package was only 20 pages, and the requirements for use of budget funds were not formulated. In the last 14 years, ERC has evolved to be a prominent and well-known think tank not only in Azerbaijan, but in the region and CIS countries as well.

Azerbaijan is living its post peak oil period and the period of rapid economic growth achieved by oil production will soon be left behind. In the post-oil period, Azerbaijan will face tremendous challenges ensuring continuous and sustainable economic growth. Consequently, the Azerbaijani government will face difficulties in continuing its current policies on poverty reduction and addressing issues of employment and access to social welfare. Therefore, independent non-governmental organizations like ERC need to keep its management practices updated and at international standards by involving diverse experts, taking internal steps to build capacity, and diversifying their financial sources.

To address the need for policy analysis and recommendations, a number of government-based research institutions were established in recent years – the Strategic Research Center under the President of Azerbaijan Republic, the Analytical Information Centre of Parliament, the Economic Research Institute of State Economic University, and the Research & Development Center of Central Bank. However, these institutions – restrained in their research by existing political dogma – are incapable of examining a full spectrum of alternative policy options. This gap is filled by non-state think tanks such as ERC. Particularly in the current situation, where pressure and restrictions are imposed by the Azeri government against independent think tanks, implementation of such projects has become challenging.

Therefore, ERC leadership believes it imperative for private think tanks to produce and excellent analytic work and communicate it effectively to succeed in the policy market place. Strong management is a critical element in realizing this objective. During 2007-2008, ERC was able to make major upgrades in its administrative practices—ranging from public relations and HR to financial management—with resources provided by a Think Tank Fund grant.

Initiative to strengthen think tank operations

The Center has a tradition of seeking to support other think tanks in Azerbaijan and contributing to improvement of these organizations. Therefore, ERC led establishment of the Azerbaijan Think Tank Alliance (ATTA) (www.thinktank.az) in May 2013. ATTA was established through the initiative, "Enhancing the effectiveness of government by strengthening the role of think tanks in decision-making arena," which was funded by the European Union (EU) in partnership with Policy Association for an Open Society (PASOS) and "Intelligent Citizen" Enlightenment Center (ICEC). Its aim is to increase the institutional and research capacities of think tanks and to expand their impact, including fostering their participation in decision making process through mobilizing funds from diverse, particularly domestic, sources.

Problems of Azeri think tanks. The main challenges faced by think tanks include: (i) lack of institutional capacity in strategic management, quality control, and financial sustainability; (ii) lack of policy-analysis research skills, particularly in modern research methods and technologies, and (iii) poor policy dialogue between government structures and non-state think tanks.

The initiative. To address these problems, ERC decided to design and implement the "Enhancing the effectiveness of government by strengthening the role of think tanks in decision-making arena" project, which aimed at de-monopolizing public policy decisions in Azerbaijan by (i) building the institutional and research capacity of 18 non-state think tanks, and (ii) empowering informed and responsible participation of these think tanks in inclusive policy making in the country.

In terms of institutional development, ERC implemented a series of trainings to support strengthening the institutional capacities of partner think tanks. These trainings included "Strategic management of think tanks," "Strategic planning in think tanks," "Fundraising and accounting policy in think tanks," "Evidence-based advocacy strategy training," "Think tanks-media: perspectives on mutual synergies," "Making Contact: Tools for building effective communication," and "Introduction to SPSS." These course were supplemented with mentoring sessions given primarily by ERC staff. Additionally, ERC developed the Journal of Policy, which publishes papers written by partner think tanks' staff and published in a journal format. Besides this, ERC organized meetings of partner think tanks with governmental agencies in a roundtable format and similar meeting for Azerbaijan's business community.

Less important activities including stimulation of more rigorous research through the" Best Policy Paper" contest among ATTA members, which generated a robust response. Another way of bringing together partner think tanks under ATTA is by members presenting their ideas at the Board and Assembly of ATTA. Lastly, the first National Exhibition of Azerbaijan think tanks was organized. During this exhibition, think tanks had numerous opportunities to demonstrate their products, research, and projects before state agencies, business community members, international organizations and the public as well.

Outcomes realized

The formal project terminated in December, 2013 and by that time ERC had reached the following outcomes:

- 75 percent of think tanks had raised 25 percent of their budgets from local sources;
- The www.thinktank.az online payment (e-commerce) system was created, which allows think tanks to sell their policy products via an online platform;
- A bilingual (English/Azerbaijani) journal containing policy papers produced by local think tanks was produced in two editions and widely distributed;
- Over 10 evidence-based policy documents were produced and based on robust data analyses rather than mere data description;
- 95 percent of members now have quality control systems in place;
- The majority of beneficiary think tanks have (i) a strategic plan, (ii) a Public Relations (PR) policy in place and operating, (iii) an advocacy strategy,; and (iv) accounting and financial management policy and procedures in place.
- A formal think tank network with a realistic structure was created that will continue to operate.

Remaining challenges

Through realization of the "Enhancing the effectiveness…" project and establishment of Azerbaijan Think Tank Alliance, ERC management changed the way think tanks in Azerbaijan operate. However, there are still some gaps in this field:

- While funding diversification has improved, more is to be done.

- Relationships and involvement in dialogues with state agencies and business communities remain limited.

- A base of strong policy papers in Azerbaijan has not been createded yet, so the penetration of think tanks' analysis has been limited in the international market.

The future

By mobilizing the resources of both ATTA and ERC, the plan is to implement more joint advocacy activities. ERC with the support of members of ATTA is planning to advocate for hotly debated issues concerning Azerbaijan's civil society and will try to resolve key existing problems. Additionally, the publication of the semi-annual journal of policy papers will be continued. Also, additional issues of a newsletter about the activities of partner think tanks in ATTA are planned.

Galib Bayramov, Chairman[152]
Economic Research Center
Baku Azerbaijan

---

152   Mr. Bayramov has since become Chairman of ATTA's Board. www.erc.az; gibadoglu@erc.az

ANNEX 1.2 ADDITIONAL INFORMATION ON SURVEY DATA EMPLOYED

The GDN-15. The "Strengthening Institutions to Improve Public Expenditure Accountability" project aimed to strengthen the capacity of the 15 participating policy research organizations to monitor and analyze public expenditure choices, processes, and impacts and to engage constructively with policy officials to recommend improvements. The four and a half-year project, launched in 2008, had as its ultimate goal more capable, accountable, and responsive governments in the countries where the project operated. Populations in the countries where participating organizations were located were anticipated to benefit tangibly in the mid-term from improved government performance. The project management team consisted of representatives from the Global Development Network (GDN), the lead organization; the Results for Development Institute (R4D), the technical partner; and NORC at the University of Chicago, the monitoring and evaluation contractor.[153]

The evaluation program collected data on management practices at baseline (2009 survey), in monitoring surveys in 2010 and 2011, and during a final survey for evaluation purposes in 2013.[154] Overall, the surveys give us a picture of staffing composition and levels and a window on turnover and training, communications planning and practices, quality control, funding sources and composition, among other practices. The data I present in later chapters are generally from the 2011 survey; for some important questions that were not repeated in 2011, I show data from the 2009/2010 surveys.

The TTI-48. The Think Tank Initiative is a large-scale support-and-technical assistance project for an impressive number of think tanks (48 in 2013) administered by the International Development Research Centre (IDRC) and funded by a group of foundations and national aid agencies. Participating think tanks were selected, beginning in 2008, in regional cohorts from West Africa, East Africa, Latin America, and South Asia. The project has funding to continue through 2017.

TTI has three objectives whose summary statements indicate the program's approach:

1. Select a group of promising independent policy research organizations and assist them in assessing critical areas of strength and weakness and identifying opportunities for improved organizational performance.

---

153   Mid-Term evaluation results are in Struyk and Haddaway (2012).
154   Additional surveys were done of policy communities in each country to measure policy impacts, and research reports were reviewed by external experienced social scientists to rate research quality changes.

2. Provide a combination of general support funding and access to training and technical assistance to permit organizations to achieve improvements in research quality, organizational performance, and policy linkages.

3. Capture and share project learning about strategies for supporting and managing policy research organizations, in order to influence the future activities of the funding partners, participating think tanks, and other development actors. (Young, Huack, and Engel, 2013).

TTI conducted baseline surveys in 2008 and 2009 (think tanks were admitted to the program in two waves) and an annual monitoring survey from 2010 through 2013. Most data used here are from the 2011 survey to maximize comparability with the GDN data. Certain important questions – about quality control practices and comprehensive staffing information, for example – were only asked at baseline and therefore are shown for the earlier years. Generally, the survey year for data items is indicated in the tables. Where only one dataset is presented (GDN or TTI) there is only one year in parentheses. When data from both GDN and TTI are presented, the year for GDN is noted first, followed by the year for TTI.

The TTI data are for the 48 think tanks still participating in 2013 (listed at the end of this Annex), a few initial participants having left the program in earlier years. In some instances not all 48 responded to all questions. Because four think tanks participated in both the GDN and TTI programs, the maximum sample size in any table is 59 think tanks (15 + 48 − 4). When data are presented for the GDN and TTI programs separately, the four think tanks common to both programs are included in both tabulations. In tabulations for all think tanks combined, they are included only once (among the GDN think tanks).

Many of the questions used by TTI were the same as those in the parallel GDN-15 survey, although some additional areas are covered, e.g., strategy development in the TTI survey. Where possible, responses from the two surveys are combined to provide a larger sample size. When questions differ between the GDN and TTI surveys or are missing in one of them, data from only one or the other are used.

In all tabulations, "Stage 1" think tanks are defined as those with fewer than 10 full-time researchers. Where there are significant differences between Stage 1 and later-stage think tanks in staffing patterns and other areas, data for the Stage 1 group are presented separately from data for the larger organizations (a grouping that combines Stage 2 and Stage 3 institutions).

Neither the GDN-15 nor the TTI-48 is in any way a representative sample of think tanks, as they were selected from among think tanks that applied to participate in the program in response to widely disseminated proposal calls. Important characteristics of the two samples are shown in Table A.1.2.1, size (as indicated by the number of full-time staff), work mix of research and advocacy, and age in 2009.

Table A.1.2.1 Selected Characteristics at Baseline of Think Tanks Participating in the GDN and TTI Programs

Percent distributions

	GDN-15	TTI-48	Combined[b]
Size by Full-Time Employees (2008-2009)			
1-15	53	10	20
16-30	13	33	29
31-50	13	23	19
51-100	20	25	25
101 and up	0	8	7
Work Mix (2011)			
25% research - 75% advocacy	0	2	2
40% research – 60% advocacy	0	0	0
60% research - 40% advocacy	33	33	34
75% research - 25% advocacy	53	33	41
90% research - 10% advocacy	13	31	24
Organization age (2008-2009)[a]			
1-10 Years	33	46	44
11-16 Years	40	21	22
17 Years and Older	27	33	34

a.   Age in 2009
b.   Some values in this column may appear not to be the mean of the values in the previous two columns. Recall that the four organizations that participated in both projects are included for both programs but only once in the combined column.

The size distribution of think tanks in the two groups differs considerably, with half of the GDN-15 think tanks having fewer than 15 staff, compared with only 10 percent of the TTI-48 group. At the other end of the spectrum, 20 percent of the GDN-15 think tanks has over 50 staff members, compared with fully one-third of the TTI-48 group. Hence, the combined sample affords a higher share of observations among larger organizations, usefully augmenting the representation of small organizations.

Table A.1.2.2 GDN-15 Think Tanks

Organization Name	Abbreviation	Country
Advanced Social Technologies	AST	Armenia
Center for Economics and Development Studies, Faculty of Economics, Padjadjaran University	CEDS	Indonesia
Center for Research and Communication	CRC	Philippines
Research Center of the University of the Pacific	CIUP	Peru
Center for the Implementation of Public Policies Promoting Equity and Growth	CIPPEC	Argentina
Graduate School of Public Administration and Public Policy, Tecnológico de Monterrey	EGAP	Mexico
Fundación para el Desarrollo de Guatemala	FUNDESA*	Guatemala
Centre for Budget and Policy Studies	CBPS	India
Policy Research and Development	PRAD	Nepal
Unnayan Shamannay	US	Bangladesh
Integrated Social Development Centre	ISODEC	Ghana
Institute of Economic Affairs	IEA*	Kenya
Economic Policy Research Centre	EPRC*	Uganda
Economic and Social Research Foundation	ESRF*	Tanzania
Center for the Study of the Economies of Africa	CSEA	Nigeria

*Also in the TTI program.

The research-advocacy work mix distribution indicates that 41 percent of the combined sample reports doing 75 percent research and 25 percent advocacy, which is the most common split. The second most common split (containing 34 percent of the sample) is 60 percent research to 40 percent advocacy. While the two think tank groups are broadly similar, there is one startling difference: TTI-48 has 31 percent with a 90-10 percent research-advocacy split in contrast to only 13 percent for GDN 15. This may seem a startling difference, but it should be interpreted in combination with the fact that 53 percent of the GDN are in the next most research-concentrated category (75-25 percent research-advocacy spilt), vs. only 33 percent for TTI-48.

Table A.1.2.3 List of TTI-48 Think Tanks

Name	Abbreviation	Country
Latin America		
Asociación de Investigación y Estudios Sociales	ASIES	Guatemala
Centro de Análisis y Difusión de la Economía Paraguaya	CADEP	Paraguay
Centro Ecuatoriano de Derecho Ambiental	CEDA	Ecuador
Foro Social de Deuda Externa y Desarrollo de Honduras	FOSDEH	Honduras
Fundación ARU	ARU	Bolivia
Fundación Dr. Guillermo Manuel Ungo	FUNDAUNGA	El Salvador
Fundación para el Avance de las Reformas y las Oportunidades	Grupo FARO	Ecuador
Fundación Salvadoreña para el Desarrollo Económico y Social / Departamento de Estudios Económicos y Sociales	FUSADES	El Salvador
Grupo de Análisis para el Desarrollo	GRADE	Peru
Instituto de Estudios Avanzados en Desarrollo	INESAD	Bolivia
Instituto de Estudios Peruanos	IRP	Peru
Instituto Desarrollo	ID	Paraguay
Sub-Saharan Africa		
Advocates Coalition for Development and Environment	ACODE	Uganda
African Heritage Institution	AfriHeritage	Nigeria
Center for the Study of the Economies of Africa	CESA	Nigeria
Centre d'études, de documentation et de recherches économiques et sociales	CEDRES	Burkina Faso
Centre for Population and Environmental Development	CREP	Nigeria
Consortium pour la recherche économique et sociale	CRES	Senegal
Economic and Social Research Foundation	ESRF	Tanzania
Economic Policy Research Centre	EPRC	Uganda
Ethiopian Development Research Institute	EDRI	Ethiopia
Ethiopian Economic Association / Ethiopian Economic Policy Research Institute	EEA	Ethiopia
Initiative prospective agricole et rurale	IPAR	Senegal
Institut de recherche empirique en économie politique	IERPE	Benin
Institute of Economic Affairs	IEA-Kenya	Kenya
Institute of Economic Affairs – Ghana	IEA-Ghana	Ghana
Institute of Policy Analysis and Research – Rwanda	IPAR-Rwanda	Rwanda
Institute of Statistical, Social and Economic Research	ISSER	Ghana
Kenya Institute for Public Policy Research and Analysis	KIPPRA	Kenya
Makerere Institute of Social Research	MISR	Uganda
Research on Poverty Alleviation	REPOA	Tanzania
Science, Technology and Innovation Policy Research Organization	STIPRO	Tanzania
South Asia		
Center for Study of Science, Technology and Policy	CSTEP	India
Centre for Budget and Governance Accountability	CBGA	India
Centre for Policy Dialogue	CBD	Bangladesh
Centre for Policy Research	CPR	India
Centre for Poverty Analysis	CEPA	Sri Lanka
Centre for the Study of Developing Societies	CSDS	India
Indian Institute of Dalit Studies	IIDS	India
Institute for Social and Environmental Transition – Nepal	ISET-N	Nepal
Institute of Economic Growth	IEG	India
Institute of Governance Studies	IGS	Bangladesh
Institute of Policy Studies of Sri Lanka	IPS	Sri Lanka
Institute of Rural Management Anand	IRMA	India
National Council of Applied Economic Research	NCAER	India

Lastly, the age distribution of the combined sample is quite broad, with 44 percent relatively new (10 years old or less) and 34 percent very well established (17 years or older)—offering a good range of maturity. It often takes a think tank a decade to really establish itself as an important player in the policy arena, particularly in well-developed markets. If the think tank focuses on an area not well covered by existing think tanks that is also of significant policy attention, less time may be needed. The TTI-48 is slightly more concentrated in the oldest group (33 percent vs. 27 percent for the GDN-15).

The CEE-6. I supplement the information from the previous two surveys in a few places where useful information is not available for them with data from this third data set, representing six think tanks in Central and Eastern Europe (CEE) (Struyk 2006). The general criteria for inclusion of a think tank in the sample used here were that it had a minimum of 10 full-time researchers and had to be operating at about this level for the past five years (i.e., sufficient time to adequately address the personnel questions faced by an organization of this size).[155] The six think tanks included in the sample come from two groups. Three are organizations with which I had long-standing working relations and I understood to have a particular interest in management questions. The other three were among those interviewed in 1997 for a prior study of think tanks in the region (Struyk 1999). They were invited to participate based on information obtained in 1997 and on recommendations from the first three think tanks selected. The data on these six think tanks are for about the year 2000, when these organizations were mostly 5-10 years old and led by their first president (generally a person who had previously worked as a researcher in a soviet-style research institute). They were all Stage 2 think tanks. Information gathered includes staff practices and related data on turnover and the ways in which they developed their agendas, as discussed further in Chapter 2 where the information is first used. Again the sample is non-representative.

---

155   Interviews on personnel practices were conducted with two smaller think tanks in the region, and the results confirmed that these practices were quite unstructured at that time.

ANNEX 3.1 ESTABLISHING A POSITION

THE URBAN INSTITUTE

Human Resources Office   Project No.:_____

REQUEST FOR POSITION/JOB SPECIFICATIONS FORM

Instructions: To be completed by hiring supervisor and returned to the HR Office.

Center/Office:	Supervisor:
Position Title:	Budgeted Salary Range:
This Position Is: ☐ New ☐ Replacing: _____	This Position Is: ☐ Supervisory Not ☐ Supervisory

Employment Status: Regular ☐ Intermittent ☐ Temporary ☐ Expatriate ☐	Schedule: ☐ Full-time ☐ Part-time (_____%) ☐ *Casual (_____ hrs/wk)*	Location: ☐ On-site ☐ Off-site: _____ Site name

Length of Assignment (if term):	Desired Start Date:

Recruitment suggestions

Brief summary of job responsibilities:

SIGNATURES:

Hiring Supervisor Date	Center/Office Director Date
Director of Human Resources Date :	Senior vice President Date
Approval: ☐ Position authorized ☐ Disapproved (state reason)	

Date: **2/28/03**

THE URBAN INSTITUTE
Personnel Policies and Procedures

Subject: ESTABLISHING A POSITION

POLICY

Prior to hiring an employee, a position must first be established and a salary range and grade assigned based on the specifications of the job to be performed. In addition, a determination must be made about the expected duration of the position, the work schedule, and the status of the position with respect to the Fair Labor Standards Act (FLSA).

Eligibility for participation in the Institute's employee benefits programs is determined in part by employment status. Attachment A summarizes benefits eligibility by employment status. For complete benefits information and eligibility requirements, refer to the appropriate summary plan description or the Urban Institute policy and procedure for each benefit.

EMPLOYMENT STATUS DESCRIPTIONS

Positions may be classified as regular, intermittent, temporary, intermittent fellow, or expatriate according to the definitions listed below:

"Regular" means a position of indefinite duration or one with a set term of employment of more than 1000 hours and having a regular, predictable, full- or part-time work schedule as described below. Most Institute positions are regular status. Regular positions bear full fringe, overhead and G&A burdens for pricing and billing purposes.

"Temporary" means a position authorized for fewer than 1000 hours during any twelve-month period. Temporary employees may not work for the Institute in any other employment status for a period of eight months from the date last worked as a temporary employee (creating, in effect, an eight-month cooling off period after a temporary assignment). Similarly, a regular employee may not be rehired or converted to temporary status unless eight months has elapsed since the last day of employment as a regular employee. A temporary position may have a full-time, part-time, or casual work schedule. Temporary positions bear statutory fringe and full G&A, but no overhead for pricing and billing purposes.

"Intermittent" means a position (like a temporary position) that is of indefinite duration and has a casual work schedule and is a position authorized for fewer than 1000 hours in a calendar year.

It is, however, used only when a regular employee is rehired or converts to a casual work schedule before the eight-month cooling off period has elapsed or as an alternative to temporary status when the employing center or office wishes to consider the employee for regular employment following the assignment. Intermittent positions bear full fringe, overhead and G&A burdens for pricing and billing purposes.

"Intermittent Fellow" means a position that is of indefinite duration and is authorized for greater than 1000 hours in a calendar year. It is used only at the discretion of the president. Intermittent fellow positions bear statutory fringe, plus full overhead and G&A burdens for pricing and billing purposes.

"Expatriate" means a position whose duty post is outside the U.S., whose assignment outside the U.S. is anticipated to last 6 months or longer, and whose direct labor costs are covered primarily by a contract/grant to UI by an outside funding source. Expatriate positions bear full fringe, overhead, and G&A for pricing and billing purposes.

WORK SCHEDULE DESCRIPTIONS

"Full-time" means a regular, predictable work schedule of 40 hours per week.

"Part-time" means a regular, predictable work schedule of at least 20 but fewer than 40 hours per week.

"Casual" means a work schedule on average of fewer than 20 hours per week or one that averages fewer than 20 hours per week over the duration of the assignment.

PROCEDURES

Obtaining Authorization for a Position

To establish a new position, replace a terminating employee in an existing position, or hire a temporary employee, the hiring supervisor completes a **Request for Position/Job Specifications Form** (Attachment B) available from the human resources office. The form requires the hiring supervisor to specify the budgeted salary range, on-site or off-site status, employment status, supervisor, desired starting date, and whether the position has supervisory responsibilities. The hiring supervisor also describes the position's major responsibilities and duties and the qualifications and skills required to perform the job successfully, and makes recruitment suggestions for attracting qualified applicants. The center or office director must sign and approve the request.

The completed form is forwarded to the director of human resources, who reviews the job specifications and classifies the position according to the Institute's job evaluation procedures (see

Urban Institute Policy and Procedure No. 108 - Salary Administration). Once classified, requests for new positions are sent to the senior vice president for approval. The director of human resources approves requests for replacement positions, notifies the supervisor when new and replacement positions are approved, and maintains a log of approved positions.

Temporary assignments allow researchers to fill short-term hiring needs quickly and cost-effectively. <u>As is the policy for all job offers, offers of employment regardless of employment status may be extended only through the human resources office.</u>

Publicizing Vacant Positions

All vacant regular positions, with the exception of senior fellow, will be posted internally in common areas and sent to appropriate external sources, except in cases where employees are promoted or transferred within the same center or office, or where a written request for a waiver of the job posting requirement has been approved by the senior vice president. Senior fellows serve at the invitation of the Institute's president and are selected based on their nationally recognized expertise in a specific field of study.

Exempt positions will be posted for a minimum of two weeks, non-exempt positions for a minimum of one week. Temporary and intermittent positions are not required to be posted.

Canceling a Vacant Position

A posted exempt position that remains vacant for longer than six months will be canceled unless the hiring supervisor makes a written request to the director of human resources that the position remain open for an additional three months.

A posted non-exempt position that remains vacant for longer than three months will be canceled unless the hiring supervisor makes a written request to the director of human resources that the position remain open for an additional three months.

ANNEX 4.1 SHARING OF INFORMATION GAINED AT SKILLS ACQUISITION WORKSHOPS[156]

The GDN Project strived to increase participating organizations' competence in policy research and communicating the results of their analysis in part through transferring knowledge gained a workshops to other members of each think tank's staff. During the period under observation, two workshops were held in the course of the project: the launch workshops, one in Asia and one in Africa, in summer 2009, and another held in March 2010 aimed primarily at peer-reviewing work accomplished since the launch workshop. The topics of the presentations made are summarized in Table A4.1.1.

Table A4.1.1 Topics of Presentations at Project Workshops

Area	Workshop	
	Summer 2009	March 2010
Analysis	PETS[a] and absenteeism study methods and examples of such studies	Cost effectiveness analysis
	"Technical support" in sampling, survey design, and data analysis	
Communications	Advocacy: case studies from past grantees	Constructive engagement & communications to achieve results
	Advocacy: best practices	

a. Public Expenditure Tracking System

The discussion presents information on how the knowledge gained through participation in the workshops was shared with other staff at the participating organizations and the effectiveness of the workshops in improving Participating Organizations' (POs) communications practices.

Dissemination of Knowledge Gained at Project Workshops

To know whether the training of one or two staff from a project workshop is transformed into organizational capacity, one must determine the degree to which workshop attendees share information obtained in the workshop with others at the organization. If there is little sharing, the institution-level effects will be small, even though the individuals may have learned a lot and are using the new knowledge effectively. With workshop participants being researchers, it is especially important for communications staff to be informed about the content of presentations in this sphere.

Table A4.1.2 summarizes the information on within-institution sharing reported by POs. The questionnaire included the list of possible actions that could have been taken shown in the table and included pace for other action types to be included.

---

156   Source: Struyk, Damon and Haddaway (2010).

Table A4.1.2 Actions Undertaken After Project Workshops

	Percent			
	Yes, we did this	No, because staff know about this already	No, for other reasons	N
May-09 – Launch workshop				
Analytic presentations				
· Distributed the materials obtained or a list of them to other researchers	86.7	6.7	6.7	15
· Led an informal discussion about program budgeting analyses	78.6	14.3	7.1	14
· Gave a formal presentation on program budgeting analyses	41.7	33.3	25.0	12
· Led an informal discussion on benefit incidence analyses	78.6	14.3	7.1	14
· Gave a formal presentation on benefit incidence analyses	53.8	30.8	15.4	13
Communications presentations				
· Gave materials on communications and impact strategies to your communications team	57.1	7.1	35.7	14
· Met with the communications team to explain what the sessions on communications strategies were about	53.3	0.0	46.7	15
· Other	100	0	0	2
Jan-10 – Review workshop				
Analytic presentations				
· Distributed the materials obtained or a list of them to other researchers	92.3	0.0	7.7	13
· Led an informal discussion about cost effectiveness studies	91.7	8.3	0.0	12
· Gave a formal presentation on cost effectiveness studies	50.0	16.7	33.3	12
Communications				
· Gave materials on communications best practices to your communications team	58.3	0.0	41.7	12
· Met with the communications team to explain what the sessions on communications techniques were about	58.3	0.0	41.7	12
· Other (specify)	100	0	0	1

The table shows a high degree of sharing the materials. Forty percent of POs reported having 3-5 sharing activities after the launch workshop and 60 percent after the review workshop. One-third reported 6 or more activities after the launch workshop.[157] (Respondents were asked to indicate all activities they had undertaken; so there are multiple responses.)

---

157   Figures are not in the table.

Substantial activity at nearly all POs is evident for the knowledge gained on research techniques at both workshops, ranging from sending around a list of the materials obtained to making formal presentations. The incidence of sharing materials and leading informal discussions is in the 78-87 percent range. The pattern indicates that organization-level benefits on the research side should accrue from participation in the Project. There was a substantial increase in sharing of research technique material between the first and second workshops.

The pattern for the content of communications events at the workshops is quite different. For both workshops attendees from about half of the participating organizations passed on to the communications staff the materials from the "best practices in communications" session to the communications staff and met with them to review the material. Staff participating in the workshop who did not share the information from the analytic session fairly often said this was because other staff already was familiar with it. This is not the case for the communications information, where it appears that half of attendees just did not bother to share it.

We can explore this point further by examining how PO senior managers perceived the change in their staffs' advocacy communications knowledge resulting from the GDN presentations. As shown below, there is essentially a normal distribution of responses, with 73 percent of managers reporting modest to large increases. Table A4.1.3 illustrates a clear relationship between a modest or greater capacity increase and the number of transfer activities undertaken, i.e., managers perceive real improvement where greater effort was made by those attending the workshops to inform their colleagues charged with communications responsibilities. For the two workshops, those reporting negligible increases in capacity had a total 10 transfer actions, while those with modest increases and large increases had 44 and 37 actions, respectively.

Table A4.1.3 Management Rating of Increased Communications Capacity from TAP Events

How would you rate the increase in your organization's knowledge of advocacy and communications abilities as a result of GDN presentations on these topics?	
Negligible increase	13.3
Modest increase	40.0
Large increase	33.3
Fundamental improvement	13.3

Further to the issue of effectiveness of the communications sessions, 60 percent of respondents named a change in communications practice in response to the following question: "Can you name a major change you organization made to your communications practices due to what you learned at the GDN events?" The questionnaire asked for a short summary of these changes. Examples include: "Address issues systematically, convince with reasons," and "We learned about the pitfalls to avoid when granting interviews to media networks."

ANNEX 5.1 POSITION DESCRIPTION FOR TEAM LEADERS AT THE DATA POLICY INSTITUTE

Responsibilities and Expectations for Institute Center Directors[158]

Institutional leadership: Center directors are members of the Data Policy Institute's senior leadership team, contributing to planning and management that advances a shared vision and strategy for the success of the organization as a whole—today and in the future.

- Participate regularly in monthly meetings of center directors and the larger strategic management group.
- Actively engage in DPI-wide thinking, planning, and problem-solving.
- Help implement new DPI-wide policies and procedures within their centers, working constructively with administrative offices.
- Connect relevant center staff to cross-center teams working on new initiatives (e.g., big data, subcontract process improvements, IT modernization) and provide the support they need to represent the center effectively.
- Encourage and facilitate collaborative, cross-center research endeavors.

Intellectual and substantive leadership: Center directors are responsible for sustaining and advancing the quality and relevance of Institute research.

- Maintain and enhance the center's reputation for technical sophistication, rigor, and independence.
- Lead the center in framing a forward-looking agenda of research—building on current areas of expertise, but expanding to address issues of emerging importance.
- Produce timely analysis (including policy briefs, fact sheets, and other products) that responds to current events in the news cycle.
- Find opportunities for innovation in data, methods, and scope.
- Manage quality control, particularly for high-profile/high-risk projects.
- Encourage center researchers to work collaboratively with colleagues in other centers to capitalize on DPI's strengths.
- Actively participate in the center's research, as principle investigator, collaborator, and/or senior adviser.

---

158   This description is used by a stage 3 think tank which permit use of the description in this book but asked that the organization not be identified.

External engagement: Center directors ensure that the center has successful efforts to engage with the full range of audiences for its research and actively participates in new institutional strategies for raising visibility and impact.

- Systematically reach out and build relationships with diverse audiences (including academics, media, policymakers, practitioners, business, and advocates).

- Empower and encourage appropriate center staff to publicly represent the center's work to a variety of audiences, helping to make them available for interviews and other relationship cultivation activities.

- Work with communications and outreach staff to identify and engage new audiences (including early identification of products and events).

- Expand the policy and communications capacities within the center (through training, practice, and possibly recruitment) to communicate key findings and engage with external audiences to gain insight on key questions for further exploration.

Fundraising: Center directors are responsible for planning and coordinating their centers' fundraising activities so as to maintain a diverse and healthy portfolio of funding sources.

- Manage and sustain good relationships with funders, guide bidding strategies, and develop and promote new funding proposals.

- Partner with development staff to cultivate new funding sources, including individuals and corporations.

- Pursue opportunities for more flexible, programmatic funding that supports outreach and communications as well as self-defined research.

- Encourage and support collaboration with other centers on cross-cutting idea development and fundraising strategies.

Staff mentoring and recruitment: Center directors are responsible for building a well-qualified and effective team of researchers and other professionals so that together the center has the research, policy, communication, and support skills necessary to sustain the center's success into the future.

- Attract new, high caliber researchers, policy experts, and communicators to the team.
- Work with executive office staff to overcome hiring disincentives perceived by senior researchers.
- Work with human resources staff to recruit the right mix of staff and set salaries that effectively attract and retain talent.

- Support the professional development and morale of existing staff at all levels, including through mentoring and by providing training and skill-building opportunities.

- Communicate effectively with center staff at all levels about all relevant goals, strategies, new initiatives, research learning, and procedures.

- Foster a sense of community and belonging to both the center and the Institute as a whole.

Internal management: Center directors oversee and are accountable for the day-to-day management of project budgets and schedules, internal controls and reporting, and use of institutional resources.

- Ensure that the center meets contract and grant obligations on time and within budget.

- Ensure that center staff complies with institutional procedures and reporting requirements.

- Deploy institutional resources strategically and responsibly.

- Oversee staffing plans, work assignments, mentoring, and quality control processes.

- Establish and monitor work schedules and flexible work arrangements.

- Keep staff at all levels informed and involve them in planning for the center's future.

ANNEX 6.1 REVIEWER'S CHECK LIST TO USE IN ASSESSING ANALYTIC REPORTS

Document Name	
Author	
Name of Reviewer	
Date:	

	Question
A	General
A.1	Is the issue well-defined and the case for its policy importance effectively made?
A.2	Is the issue defined or structured in such a way that a clear hypothesis or researchable question is stated?
A.3	Are all the relevant aspects of the issue included for analysis?
A.4	Are relevant previous studies on the issue in the country cited and built on?
A.5	Do the authors show knowledge of the relevant international studies on this topic?
A.6	Has the right type of information and data been assembled to address the issue? If not, what was omitted that should have been included? Where sample data are employed, is the sample correctly drawn to be representative? Is it sufficiently large for the necessary tests?
A.7	Are the methods employed appropriate? Are statistical tests used where needed?
A.8	Is the report well-organized and clearly and succinctly written?
B	**Conclusions and recommendations**
B.1	Are the conclusions based squarely on the paper's findings? (or do the authors go beyond the findings in effect expressing personal views or political opinions?)
B.2	If the conclusions call for action through government programs, is the cost realistically estimated? Is the administrative feasibility and complexity of the program considered?
B.3	Do the authors consider various options for addressing the issue and the merits of each, or focus exclusively on a single approach?
B.4	In general, do the authors draw out the full policy implications of the findings and make realistic suggestions for their use in changing current policies?
B.5	Where appropriate, do the authors suggest what additional data could be collected and/or analysis undertaken to better answer the question posed or to answer additional questions the study raised?
C	**Reviewer's summary comments** (use as much space as needed)

Guidelines for Rating Policy Research Reports

	Question	Very Weak	Very Strong
A	**General**		
A.1	Is the issue well-defined and the case for its policy importance effectively made?	Hard to identify the issue under discussion, possibly because it is confused with others; or issue is stated but there is no attempt to explain why it merits public policy attention.	Issue crisply and clearly defined and a cogent case for its policy importance and timeliness is made.
A.2	Is the issue defined or structured in such a way that a clear hypothesis or researchable question is stated?	Difficult-to-impossible to understand the specific question or hypothesis that is the research subject.	The basic policy issue is expressed in a way that makes addressing it empirically straightforward and accessible to the reader.
A.3	Are all the relevant aspects of the issue included for analysis?	Author leaves out key point, e.g., the distribution of benefits or subsidies or the efficiency with which they are employed, while focusing only on the total amount	All relevant elements are noted. (It is not necessary that they all be covered in the paper, but enough information should be provided to fully understand the situation.)
A.4	Are relevant previous studies on the issue in the country cited and built on?[b]	No prior studies are cited.	There is a good review of the prior studies and the advances that the current research makes over the prior is clearly articulated.
A.5	Do the authors show knowledge of the relevant international studies on this topic?[b]	Such studies are not mentioned.	This study exhibits knowledge of the relevant literature and states or implies its influence on the current study.
A.6	Has the right type of information and data been assembled to address the issue? If not, what was omitted that should have been included? Where sample data are employed, is the sample correctly drawn to be representative? Is it sufficiently large for the necessary tests?	The selection of data seems arbitrary and not well-suited to the study. Where survey data are used, insufficient information is provided to judge its quality, or the information provided makes problems with the sample clear.	The data employed are ideal for the study. Where survey data are used, the sample is well-described and clearly appropriate for the task at hand.
A.7	Are the methods employed appropriate? Are statistical tests used where needed?	The authors do not employ the relevant statistical tests but rather just describe qualitatively the patterns in the data.	Relevant statistical tests are used throughout. The author interprets the results of the tests effectively.
A.8	Is the report well-organized and clearly and succinctly written?	The report is very poorly structured, with little logic to the sequencing of the presentation. The writing style is very wordy or otherwise makes it hard for the reader to	The report is well-organized and tightly written. The flow of language makes it easy to read. There are few extra words. The author exercises good judgment in allocating material to

Reviewer's Check List to Use in Assessing Policy Briefs or Other Documents Aimed Explicitly at Advancing a Policy Position

	Document Name	
	Author	
	Name of Reviewer	
	Date:	

	Question	
A.1	What is the purpose of the paper? (record number in next column) 1. Call attention to a pressing policy issue 2. Define an issue and propose a way to address it 3. Other (name) -- Reviewers will use sections A and D for all documents; and will choose one of either section B or C depending on the type of document. B is for documents identified above as type #2; and C for those identified as #1. For those identified as #3 select either B or C as appropriate.	
A.2	Purpose of the Brief is clear and the issue well-defined	
B	**For Briefs that define an issue and ways to address it (item 2) in A.1**	
B.1	Is the problem definition supported properly with facts?	
B.2	Are options for addressing the issue articulated well? (A stronger presentation is one that does advance only a single solution.)	
B.3	Are the criteria for judging the alternative solutions well-articulated?	
B.4	Are the reasons for the superiority of the recommended solution clearly stated?	
B.5	Is the analysis underlying the recommendation sufficiently explained that the reader can judge it?	
B.6	Is the presentation of the recommended action comprehensive, i.e., addresses costs, administrative issues, as well as the program or other action to be taken?	
C	**For briefs that define a pressing policy issue**	
C.1	Are the public policy dimensions of the problem well developed and presented, i.e., why is this an issue deserving policy attention?	
C.2	Is the dimension of the problem, e.g., the share of children not attending classes, well-developed and based on credible sources and analysis?	
C.3	Are "next steps" defined, i.e., now that the problem is defined, who should take responsibility for addressing it in some way?	
C.4	Is the recommendation (C.3) sensible and well-justified?	
D	**All Briefs**	
D.1	Is the presentation engaging, i.e., is the reader motivated to continue to read?	
D.2	Is the level of presentation suitable for the policymaker or "intelligent layman"?	
D.3	Is the presentation succinct, closely reasoned, and of the appropriate length?	

Explanation of Ratings for Policy Briefs

	Question	Very Weak	Very Strong
B	**For Briefs that define an issue and ways to address it in A.1 of the scoring sheet**		
B.1	Is the problem definition supported properly with facts?	Essentially no facts are presented. There seems to be an assumption that everyone agrees that this is a problem and no further explanation is needed.	Facts are succinctly and effectively marshaled to document the problem.
B.2	Are options for addressing the issue articulated well? (A stronger presentation is one that does not advance only a single solution.)	No options other than the one favored by the authors is even described, not to mention being assessed.	The relevant options are fairly stated and described.
B.3	Are the criteria for judging the alternative solutions well-articulated?	No criteria are explicitly or even implicitly stated. Everything seems to hinge on the authors' judgment.	The criteria are stated clearly and the set is complete, i.e., the criteria are not biased through omission.
B.4	Are the reasons for the superiority of the recommended solution clearly stated?	No. The reader is in effect asked to accept the recommendation simply on the basis of the authors' judgment.	A full discussion of the reasons for the selection of the favored options is presented.
B.5	Is the analysis underlying the recommendation sufficiently explained that the reader can judge it?	The analysis is simply missing or so obscure that the reader really cannot understand it. The author does not reference other documents where a full explanation can be found.	The analysis is carefully explained and presented, given the space limitations of the policy brief. Other supporting studies are cited.
B.6	Is the presentation of the recommended action comprehensive, i.e., addresses costs, administrative issues, as well as the program or other action to be taken?	Little-to-nothing is said about the short-term to long-term costs or administrative issues. The brief does not raise transition issues (from the current to the new policy) that are involved.	The author provides careful and comprehensive cost estimates over a reasonable time period (5-years) and accurately describes the administrative issues that will be involved in the new action.
C	**For briefs that define a pressing policy issue**		
C.1	Are the public policy dimensions of the problem well developed and presented,	It is unclear why the issue raised in the brief is a matter to	A compelling case is made for the public's interest in the issue. Both the most obvious

ANNEX 7.2 MORE INFORMATION ON RECRUITING NEW BOARD MEMBERS

Recruiting: What Board Members Want

Most people who serve as members of a think tank's board do so for some combination of three reasons. First, they would like to enjoy the company of their fellow board members. This can be an especially powerful draw if the institution's board is populated with prestigious individuals. Second, members want to feel that they are doing good work, that they are giving something back to their community through serving without compensation.[159] Third, board members want to be associated with an organization doing high-quality work that may have significant positive effects on national living standards and governance. Highly regarded think tanks active in the public domain will have an easier job than others in attracting their most desired candidates.

Over time, boards can become more attractive to potential new members by helping the think tank achieve its primary objectives and by recruiting excellent new members for the board. Here, success breeds further success. Given the board's central place in a think tank's life and the intangible benefits board members seek from serving on the board, it is not surprising that boards typically devote substantial energy to recruiting new members.

Many candidate board members will want to be assured that the institute will purchase for them directors' and officers' liability insurance—in other words, insurance to cover the costs of defending themselves against allegations that they acted wrongfully in discharging their duties as a board member. (See article VII in the board bylaws presented in Annex 7.1 for specific language.) This insurance is payable to the directors and officers of an organization or to the organization itself, as indemnification (reimbursement) for losses or advancement of defense costs in the event an insured suffers such a loss as a result of a legal action brought for alleged wrongful acts in their capacity as directors and officers. Such coverage can extend to defense costs arising out of criminal and regulatory investigations/trials as well; in fact, often civil and criminal actions are brought against directors/officers simultaneously.

How to Recruit

Before approaching a candidate for board membership, the board needs to clearly define the minimum expectations for successful service on the board. How much time should it take? Does it just involve attending the board meetings, or is something also expected between meetings? The board member who knows the candidate best is usually asked to make the initial contact. Robinson (2001, 126–27) provides a good list of questions the board needs to answer before a member approaches a candidate.

---

159   These two reasons are noted in Robinson (2001, 22).

What major issues is the board currently focused on?

What talents, expertise, qualities, or characteristics is the board seeking in new members?

How often does the board meet and for how long?

Is everyone asked to serve on a committee? How are committee assignments made?

What kind of fund-raising is required of board members?

What is the relationship between the board and the executive director and between the board and other staff?

Is an orientation program in place? Are other board education activities offered?

Does the board have an annual retreat of any kind?

Are there changes on the horizon that a new board member should know about?

Many recruitment conversations stress how little time will be required of the new board member. This is a mistake for two reasons. It may lead to unrealistic expectations on the part of the new member, possibly resulting in lower involvement than actually required. More important, it diminishes the real reason for which the person is being recruited: Their talent and experience would be valuable in helping to shape the institution's work and future agenda. In short, apologizing for the inconvenience of serving usually backfires.

The tradition among think tanks has been *not* to expect board members to personally contribute funds to the organization. This was contrary to the practice of many service-providing NGOs. Many in the business or communications may not understand this distinction, and it is certainly worth pointing it out when approaching a candidate. At times the president may gently ask the chairman or a board member with a specific connection to a possible donor to make introductions or even participate in an initial meeting.

While this tradition still holds in many countries, in the west the last decade has witnessed an evolution toward members being contributors. This is particularly true in the U.S., where annual contributions are often expected from members in a position to make them. The board-as-revenue source is one explanation for the steady increase in the size of U.S. boards.

New Member Orientation

Orientation programs, formal or informal, make it easier for new board members to make a contribution right away. While private firms in many countries offer formal training programs for the directors of nonprofit organizations, these programs are likely ill-suited for most think tanks, for two reasons. First, most such programs are oriented to a wide range of service delivery nongovernmental organizations (NGOs), with which think tanks have little in common. Think tanks often more closely resemble for-profit consulting firms or university research centers than the typical NGO that provides human services (e.g., counseling, training, and various social services). Second, the kind of people recruited to think tank boards are unlikely to have the inclination or time to attend such training events.

A simple program organized by the chairman of the board and the think tank's president can deliver the necessary information. For orientation at many think tanks, the new board member is invited to the think tank for an extended meeting with the president and introductions to key staff members. When the new member resides in another city, rules of common courtesy suggest that the president should visit the new member to provide the orientation, or at least offer to do so.

The orientation should include a summary of the organization's history, because the current activities and attitudes are often heavily conditioned by its roots and early development. Additional topics to cover include:

> goals and objectives
> the current program of work
> recent successes in research and the policy process
> the organization's communications and dissemination programs
> recent financial history
> fund-raising, especially if this has been a problem and year-to-year swings in financing have been significant, along with the strategy for dealing with funding problems
> any other current or impending problems that have been discussed with the board
> a quick review of the performance indicators being employed
> the institution's key staff, highlighting each member's special contributions.

Each new member should be given a package of materials about the organization: its charter and other legal documents are a must, as are current financial statements and the strategic plan if one exists. Annual reports for the past two or three years and examples of the think tank's written products should also be included. It is doubtful that the new member will study these immediately. But he may turn to them if a particular issue arises, especially an urgent one. Lastly, provide him with a copy of this book or a similar guide that provides an in-depth discussion of not only boards' responsibilities but think tank management more generally.

It is often said that board members learn best by asking questions.[160] The one-on-one meeting with the president offers significant scope for such questions. But the president should also encourage any new member who wants to talk with senior staff members—both researchers and administrators—to go ahead.

---

160   This paragraph draws on Robinson (2001, 76–77).

No orientation is complete without a discussion of the new board member's duties and the kind of role the organization hopes the member will play. This conversation can be led by the president or the chairman of the board. In either case, it should be guided by a statement produced by the board, ideally at the same time the board discusses specific candidates to serve. Most duties will be common to all members, including attendance at board meetings, active participation in the meetings, and so forth. But there may be particular tasks for some members. For example, a member with a strong financial background could be asked to take the lead in monitoring the organization's financial condition and controls, presumably mostly by reviewing the annual external audit of the institution's finances.

ANNEX 8.1 WHITE BOOK—TABLE OF CONTENTS

A) Private sources and institutional development
6.3 Responsibilities
6.4 Donor Loyalty
6.5 CIPPEC' Annual Dinner
6.6 Accountability
6.7 Payments' management and monitoring
6.8 Billing meeting
6.9 Processes by source of funding
B) Public sources and political linkages

Chapter 7: Administration and Finance
7.1 Billing and collection of non-allocated donations
7.1.1 Origin of the process: Donation
7.1.2 Register of donation
7.1.3 Billing Process
7.1.4 Collection Process
7.1.5 Policies
7.1.6 Monthly Reports' Process
7.2 Projects' Billing and Collection Process
7.3 Payments' Process
7.4 Petty cash's Process
7.5 Expenses' Accountability Process
7.6 Monthly Closure process
7.7 Auditing Process

Chapter 8: Human Resources
8.1 Linkage Modalities
8.2 Internal policies and benefits 98
8.3 Labour Unlinking
8.4 Selection of Directors Policy

Chapter 9: Communication
9.1 Information and Confidentiality
9.2 Publications Policy
9.3 Media Policy
9.4 Events
9.5 Individual participation in external events
9.6 Internal communication program
9.7 Communication of crisis
9.8 Institutional Cards
9.9 Web

ANNEX 9.1 SEVEN INNOVATIONS UNDERTAKEN BY EASTERN EUROPEAN AND RUSSIAN THINK TANKS

Overview of Initiatives

How many and what types of initiatives did these think tanks undertake? Why did they do it? How important are such initiatives to the institutions? Table A9.1.1 and Box A.9.1.1 provide summary information; the box includes a short description of each initiative.[161]

Table A9.1.1 Number, Timing, and Importance of Initiatives

Item	CSD	IUE	CDFE	CASE
Timing				
Year institute founded	1989	1995	1991	1991
Year institute began thinking seriously about diversification	1994	1996	1996	1992
Motivation				
Reduce dependence on primary funding source	No	Yes	Yes	Yes
Necessary to engage in new type of work	Yes	Yes	No	Yes
Number of initiatives				
Number allied to principal activity	1	2	1	2
Number separate from principal activity	1	0	0	2
Importance of all initiatives to revenue of main company	30%	10%	20 to –30%	40 to 55%
Size				
Number of professional staff (full-time equivalent)	28	36	6[a]	40

CSD = Center for the Study of Democracy
IUE = Institute for Urban Economics
CDFE = Center for Democracy and Free Enterprise
CASE = Center for Social and Economic Research
[a] Excludes parliamentary interns.

Of the four study firms, three were clearly in Stage 2, meaning that they had more than five full-time researchers, had stable funding, and were well established in their markets. All three were all large by regional standards. The fourth, the Center for Democracy and Free Enterprise (CDFE), was nearly there.

Each firm cited one or two initiatives that had progressed enough to be reported upon. Initiatives were wide-ranging and included setting up a market survey operation, a credit rating agency,

---

161   Note that not all actions cited as entrepreneurial by the respondents have been included. Some had begun too recently at the time of the interview to be of interest, and others were simply a somewhat different approach to marketing to prior clients.

customized corporate training programs, and an in-house consulting center for working in other transition countries.

Most initiatives had been undertaken after the think tank had been in operation for two or three years, but there are exceptions to this rule. One is the radio station established by the Center for the Study of Democracy (CSD); founding the station was one of the center's first activities, and was meant to break the government's monopoly on local news broadcasts by rebroadcasting Voice of America programs. Over the years the programming format has changed in line with evolving consumer preferences. Another example is the Center for Social and Economic Research (CASE), which began advising other transitional countries very early in its life, when a foundation invited one of CASE's senior staff to work with Russian reformers on macroeconomic policies.

The Institute for Urban Economics (IUE) was also a fast starter because it believed it could survive only if it aggressively diversified its activities and client base from the initial project—a large housing and real estate reform project supported by the U.S. Agency for International Development.

Motivation for the initiatives varied. CDFE was facing very tough times financially and diversified out of necessity. CASE's "corporate sponsors" initiative was also a straightforward attempt to diversify funding sources. On the other hand, CSD set up its marketing research operation primarily because it offered the chance to become engaged in new topic areas. Similarly, CASE's technical assistance to transitional economies resulted from its desire to share its staff expertise. IUE was motivated by wanting both to reduce dependency on its primary sponsor and to enter new fields.

One key element in determining the nature of the initiative was the institution's initial activity base. CSD built its marketing survey operation on its existing survey capacity, and IUE created its credit rating agency for local government bonds around a team already doing related municipal-finance projects. Similarly, CDFE was able to exploit its established reputation for conducting training projects in preparing its custom training packages for corporate clients. CASE's international consulting operation built squarely on the group's work on similar topics in Poland.

In short, the firms generally built on the positive reputation they had established for related activities and exploited the capabilities of existing staff in selecting an initiative. Building on strength is a common business strategy. However, the modest capital available to underwrite the start-up costs of an initiative also prevented these institutions from launching any initiative further afield from their core activities.

Identifying and Launching Initiatives
The most common pattern for the launch of an initiative was for the basic idea to come from the president of the organization or from a staff member (Table A.9.1.2). The idea was then discussed among the staff and a few people outside the organization and usually with the Board. If it was agreed upon as probably feasible, then the new line of work was marketed by word of mouth and

participation in seminars, where this specific expertise could be demonstrated and promotional material distributed. In short, these were low-tech, often rather informal processes. Instinct played at least as large a role as analysis in making the decision to proceed.

Table A9.1.2 Origin, Development, and Rating of Each Initiative

Firm and initiative	Source of idea	Type of analysis undertaken[a]	Promotion effort[b] (yes/no)	Annual number of orders	Financial success (yes/no)
CSD: radio station	USG rep.; CSD president	2	No	NA	Yes
CSD: marketing surveys	Staff	2, 4	No	25 to 30	Yes
IUE: credit rating	Staff	1, 3, 4	y2	3 to 5[c]	Yes
IUE: municipal economic development	Staff	1	y2	2	Too early to tell
CDFE: corporate training	CDFE president	1	No	varies	Yes
CASE: tech assist to transition economy	Staff	1	y1	5 to 6 countries, 3 to 4 sponsors[d]	Yes
CASE: corporate sponsors	Staff	1	y2	8 sponsors	Yes

[a] 1 = discussed among staff; 2 = sought outside advice from knowledgeable people (volunteers); 3 = paid for outside expert advice; 4 = prepared professional-standard business plan.
[b] y1 = Promotion consisted of actively seeking opportunities to make presentations at seminars and conferences; preparing and distributing reports; and mentioning the activity on the organization's web site.
y2 = Formal marketing activities undertaken beyond those listed in y1, such as holding a press conference, organizing seminars, or publishing and distributing special promotional brochures. Also, in rare cases, pilot projects were carried out to provide a "product" to demonstrate (e.g., IUE's economic development team worked on a nonfee basis with a mid-sized Russian city to develop an economic development strategy that the institute could then show other cities).
[c] A single "order" can involve ratings for a number of cities (e.g., a multilateral donor requesting information on debt-carrying capacity of several cities).
[d] A sponsor sometimes supports work in more than one country.

Preparation of a formal business plan to test the feasibility of an initiative was relatively rare, with plans prepared for only two initiatives—CSD's marketing survey initiative and IUE's credit rating facility. IUE was the only group surveyed that contracted for assistance in analyzing its initiative. It hired an international management consulting firm to help prepare the business plan. IUE believes this was a good investment, because the strong business plan was instrumental in inducing Standard & Poor's (S&P) to sign a strategic affiliation agreement with the credit rating agency less than a year after it began operations.

Similarly, formal promotional efforts beyond seminar participation to launch a new initiative were exceptional. IUE has been more aggressive than most think tanks in explicitly marketing an initiative. For its credit rating initiative, for example, it sponsored presentations by the key researcher at numerous seminars within Russia, gave the activity prominence on its home page, produced a slick three-fold marketing brochure and distributed it widely at conferences, and sponsored a session at a major international conference in London on credit ratings in the Commonwealth of Independent States. The affiliation with Standard & Poor's was announced at a splashy press conference in a five-star Moscow hotel. CASE launched its "corporate patrons" program with a customized sophisticated mailing to 70 of the largest corporations and banks in Poland, with telephone follow-up to recruit patrons.

Common, if modest, promotional efforts included devoting space in the institute's newsletter and on its web site to the initiative, where these vehicles were available. Since most projects resulted in reports, these, too, were available to show to new potential clients.[162]

Of those interviewed, only CASE cited an example of an initiative that had not worked. CASE attempted to obtain contracts from the Polish government for carrying out research and policy analysis; while government offices used the Center's work, they resisted paying for it. This initiative was handled very informally. The practice of Polish ministries in contracting out has changed dramatically since 2000, so by 2005 ministries were major research clients. (See the next chapter for more on government procurement of policy research and evaluation services.)

Rewards and Challenges

How did the pluses and minuses of introducing innovations balance for these think tanks? Table A9.1.3 provides an overview using the same factors listed above.

Table A9.1.3 Summary of Responses on Challenges and Rewards

Reward/Challenge	Number of firms citing reward/challenge
Rewards	
Broader base of experience for policy development	3
Improved efficiency	2
Support for overhead functions	0
Improved visibility and marketing possibilities	4
Challenges	
Agenda-setting and lack of focus	0
Restricted use of data and publications	0
Perceived lack of independence	0
Conflict of cultures within the think tank	0
Restive clients or sponsors	0
Management challenges	2

---

162   CDFE was not anxious to advertise its special corporate training activities, because some viewed the training as not fully consistent with its primary mission, so it used none of these tools.

Rewards

Financially, the revenues generated by the initiatives have generally been moderately important, representing 10 to 30 percent of total revenues (Table A9.1.1). But CASE's assistance to transition economies was uniquely successful, with revenues from this activity accounting for 40 to 55 percent of total revenues in the two years before the interview.

The directors of the think tanks rated the initiatives as financially successful. This is, however, a fairly imprecise term. While each initiative is generating significant revenue, as seen above, the rating of financial success is *not* based on revenues net of start-up costs. For many initiatives these costs were quite modest, so the needed adjustment would be small. But in a few cases, such as IUE's substantial promotional efforts and paid assistance in business-plan development, the rating of financial success could be affected. Unfortunately, these think tanks do not keep records in a way that permits all relevant costs to be readily identified.

Some respondents emphasized that the form in which the funds were received made them especially valuable. Both CDFE and CSD reported that the use of profits from corporate training and the radio station, respectively, had no restrictions and could be used very flexibly. For example, they could serve as matching funds for foundation grants or be used for computer purchases or other institution-building tasks. On the other hand, if the activity increases total operations but leaves profits unchanged, then funds in the overhead accounts increase—but these are all dedicated to specific purposes.

All four think tanks believed their initiatives improved their reputation and/or visibility with certain local communities, especially the business community. IUE's credit ratings made the young institute visible to financial circles. CASE's corporate patrons program helped establish a firmer relationship with the business community. CDFE's customized training courses were more important in giving the Center access to other projects than for its reputation per se. Finally, CSD saw its market survey work for major multinational firms as a recognition of its capabilities—recognition that it could use to woo future clients.

Three of the sample think tanks also saw various aspects of their initiatives as broadening their experience base for policy development. Working in these new areas expanded the perspective of the researchers involved, and in some instances informed other policy analyses. IUE's ratings of municipal bonds gave analysts new insights into the actual financial condition of local governments and the structure of intergovernmental fiscal relations.

Interestingly, certain unanticipated benefits were cited important to the overall success of the new ventures. First, CSD thought its market survey operation helped the group retain staff, by giving analysts a change from the typical research and writing assignments. CASE also thought the change of pace provided by foreign travel and somewhat different assignments made the center a generally more attractive place to work for some staff members.

IUE and CASE cited a second unexpected benefit: the new activities generated important staff training. For IUE, the training in the credit rating initiative came from the classroom training provided by Standard & Poor's and by IUE staff working directly with the S&P staff on benchmarking and other tasks. The leadership at CASE stated that young staff members were challenged by working largely on their own in other countries of the region, helping them mature quickly as researchers and policy analysts. The training and adjustments to management (described below) can be counted as indicating improved operational efficiency.

None of the think tanks spoke about the benefits of expanded overhead revenues, although this may have been implied in the positive statements on financial success.

Challenges
Think tank leaders reported remarkably little in the way of problems accompanying the new, more commercially oriented initiatives. The interview included explicit questions about the half-dozen different types of problems the institution might have encountered (listed above), so the respondents were thoroughly prompted to recall any problems.

Neither IUE nor CDFE could identify any. The IUE director said she thought this was due in part to the orientation of the organization, which from the beginning had worked on multiple demonstration projects that involved close relationships with local government officials and banks. CDFE stated that the financial pressures were so severe that the staff understood the organization had to change direction if it was to survive.

CSD reported no philosophical problems with the staff, the Board, or foundation clients. Rather, the problem was in changing employees' task orientation; staff shied away from doing the necessary marketing. At CASE, the only problems encountered were managerial. There was a certain conflict between the demands of short-term consulting jobs in other transition countries and keeping the larger home-based projects on schedule: the major projects fell behind as staff dashed off on short-term assignments. This conflict was finally resolved by expanding the size of the permanent and associate staff. Both these difficulties can be classified as management challenges.

It is important to note that none of the four institutions reported problems with dilution of the focus of their work, perceived independence in the policy process, or cultural conflicts within the organization. This happy record may result from the fact that the new lines of work were all closely aligned with each institution's main activities and that these were young organizations whose identities were not yet carved in stone and hence were still able to be quite flexible in creating or responding to opportunities.

Status in 2013
An important question is whether the seven innovations described above proved to be successful. At a minimum, success is indicated by the program undertaken still being part of the think tank's

program. I was able to determine the status as of December 2013 of five of the seven innovations reviewed.[163] The results for the five are listed in Table A9.1.4. Four of the five were clear successes. Of these four, three are still operational within the think tank and one was sold profitably as an investment to an international firm.

Table A9.1.4 Summary Status of Innovations as of December 2013[a]

Organization		Innovation	Status
Abbrev	**Name**		
CSD	Center for Study of Democracy	Radio station	Limited success. Station sold when competition reduced performance level
		Marketing surveys	Success. Vitosha Research evolved into substantial research and survey firm, doing much its work for the EU.
IUE	Institute for Urban Economics	Credit rating agency	Success. After the agency established itself, it was purchased by S&P, which provided a basis for an IUE endowment.
		Municipal economic development	Success. The work program in this sphere has been a significant part of the IUE research-policy program.
CASE	Center for Social and Economic Research	Technical assistance to transitional countries	Success. CASE is still active in former Soviet Union countries, primarily through sister think tanks it helped establish in them. Staff is also active in the Middle East and Africa.

a.   Only innovations for which current information could be obtained are listed.

The one unsuccessful innovation was establishment of a radio station in Sofia by the Center for the Study of Democracy. Over time, competition increased and its market share decreased. The station was sold. CSD's executive director draws the conclusion that major new undertakings should be closely related to a think tank's core competencies.[164]

---

163   It appears that the Center for Democracy and Free Enterprise in Prague no longer exists. An inquiry to CASE to clarify the status of the corporate sponsors program was not answered. A review of the CASE 2012 annual report shows that private giving is significant but it is unclear if this is associated with the program.

164   Private communication from Ognian Shentov, December 9, 2013.

Box A9.1.1 Summary of Initiatives

Firm	*Initiative title and summary*
CSD	*Radio station.* Began in April 1991, rebroadcasting Voice of America programs. Received early U.S. government and other support for equipment and otherwise establishing the station. Once the transition began, the station tried a strong news format but soon discovered that this was not appealing. In response to lost market share, in 1993 the station shifted to a music format with news briefs, and expanded to three stations. Under this format, the station is profitable.
	Marketing surveys. Although CSD's first survey was conducted in 1990, Vitosha Research (VR), which conducts marketing surveys and analysis for commercial clients, was not created until 1994. VR has a number of international clients and specializes in more demanding survey research tasks.
IUE	*Credit rating agency.* IUE created the first Russian credit agency in 1997; initially the activity focused on rating bonds issued by municipalities and subjects of the Federation. In summer 1998, it was spun off as a wholly owned subsidiary (E-A Ratings Service) and signed a strategic affiliation agreement with Standard & Poor's. In 2001, S&P purchased a 70 percent interest in E-A Ratings.
	Municipal economic development. Established in fall 1997, a team within IUE provides consultancy services to mid-sized cities in the creation of their economic development plans.
CDFE	*Corporate training.* The program provides development and management of customized education programs for senior staff of banks and enterprises.
CASE	*Technical assistance to transitional countries.* In 1992, a foundation invited CASE staff to provide technical assistance to Russia on its evolving macroeconomic policy. Further requests from donor organizations followed and activity expanded. In 1994–95, CASE more actively sought support for such work.
	Corporate sponsors. CASE recruited "corporate patrons" from among Poland's 70 largest and most respected corporations and banks. Patrons make a fixed contribution and receive CASE's publications, invitations to open seminars, and invitations to occasional "patrons only" events.

ANNEX 10.1 TASKS INVOLVED IN GOVERNMENT OUTSOURCING FOR POLICY RESEARCH

Any agency originating a contract for research undertakes a series of actions. Each action is discussed below. Where appropriate, differences in the way the task is executed depending on how the agency has organized such procurements (the three models) are noted. Think tanks are well advised to understand the procurement cycle, since this is the first step in developing a strategy on how they can operate effectively in this environment.

Determining the annual budget. As part of regular budget preparation, the agency determines the research budget for each office. The process begins the year before the budget year—that is, the year the funds are spent. In model A, the centralized research and evaluation office, after consulting with the program offices, prepares its recommended budget along with a general description of how it will be used. Its proposal is scrutinized and possibly adjusted by the ministry before being sent to the Ministry of Finance, which performs another round of reviews and determines the amount included in the final budget. In the other models, the overall process is similar, except that each program office prepares the proposed budget and research plan. In some instances, only a budget figure is required without a justification statement. Internal review and coordination within the ministry are typically handled by the procurement office. Under all models, detailed research agendas for the year are developed only when the resources available are known.

Two points should be noted. First, the program office is setting the agenda, except in model A. If a think tank wants to influence an agency's future research agenda, then this office is its target. Second, staff in every program office I interviewed stated that the research budget available was far below what they needed. In other words, the process for determining the budget systematically results in underfunding research. *This means that price may often be the paramount consideration in deciding the winner among competing firms.*

Preparing the terms of reference (TOR). In models B and C, the program office often drafts the TOR. In model B, the TOR is then reviewed and possibly modified by the procurement office. In some countries, the agency creates a panel to prepare the TOR that includes staff from the program and procurement offices and other offices in the agency with interest in the subject matter. In model A, the TOR is drafted by the central research office and reviewed by the program office.

Distributing the request for proposals (RFP). The standard procedure is for an RFP to be made widely available. Often, this means it is placed on the agency's web site on a page where all procurements appear. In some instances, an agency also sends a notice to firms who have submitted proposals in the past.

For procurements with values below critical thresholds, more limited notification is the rule. As noted, in the case of a limited competition usually three proposals are needed. For very small contracts, a single contractor can be invited to submit a proposal. Many program offices are structuring their procurements to avoid full competitions—a practice that can afford certain firms a clear advantage.

This is typically not a matter of corruption. The general view of program office staff is that they know the firms doing research in their area very well; they know the relative strengths and weaknesses of each on various topics. So they want to choose the firm to do the work. In part this reflects the frequent reality of limited capabilities among firms and therefore limited possibilities for true competition. But it obviously discourages existing firms from expanding their areas of expertise if they believe they will not be selected for a contract when there is an established leader. It is even more discouraging to those considering starting a new think tank to work in such an area. The value (and perhaps necessity) of team leaders marketing to the leaders of these offices is obvious.

Scoring the proposals. For a full and open competition, proposals are formally scored using factors for award announced in the RFP. Under model B, a panel consisting of staff from the program and procurement offices is usually appointed for this task. In Russia, staff from the program office scores the proposals and two or three experts from outside the agency also score them independently. Both use a standard set of 15 factors. The two sets of scores are discussed and reconciled at a meeting that includes those who scored the proposals, along with representatives from the procurement office and other interested offices within the agency. In the next stage, the program office recommends a winner and the same commission meets to review it. Technical quality and price are both considered.

In model A, the panel scoring the proposals consists of a staff member or two from the program and several from the central research office. The panel recommends the winner to a senior official, who usually makes only a pro forma review before giving approval.

For smaller competitions, the procedures are less rigorous. In Hungary, only the program office assesses the proposals for such procurements. Indeed, the competition in some agencies is strictly on the basis of price. Those interviewed in offices with this practice asserted that research proposals were too subjective to use standard criteria for assessment. The RFP requires that a bidder demonstrate it has the basic competence to do the work, but the RFP does not require the proposal to discuss how the contractor would carry out the work. The deliverables required are stated in the RFP. The winner is the firm offering the lowest price among those firms deemed qualified to do the work. Clearly, with only three firms necessary for a competition and with these firms being invited by the program office, considerable scope for collusion and favoritism exists.

Negotiating the contract. For full and open competitions, the universal practice is that strictly contractual matters, such as the conditions stated in the draft contract about the firm's right to publish the results, are the responsibility of the procurement office. Under model B, the procurement office also negotiates with the contractor about adjustments to the scope of work, presumably on the advice of the program office. In model A, the central research office has a more active role in negotiating these changes but works closely with the procurement office.

Again, practices differ for the smaller awards. In many instances the program office negotiates and signs the contract. In other cases the procurement office executes the contract on the recommendation of the program office.

Quality control and acceptance of deliverables. In both models B and C, the program office is responsible for working with the contractor over the life of the project to insure that acceptable quality work is prepared. The same office formally accepts contract deliverables. In model A, these are tasks of the central research office. In short, the program office or central research office is the real client for the research.

In most countries, the responsible offices have some kind of external review of the work being done. In Hungary, one office reported that the oversight consists of checking the physical presence of reports and CD-ROMs submitted for each project. In Russia's Ministry of Economy, an especially appointed commission reviews the products to certify they meet the contract's requirements.

The foregoing outlines the workings of the research acquisition cycle common to government agencies in many countries. The starting point for a think tank to be successful in winning contracts is understanding the specifics of the contracting process of the agencies with which it works. As indicated, not all agencies have the same practices. How to market effectively to each office depends critically on how it organizes its procurement process.

ANNEX 10.2 BEING COMPETITIVE IN PURSUING GOVERNMENT SUPPORT

Winning contracts from government agencies is only partly about writing good proposals. Indeed, the earlier section on challenges and opportunities points to various ways a firm can gain advantage in what appears to be a highly objective process. This section is not about writing proposals. Most think tanks learn this part of the craft early from the requirements of international foundations and donors. Rather, I concentrate here on how to cultivate relationships and develop advantages.

Influencing the Agenda

A good way for an organization to establish itself as keenly aware of policy developments, and to help a government office organize its future research agenda, is to offer ideas for analytic projects that will support upcoming policy considerations. Proposed program evaluations are also good topics in principle, although most managers still do not appreciate the constructive role evaluations can play in improving program performance. Many think tanks use this "insiders" approach, both because it is good marketing and because they sincerely believe the research proposal is in the public interest.

The process of exploring a research idea with a government office begins by looking ahead a year or more to forecast what the office's analytic needs may be then: what policy topics will be under active consideration? Once a topic is identified where your organization has some credibility, related policy research is identified and carefully considered. It is critical to have a meeting with the relevant officials rather than simply sending a document. The goal is to strengthen personal relationships as well as having a stimulating policy research discussion. Try to organize the meeting through an informal conversation with the official at an event or during a phone call.

It is good practice to have a one- to two-page summary to hand over—this leaves a record of the idea with the officials and indicates seriousness of purpose on the think tank's part. While the officials will understand that this is a marketing meeting, it is important to focus on the substance of the research. The officials will appreciate the firm's capabilities from the quality of the presentation and discussion. A successful meeting concludes with the officials believing the analysis will genuinely meet their needs.

Meetings of this type are also good opportunities to inquire about upcoming procurements so the organization can prepare to compete for these contracts. A particular "first mover" advantage is to be able to form a consortium with the best qualified partners.

A common mistake of think tanks is to stay on the same topic too long—that is, to keep proposing additional work on a topic on which analysis has already been done, usually by the firm proposing more analysis. With limited resources, program offices need to address many areas, and continuing to invest in a particular topic is unlikely. If the think tank continues to press, its leaders may find it harder to get appointments with the agency staff.

Reputation

Officials often know what firm they want to do a specific task and work hard to structure the procurement so they get their choice. This means a firm's reputation in particular areas is critical to being invited to bid on limited competition contracts. Past performance is obviously a factor; and if there is reason to believe the official (perhaps a new official) does not fully appreciate the institute's record, sending a well-crafted, targeted letter and brochure can be effective.

But it is equally important from time to time to remind these officials of the think tank's capabilities. Common ways of doing this include sending them hard copies of reports that are expected to be of special interest to a particular office; including relevant clients and potential clients on the distribution list for e-mails that summarize new research and include links to reports that can be downloaded; and inviting clients to relevant events the institute organizes, such as roundtable discussions or particularly relevant staff presentations—a personal phone call is often very effective in this all-internet era in encouraging attendance. Where appropriate invite clients to make comments.

Being Attentive

Actions on this list go beyond those designed to keep the institution's good name and reputation before the relevant officials. The following are examples of actual think tank actions to promote themselves to government clients:

- Most think tanks have annual parties of some type to which clients can be invited. Christmas and New Year are common occasions. Some have summer outings—picnics or boat cruises.
- Many think tanks send greeting cards on the major holidays and remember the milestone birthdays.
- One think tank offered to brief a new deputy minister unfamiliar with the subject of his new responsibilities on the general structure and key issues in the sector. The official accepted and spent a half-day being briefed.
- A think tank learned that a senior official liked to interact professionally with young people. The institution had several staff who regularly taught university courses and arranged for the official to give a guest presentation to one of the classes.
- Occasionally a think tank has the chance to influence the composition of a team being sent abroad on a study tour. Including an important client when the topic is appropriate is generally very appreciated.

Many think tanks take the kind of initiatives listed just above and those under "Reputation." It is important to implement these initiatives systematically and not just as an impulse or afterthought. A junior staffer can easily be tasked with managing the process of keeping track of opportunities and asking his/her superior if certain actions should be taken.

Respect

At a conference in summer 2005 on cooperation between government agencies and policy research organizations, presentations were made on contracting out.[165] Government officials from several countries made the point that it is critical for think tank leaders and experts to show a certain level of respect to the officials. This is not about respect for the office. Rather, the problem is that analysts talk down to officials, making it far too evident that the experts are just that and the officials are not. This may seem a small point, but it is not to the officials. Think tank senior managers should be very alert to the attitudes of their staff and, where required, do the coaching required.

Partnering

A central point in the section on doing business with government agencies is that winning awards in many countries is an insiders' game. An established reputation in the topic area at hand is very important. One way to become more competitive for certain contracts is to partner with another firm with complementary skills. In other words, both organizations benefit from adding the other's capabilities in competing for a specific project.

Consider the example of a housing ministry interested in improving the targeting of its housing allowance program, so subsidies are concentrated on very low income families. One firm has detailed knowledge of the country's housing programs but does not know much about targeting social programs. The second firm has a strong reputation in the social assistance area, including the targeting of benefits under cash transfer programs to the very poor, but it knows nothing about housing programs. The combined expertise of the two firms yields very strong credentials for the project. Naturally, not all competitions will lend themselves to such combinations, but it is certainly an option to consider regularly.

Forming the partnership in such cases is clearly very important. But it is equally important to make sure the client office appreciates the capabilities of the combined firms. A joint meeting of the two firms with the program office is a necessity if at all possible, particularly under a limited competition when the program office decides which firms are invited to submit proposals. Sending a written statement about the combination and the intentions to work together on this type of project is probably the next best approach. A follow-up phone call is very important.

A frequent problem is that proposal managers wait too long to identify possible partners and even

---

165   "Beyond Analysis—The Broader Role of Policy Research Organizations in BiH," Jahorina (Sarajevo), Bosnia, July 14–16, 2005.

longer to initiate contact. As soon as there is a reasonable expectation that a competition will be held and the topic fairly well defined, the first task is securing highly qualified partners—both firms and individual consultants.

Learning from Failed Efforts

Most think tanks lose at least as many competitions as they win. Sometimes the reasons for losing are idiosyncratic, but there may be systematic problems with the firm's approach as well. The great majority of think tanks (and for-profit firms for that matter) do not devote sufficient resources to learning from lost bids.[166]

Institutions can undertake at least two actions to improve future proposals' chances of success. The first is to request a debriefing from the agency that held the competition. At such debriefings, someone involved in the selection process will inform the think tank representatives of the strengths and weaknesses of the proposal compared with those submitted by other firms. Perhaps the price was too high, insufficient time was budgeted for the project director, or the proposed approach overlooked a key methodological point. Usually statements will be fairly general; but, if listened to carefully, they will signal the significant problems. This information is clearly very useful for a losing firm. Another, indirect benefit: agency staff often takes note of which firms ask for debriefings and are often impressed by the diligence of those who make the effort to learn for the future.

Think tank leaders participating in such debriefings must guard against complaining and challenging statements made by the official, unless there is clear evidence that the basic procedures governing the competition were violated. Complaining will leave an unconstructive impression and may negatively affect the attitude of those reviewing proposals in the future.

Not all agencies routinely provide such briefings. Whether they are obliged to do so depends on the procurement regulations. It is difficult to generalize on this point, as the provisions differ among countries. If the regulations give bidders the right to a debriefing but the agency resists giving one, the contractor will have to weigh whether it is worth aggravating the agency to get the debriefing.

The second action a think tank can take is to convene a meeting of those who took part in preparing the proposal and systematically go through their technical proposal—both technical and cost elements. The main elements to consider in the technical proposal are the following:

- Quality of staff proposed—did they really have the right qualifications and experience for their assigned tasks?
- The project's organizational structure—was the amount of time proposed for each person

---

166   Darling and others (2005) include an excellent discussion about learning from mistakes.

adequate? Was control over certain functions (for example, a household survey) adequate? If subcontractors were involved, were lines of authority among all parties clear? Was it clear who would be directly answerable to the agency-customer?

- Quality of approach to the research or analysis—was what was being proposed absolutely clear? In rereading the RFP, can any issues be identified that were not explicitly addressed in the proposal? Was the scheduling of the work realistic? Did the different activities logically relate in time to each other?

After the review of this particular proposal, think tank managers should study the findings of similar reviews for other proposals in the past several months to identify patterns. In addition, it should examine the results of other competitions with the same government office to detect a pattern in what the competition offered compared with the think tank's proposal.

A similar, detailed review of the cost proposal should also be undertaken. The analysis should be especially careful if the institution lost on price by a wide margin. Comments from various think tanks, combined with discussions with government officials in offices that are contracting for research, suggest that government clients often do not really appreciate the relationship between price and the quality of the product they receive. There seems to be a sense that contractors either pad their budgets substantially or have some reserve funds to "top up" the contracted amount if it is necessary to maintain quality. The reality, of course, is that think tanks generally do neither. Unfortunately, it will probably take some years before typical officials contracting for research become more discerning in terms of product quality.

ANNEX 11.1 ADDITIONAL INFORMATION ON INDIRECT RATES

Alternative Classifications of Direct and Indirect Cost Items

Two definitions in use for nonprofit organizations in the United States are provided by the Financial Accounting Standards Board (FASB) and by the U.S. Office of Management and Budget (OMB).

FASB Statement of Financial Accounting Standards No. 117 requires nonprofit organizations to report expenses by "functional classification." The two primary functional classifications are "program services" (direct project costs) and "supporting activities" (management and general administration, fund-raising, and membership development); they are defined as follows:

> Program services are activities that result in goods and services being distributed to beneficiaries, customers, or members that fulfill the purposes or mission for which the organization exists. Supporting activities are all activities of a not-for-profit organization other than program services. Management and general activities include oversight, business management, general recordkeeping, budgeting, financing and related administrative activities, and all management and administration except for direct conduct of program services or fundraising activities. Fundraising activities include publicizing and conducting fundraising campaigns; maintaining donor mailing lists; conducting special fundraising events; preparing and distributing fundraising manuals, instructions and other materials; and conducting other activities involved with soliciting contributions from individuals, foundations, government agencies and others. Membership-development activities include soliciting for prospective members and membership dues, membership relations, and similar activities. (FASB Statement No. 117, paragraphs 27 and 28).

OMB Budget Circular A-122, *Cost Principles for Nonprofit Organizations,* provides the following definition of indirect costs for projects funded by the U.S. government (Attachment A, Paragraphs C.1–C.3):[167]

1. Indirect costs are those that have been incurred for common or joint objectives and cannot be readily identified with a particular final cost objective. [Any direct cost of a minor

---

167   On December 26, 2013, OMB published a new "supercircular" that supersedes and streamlines requirements from OMB Circulars A-21, A-87, A-110, and A-122 (which have been placed in OMB guidance); Circulars A-89, A-102, and A-133; and the guidance in Circular A-50 on Single Audit Act follow-up. This new document is available online at http://federalregister.gov/a/2013-30465. As general guidance, however, A-122 remains a useful resource.

amount may be treated as an indirect cost for reasons of practicality where the accounting treatment for such cost is consistently applied to all final cost objectives.]…After direct costs have been determined and assigned directly to awards or other work as appropriate, indirect costs are those remaining to be allocated to benefiting cost objectives. A cost may not be allocated to an award as an indirect cost if any other cost incurred for the same purpose, in like circumstances, has been assigned to an award as a direct cost.

2. Because of the diverse characteristics and accounting practices of nonprofit organizations, it is not possible to specify the types of cost that may be classified as indirect cost in all situations. However, typical examples of indirect cost for many nonprofit organizations may include depreciation or use allowances on buildings and equipment, the costs of operating and maintaining facilities, and general administration and general expenses, such as the salaries and expenses of executive officers, personnel administration, and accounting.

3. Indirect costs shall be classified within two broad categories: "Facilities" and "Administration." "Facilities" is defined as depreciation and use allowances on buildings, equipment and capital improvement, interest on debt associated with certain buildings, equipment and capital improvements, and operations and maintenance expenses. "Administration" is defined as general administration and general expenses such as the director's office, accounting, personnel, library expenses, and all other types of expenditures not listed specifically under one of the subcategories of "Facilities" (including cross allocations from other pools, where applicable).

In addition, Attachment B to OMB Circular No. A-122 specifies categories of cost that are allowable, allowable under certain limitations or conditions, or unallowable for funding by U.S. government grants and contracts. Table A11.1.1 summarizes Attachment B.

Nonetheless, the above guidance still allows a range of differing practices and policies for allocating expenses among the indirect and direct cost categories. As a result, how expenses are allocated between categories varies widely from organization to organization. For example, time spent by the executive director developing and overseeing programs can legitimately be considered a program expense, yet some organizations will place the entire director's salary into the indirect cost category. Similarly, while rent, utilities, insurance, supplies, and other general expenses are typically included in the indirect cost category, there may be circumstances in which it is more appropriate for an organization to allocate these costs directly to projects. Each organization needs to decide which expenses are legitimately programmatic and which are supportive in order to define its direct and indirect costs. The acceptability of these allocations by auditors and funders will depend on how reasonable and justifiable is the rationale for the decision.

Case-by-Case Allocation of Indirect Costs

The case-by-case method of allocating indirect costs is to determine a rate of actual usage for each activity in the organization. In its simplest forms, this approach can be used to account for costs that can easily be tracked. Examples of this approach include keeping track of long distance telephone calls, using a counter or log for photocopying, or using time sheets as a means of allocating the salary cost of managers and administrative staff (such as the executive director, financial manager, or administrative assistant) whose work benefits more than one program or activity. As shown by the example above, a different method can be adopted for each type of cost.

The advantage of this method is that it creates a strong connection between activities and the indirect costs that support them. The disadvantage, however, is that this approach can require a great deal of time-intensive record keeping, even for relatively minor costs. Further, even if complete records are kept, there will still be shared costs that cannot be precisely allocated. (For example, office space costs can be allocated on the basis of the work done by those occupying the space and the amount of space occupied. But how then should the cost of common space, such as hallways, be allocated? Similarly, local telephone service and Internet connections typically have fixed monthly costs, regardless of use, and so do not easily lend themselves to being tracked.)

As a result, most organizations do not rely solely on case-by-case allocation for distributing indirect costs. The choice of whether to rely on case-by-case allocation or use of an indirect cost rate (as described below) depends on two factors:

> *Ease of record keeping.* Where automated systems can track costs by project with minimal effort (such as computerized tracking systems for long distance telephone calls or photocopies), using case-by-case allocation distributes costs more accurately.

> *Variability of cost across projects.* Where costs vary significantly across projects, case-by-case allocation helps limit cross-subsidization of indirect costs. For example, if the typical project of an organization requires only a nominal number of photocopies, but one project requires a large number of copies (because of a requirement for large-scale distribution of reports, for example), case-by-case allocation will ensure the typical projects do not have to bear a disproportionate share of photocopy costs.

Because of the disadvantages outlined above, the indirect cost rate described in the text may be a more appropriate way to allocate those shared costs that cannot be easily allocated directly to specific activities or projects. That said, there are examples of organizations that use the case-by-case approach. One is the National Council of Family Affairs in Jordan.

Types of Indirect Cost Rates

As described earlier in Chapter 11, the calculation of indirect cost rates is based on the ratio of indirect costs to a defined direct cost base. The actual ratio of indirect to direct costs can be known only after the accounting period (typically an organization's fiscal year) for which the rate is defined has been completed; this is typically called a "final" rate. However, because both the organization and funders typically cannot wait until the accounting period is over to bill expenses and pay these bills, indirect rate structures based on a prospective analysis of costs ("provisional" rates or "predetermined" rates) are often used. These different kinds of rates are described below:

Final rate. A final indirect cost rate is established after an organization's actual costs for a given accounting period are known. Once established, a final indirect cost rate is used to adjust the indirect costs initially claimed through provisional rates (see below). The adjustment to actual costs is for the period in which the actual costs were incurred and thus cannot be determined until the end of the period.

Provisional rate. A temporary indirect cost rate is established for a future prospective period to permit budgeting and billing/payment of expenses to/by funders until the actual indirect costs can be determined and a final rate established. The provisional rate is usually based on the planned budget of an organization (based on expected expenses and activities). A final rate for a particular year may also be used as a provisional rate in the ensuing year, if anticipated changes in funding levels or costs are expected to be small.

Because the provisional rate is based on the expected activity of the organization (which is likely to be somewhat different than the actual outcome), a provisional rate is subject to later adjustment by issuance of a final indirect cost rate based on actual indirect costs incurred. The organization may then need to either seek additional payment from funders (if the provisional rate was too low and there was under-recovery of indirect costs) or provide refunds to funders (if the provisional rate was too high and indirect costs were over-recovered) for the cost-reimbursement type of agreements between the organization and its funders.

Not all funders ask for this kind of post project reconciliation even when a provisional rate is accepted as the basis for payment.

Predetermined rate. A fixed rate is established for a specified current or future period and is not subject to adjustment. A predetermined rate may be used on contracts or grants where there is reasonable assurance that the rate is not likely to vary significantly from a rate based on the organization's actual costs. This type of rate would be used where the organization has a consistent indirect cost rate over time (for example, because it has a very stable cost structure and funding).[168] Organizations can incur significant financial risk in using this rate, particularly for projects lasting several years.

The use of provisional and final rates is preferable for most organizations for the following reasons:

actual indirect costs are allocated to projects in the period incurred, creating accurate cost information;

there are no prior period indirect costs carried into a future period to burden new or continuing funding;

all indirect costs are properly funded in the period incurred, creating no profit or loss for the organization;

the organization's accounting system must determine actual costs each year, a capability that ultimately must exist to synchronize accounting, budgeting, and cost allocation; and

the actual cost of services or programs is determined annually and is therefore available for internal management and informed budgeting.

---

168   Another type of indirect cost rate is a "fixed rate with carry-forward." In this structure, a fixed rate is established for a period of time to permit budgeting and billing/payment of expenses to/by funders. Actual costs are determined by the organization's accounting system and the difference in indirect costs as calculated by the fixed indirect cost rate and actual indirect costs is carried forward to a future period (usually the organization's fiscal year) in order to adjust the fixed rate in the next period for any over- or under-recovery of indirect costs. This structure would only be used where the structure of funding for an organization remains stable over time; otherwise, the structure could result in inappropriate allocation of indirect costs to funders because of the mismatch between a changing funding structure and the shifting of indirect cost recovery out of the period in which the costs were incurred.

Table A11.1.1 Allowability of Costs under OMB Circular No. A-122

Allowable costs	Allowable costs (limited)	Unallowable costs
Bid and proposal costs	Advertising and public relations	Alcoholic beverages
Bonding	Defense/prosecution of	Bad debts
Communications	criminal/civil proceedings	Contingency provisions
Compensation for staff	Equipment/capital improvements	Contributions/donations to
Depreciation/use allowances	Fringe benefits (including	other organizations
Employee	pensions)	Entertainment
morale/health/welfare	Housing and personal living	Fines and penalties
Independent research and	expenses	Fundraising
development	Idle facilities/idle capacity	Goods/services for personal use
Insurance and indemnification	Indirect costs associated with	Interest on borrowed capital
Labor relations costs	donated labor	Investment management costs
Maintenance and repair costs	Interest on debt for capital asset	Lobbying
Materials and supplies	acquisition	Losses on other projects
Meetings and conferences	Overtime	Organization costs (in
Memberships, subscriptions,	Patent costs	connection with
and professional activity costs	Pre-award costs	establishment/reorganization)
Page charges in professional	Profits/losses on disposition of	
journals	depreciable property or other	
Participant support costs	capital assets	
Plant security costs	Publication and printing costs	
Professional service	Rearrangement/alteration costs	
costs/consultant fees	Reconversion costs	
Rental costs	Recruiting costs	
Royalties/costs for use of	Relocation costs for staff	
patents and copyrights	Selling and marketing costs	
Taxes	Severance pay	
Training and education for staff	Specialized facilities	
Transportation costs	Termination costs	
	Travel costs for staff	
	Travel costs for trustees	

Annex 11.2 Model Cost Policy Statement

The model Cost Policy Statement in this annex is adapted from the U.S. Department of Labor *Indirect Cost Rate Determination Guide: Cost Principles and Procedures for Non-Profit Organizations.* It is provided here as an example of the kind of documentation organizations should develop in order to demonstrate to funders that they have a well-defined, reasonable, and justifiable method of allocating and recovering indirect costs. Of course, individual funders may have particular requirements for indirect costs (such as a ceiling on the amount of indirect costs that can be reimbursed or particular types of costs that cannot be reimbursed) that may be in conflict with the example provided below. Each organization must decide how to structure its indirect cost recovery to reflect its own particular funding situation.

This model Statement assumes that the example organization (EO) uses the direct allocation method of charging costs (i.e., in addition to direct costs), and that EO has in place accounting procedures that enable it to direct charge some costs that would otherwise be considered indirect costs (see, for example, the description below on how the photocopy costs are charged).

COST POLICY STATEMENT EXAMPLE ORGANIZATION

I. General Accounting Policies

A.	Basis of account	Accrual basis
B.	Fiscal period	July 1 through June 30
C.	Allocation basis	Direct allocation basis
D.	Indirect cost rate allocation base	Direct salaries and wages including applicable fringe benefits

A. Example Organization (EO) Fringe Benefit Base-Direct Salaries.

B. EO maintains adequate internal controls to insure that no cost is charged both directly and indirectly to contracts or grants.

C. EO accumulates all indirect costs and revenues in accounts titled "Indirect Cost-Expense" and "Indirect Cost-Revenue," respectively.

II. Description of Cost Allocation Methodology

A. Salaries and Wages

1. Direct Costs—The majority of EO's personnel direct-charge their salary costs since their work is specifically identifiable to specific grants, contracts, or other activities of the organization. The charges are supported by auditable labor distribution reports that reflect the actual activities of employees.

2. Indirect Costs—The following personnel charge 100 percent of their salary costs indirectly:
   Financial Manager
   Administrative Assistant

3. Mixed Charges—The following personnel may charge their salary costs to both direct and indirect activities:
   Executive Director
   Technical Staff

The distinction between direct and indirect is primarily based on the functions performed. For example, when the positions shown are performing functions that are necessary and beneficial to all programs they are indirect. When functions are specific to one or more programs they are direct because they do not benefit all programs.

Auditable labor distribution records that reflect the actual activities of employees are maintained to support the mix of direct/indirect charges. The time records are certified by the executive director.

B. Fringe Benefits

Leave time costs (vacation leave earned, sick leave used, and holiday pay) are considered fringe benefit costs. EO's accounting system records leave time as a fringe benefit cost in the same manner that salary costs are recorded. Vacation leave earned but not used during each fiscal period is recorded as a cost in the period earned.

EO contributes to the following fringe benefits for its personnel: social/health insurance (including unemployment insurance and worker's compensation) and matching contributions to retirement fund.

C. Travel

Travel costs may be charged as either direct or indirect costs depending on the purpose of the trip. For example, the executive director travels to a regional office to give employees a quarterly update. This trip is indirect in nature and should be charged as an indirect cost. However, if the executive director travels to a regional office to perform a specific task for a contract, the trip would be considered a direct cost.

D. Board Expenses

Board expenses charged on an indirect basis are for travel to/from board meetings and an annual fee of $250 paid to each board member. Other board expenses are absorbed by EO and are not charged either directly or indirectly to contracts or grants.

E. Supplies and Material

To the maximum extent possible, office supplies and materials are direct-charged to the contract/grant that uses the supplies or materials. Supplies and materials used by personnel engaged in indirect activities will be charged on an indirect basis.

F. Facility Expenses

EO occupies space it leases from Lessor Corporation. The lease provides for equal monthly payments during the term of the lease. All rent is charged as an indirect cost.

EO's lease includes the cost of all utilities except electricity. The cost of electricity is charged as an indirect cost.

G.   Communications

1. A log is maintained of all fax transmissions. The cost of fax services is charged either directly or indirectly based upon whether a direct or indirect activity benefits from the transmission.
2. Long distance telephone calls are charged either directly or indirectly based upon whether a direct or indirect activity benefits from the transmission.
3. Local telephone service costs are treated as indirect charges.
4. EO uses a meter system for postage charges. The postage meter has been programmed to identify the specific project or activity to charge costs against. Express mail costs are also specifically identified to the project or activity incurring the cost.

H.   Photocopying and Printing

EO maintains a photocopy activity log. From this log, EO is able to prorate its photocopy expenses to each project based on the specific volume of copies made for each program. Administrative personnel will record copies made to the benefiting project to the maximum extent practical. In situations where the photocopies being made by administrative personnel cannot be identified to a specific project and the matter being copied relates to the activities of EO in general, the cost of such copies will be charged to the "Indirect Cost-Expense" account.

Printing expenses are charged to the benefiting activity.

I.   Outside Services

EO incurs outside services costs for its annual audit, legal fees, and for staff development specialists.
1. The cost of the annual audit is charged indirectly.
2. In general, legal fees are charged directly to the benefiting project or activity.
3. Legal fees not identifiable to specific direct projects are charged indirectly.

J.   Capital Items

Capital expenditures are charged directly to projects only in cases where a contract or grant specifically authorizes such charges. No capital item is charged indirectly. The cost of capital items purchased with non-contract/grant funds is recovered through depreciation charges. EO's capitalization threshold is $500.

K.   Depreciation

The cost of capital items purchased with non-contract/grant funds used in a manner that benefits projects is recovered through depreciation charges. EO recovers the cost of capital items using straight line depreciation methods in accordance with generally accepted accounting principles. Depreciation is charged indirectly.

L.   Unallowable Costs

EO recognizes that the costs listed below are unallowable charges to contracts/grants and has internal controls in place to insure that such costs are not charged to contracts/grants:

- Advertising and public relations
- Entertainment/alcoholic beverages
- Capital expenditures
- Bad debts
- Interest
- Lobbying and fund-raising

_____   _____
(Signature)   (Date)

_____
(Title)
Example Organization
(Address)

ANNEX 12.1 EXAMPLE TABLES FOR PERFORMANCE REPORTS TO MANAGEMENT

Table A12.1.1 Performance Indicators from the Funder Perspective: Project Work

Indicator	Period 1	Period 2	Period 3	Period 4
No. of reports **not** delivered to clients on time as a percent of all reports delivered				
No. of projects with cost overruns				
No. of projects with cost overruns that were closed this period—total • No. of projects where additional funds were received from the sponsor • No. of projects where overrun was funded internally				
No. of grants and contracts in past 12 months from prior clients • No. as percent of all grants and contracts No. of contracts/grants in past 12 months from established clients as percentage of all contracts/grants				
Seminar on municipal budgeting				
Date course offered				
Mean student evaluation score % of scores < 3.5[a]				
No. of attendees				
Certified Mortgage Lender course				
Date course offered				
Mean student evaluation score % of scores < 3.5				
No. of attendees				
Course on municipal economic development				
Date course offered				
Mean student evaluation score % of scores < 3.5				
No. of attendees				
Transparency • Think tank's rating for transparency in its funding sources computed using the Tranparify 5-star rating protocol[b]				

[a] Using a scale from 1 to 5, with 5 indicating the highest level of student satisfaction.
[b] This is described in Tranparify (2014); a slightly easier to compute 5-star system is presented in Mendizabal (2014c).

Table A12.1.2
Performance Indicators from the Internal Business Perspective: Project Expenditures

Project number	Project title	Total budget[a]	% spent to date	Work period (months)	% period elapsed	% spent/% elapsed
0722-00	Economic forecasting	$120,000	35	12	42	0.83
0745-00	Regional seminars	32,000	75	6	50	1.50

[a] Excludes fixed fee or profit, if included in the award amount.

Table A12.1.3
Performance Indicators from the Internal Business Perspective: Staff Utilization—January–August 2013 (percentage distribution of hours)

Center	Proposals	Overhead Accounts						Fringes	Total
		General admin.	Center develop.	Center management	Other	External research[a]	General support[b]		
Research									
Housing	6.5	—	4.5	13.7	0.4	64.1	—	10.9	100.0
Law Reform	4.7	—	1.3	6.5	—	75.1	0.2	12.2	100.0
Local Gov.	7.4	—	3.1	4.4	—	71.1	0.1	14.0	100.0
Social Asst.	5.3	—	4.5	3.2	—	74.1	—	13.0	100.0
Health	6.2	—	5.4	3.0	—	70.4	0.3	14.7	100.0
Support									
Accting	—	88.0	—	—	—	—	—	11.2	100.0
Comm/PR	—	—	14.3	0.5	36.8	9.0	26.2	13.3	100.0
Ex. Office	—	78.2	0.4	—	7.1	0.1	2.8	11.4	100.0
Human Res.	—	4.1	0.9	6.3	1.8	3.6	10.9	72.4	100.0
IT	1.3	—	0.1	—	55.8	30.5	—	12.4	100.0
Office Mngt.	0.1	61.1	—	—	24.1	0.1	—	14.6	100.0
Total	5.2	8.5	4.7	3.6	6.3	56.2	1.7	13.7	100.0

Note: A similar table can also be prepared for the staff in each center to track billable hours and utilization of individual researchers.

[a] Funded by grants for specific projects and contracts.

[b] Funded from fee income and unrestricted grants to the institution.

Table A12.1.4
Performance Indicators from the Internal Business Perspective: Proposal Funds Efficiency—2013

Center	Proposals submitted with results known			Proposals won		Efficiency measures[a]	
	No.	Award amt	PD funds[b]	No.	Award amt	PD$/no. won	Award$/PD$
Housing	2	$35,000	$2,400	1	$20,000	$2,400	8.33
Law Reform	5	240,000	6,000	2	97,000	3,000	16.16
Local Gov.	12	74,000	9,000	6	48,000	1,500	5.33
Social Asst.	3	640,000	7,500	1	450,000	7,500	60.00
Health	7	370,000	6,600	3	220,000	2,200	33.33
Total	29	1,359,000	31,500	13	825,000	2,423	26.19

Note: Includes proposals submitted in 2012 on which funders made decisions in 2013.
[a] Proposal development funds expended on all proposals. [b] Proposal development funds expended.

Table A12.1.5
Performance Indicators from the Internal Business Perspective: Accounting Office, Aged Receivables–August 15, 2013

Project number	Project name	Invoice number	Invoice date	Invoice amount	Amount unpaid	0–30 days	31–60 days	61-90 days	>90 days	Total
07230	Armenia	2131	9/27/12	23,400	23,400				23,400	23,400
		3154	12/12/12	37,500	19,600				19,600	19,600
07274	Local Gov.	4431	6/20/13	44,736	21,678		21,678			21,678

Note: Includes only those projects with outstanding invoiced amounts.

Sample Table A12.1.6
Performance Indicators from the Internal Business Perspective: Accounting Office, Aged Invoicing Delays, August 15, 2013

Project number	Project name	Payment type[a]	Target invoice date	Invoice amount	0-30 days[b]	31-60 days	>60 days
7188	Banking seminars	M	6/30/13	30,000		30,000	
7201	Ag evaluation	TM	4/30/13	7,491			7,491

a. M = mobilization payment; WP = payment against completion of work product, e.g., specific report accepted; TM = payment for time and materials
b. Delays are days after the end of the earliest month when an invoice could be submitted.

Sample Table A12.1. 7
Performance Indicators from the Internal Business Perspective:
Annual Accounting Office Review—2013

Indicator	2013	2012	2011	2010
Total projects under contract				
No. of projects from bilateral and multilateral donors				
No. of projects from foundations				
No. of projects supported by other sponsors				
Total projects under contract/staff[a]				
No. of projects closed				
No. of projects closed/staff				
No. of proposal budgets prepared/reviewed				
No. of proposal budgets/staff				
No. of new employees and employees leaving the institution[b]				
No. of new employees and employees leaving the institution/staff				
No. of business trips taken by staff[c]				
No. of business trips taken by staff/staff				

[a] Full-time equivalent members of the accounting staff
[b] Extra work is required to set up income and other payroll tax deductions and, in some cases, arrange for direct bank deposit of pay.
[c] This entry is an example to illustrate certain special features of a tax system that require extra accounting staff effort. In some countries such as Russia, per diem payments above a very low minimum are counted as income to traveler. This extra income must be recorded and taxes assessed, which is a significant burden at a think tank with a high volume of travel.

INDEX

CPSIA information can be obtained at www.ICGtesting.com
Printed in the USA
LVOW03s0225090715

445553LV00007B/116/P